The History of Crime &

Criminal Justice Series

The History of Crime and Criminal Justice Series

David R. Johnson and Jeffrey S. Adler, Series Editors

The series explores the history of crime and criminality, violence, criminal justice, and legal systems without restrictions as to chronological scope, geographical focus, or methodological approach.

> *Murder in America: A History*
> Roger Lane
>
> *Men and Violence: Gender, Honor, and Rituals*
> *in Modern Europe and America*
> Edited by Pieter Spierenburg

Martha A. Myers

Race,

Labor,

and

Punishment

in the New South

Ohio State University Press

Columbus

Copyright © 1998 by The Ohio State University.
All rights reserved.
Myers, Martha A.
  Race, labor, and punishment in the New South / Martha A. Myers.
    p. cm. — (The history of crime and criminal justice series)
  Includes bibliographical references (p.   ) and index.
  ISBN 0-8142-0797-9 (cloth : alk. paper). — ISBN 0-8142-5001-7 (pbk. : alk. paper)
    1. Criminal justice, Administration of—Southern States—History.   2. Convict labor—
Southern States—History.   3. Prisoners—Southern States—History.   4. Prison
industries—Southern States—History.   5. Urbanization—Southern States—History.
6. Industrialization—Southern States—History.   [1. Southern States—Race relations—
History.]   I. Title.   II. Series.
HV9475.S65M94   1998
364.6'0975—dc21   98-20124
                                                                           CIP

Text and jacket design by Diane Gleba Hall.
Typeset in Adobe Caslon and Syntax by Keystone Typesetting, Inc.
Printed by Maple-Vail Book Mfg. Group.

9 8 7 6 5 4 3 2 1

To my father

We shall not cease from exploration

And the end of all our exploring

Will be to arrive where we started

And know the place for the first time.

T. S. Eliot

Contents

Acknowledgments   viii

Prologue   1

1. Social Change and the Rise of the Penitentiary   5

2. Forms of Punishment in Georgia   12

3. Social Change and the Use of the Penitentiary   34

4. Modeling Use of the Penitentiary in Georgia   44

5. Admissions to the Penitentiary   81

6. Prison Sentences   121

7. Release from the Penitentiary   160

8. The Self-Regulation of Punishment   198

9. Understanding Punishment in Georgia   225

Appendix A. The Relationship among Social Change Series   265

Appendix B. Conditional and Unconditional Release
from the Penitentiary   279

Appendix C. Black Property Values and Prison Sentences   291

Notes   293

References   301

Index   317

Acknowledgments

A mountain journey is unlike any other undertaking. Long and arduous, it is a mixed blessing. Some days are so sunny and the trail so wide that progress is swift. The landscape at nightfall bears only passing resemblance to the terrain that greeted the morning's sunrise. Other days are so overcast and the trail so steep and snow-filled that progress is glacial and a backward glance poses more dangers than the next forward step. The sojourn at the summit is altogether too brief. It is filled with a complex mixture of disbelief, relief, and regret. The downhill journey also ends too quickly, rarely allowing for more than a passing backward glance. The journey closes like a book, leaving behind images and a returning disbelief that it was ever begun much less completed.

So it was with this book. The research journey it represents could never have been undertaken without the Georgia Department of Corrections, which gave permission to use their data in 1987. Since then, the Georgia Department of Archives and History has generously contributed to an understanding of the context that generated the data. Neither agency is responsible for the directions in which I took their information. Melissa Landers shared the challenge of transforming nineteenth-century script, filled with references to "ginger coke mulattos," into more prosaic twentieth-century data. Each scholar cited in the manuscript lightened the intellectual burden of the journey. I am especially indebted to Edward L. Ayers, E. M. Beck, Stanley Cohen, David Garland, Alex Lichtenstein, Allen Liska, Charles Tittle, and Stewart Tolnay. None of these colleagues should be held responsible for the unexpected turns I might have taken with their thoughts and inspiration.

I owe a special debt of gratitude to my husband, Andy Furlow. Never once during this long research project did he intimate that monosyllabic responses to complex questions were in any way out of the ordinary. To my parents, I am indebted the most. Nearly two decades ago, they generously enabled me to find a place that was once part of Colonel James Monroe Smith's thirty-square-mile farm in the Pleasant Hills community of Oglethorpe County. Even today, it is a place where voices from the last millennium are closer than those of the approaching one. Still indebted to cotton, its soil continues to resist diversification even into the realm of nineteenth-century heirloom varieties. The land still contains a small cabin, where a white sharecropper family worked and, during the Great Depression, paid their rent in cotton bales. In the pine woods lie the unmarked graves of a dozen black men, women, and children, who also worked the land but left on it no other trace. My chief debt, then, is to this place and its long-departed inhabitants who, no less than scholarly work, inspired and sustained this research journey.

Prologue

On September 22, 1870, twenty-six-year-old Landon Broomfield was convicted of burglary in Greene County, in the northern section of Georgia's cotton belt. He was sentenced to serve time in a new penitentiary. The buildings of the old state prison, destroyed as Sherman marched through Milledgeville, had recently been repaired. Significantly enlarged, the penitentiary could now accommodate five hundred convicts. Yet Landon Broomfield would spend no time within its walls. Nor would more than one hundred other men who were convicted of felonies the same year and sentenced to serve time in prison. Instead, they and nearly four hundred other convicts would spend their days outside, at hard labor. They would spend their nights chained together in temporary camps. This system of punishment, which Georgia shared with other southern states, involved the lease of virtually every convict to a private party. In 1870, Colonel William D. Grant was that party, and the convicts he leased repaired and constructed railroads. The state, in the person of the penitentiary's principal keeper, was little more than a supervisor in absentia.

Landon Broomfield was a black man convicted of a property crime, as were most of those admitted to the penitentiary in 1870 and most of those already serving time. Although burglary carried a maximum sentence of twenty years, Broomfield received only five. Every month of "unexceptionable" behavior reduced his sentence by two days. Shortly before his sentence expired, the state doubled the size of the reduction. As a result, Broomfield served four and one-half years and walked out of prison on May 1, 1875.

In neighboring Oglethorpe County, William Simpson had also been convicted of burglary. Although sentenced to three years in the penitentiary, he too never arrived in Milledgeville. But unlike Broomfield, Simpson managed to escape the lease as well. An exception to the rule, he was white. His punishment was exceptional as well. Convicted on April 20, 1874, Simpson was pardoned by the governor two months later.

Landon Broomfield and William Simpson exemplify the very different worlds that black and white men inhabited after Emancipation and the Civil War. Infrequently snared by the criminal justice system and more easily extricated, white men were rarely encountered working for lessees. Black men, in contrast, were more frequently caught within the system of formal punishment, and once caught, they found release from its clutches more difficult to achieve.

As Broomfield and Simpson weathered the very different storms of their penal convictions, Georgia experienced its own woes. No sooner had the state survived the political tumult of Reconstruction than it was plunged into a severe economic depression that lasted more than four years. Throughout, however, Georgia remained a society bound to the soil and increasingly bound to cotton and to credit. In 1870, only four cities exceeded the ten thousand mark, and none left its imprint on the population of convicts leased to private entrepreneurs. Like the majority of convicts, Broomfield and Simpson came from rural counties with large black populations and heavy investments in cotton production. Like many throughout the state, these counties were still wrestling with the legacy of Emancipation, which left nearly half the state's population free from the chains of slavery but enslaved by custom and by poverty. Although they escaped Sherman's destruction, the communities of Landon Broomfield and William Simpson felt with full force the consequences of war and military defeat: racial tension, neglected fields and homes, families and communities torn by death, destitution, and debt.

Seventy years later, the lease and the legacies of the Civil War were but distant memories. In 1940, over ten times the number of men, nearly 1,300, were admitted to the penitentiary. Like their 1870 counterparts, these convicts encountered a prison system that had been newly reorganized. Long departed was the position of principal keeper of the penitentiary, which was abolished in 1897. Its replacement, the Prison Commission, did not survive the Great Depression. An appointed Board of Penal Administration now supervised and controlled felons. Like Milledgeville decades earlier, prisoners could be sent to a new prison, located in Reidsville and built in 1937 to house over 2,500 convicts. But once again, few convicts would spend time inside its walls. In fact, most prisoners would never leave the counties that convicted them. For just as the state in 1870 had relied on private entrepreneurs to bear the major cost of punishment and daily responsibility for convicts, so they relied on counties in 1940. Prisoners spent their days at hard labor on roads and public works, their nights in makeshift camps.

Between 1870 and 1940, the convict population had changed little. The vast majority of men admitted to the penitentiary were black, and over 60 percent had been convicted of property offenses. The twentieth-century equivalent of Landon Broomfield could expect to receive a sentence of five and one-half years for burglary; Simpson's equivalent received only four years. Whites were still less likely to be admitted to the penitentiary and, if admitted, could still expect to receive more lenient treatment.

Despite this seeming stability, punishment in Georgia had changed, often dramatically, in the intervening decades. Modified in 1897, the convict lease was abolished in 1909. Its successor featured a continuation of hard labor but under county administration for county and state purposes. Parole was instituted in 1908, probation in 1913. For both black and white men, admissions to the penitentiary fluctuated markedly, as did sentences and rates of release. The rate at which black men were admitted, for example, tripled between 1870 and 1875, doubled between 1890 and 1893, and doubled again between 1926 and 1932. It plummeted during World War I, from a high of thirteen per ten thousand black males in 1915 to a low of five per ten thousand in 1918. The admission of white men, in contrast, saw no similar nineteenth-century increases. Nor was a sharp decline during the war evident. Relatively stable until the end of World War I, white admissions to the penitentiary only rose after the Armistice. At the height of the Great Depression, white admissions were five times higher than the postwar equivalent.

Just as punishment in Georgia surged and declined between 1870 and 1940, so too did the state itself. The population of Georgia tripled, and nearly twenty cities had at least ten thousand residents. Indeed, by 1940 one in every three Georgians lived in a town whose population exceeded 2,500. King Cotton, long unsteady on its throne, had been deposed, abetted by the Great Depression and the federal policies it spawned. No longer wedded to agrarian production, industrial development surged, albeit fitfully. The growth of urbanization and the demise of cotton hegemony found expression in the convict population. No longer did the cotton belt contribute most of the felons sentenced to prison. Nearly one of every five convicts came from the cluster of counties surrounding Atlanta; another one in five came from the wiregrass and pine barrens of Georgia's southeast. Although still racially polarized and segregated, the state had lost over 10 percent of its black population. Buffeted by fluctuating cotton prices and a succession of depressions and recessions, the economic divide that so sharply separated blacks and whites was narrowing dramatically.

The Present Study

Between 1870 and 1940, the state of Georgia and its system of punishment changed, often dramatically. This book forges a connection between those changes. It identifies social and economic forces and events that shaped punishment over a seventy-year period. To underscore its often neglected multidimensionality, several facets of punishment occupy the analytic stage: rates of admission to the penitentiary, the length of sentences, and rates of release. Chapter 1 examines in a general way the links between social change and forms of American punishment. Consideration of these links becomes more focused in chapter 2, which identifies the major transformations of punishment in Georgia between 1870 and 1940. Chapter 3 examines the relationship between social change and the extent to which the dominant form of punishment was actually used. It provides the foundation for chapter 4, which develops a model of punishment, introduces the data on incarceration, and explains the techniques used to analyze the data. Presented in chapters 5 through 8 are the results of the analysis, which focus on the admission rate, sentence severity, release rates, and the relationship among them. The final chapter summarizes the results and offers directions for future research and theorizing.

1

Social Change and the Rise of the Penitentiary

SOCIAL THEORISTS OF THE NINETEENTH CENTURY DEEPLY EMBEDDED
the punishment of criminals in the fabric of social, political, and economic life.
Durkheim (1961: 167), for example, located punishment in the moral arena. Its
essential function "is not to make the guilty expiate his crime through suffering or
to intimidate possible imitators through threats, but to buttress those consciences
which violations of a rule can and must necessarily disturb in their faith . . . ; to
show them that this faith continues to be justified." More recently, Rusche and
Kirchheimer (1939: 5) locate punishment in the economic arena, arguing that "the
bond, transparent or not, that is supposed to exist between crime and punishment
prevents any insight into the independent significance of the history of penal
systems. It must be broken."

Attempts to place punishment in its social context continue to the present day.
In concert with their forebears, contemporary theorists conceive of punishment as
an institution whose operation is shaped not simply by the nature and extent of
crime but also by other institutions and their actors (Garland 1990). Social scientists have drawn freely from these theoretical traditions to focus attention on two
major questions. First, what accounts for shifts over time in the form of punishment, in particular, the movement away from capital and corporal punishments
toward hard labor in the penitentiary? Second, once the penitentiary was established as the primary form of punishment, what social, political, and economic
forces determined the extent to which it was used?

This chapter provides an overview of research that addresses the first question, namely, the rise of the American prison and its reliance on forced manual labor. Grounded firmly in the political economy perspective, this research has embedded punishment within the capitalist mode of production and its ceaseless concern with the accumulation of capital. Hard labor in the penitentiary, under the auspices of the state, facilitated this process. Distinctive features of the southern political economy help account for its heavy reliance on a particular version of convict labor, the lease system.

Labor and the American Penitentiary

In the past two hundred years, institutions of western punishment have been transformed (Cohen 1985). Capital and corporal punishments, publicly witnessed, were once the dominant forms of punishing criminals. These deprivations of life and limb gradually ceased, to be replaced by deprivations of liberty in total institutions, often beyond public purview. The focal point of justifications for punishing criminals shifted accordingly, from retribution for past behavior to prevention of future criminality through deterrence, rehabilitation, and incapacitation.

For social scientists, these transformations pose two inseparable challenges: to document their trajectory in specific places and to identify the factors that account for them.[1] To understand the development of the American penitentiary, researchers have drawn most heavily from the political economy perspective, developed by Rusche and Kirchheimer (1939). This perspective considers transformations in punishment to be direct outcomes of transformations in the mode of economic production. The capitalist mode of production, particularly its labor market, shaped American punishment in a number of ways.[2] During the early phase of capitalism, merchant capitalists lacked the technological wherewithal to improve the productivity of labor and, therewith, to accumulate capital. To increase productivity, they added convicts to a labor pool that already included women and children, in large part because the unskilled labor of these groups could be expropriated cheaply and easily (Commons et al. 1918). During early capitalism, then, the role of prisons was part and parcel of the accumulation of capital by the private sector (Gardner 1987).[3] Hard labor for private profit was, therefore, an essential attribute of all penitentiaries (Mohler 1924–25; Gildemeister 1987).

Hard labor in northeastern penitentiaries, organized under the contract system, achieved dominance by 1840. Under this method, the state signed contracts with private entrepreneurs for the daily labor of each able-bodied convict. Less fit inmates—the sick, old, or disabled—also worked; they were simply hired at reduced rates. The state often provided contractors with the heavy machinery and energy sources needed for production within prison walls. Contractors provided workers with lighter tools and raw materials. They bore responsibility for production and distribution, in return for which they reaped all profits (Mohler 1924–25). This system derived its popularity from superior productivity and efficiency. The closest competitor was the public account system, the earliest form of convict labor. Here, the state acted as a private entrepreneur, controlling production and distribution and reaping all profits. In 1886, nearly fifteen thousand inmates labored under this system and produced goods valued at approximately $4 million. The contract and related piece-price systems, where contractors paid for each unit that inmates produced, employed only 44 percent more inmates. They nevertheless produced goods worth 400 percent more than the public account system. This amounted to nearly $21 million in 1886 alone (U.S. Department of Interior 1887).

The status of hard labor in northeastern penitentiaries—whether central, profitable, difficult, or controversial—reflected the state of the labor market (Conley 1980; Miller 1980; Petchesky 1981; Adamson 1984a, 1984b). With the surplus of labor that accompanied recessions and depressions, the rhetoric of reformation lost ground to concerns with deterrence. No longer profitable, industrial labor was replaced with harsher regimens such as treadmills and corporal punishment. In contrast, with the labor shortages accompanying economic expansion, industrial production within prison walls became more remunerative, corporal punishments declined, and policy emphasized reformation through labor.

The status of convict labor reflected as well the position of capital. As capital became more centralized, convict labor became more controversial. By the 1890s, opposition from organized labor and from business associations signaled that the contract labor system had outlived its usefulness and had become a liability (Mohler 1924–25; Gildemeister 1987). Although labor continued to be a hallmark of the penitentiary, its beneficiaries were no longer entrepreneurs pursuing private fortunes. Contracts declined precipitously and were superseded by the public account system. Labor in the penitentiary was thus harnessed to the production of goods for state agencies or for the public at large.[4]

Prison Labor and the Southern Political Economy

The link between the penitentiary and the development of a capitalist political economy was particularly close in the South, which long relied heavily on a different organization of convict labor known as the lease system.[5] In 1885, only a minority of all productively employed convicts worked under this system. In the South, however, 65 percent of all productively employed convicts were so engaged (U.S. Department of Interior 1887). Alternatively put, of all convicts leased to private entrepreneurs, a full 96 percent were in the South.

Although popular in the region, the lease system was not a southern invention. That distinction belongs to Massachusetts, which drew up the first lease in 1798

(Zimmerman 1947). Nor was the lease a unique response to the Civil War. Three southern states had leased their penitentiaries in the antebellum era: Kentucky in 1825, Louisiana in 1844, and Alabama in 1846 (Sneed 1860; Moos 1942; Carleton 1971). The lease nevertheless flourished in the postbellum South because it dovetailed with a political economy confronting the disarray wrought by a lengthy war, military defeat, and the termination of slavery.

Following the Civil War and Emancipation, the predominant form of southern punishment—incarceration at craft labor in a penitentiary—was no longer a viable option. From transportation networks to prisons, the southern infrastructure was seriously damaged. Destitute citizens clamored for relief (Conway 1966). Each Confederate state was saddled with large debts, and their treasuries had only worthless Confederate currency to offer in payment (Thompson 1915). Georgia, for example, began the decade of the 1860s with a debt of $2.67 million and ended it with a debt of $6.54 million. At its highest point (1872), the state owed creditors $20 million, about $7 million of which was incurred through the endorsement of railroad bonds. After repudiating nearly half its debts, Georgia still owed more than $10 million in 1880 (Porter 1880; Hawk 1934). Raising taxes to secure the state debt, never a popular solution, was especially inadvisable after the war. Property values plummeted, and landowners could no longer consider black workers as property (Wallenstein 1987). Tax revenues thus flowed less freely into state coffers, jeopardizing the ability of state governments to conduct business of any kind.

Crime was a new and particularly pressing feature of that business. Emancipation destroyed the informal social control system afforded by plantation slavery. In so doing, it increased by a third to a half the number of persons over which formal social control systems held jurisdiction. Reconstruction failed to redistribute land, and most freedmen were penniless. State governments, then, were faced with too little money to address too large a social control problem.

State governments were not the only ones feeling the pinch of an empty purse. Southern entrepreneurs also found capital difficult to obtain. Industrial production rebounded after the Civil War, but it was an evolutionary rather than revolutionary process, constrained by the availability of investment capital (Woodward 1971; Ransom and Sutch 1977; Goldfield 1982; Wood 1986). Internally, capital grew at a glacial pace. From the North, capital flowed more freely, but it was directed toward investments that would retain the competitive advantage of the North. Using existing technologies, capitalists with northern financing invested in railroads, real estate, and the extraction and initial processing of raw materials. The South grew, harvested, ginned, and baled cotton. Its textile mills produced yarn and coarse cloth. The North, however, dyed and finished the cloth, producing fine garments. The South cut, planed, and sometimes treated lumber, which was then shipped North for conversion into machine parts, ship timbers, building materials, and furniture (Clark and Kirwan 1967). Appalachian mines provided coal and iron ore, which found their way to northern foundries, machine shops, and other capital goods enterprises (Norrell 1991).

The absence of a strong southern technological community and the limited influx of capital conspired to generate an industrial process much like agriculture: labor-intensive rather than highly mechanized. But since wages were lower in the South than in any other region of the country, the labor needed to meet industrial demands trickled into the region. More often than not, labor deserted the South for higher wages elsewhere. Southern industrialists were thus left with an indigenous labor force. They preferred white workers in their factories, on the grounds that "Negroes were not adaptable to factory work and were to be left in the fields" (Baron 1971; Wynne 1986: 89–90). But southern industrialization meant more than factory work: it entailed hard manual labor in mines extracting coal and iron ore, on roadsides repairing and constructing roads and railroads, and in pine barrens making turpentine. Few whites were willing or needed to engage in such hard physical labor, traditionally the province of black men, at the low wages that industrialists were willing or able to offer (Blatner 1952; Carter 1964; Lichtenstein 1996; Mancini 1996).

Southern industrialists faced, then, two problems: limits on their capital and a scarcity of inexpensive and reliable labor. What had been the state's problem, convicts and their labor, became the industrialist's solution. The state entered into binding agreements with private entrepreneurs, who exploited convict labor for profit. Lease agreements tended to be much more global than the contracts so popular in the Northeast (U.S. Department of Interior 1906). Lessees received not only the labor of able-bodied convicts but also the convicts themselves and, in some instances, the physical structure and belongings of the penitentiary. Lessees paid the state a fixed fee for the convict population and bore the costs of housing, feeding, clothing, and guarding all convicts. Leased convicts were deployed to enterprises whose low wages, difficult working conditions, and black labor force generated shortages of reliable labor and little competition with white workers (Blatner 1952; Carter 1964; Lichtenstein 1996; Mancini 1996). The ten thousand miles of neglected or destroyed railroad lines typically came first (Clark and Kirwan 1967), followed by mining, lumbering, farming, turpentine distilling, brick making, and sawmilling. Twentieth-century leases deployed convicts to maintain and construct roads that the public deemed essential for industrial and agrarian development.

The State and Convict Labor

The exploitation of convict labor, whether in the North under the contract system or in the South under the lease, required the cooperation of state officials. Their active intervention and support, often in pursuit of their own political interests, strengthened the foundations of capitalism and helped create the conditions that would ensure its growth. Dual investments in the state and in the broader capitalist system made prison labor an attractive option, since "by forging an alliance with a segment of private capital, state managers were able to defer the financial cost of expanding the state apparatus. They had, in essence, successfully reproduced the conditions of their existence and legitimation" (Staples 1990: 35).

During early American capitalism (1790–1860), then, the state was no less concerned with capital accumulation than were capitalists (Staples 1990). This "accumulative state" actively intervened in many sectors of the economy. Involvement in convict labor was simply one manifestation. But as northern capital became more concentrated after the Civil War, state intervention in the economy became unwarranted "trespassing." As noted above, hitherto successful alliances with capitalists crumbled in the face of criticism not only by organized labor, which was to be expected, but also by capitalists who lacked access to cheap convict labor and found this situation intolerably unfair. To maintain its own legitimacy, the "bureaucratic state" turned its attention to the social costs incurred by capital accumulation, and in the process it was compelled to shift to types of convict labor that did not produce revenue.

The role of the "accumulative state" was particularly clear in the South (Green 1949; Blatner 1952; Ayers 1984). Alabama illustrates this more clearly than any of its neighbors. Between 1880 and 1940, 10 percent of its annual state budget came from convict labor (Lewis 1987). More generally, states using the lease generated revenues that were 372 percent of the cost of operating penitentiaries. Alternative modes of convict labor could offset only half the cost of operating penitentiaries (U.S. Department of Interior 1887).

State treasuries were not the only recipients of revenues from the lease. One historian has characterized the relationship between capitalists and politicians as a "mutual aid society" (Ayers 1984: 195). Although the state government of Georgia, for example, made less money than Alabama, its state officials did not. Dozens of state officials profited personally from the lease system (Carter 1964). The career of Joseph E. Brown illustrates the argument (Roberts 1960). Governor between 1857 and 1865 and U.S. senator between 1880 and 1891, Brown was "perhaps the single most powerful man in Georgia" for nearly thirty years (Wynne 1986: 147). Involved in numerous business ventures, he entered a bid in 1875 for one hundred convicts. Although late, it was accepted a day later. The following year, Brown competed successfully for a twenty-year lease, even though other bids exceeded his own by 400 percent (Carter 1964). Not only did Brown receive this lease under less than deserving circumstances. He was also able to obtain convicts for his coal mines three years before the official start of his twenty-year lease (Felton 1911). Of the three penitentiary companies that received twenty-year leases for the state's able-bodied convicts, the first was the Dade Coal Company, headed by Joseph E. Brown. The second was headed by John B. Gordon, a U.S. senator (1873–80, 1891–97) and later governor (1886–90). His business colleague was James M. Smith, who as governor (1872–77) appointed his brother-in-law to serve as principal keeper of the penitentiary (Felton 1911). The final penitentiary company was headed by John W. Murphy, a clerk in the state treasurer's office.[6]

While never free from criticism, the alliance between southern entrepreneurs and public officials did not generate scandal and public outrage until the early twentieth century (McKelway 1908b; Taylor 1942a). As chapter 2 will show, a severe depression generated a legitimacy crisis for Georgia's state officials. Following the well-worn footsteps of "bureaucratic states" in the Northeast, Georgia severed its link with the private sector and turned its attention and its convicts toward road construction for the "public good."

2

Forms of Punishment
in Georgia

THE STATE OF GEORGIA EXPERIENCED ITS OWN VERSION OF THE TRANS-
formations discussed in chapter 1. During the last century and a half, Georgia
shifted from capital and corporal punishments to hard labor in the penitentiary,
from the penitentiary to the convict lease, from the convict lease to county-run
chain gangs, and from chain gangs back to incarceration in prisons. This chapter
offers an overview of the first three transformations, with the greatest attention
devoted to the most neglected era: county-administered chain gangs. Two threads
bind these transformations tightly together. First, dissatisfaction with the current
punishment was perennial, and the state continually entertained drastically different alternatives. The second unifying thread was an abiding concern that the
state's responsibility to punish not place an undue financial burden on its ability to
operate in other arenas. This concern undergirded the forced expropriation of
convict labor that was, even by standards then in use, brutal and inhumane. These
commonalities aside, the periods differed in the extent to which the state or the
private sector was involved, on a daily basis, in punishment.

After describing major shifts in the form of punishment, I will consider its
severity and changes in its administration. Little more than minor variations on a
theme, these changes include modifications of criminal penalties and the introduction of specific penal policies such as probation, parole, and indeterminate sentencing. Taken together, changes in the form, severity, and administration of punishment provide the shifting backdrop for the actual imposition of punishment on
black and white offenders.

The Penitentiary Period, 1817–1868

The state of Georgia embraced the concept of the penitentiary earlier than did most of its southern neighbors. It was preceded by only three states: Virginia, Kentucky, and Maryland. Georgia's control over its felony convicts effectively began in 1817, when the state prison in Milledgeville accepted its first convict (Taylor 1940; Walden 1974).[1] Like other states, Georgia revised its penal code to lay the legal foundation for the physical structure of the penitentiary. Completed in 1816, the new penal code replaced or curtailed traditional corporal punishments imposed by counties, such as whipping, the pillory, fines, or death. In their stead were terms of imprisonment in the state penitentiary. A few examples illustrate the magnitude of this change. In the traditional code, felonies as diverse as forgery, counterfeiting, and stabbing were punishable by death (Watkins and Watkins 1800; Prince 1822). A second conviction for mayhem, the maiming of another, rendered the offender eligible for the death penalty, regardless of the injury inflicted or of the offender's degree of involvement in the crime. The new penal code imposed more modest penalties. Persons convicted of forgery received sentences of two to ten years, counterfeiters, up to ten years (Prince 1822). Stabbing was punishable either as a misdemeanor or as a felonious assault with intent to commit murder. As a misdemeanor, the most severe punishment was one year in jail; as a felony, one to five years in prison. The new code also recognized various degrees of mayhem and imposed a maximum penalty of life imprisonment. Only the gravest offenses still elicited the death penalty, most notably murder and certain forms of arson.

Approved by the legislature in 1816, the new penal code did not become effective until the governor proclaimed the penitentiary fit to receive convicts in 1817 (Lamar 1821). In philosophy and appearance, Georgia's penitentiary drew upon northern precedents, particularly the Walnut Street jail in Philadelphia (Walden 1974). Originally, a nine-person board of inspectors, appointed by the assembly, selected all penitentiary officers and devised appropriate regulations (Lamar 1821). The board's membership was reduced to three in 1820, and its authority eroded in 1828, when the power to appoint prison officials became the province of the governor (Dawson 1831). Assembly oversight rested with the Joint Standing Committee on the Penitentiary, which conducted periodic inspections. The daily affairs of the prison were in the hands of the principal keeper; the health of its convicts was the purview of the principal physician.

Critics and partisans alike expected the new penitentiary to reform inmates through labor and to be self-sufficient, if not ultimately revenue producing. Labor was to be of the "hardest and most servile kind, . . . least liable to be spoiled by ignorance, neglect, or obstinacy, and where the materials are not easily embezzled or destroyed" (Lamar 1821: 662). Among the industries at which convicts labored, six

13

days a week, eight to ten hours a day, were the manufacture of shoes, clothes, furniture, and cabinets and the construction of carriages, wagons, and railroad cars (Walden 1974). A tannery, paint shop, and grist mill were added later (Bonner 1971).

Although Georgia embraced the penitentiary regime early, it did not do so with fully open arms. As the primary institution of formal social control, the penitentiary's foothold was always tenuous. Criticism from both the press and assemblymen was unceasing (Walden 1974). The most recurring theme was its failure to achieve the stated goals of reformation and self-sufficiency. In 1818, for example, the Joint Penitentiary Committee found "no evidence of the much hoped for amendment of morals; but on the contrary, . . . the convicts, with few exceptions, [are] astonishingly dissolute, profligate and insolent. . . . There have also been instances of convicts embezzling the goods committed to their charge" (Georgia Senate 1818: 48).

The inmate pool remained small: 64 in 1820, 96 in 1830, and 155 in 1840 (Bonner 1971; Walden 1974). As a result, the financial situation of the penitentiary was, "ever since its establishment, a source of mortification, and regret to its friends" (Georgia House 1853–54: 730). The committee concluded in 1854 that the penitentiary would never become self-sustaining, having lost at least $11,000 between 1846 and 1854 alone (Georgia House 1853–54). Sales on credit and bookkeeping procedures yielded profits that were typically more apparent than real, necessitating continual state appropriations (Bonner 1971; Walden 1974). Periodic fires, set by inmates, caused considerable damage, requiring more unanticipated appropriations. The local community added its concerns to the chorus of criticism, noting the prospect of escapes and competition between convict and free labor.

Alone or in concert, these critiques provided the pretext for entertaining alternative ways of organizing punishment. The earliest (1822) and most common proposal was abolition of the penitentiary and a return to corporal punishments, administered by county authorities (Walden 1974). Only one of these proposals successfully passed the legislature, in 1831. Life without the penitentiary, however, proved too difficult, and it was reinstated within a year.

Over a decade later, critics again proposed abolishing the penitentiary (Georgia House 1843). But rather than return the duty of punishment to county authorities, critics suggested "farming out" or leasing the penitentiary and its convicts to private entrepreneurs. As noted in chapter 1, this option differed radically from the contract labor system. Unlike contractors, who in essence purchased only the labor of convicts, lessees relieved the state of virtually all expenses, including the costs of housing, feeding, and guarding inmates. The state retained limited financial responsibility, paying the salaries of the principal keeper, his assistant, and the principal physician. The state also bore responsibility for developing and enforcing general rules and regulations.

The proposal to farm out convicts met with little success, being postponed indefinitely (Georgia House 1843). Ten years elapsed before it was entertained seriously. Although deemed "unwise and impolitic" by the Penitentiary Committee (Georgia House 1853–54), a proposal to lease the penitentiary to the current principal keeper won by a wide margin (65 to 30) in the House. It nevertheless failed in the Senate, which was willing, by a slim margin (30 to 23), to request that the governor obtain information about the lease from other states and report his findings the following year (Georgia Senate 1853–54). While the governor never explicitly discussed the results of his correspondence, if any, he admitted in his 1855 message to the assembly that the penitentiary was a failure. He suggested yet another option: remove the penitentiary to a different location and enlarge it (Georgia Senate 1855–56).

With the onset of the Civil War, criticism of the prison and its role abruptly ceased. Able-bodied convicts manufactured articles for the military and continued to produce bricks, wagons, and harnesses. In 1862, the penitentiary made history when, with the labor of its 188 convicts, it paid $10,000 into the state treasury (Walden 1974). But as General Sherman's troops advanced south in 1864, state officials began to remove valuable property from the prison grounds. With the exception of twenty-five old, disabled convicts and murderers ineligible for pardon, virtually all convicts accepted the governor's offer of service in the Confederate army, in return for a pardon after sixty days of service.

The penitentiary survived the war, but not without serious fire damage, inflicted by either the convicts themselves or Sherman's troops (Walden 1974). Coupled with a rise in the number of felons, this damage compelled the legislature to appropriate funds for the support and restoration of the prison (Georgia Assembly 1866). As a result of these efforts, the penitentiary was restored, at least on the surface. In 1868, it could accommodate five hundred convicts and was reportedly in better condition than it had ever been (Bonner 1971). Yet within the space of two years, the prison stood empty and neglected. Its buildings were gradually torn down, their materials recycled for state and private uses (Walden 1974).

The Convict Lease Period, 1868–1908

Just as Georgia led the South in embracing the penitentiary, so too did it lead the region in embracing its alternative, the lease of convicts to private entrepreneurs (Lichtenstein 1996; Mancini 1996). The precipitous decline of the penitentiary described in the previous section reflected the state's inability to stem the flow of felony convicts and to bear the financial burden of their punishment. Recall that Georgia owed creditors $6.54 million in 1870 and more than $10 million in 1880 (Porter 1880). Immediately after the war, the legislature sought to limit prison admissions in two ways. First, it increased the penalties for certain crimes (viz., rape, burglary at night, stealing a horse or mule, arson) from imprisonment to death (Georgia Assembly 1865–66, 1866). Second, it reduced other felonies, most notably stabbing and simple larceny, to misdemeanors, which made them eligible for punishment by county authorities. Neither provision appreciably dampened the flow of felons into the penitentiary, and in 1866, the General Assembly authorized the governor to "farm out the institution . . . on the best terms," providing only that the lease "relieve the State from all further expense" (Georgia Assembly 1866: 155). This solution to the postbellum convict problem was, as noted in chapter 1, neither new nor distinctive. All states of the Confederacy turned to leasing after the Civil War. Georgia and Tennessee were simply among the first to authorize its use (Zimmerman 1947).

Georgia did not actually draw up a lease until 1868, when a provisional governor sympathetic to leasing was installed. Early leases, primarily for railroad construction, were short-lived (one to two years) and limited by law to five years. Within a year of the first lease, the governor divested the state of the entire penitentiary, leasing its buildings, property, and fixtures and terminating the employment of all state officials except the principal keeper (Taylor 1940). Few inmates were kept at the prison and, as noted above, its physical structures quickly fell into disrepair.

At first, lessees did little more than relieve the state of the expenses associated with maintaining and guarding inmates. Indeed, Principal Keeper John Darnell complained, "Since I came into office—August 12, 1869—I have not had a dollar in my hands belonging to the institution, nor have any collections been made" (Principal Keeper of the Penitentiary 1870: 11). Lessees made no payment into state coffers until 1872, when Grant, Alexander and Company agreed to pay the state fifty dollars per capita for inmates to work on the railroad. The total revenue from lessees in 1874 was more than $14,000 and nearly $11,000 the following year (Principal Keeper of the Penitentiary, 1874, 1875). The legislature soon authorized much longer and ultimately more profitable leases.[2] In 1876, the assembly empowered the governor to lease convicts for twenty years, effective upon expiration of previous leases. Long-term leases were signed by groups of entrepreneurs or "penitentiary companies," which used convict labor on farms and in coal and iron ore mines, rock quarries, and brick factories. Over the length of the twenty-year lease, the state received an annual income of $25,000.

Although profitable, the convict lease proved to be no less immune to criticism than the penitentiary. Legislative committees perennially issued critical reports, and even principal keepers and governors expressed reservations (e.g., Georgia House 1886, 1897).[3] Despite the diversity of sources, criticisms focused, either alone or in concert, on two issues. The first was the failure of lessees to comply with rules and regulations, the result being inhumane conditions, escapes, brutal treatment, and untimely deaths. Second and more fundamental were criticisms of the appropriateness of turning convicts over to the control of the private sector for its profit.

Until the turn of the century, the first criticism was voiced more frequently. The House Penitentiary Committee, for example, issued a generally favorable report in 1870 that nonetheless itemized violations of regulations and incidents of cruel whipping (Joint Committee on the Penitentiary [1870] 1974). Seven years later, its Senate counterpart considered the "lease system, at best, . . . a very bad one," and recommended that several camps be closed and leases canceled (Georgia Senate 1878). Although the same committee spoke in more glowing terms three years later, referring "with pride" to the convict system (Georgia Senate 1881), its assessment was not shared by members of the House committee. Numerous abuses compelled this committee to note the need for "a central authority employed to exercise a supervisory control over all persons, companies, and corporations . . . as to government, discipline and management of the convicts, with full power and authority to frame all suitable rules and regulations for the proper control of said convicts" (Georgia House 1881: 75). The penitentiary committee also saw the need for a state official to "stand between the convict and lessee" and enforce state rules (Georgia House 1881: 76).

With the rise of the Populist Party in the 1890s and its public stance against the convict lease (Shaw 1984), the House committee grew increasingly critical. In 1890, it noted many abuses that should be corrected (Georgia House 1890). Two years later, the committee enumerated shocking incidents of gambling and "that crime which cannot be named or written without a revulsion of feeling amounting to horror" (Georgia House 1892: 655). By 1895 the penitentiary committee considered the lease "a blot on the fair name of our beloved State" (Georgia House 1895: 830).

The earliest and least common state response to criticisms involving violations of rules and regulations was annulment of individual leases (Taylor 1942b). In 1875, the lease with Wallis, Haley and Company was annulled on two grounds: negligent care of convicts and the division and removal of convicts to another part of the state without consulting the governor. George D. Harris lost his lease in May 10, 1875, because of improper treatment. A few months later, John Howard's lease was voided because of improper care and failure to pay the lease. As the consortia of entrepreneurs became more powerful and difficult to control, reactions to rule violations became less drastic (Ward 1947). Two penitentiary companies were fined the modest sum of $2,500 for cruelty to inmates in 1886, the first fine ever levied on a lessee (Wynne 1986). A decade later, similar abuse of his power as "whipping boss" led to termination of the employee and a $1,400 fine on the lessees. When the penitentiary company refused to pay the fine, approximately four hundred convicts were delivered to the presidents of the companies, who simply distributed them to other lessees within the company (Principal Keeper of the Penitentiary 1896).

17

Fundamental criticisms of the lease surfaced only intermittently before 1900. Principal Keeper Darnell believed that "the convict element should not . . . be thrown into the channel of commercial speculation, subject to the highest bidder, to the loss and serious inconvenience of the people of the whole State. Convicts, during their time of confinement, belong exclusively to the State" (Principal Keeper of the Penitentiary 1870: 10). By 1898, the Prison Commission, which replaced the principal keeper, considered the use of the penitentiary as a source of revenue "entirely foreign to the most advanced idea of prison management and unheard of in the most prosperous states" (Prison Commission 1898: 23).

Fundamental critiques of the convict lease elicited recommendations for equally fundamental change (Taylor 1940). As was the case with the penitentiary, a perennial but unsuccessful response was abolition of the lease system entirely. This proposal continually fell on deaf ears in the assembly. Shortly after the Joint Penitentiary Committee enumerated problems with the lease in 1870, for example, the House referred to the Committee of the Judiciary a resolution to return convicts to the penitentiary; it never emerged as a bill (Georgia House 1870). Soon after the legislature authorized twenty-year leases, a bill to repeal authorization was read in the House, but the penitentiary committee refused to recommend it (Georgia House 1877). And in 1897, assemblymen soundly defeated a proposal to abolish the lease and replace it with the use of short-term inmates on public roads and a penal island for long-term convicts.

The most common response to criticisms of the lease, whether about its appropriateness or its implementation, was to enlarge the state's role in punishment through increased oversight and tighter regulations. The principal keeper, the only state official responsible for the supervision and care of the inmates, was initially given little guidance and no budget for camp inspections. Indeed, during the earliest leases, not all inmates passed through the principal keeper's office on their way from county authorities to lessees. This situation caused John Darnell "considerable embarrassment in the discharge of [his] official duties" (Principal Keeper of the Penitentiary 1870: 6). By 1871, the assembly had devised regulations governing work, corporal punishment, and discharge (Georgia Assembly 1871). Rules on subleasing, escapes, cruelty, and the use of convict guards followed (Georgia Assembly 1876). The governor specifically ordered general notices to be issued to the lessees in 1875, 1880, and 1885 (Principal Keeper of the Penitentiary 1875, 1880, 1886). These notices enumerated regulations that governed an increasingly broad range of issues including mail privileges, health, diet, housing, food, living quarters, and work requirements. Indeed, by 1890, the principal physician had developed a detailed set of rules governing physicians in charge of penitentiary camps (Principal Physician of the Penitentiary 1890).

Along with greater regulation, the assembly introduced penalties for noncompliance. Legislation authorized fines for negligent escapes, cruelty, subleasing, and the use of convicts as guards (Georgia Assembly 1876). The sanctions were virtually toothless: fines were modest and rarely imposed. The penitentiary committee concluded in 1878 that, although there had been more than five hundred escapes, the state received not a penny in fines for negligence. Even worse, every camp was using convicts as guards, in direct violation of the law (Georgia House 1878). To strengthen enforcement, the assembly quickly authorized grand juries to prosecute lessees who violated state laws governing the treatment of convicts (Georgia Assembly 1879). The negative penitentiary committee report of 1881 precipitated a measure that subjected any employee who inflicted unauthorized punishment on a prisoner to conviction of a felony and a term of six months to two years in prison (Georgia Assembly 1881).

Apart from devising regulations and introducing penalties for noncompliance, the assembly gradually increased personnel and delimited their duties more clearly. The position of principal physician was reestablished in 1876, bringing with it the duty of attending to sick or diseased convicts (Georgia Assembly 1876). The following year, the physician was required to inspect camp conditions and to report on the health of all convicts (Georgia Assembly 1877). While the state assumed the costs of the principal physician, lessees continued to bear full responsibility for the costs of hiring a camp physician and of providing the medical care he prescribed. "To aid in reforming the moral character of the convicts," a chaplain to the penitentiary was authorized in 1876. The position of assistant principal keeper was reestablished in 1881 (Georgia Assembly 1876, 1881). His primary duty was to assist the principal keeper in monthly inspections and in reports to the governor about conditions, diet, treatment, and compliance with regulations. Also authorized in 1881 was the "whipping boss," responsible for disciplining recalcitrant convicts in each camp. Although selected and compensated by lessees, whipping bosses were required to submit monthly reports under oath to the governor, listing the names, causes, and extent of all disciplinary actions taken. Finally, the assembly approved public oversight of the penitentiary in 1879, when it required grand juries to inspect convict camps in their counties at each term and file a report on their condition in the county and to the principal keeper. Grand juries were also required to appoint a chaplain, whose compensation was to be paid out of money received from the lease (Georgia Assembly 1879).

In the wake of sustained criticism by the Populist Party (Shaw 1984) and by penitentiary committee reports in 1895 and 1896, the assembly reorganized punishment in 1897. Complete management and control of felons became the responsibility of an elected three-person Prison Commission. At the same time, however, the assembly abolished the position of principal physician, leaving lessees responsible for engaging local doctors to care for convicts. Moreover, the assembly allowed the subleasing of convicts, which over time elevated the cost of convict labor to a point rivaling that of free labor (Mancini 1996). The essential elements of the lease thus remained. Contractors paid not only for the annual labor of convicts. They also paid for "transportation, maintenance, medicine, clothing and all other necessaries, and such buildings as may be required" for convicts who worked outside prison walls (Georgia Assembly 1897: 76). State oversight continued to be illusory and, in many respects, lessees controlled both the labor and the person of the convict just as firmly as they had under the principal keeper system (Lichtenstein 1996).

Initial penitentiary committee reports were nonetheless positive (Georgia House 1898, 1903; Georgia Senate 1899), and the Prison Commission cited the "wonderful change for the better" wrought by reorganization (Prison Commission 1902: 17). The modified lease continued to be profitable as well. The first two five-year contracts yielded a net profit of $2.3 million to the state treasury (Prison Commission 1908).

In the midst of a severe depression (1907–8), with the profitability of the lease in doubt, public and legislative opinion shifted dramatically (Taylor 1942a; Fierce 1994; Mancini 1996). The press, particularly the *Atlanta Georgian,* gave the issue sustained attention in 1908, and many towns held mass meetings to protest the lease system. The State Democratic Convention, also held in 1908, announced its opposition. In its regular session, the assembly considered but failed to pass several bills. In August, the governor called an extraordinary session to hear the report of the penitentiary committee, authorized in 1907, and to take appropriate action.

In considerable detail, the committee's report enumerated the vices of the lease system. The most egregious rule violations took the form of unauthorized subleasing, inhumane conditions, and excessive brutality. But most damaging was evidence that cast state officials as violators of the public trust. Testimony revealed evidence of nepotism, neglect of duty by prison commissioners, and conflicts of interest involving state employees. Witnesses indicated that the state warden, appointed by the Prison Commission, had been paid by contractors for arranging subleases and was a business partner with the largest contractor for prison labor. Deputy wardens, physicians, and guards had been paid not only by the state but also by the lessees whose behavior they were charged with regulating: "For these trusted State officers to become also the employees of the lessees, and to receive from them compensation frequently as large as that paid by the State and ofttimes from twenty-five to one hundred and fifty percent larger, was to place themselves under such obligations as would interfere with, if not render impossible, honest discharge of their duties to the State or its wards. No mere man can serve two masters with conflicting interests" (Georgia House 1908: 34).

In the wake of these revelations, the Senate passed a bill abolishing the lease system, effective with the expiration of the last lease on March 31, 1909. The House followed suit with minor modifications four days later, and the subsequent law marks the end of private sector intervention in punishment (Georgia Assembly 1908). The state continued to bear ultimate responsibility for supervising felons. County authorities were responsible for supervision on a daily basis. The state did not completely shirk its financial responsibility, as it paid the salaries of camp wardens, inspectors, and supervisors. Counties were responsible for the salaries of physicians and guards.

The Chain Gang Period, 1908-1944

With abolition of the lease, all able-bodied men convicted of felonies became eligible for work on public roads, bridges, and other works undertaken by counties and municipalities. While the number of convicts that each county received depended on its post road mileage, counties could obtain more convicts by petitioning the Prison Commission. They also could deliver unused shares of convicts to more needy counties. Although the state would, if possible, "equip and organize road-working forces," counties bore the cost of maintaining both the equipment and the convicts (Georgia Assembly 1908: 1121–22).

Like the penitentiary and the lease, Georgia's reliance on chain gangs was not new. The sight of convicts on public roads and works was a common feature of nineteenth-century American punishment (Stone 1895). This was true in Georgia as early as 1866, when persons convicted of misdemeanors could be sentenced to a fine, jail, or work on the public roads in the chain gang (Georgia Assembly 1866). What distinguished Georgia from other states was its wholesale use of state prisoners on public roads and the decentralized nature of that use over a lengthy period of time. Its solution most closely resembled North Carolina's, where after 1887 felons sentenced to less than ten years could be retained by counties for their use on roads (McKay 1942; Steiner and Brown [1927] 1970; Hawkins 1984). North Carolina was exceptional, however. At the turn of the century, it was one of only three states, with Alabama and South Carolina, that allowed any felons to work on public roads (Holmes 1901b). With the flowering of the good-roads movement, discussed below, more states permitted this option and set fewer restrictions on which convicts could be used.[4] Permission to use state prisoners rarely implied their actual use, however. The exceptions to the rule were all southern states. In 1912, for example, Alabama reported using 300 convicts; Virginia, 735 convicts; North Carolina, 2,300; and Georgia, 4,744 (McCallie 1912; American Highway Association 1913).

The use of serious felons on chain gangs was an outgrowth of the movement to improve transportation, which swept the United States in general and Georgia in particular (Dearing 1941; Hilles 1958; Wallenstein 1987; Lichtenstein 1996). The good-roads movement began in the 1880s and gained momentum in 1892, when the first national good-roads convention was held and the National League for Good Roads was founded (Hilles 1958). The Southern Road Congress quickly merged with the National League. The League, the National Good Roads Association (founded in 1900), and thousands of their counterparts at the state and local levels campaigned vigorously for improved public roads.[5]

With the expansion of cotton production into new areas of the Piedmont, the state of Georgia was one of the most active partisans of the movement. It led the South in forming a state good-roads association in 1901, following Alabama by only a week (Preston 1991). Years earlier, the state had laid the groundwork for the association by hosting a Good Roads Congress (1889) and a National Road Parliament (1895). The regional magazine, *Southern Good Roads*, considered Georgia the southern exemplar in its commitment to road improvement: "Every farmer wants the best part of the road in front of his place, and he is so anxious for it that he not only stands his proportion of the burden of taxes, but also digs down into his pocket and gets more coin and gives more labor in order that his road may be as he desires" (quoted in Varner 1910b: 21). Between 1904 and 1909, Georgia led the nation in increasing the total mileage of improved roads: from 1,634 to 5,978, for an increase of more than 4,000 miles. The state of Washington was a distant second, with an increase of only 2,500 miles (Pennybacker and Eldridge 1912).

The demand for roads brought with it a particularly thorny problem: how best to finance them. Convict labor quickly emerged as a viable alternative to labor required by statute.[6] Early and often, good-roads associations proposed and supported the use of convicts (Mason 1957). The Georgia Road Congress went on record in 1889 as mounting concerted efforts to obtain the state's convicts for this purpose (Eve 1895). Hardly unique, its advocacy was echoed in some of the earliest bulletins issued by the federal and state governments (Sheffield 1894; Stone 1898; Holmes 1901a; McCallie 1901).

H. B. Varner, editor of *Southern Good Roads*, best summarized popular arguments for using convict labor:

> It engages convict labor in healthful occupation without competition with free labor; it permits of a permanent, organized force for road building which can be better maintained than with free labor; it is cheaper to the state than free labor and all the people of the state derive a direct benefit from its employment; it frees the state from the expense of keeping prisoners without any return value, or of obtaining a revenue and the convicts in competition with free labor; it is the best possible punishment of the common criminal; it will free our cities and county of the tramp nuisance; and the result will be good roads throughout the state, which is a benefit and blessing to all. (Varner 1910a: 18)

In less florid prose, E. Stagg Whitin, closer to the scene as general secretary for the National Committee on Prison Labor, offered a quite different justification:

> The underlying motive in convict road building must be to secure the greatest efficiency for the state out of its possession. The convict is the property of the state; the road is the property of the state or of its subdivisions; the working of the convict upon the roads brings together two elements similar in their possession thereby eliminating many elements of waste in their joint operation. (Whitin 1912: 12)

Widespread use of convict labor on roads met resistance in the North on a number of grounds: the cost of maintaining convicts, competition with free labor, demoralization of the public, and degradation to convicts (Hilles 1958). As a result, convicts did little more than prepare road materials (Mason 1957). For southern states, however, competition with free labor was not an issue. The symbolic costs of degradation and demoralization did not figure prominently until much later. Initial resistance to improved roads derived from agrarian fears that higher taxes would be levied to finance them. Convict labor won strong approval precisely because, at least on the surface, it allayed these fears.

While there was strong public interest in good roads and in the use of convicts for that purpose, Georgia's assembly proceeded with caution and embraced the alternative slowly and grudgingly. Early proposals to use felons on public roads were rejected because of two obstacles: cost and the danger posed by escaped convicts. As early as 1886, Governor Gordon spoke favorably of the possibility, noting that it would be an improvement over the lease system and would produce "great and lasting benefits" to the public (Georgia House 1886: 298). Implementation faced two major hurdles. To maintain a force of guards would require direct taxation; to distribute convicts equitably among the counties would require a plan. The governor preferred the simpler alternative of self-sustaining farms.

A decade later, the principal keeper of the penitentiary returned to the option and concluded that it would be dangerous and unwise to place convicts on public roads (Principal Keeper of the Penitentiary 1896). His report in 1897 echoed early concerns about the prohibitive cost of this option: "To place the convicts on the road will cost the tax-payers each year for maintenance, $209,875, a like amount the first year for equipments and material, and large sums each year thereafter for repairs, new equipments and material, and the State will have neither permanent prisons, or a permanent system" (Principal Keeper of the Penitentiary 1897: 16).

While the governor thought convict road labor was "an alluring and captivating suggestion," he too had reservations. The construction and maintenance of county roads by the state posed "the danger of State centralization." Should this course be taken, the slope would indeed become slippery: "When this new obligation is assumed there will necessarily go with it the obligation to build and repair all bridges now built and maintained by the respective Counties. When this step is taken there is no halting place until the State builds all court-houses and jails, pays all court expenses—all County taxes are abolished, all County authority over local affairs surrendered, and the General Assembly of the State becomes the arena where Counties must contest for such a share of State taxes as can be secured by carrying on their local affairs" (Georgia House 1897: 53).

Not surprisingly, Governor Atkinson was "unalterably opposed" to a plan that would require the state to supervise and fund the work of state convicts on public roads (Georgia House 1897: 54). Less vociferously, he also expressed reservations about transferring jurisdiction of state convicts to county authorities, citing management problems and mismatches between the supply of convicts and the demand for public roads. As noted earlier, the initial proposal to extend the chain gang to short-term felony convicts, while keeping the remainder on a penal island, was soundly defeated in the assembly the same year (Taylor 1940).

The modified lease system, adopted in 1897, posed a compromise. Less dangerous felons, those with terms less than two years, could indeed be worked on the public roads of those counties already making full use of their misdemeanants. State convicts were not offered free of charge, however. Counties were required to pay the state thirty-six dollars a year for each convict and to furnish "transportation, maintenance, guards and other necessaries" (Georgia Assembly 1897: 75). Not surprisingly, no county leaped at this opportunity (Prison Commission 1908).

The penitentiary committee again brought up the issue of road work by state convicts in 1902, when it estimated that implementation would cost $500,000 and would increase opportunities for escape (Georgia House 1902). In a rare display of dissension, the chair of the committee issued a minority report strongly favoring the use of all felons on county roads. His proposal was simple. Thirty-three counties provided the Prison Commission with half its felons. Each county currently had misdemeanor chain gangs, within which felons could easily be integrated. To encourage road expansion and thus the prospect of long-term employment, the state should make the remaining convicts available to the counties on demand and at no cost. Short-term contracts with private parties would use the labor of the remaining convicts.

The following year, the legislature adopted part of this proposal: counties obtained the right to secure, at no cost, felons whose sentences did not exceed five years (Georgia Assembly 1903). Within a year, twenty-nine counties were using felons on their roads, and a quarter of all prisoners were so engaged (Prison Commission 1904). Four years later, with the lease discredited and no penitentiary able to house more than 2,500 convicts, the assembly once again divested the state of the expense of maintaining state prisoners, and it transferred them to the care and keeping of the counties in which they were convicted. By 1912, 116 of the state's 146 counties used prisoners on their public roads, and more than 4,700 felons and misdemeanants were so engaged (McCallie 1912). Three years later, the number of convicts working on roads increased by 48.7 percent (from about 4,700 to more than 7,000). The total value of their labor increased by 85.9 percent (from $1.4 to $2.6 million). Georgia's total mileage of public roads rose by 17 percent, from 84,000 to 101,000 miles (Varner 1915: 19).

While northern states turned to hired labor on roads in the early twentieth century (Wallenstein 1987), Georgia continued to use felons and misdemeanants until the mid-twentieth century. In its early years, this solution to the prisoner problem met with little criticism. In 1911, few counties (11 of 146) used no convict labor on roads, a "splendid showing" for the new system, according to the Prison Commission (1910–11: 7). Indeed, the commission considered the current situation the " 'come back' solution of the penitentiary problem" (Prison Commission 1914–15: 7).

Until its reports ceased in 1936, the Prison Commission offered no critique of the chain gang system. Its concerns lay elsewhere. Each year, more convicts were sent to the prison farm, known as a "refuge for old, worn-out, sick, maimed and crippled prisoners" (Prison Commission 1916–17: 4). Three camps at the state farm held 462 convicts in 1924, 701 in 1930, and 1,055 in 1936. The Prison Commission considered "less than 40 per cent of these unfortunates . . . physically fit for labor in the field and on the buildings. The production of the farm is thus handicapped, and 100 per cent must eat and be cared for with less than 40 per cent of the inmates fit for outdoor work" (Prison Commission 1931: 5).

Although recommended by the warden and superintendent in 1923, light industry for state use conflicted with state law (Prison Commission 1923, 1926). The first prison industry was not begun until 1930, when a small number of convicts produced automobile license tags (Prison Commission 1929–30). In the absence of revenue-producing labor and a population fit enough to make the prison self-sustaining, the Prison Commission annually requested larger appropriations to cover building expansion and repairs.

In addition to financial concerns about prison maintenance, two related events ensured that the prison farm was never filled to any level resembling capacity. The Federal Aid Road Act (U.S. Statutes at Large 1917: 355–59), passed in 1916, was the culmination of sustained efforts by diverse organizations to ensure that the federal government accompany its symbolic interest in good roads with practical assistance. The act allowed for matching funds to assist states in the construction of rural post roads. Such roads were defined as public roads in places with a population of less than 2,500 over which the U.S. mail was or might afterwards be transported (Holt 1923). Applications for funding required an agreement between

25

the U.S. Secretary of Agriculture and the highway department of the state seeking funding. Georgia quickly assented to the act's provisions and, lacking such an entity, created a state highway commission the same year that the federal act was passed (Georgia Assembly 1916).[7] Despite technical difficulties, Georgia applied for federal funding and quickly established itself as one of the top five states in federal aid mileage completed and in federal assistance received (Georgia Highway Department 1922). By the end of fiscal year 1932, Georgia had received nearly $34 million in federal aid, and consistently led the South in the number of miles completed with federal assistance (Georgia Highway Board 1932, 1934).

Since Georgia's constitution prohibited the state from engaging in internal improvements, the State Highway Commission operated as a conduit for dispensing federal money to the counties. It released federal money to counties or groups of counties that met federal regulations and provided the "proportion or share" needed to be eligible for assistance. In Georgia, "proportion" was interpreted loosely to mean "sufficient funds, or a combination of funds and county forces, to meet fifty per cent of the cost of the proposed work" (Georgia Highway Department 1919). "County forces" referred to convicts, who were used to construct federal highways until 1935, when a new law ended this practice (U.S. Statutes at Large 1936).

The 1935 prohibition against convict labor on federally funded highways in no way diminished the demand for and use of convict labor on roads. The State Highway Department, reorganized in 1919, was empowered to establish a system of state highways (Georgia Assembly 1919). In 1924, the assembly allowed the use of felony convicts, under the supervision of the State Highway Department, when constructing any part of the state-aid road system (Georgia Assembly 1924). While clearly not its intent, this legislation made it possible for counties to profit from felony convicts by providing them to the State Highway Department, in return for a daily allowance of one dollar per convict (Herndon 1974). For the county to receive payment, its felony convict need only remove four cubic feet of earth (Collier 1938). Once that task was completed, the county could use the convict for the remainder of the day.

Fueled by revenues from vehicle registration and gasoline taxes, the state highway system grew and slowly absorbed roads formerly maintained by counties (Foster 1949). Counties closed their work camps. In 1936, for example, 115 counties maintained camps and employed about 75 percent of all inmates (Prison Commission 1936). In 1940, only eighty counties worked felons on roads (Collier 1940). State highway camps correspondingly grew more numerous and concentrated: from five camps each housing between 100 and 150 prisoners in 1938 to fourteen camps housing between 75 and 150 convicts in 1942 (Georgia Highway Board 1937–38, 1941–42).

In sum, sustained interest in road building on the part of local, state, and federal governments ensured that all able-bodied felony convicts spent their terms of imprisonment laboring throughout Georgia in dozens of public road camps. Theoretically, the Prison Commission retained complete control and supervisory powers, manifested in its rules and regulations and in the appointment of camp personnel. In reality, supervision and control rested with those who paid the price, that is, with county and state highway authorities who bore the financial burden of constructing and maintaining camps and of compensating their personnel (U.S. Prison Industries Reorganization Administration 1937).

As the Great Depression deepened, criticism of the chain gang grew, from both within and outside Georgia. In most respects, these critiques were reprises of earlier objections to the convict lease: brutality toward inmates, inhumane conditions at the camps, and lack of state supervision and control of its own convicts (Zimmerman 1947). In reviewing southern penal systems just before the Great Depression, Haynes (1939: 203) was forced to conclude that "in no other state is the actual control of the state board over the state prisoners so limited as in Georgia. . . . It has authority to inspect, but this power has been rendered futile through lack of sufficient appropriations to cover the employment of a staff of competent inspectors. Furthermore, the counties can and probably would refuse to take state prisoners if standards were raised to a proper level."

County camps were more notorious than state highway camps, both for their profiteering activities and for their unwillingness to spend the funds needed to ensure secure and sanitary conditions. Exposés from several sources fueled condemnations of the system. As early as 1928, William B. Cox, secretary of the National Society of Penal Information, publicly stated that of the states operating road camps, "Georgia may be classed as having the worst" (Cox 1928: 214). His address to the American Prison Association seven years later indicated that deplorable conditions had not changed (Cox 1935).

When Governor Talmadge was in office, such criticism was ignored. Indeed, a legislative investigation concluded that, with some exceptions, conditions in the camps were "fairly good" (Page 1935: 562). Only when Governor Eurith Rivers took office in 1937 did penal reform became possible. Although he considered reports of chain gang abuses to be exaggerated, the governor recommended, and the assembly quickly passed, a variety of organizational changes. The functions of the Prison Commission were assigned to two separate entities. The Board of Penal Administration had authority, supervision, and control over all prisons and work camps (Georgia Assembly 1937–38). The governor appointed its members to staggered five-year terms. The Georgia Prison and Parole Commission was responsible for granting pardons and parole and could do so without approval from the governor. The public elected its members. Chain gangs, the subject of so much public opprobrium, were renamed public work camps, but they changed little. Although the state agreed to lease a large prison in 1937, built by the federal Works Progress Administration, continued interest in state and local road building ensured that this prison, capable of housing 2,500 prisoners, was underused. Only 913 male convicts were held in the Reidsville prison in 1943, on the grounds that they were unfit for road duty (Georgia House 1943: 22).

The Board of Penal Administration operated for only fourteen months. It was then abolished, and its functions were assumed by the Board of Penal Corrections, whose three members were appointed by the governor. In clear terms, the assembly gave the board the power to hire and discharge at will, with or without cause, all personnel needed to carry out its duties, including wardens and guards (Georgia Assembly 1939). This board also proved to be short-lived. In 1941, its responsibilities were merged with those of the Prison and Parole Commission, which continued to be elected (Georgia Assembly 1941). Until 1943, this single entity functioned as the defunct Prison Commission once had, exercising both administrative and quasi-judicial powers.

In its regular 1943–44 session, the assembly again divorced the supervisory function from the granting of pardons and parole. The Prison and Parole Commission was renamed the Georgia Board of Prisons. Composed of elected members, the board was responsible for control and supervision of the inmate population (Georgia Assembly 1943a: 185–95). Pardons and paroles became the responsibility of the Georgia Board of Pardons and Parole, appointed by the governor.

Mass escapes from prison and reported abuses in both the state and county work camps surfaced anew in 1943. In September, the presiding officers of the House and Senate drew sharp and unflattering comparisons between Georgia and the penal systems of the nine southern states they had recently visited. In no other state prison did they see the idleness and poor treatment that were common at the prison in Reidsville. No other state highway department continued to use convicts for road work, and no other system operated at such expense to the state. Members of the penitentiary committee, who had visited each of Georgia's state and county work camps, concurred with this assessment. Conditions were cruel and inhumane; camps were inefficiently run.

Assembly reports placed the blame for Georgia's penal problems squarely on the shoulders of the Board of Prisons. Its feuding members engendered a "complete lack of intelligent direction" in the penal system (Georgia Senate 1943: 35), which the governor found acutely embarrassing (Henderson 1991). Legislative action was swift and broad. It created a Department of Corrections, whose director was appointed by and served at the pleasure of the governor. The Georgia Board of Prisons became an advisory commission to the director until its members' terms expired. No successors were named. The director of corrections was authorized to remove all "shackles, manicles [sic], picks, leg irons and chains" immediately and to abolish work camps run by the State Highway Department "as soon as practical" (Georgia Assembly 1943b: 2).

For the most part, legislation left untouched county public work camps, where most convicts continued to labor. These camps continued to receive the quota of prisoners to which they were entitled by law, the preference being for offenders convicted in the county. Nevertheless, county camps were now subject to closer state inspection, initially conducted with assistance from the Federal Bureau of Prisons. By February 1944, the director of corrections had devised rules and regulations and distributed them to county commissioners and the wardens of county camps. Five months later, he reported improvement in supervision, treatment, and living conditions in the work camps located in eighty-seven of the state's counties (Director of Corrections 1943–44). Thus, the use of state convicts for county public works continued during World War II.

Changing Penalties and Policies

As the preceding sections made clear, Georgia's assembly was willing, though often at the eleventh hour, to change the *form* of punishment. It eschewed incarceration for leases and abolished the lease in favor of county-administered punishment. At the same time, the state was considerably less willing to alter the *severity* of punishment imposed on offenders (table 2.1). Penalties were remarkably stable over time. For example, murder was punishable by death or life imprisonment, and assault with intent to murder was punishable by two to ten years in the penitentiary. Despite intensified concern with rape at the turn of the century (Myers 1995b), the law continued to permit one- to twenty-year sentences for rape and one- to twenty-year sentences for assault with intent to rape. Although minor, the only noteworthy changes involved longer terms for various forms of larceny and robbery and shorter terms for arson and burglary.

Of greater significance for punishment in the penitentiary were changes in the nature of judicial discretion. In 1895, the assembly empowered judges to punish certain felonies as misdemeanors. This power was discretionary during bench trials and, during jury trials, upon recommendation from the jury. Only the most serious crimes (e.g., homicide, rape) were exempt (Georgia Assembly 1895).[8] In 1913, Georgia became the third southern state and the twenty-seventh state of the union to extend probation to adults whose felonies had been reduced to misdemeanors (Morse 1939; Timasheff 1941). Instead of a fine, jail term, or imprisonment on the chain gang, offenders could receive service without confinement under supervision

Table 2.1 Penalties for major offenses, state of Georgia, 1866–1940

Offense	Penalty, in Years
Violent Offenses	
Assault, intent to murder	2–10
Assault, intent to rape	1–20
Assault, intent to rob	2–4
	2–4, as misdemeanor (1895)
Kidnapping	4–7
	4–7, as misdemeanor (1895)
Kidnapping for ransom	4–20 (1933)
	Life, death (1937)
Manslaughter, voluntary	1–20
Manslaughter, involuntary	1–3
Murder	Life, death
Rape	1–20, death
Shooting at another	1–4, as misdemeanor
Sodomy	Life
Property Offenses	
Arson, occupied dwelling	Death
	Life, death (December 1866)
	5–20 (1899)
	2–20 (1924)
Burglary, night	Death
	Life, death (December 1866)
	5–20 (1868)
	1–20 (1879)
	1–20, as misdemeanor (1895)
Burglary, day	3–5
	1–20 (1879)
	1–20, as misdemeanor (1895)
Forgery	2–10
Larceny after trust	1–5
Larceny, auto	1–5
Larceny (>$50) from a person	As misdemeanor
	2–5 (1879)
Larceny, horse	2–5, death
	4–20 (1868)
	4–20, as misdemeanor (1895)
Robbery by intimidation	2–5
	2–20 (1891)
	2–20, as misdemeanor (1895)
	4–20, life, death (1937)

Sources: Georgia Code (1867, 1873, 1882, 1896, 1911, 1926, 1935); Georgia Assembly (1937).

Note: Misdemeanors were punishable by a fine, imprisonment in jail for up to six months, or work on county chain gangs for up to one year.

and on conditions specified by the sentencing judge (Georgia Assembly 1913). Counties, rather than the state, bore administrative and financial responsibility when exercising this option.

While these policies affected the number of convicts admitted to the penitentiary, Progressive-era reforms gave state officials greater flexibility in determining the speed with which offenders left prison. Georgia was the sixth southern state and the thirtieth of the union to pass a parole law (Lindsey 1925; Morse 1939; Barnes and Teeters 1945). It was the seventh southern state and thirty-ninth state of the union to accept indeterminate sentencing and the only state to place this power squarely in the hands of the jury.

Parole, the first innovation, provided for conditional discharge of convicts after they had served part of their sentence. Like most states, Georgia had long provided for the *unconditional* early release of convicts who had served "good time." As early as 1856, each month served reduced the sentences of "unexceptionable" offenders by two days (Georgia Assembly 1856). During the early years of the lease, the legislature doubled this allowance (Georgia Assembly 1874). In 1887, a more complicated formula was devised. For the third through tenth year of incarceration, convicts who comported themselves "uprightly" received a three-month deduction per year, and each good year thereafter earned a four-month deduction (Georgia Assembly 1887: 38).

"Good time" implied a straightforward reduction in sentence length and unconditional discharge. The closest forerunner to parole, as a form of conditional discharge, was executive clemency, which allowed convicts to petition the governor and, if their cases were compelling, to receive pardons or commutations of sentence to time served (Prison Commission 1901). Theoretically, governors could set conditions on any discharge and, in effect, grant parole, but apparently none had done so. In 1897, legislation authorized the Prison Commission to operate as a board of pardons. It could both initiate and respond to applications for clemency and recommend action to the governor (Georgia Assembly 1897). The Prison Commission called for more sweeping legislation in 1901; it wished to issue conditional pardons or paroles itself. To support its position, the commission cited the satisfactory use of this policy in other states. To guide the assembly, the commission reproduced the Ohio parole statute, the country's first, in its entirety (Prison Commission 1901). Its request was ignored until 1908, when abolition of the lease became a distinct possibility. Like other states faced with limits on prison labor (Simon 1993), Georgia's assembly gave the Prison Commission "full power to establish rules and regulations under which prisoners within the penitentiary may be allowed to go upon parole" (Georgia Assembly 1908).

Eleven years later, the assembly increased the discretionary powers of the commission again by providing for indeterminate sentencing. Before 1919, judges selected a specific term of imprisonment that fell within statutory limits (Cobb 1850). Where imprisonment was discretionary, the judge again determined punishment, "paying due respect to any recommendation which the jury may think proper to make in that regard" (Prince 1837: 661). Judicial sentencing powers were absolute, and judges' decisions were final. The Prison Commission first expressed dissatisfaction with this method of sentencing in 1916, noting that "one of the defects of the Georgia criminal procedure is the inequalities of punishment in the various judicatories of the State. In each case the punishment is determined by the opinion of the trial judge about particular offenses, and on account of there being so many judges their ideas, of course, vary, and we have a great variety of sentences for the same crime" (Prison Commission 1915–16: 4). The commission reiterated the recommendation for indeterminate sentencing in its next three reports. The assembly finally acted in 1919 and gave juries the power to set a minimum and maximum term for all felonies not requiring life imprisonment. Juries held this power until February 16, 1938, when judges regained the power to set prison terms (Georgia Assembly 1937–38). Until then, the only stipulation was that the minimum and maximum lie within the bounds established by statute. Once the minimum sentence was served, the Prison Commission was given the power to fix the rules "by which said convict . . . may be allowed to complete his term without the confines of the penitentiary upon complying with said rules" (Georgia Assembly 1919: 387). In a real sense, then, neither judges nor juries established the duration of punishment after 1919. That decision was in the hands of the Prison Commission and its administrative descendants.

Conclusion

From the vantage point of the Great Depression, an observer eloquently remarked that the Civil War "fell like a huge boulder into the stream of American prison developments, sending large eddies across the main current that swept around to the north, and sharply diverting into a separate southern channel but a small portion of the old Auburn tradition. . . . The war and its aftermath were the dominant factors in separating the South from the Union in penological matters for at least half a century" (McKelvey 1935: 153). As the foregoing narrative makes clear, the southern political economy, altered by the war, did indeed shape Georgia's long-standing commitment to minimize the costs of punishment by expropriating the labor of its convicts. To minimize costs meant initial alliances with private capitalists, followed by alliances with county authorities. For decades after the Civil War, then, the burden of punishing its prisoners fell lightly on the state's shoulders. It took the form of symbolic control through legislative regulation and the modest financial costs of maintaining a little-used penitentiary and a relatively small staff.

Weak state intervention in the punishment of state convicts reflects, in part, the operation of a political economy noted for an enduring and heavy dependence on a volatile cash crop. As we saw in chapter 1, the volatility of cotton prices and harvests affected the well-being of individuals and their communities. Ultimately the state, its revenues, and its reputation were affected. Not surprisingly, major transformations in punishment followed closely on the heels of unsettled economic conditions. Shortly after the depression of 1893–94 and the ensuing recession, the state was forced to modify the lease system in such a way that greater attention was paid to the public interest. Some convicts were diverted from the accumulation of private profit to the construction of roads, which the public deemed essential to the production and distribution of cotton. During the depression of 1907–8, the state once again was forced to consider the public good. This time, it released all convicts for work on the transportation infrastructure. Connections between the private and public sector, once considered appropriate or tolerable, became unseemly and were severed. The Great Depression focused attention once again on the conduct of the state, which yet again was found wanting. While no basic shift in punishment occurred, a series of bureaucratic reorganizations represented renewed attempts to tighten state control over the conditions under which convicts labored.

Interspersed among changes in the form and administration of punishment were modifications in the penalties associated with crimes and policy innovations that had won widespread acceptance elsewhere in the country. In their entirety, these changes and innovations defined the shifting parameters within which judges, juries, and parole boards acted to punish criminals. The next two chapters consider the consequences of their actions: the frequency with which black and white men were admitted to the penitentiary, the severity of punishments they received, and the frequency with which they secured release. Chapter 3 returns to the general literature for guidance in identifying the social changes and events that shaped punishment in other contexts. Chapter 4 adapts this literature to develop models that account for patterns of punishment in Georgia.

3

Social Change and the
Use of the Penitentiary

OUR ATTENTION THUS FAR HAS FOCUSED ON THE FIRST ISSUE ANIMATING social science research on punishment: how and why punishment became wedded to the labor of convicts within penitentiaries. Of interest in this chapter is research addressing the second issue: how the actual use of the penitentiary was linked to specific social, political, and economic changes. Considered first are studies of twentieth-century trends in incarceration. They draw their inspiration not only from the political economy perspective but also from Durkheimian notions about the stability of punishment and from twentieth-century interest in intergroup competition. The focus then shifts to the nineteenth century, where research emphasizes the dual importance of race and region to an understanding of punishment. Taken together, these research traditions constitute the foundation for the models that are developed and tested in the following chapters.

Patterns of Imprisonment in the Twentieth Century

Analysts who examine incarceration in the twentieth century begin their work, as do theorists, by abandoning the commonsense notion of a simple equivalency between criminality and punishment. Intensified levels of punishment do not necessarily spring from elevated levels of criminality. Nor does a decline in criminality invariably lower rates of incarceration. Instead, the notion of threat is an indispensable tool for understanding changing levels of punishment over time

(Liska 1994). What distinguishes current research are the divergent avenues that scholars have taken to reach this common focus on threat.

Stability of Punishment

The earliest analysts of trends in punishment turned to Durkheim's thoughts about punishment and its consequences (for reviews, see Liska 1992). For Durkheim, punishment is an essential element of social life: "It does not serve, or else only serves quite secondarily, in correcting the culpable or in intimidating possible followers. From this point of view, its efficacy is justly doubtful and, in any case, mediocre. Its true function is to maintain social cohesion intact, while maintaining all its vitality in the common conscience" (Durkheim 1933: 108). From the functionality of punishment as a source of order and cohesion flows the "stability of punishment" hypothesis, originally developed by Blumstein and Cohen (1973). Like other functional aspects of a society, including levels of crime, the level of punished criminal acts will be stable over time. This is not to say that punishment will never vary. Rates of punishment will fluctuate but around a relatively unchanging level. This is so because "if too large a portion of the society is declared deviant, then the fundamental stability of the society may well be disrupted. Likewise, if too few are punished, the basic identifying values of the society will not be adequately articulated and reinforced, again leading to social instability" (Blumstein, Cohen, and Nagin 1977: 320).

To maintain stable levels of punishment requires the use of adaptive self-regulating mechanisms within the larger system for controlling crime. Should incarcerated populations become too large and exceed the stable level, discretionary decisions all along the process will compensate and exercise a dampening influence. Police will ignore behavior previously considered harmful and prosecutors will refuse to invest the time and personnel to prosecute such acts. Parole boards will increase the number of convicts released on parole. On the other hand, should incarcerated populations fall below the stable level, discretionary decisions will tend to reflect a growing intolerance for behavior once considered harmless or annoying. More arrests, prosecutions, and convictions will ensue, as will fewer early releases from prison (Blumstein and Moitra 1979).

The long-term stability of punishment presumes the absence of social upheavals. Levels of punishment may nevertheless shift dramatically, when conditions or events threaten the normal functioning of society. Abrupt changes such as depressions and the demobilization following a global conflict pose general and diffuse threats to the social order. As such, they lower tolerance for criminality and so intensify social control efforts. The ultimate purpose of such intensification is to reestablish moral boundaries and social order. Once accomplished, levels of

35

punishment may stabilize at new, possibly higher levels, around which occur minor fluctuations requiring the use of self-regulating mechanisms (Blumstein and Moitra 1980).

Although continuing to the present day (e.g., Tremblay 1986; Fiselier 1992), research based on the Durkheimian tradition has generally failed to document the stability of punishment in a consistent way. Indeed, what constitutes clear evidence of stability is subject to debate. There is no single test for determining whether a given trend in punishment is stationary, that is, stable. Some trends can be modeled successfully as outcomes of either stationary or nonstationary processes (Rauma 1981). Neither has the tradition successfully located the mechanisms through which this stability, where it appears to exist, is achieved (Liska 1992).

The continued vitality of the perspective rests on two insights. First, research based on the stability of punishment tradition has initiated inquiries into the nature of the relationship between social changes, often abrupt in nature, and punishment. Berk et al. (1981, 1983), for example, discovered that admission rates rose in California (1851–1970) during periods of military demobilization and economic distress. Lessan and Sheley (1992) presented evidence that incarceration rates in the United States fell during wars. The first insight from this tradition, then, is the possibility that traumatic social changes fundamentally alter the extent to which incarceration is used. As yet unestablished are which changes, if any, are consistently important.

The second insight from the stability of punishment tradition is its recognition that the punishment process has its own inner dynamic. Although most research has focused on admissions (e.g., Sabol 1989) or on the number of persons incarcerated (Berk et al. 1981; Rauma 1981), Tremblay (1986) draws a crucial distinction between how *often* a society punishes (admission rates) and how *severely* a society punishes (sentence severity). One possible mechanism for maintaining stable punishment is self-regulation: to compensate for more severe punishment simply by punishing less often. A narrow focus on a single aspect of punishment, such as the incarceration rate, obscures this process. It fuses the amount of punishment with its severity (Waller and Chan 1974; Rauma 1981; Moitra 1987), thereby precluding an exploration of the relationship between the two processes.

In sum, research based on the stability of punishment tradition has initiated two very different inquiries. The first is the relationship between punishment and a variety of social changes and events. The second is the relationship among discrete dimensions of punishment. Both relationships lie at the heart of the present work.

Political Economy

The second and currently dominant avenue for research rests on the work of Rusche and Kirchheimer (1939) and later neo-Marxian analysts (e.g., Spitzer 1975;

Adamson 1983, 1984b). Of central concern is the political economy, particularly the relationship between labor supply and demand. Surplus labor, in the form of a large unemployed population, constitutes a reserve upon which capitalists can draw when accumulating capital. At the same time, this "reserve army of the unemployed" is a problem population. Its sheer existence and size pose symbolic and real threats to the stability of the economic, political, and social order. In this perspective, then, the source of threat is localized in the economic arena. Its disconcerting influence nevertheless ripples outward, necessitating more coercive social control responses as economic threats become more severe.

For the most part, analysts have successfully verified the link between a labor surplus, indicated by rates of unemployment, and higher levels of contemporary punishment. The most comprehensive literature review (Chiricos and DeLone 1992) concluded that 83 percent of all studies (n = 262) found a positive relationship between unemployment and punishment, once levels of reported criminality were held constant. Over half of all studies reported relationships that were not only positive but also statistically significant, again with the level of crime controlled.

Research applying the political economy perspective to early twentieth-century trends in punishment has reached a similar conclusion (Myers and Sabol 1987). Growing black unemployment increased the rate at which blacks were incarcerated between 1925 and 1950. White unemployment did the same for the rate at which whites were incarcerated. Of direct relevance here is the fact that these findings apply only to punishment in the North. Industrial production, a dominant feature of the northern economy, produced wider oscillations in unemployment than did agricultural production, which predominated in the South. As a result, the link between unemployment, especially black unemployment, and incarceration rates existed only in the North. Agricultural output proved to be the key to understanding punishment in the South. As this output declined, signifying lower demand for labor, incarceration rates increased.

Research drawing from the political economy perspective yields two insights of relevance here. First is the realization that the relationship between the labor market and punishment is hardly invariant (D'Alessio and Stolzenberg 1995). It appears to be a stronger determinant of how *often* a society punishes than of how *severely* it punishes. In emphasizing several dimensions of punishment, the present work affords us an opportunity to assess explicitly the variability of the labor-punishment relationship not only over time but across the various facets of punishment.

The second insight of the political economic perspective is its forcible reminder of regional differences in political economies. A proper understanding of punishment rests on a clear understanding of the specific political economy from which it emanates. By the early twentieth century, the Northeast had virtually completed

37

the transition to industrial capitalism;[1] the South had just begun (Fields 1983). Focused as it is on an agrarian political economy undergoing a distinctive industrialization process, this examination attends in equal measure to variations in agrarian and industrial production over time.

Interracial Competition

The final perspective grounds threat in yet a third source: problematic minority populations and their size vis-à-vis the dominant population (Blalock 1967). This perspective is particularly relevant in the South, with its large black population. The central contention is that as minority populations increase in relative size, economic competition with the dominant group ensues, interracial inequalities decline, and perceptions of economic threat intensify. Social control efforts—both legal and extralegal—intensify in an effort to ensure economic dominance.

The earliest applications of this perspective focused on the link between percentage black in the population and social control mechanisms other than punishment. In general, results have been supportive. Growth in the size of minority populations or in economic inequalities between minority and majority populations tends to increase the size of police forces (Chamlin 1989; Jackson 1992) and arrest rates (Chamlin and Liska 1992). Moreover, it does so independently of levels of criminality. The link between interracial competition and punishment has also occupied researchers focusing on nineteenth-century trends in southern punishment. It is to this literature that we now turn.

Imprisonment in the Nineteenth Century

As the previous section makes clear, the notion of threat unifies theorizing and empirical work on punishment in the twentieth century. From the Durkheimian tradition emanates a focus on threatening "times," that is, certain events and conditions. From neo-Marxian roots springs a concern with the state of the labor market. And from an intergroup conflict perspective derives an interest in threats posed by the relative position or distribution of minorities in the economic and political arenas. Of what utility are these perspectives when our field of vision shifts to the nineteenth century in general and to the South in particular? Although often grounded in the same theoretical traditions, research on historical trends in punishment has posed different questions and, in so doing, has focused attention on race and region, issues of peripheral concern to researchers examining contemporary punishment. This section considers two issues, both of which bear on analysis presented in later chapters: regional differences in the use of incarceration and racial differences in factors that account for punishment.

Region and Punishment

Research examining regional differences in punishment addresses the question of punishment's stability. It has generated two quite different conclusions (Myers and Sabol 1986). First, the rate at which whites were incarcerated in penitentiaries tended to be stable. In the North, this was the case between 1850 and 1980. In the South, stability characterized the punishment of whites for a shorter period, between 1850 and 1920. Second, the rate at which blacks were incarcerated tended to be *unstable,* and this was particularly true in the North. In short, a single question about the stability of punishment or lack thereof yields several answers, depending on how punishment is conceptualized. Resolution of the issue hinges on a conception of punishment that distinguishes its black and white, northern and southern manifestations.

Race and Southern "Punishment"

Southern punishment in the nineteenth century has traditionally been equated with the punishment of black men, for they filled the penitentiary and worked on chain gangs. Less frequently encountered and less intense, the punishment of whites has generated, until recently, little more than a footnote.

To account for the punishment of black men in the nineteenth century, researchers have drawn from the political economy and intergroup competition perspectives. The price of cotton has been the leading indicator of economic health or distress. With falling cotton prices and, by extension, deteriorating economic conditions, the rate at which black men were lynched, incarcerated, or sentenced to work on the chain gang rose (Hepworth and West 1988; Beck and Tolnay 1990; Olzak 1990; Myers 1991, 1993; Tolnay and Beck 1994). Indeed, the sheer expansion of the cotton economy stimulated the forceful expropriation of black labor in the penitentiary (Myers 1991).

Apart from the political economy, research on the social control of black men in the nineteenth century draws inspiration from the interracial competition perspective. Conflicting results underscore the need to consider which aspects of the minority population threatened which groups within the dominant population (Myers 1990a; Tolnay and Beck 1992). A declining population of black men may indeed have eased fears of interracial competition among lower-class whites. This could account for reductions in coercive sanctions against blacks, the most prominent being lynching (Tolnay, Beck, and Massey 1989; Tolnay and Beck 1990). Yet the very same phenomenon fueled anxiety among upper-class white landowners over the adequacy of the labor supply. This anxiety helps explain the increase in incarceration rates that followed reductions in the size of the black male population (Myers 1990b).

39

If we focus directly on interracial economic competition, we find that greater competition did not always disadvantage blacks. As the economic gap between whites and blacks narrowed, black men were indeed more likely to be executed and lynched around the turn of the century (Corzine, Huff-Corzine, and Creech 1988; Tolnay, Beck, and Massey 1989, 1992). Yet the blurring of traditional caste boundaries did not adversely affect their risk of being incarcerated in the penitentiary or of being sent to work on misdemeanor chain gangs (Myers 1993).

Thus far, we have spoken only of the punishment of southern black men in the nineteenth and early twentieth centuries. Of what use are the political economy and interracial competition perspectives to the punishment of white men? The price of cotton, a global indicator of the South's economic health, had similar consequences for the social control of whites. Declines in the price of cotton intensified incarceration in the penitentiary and on chain gangs (Myers 1993). Moreover, even though the demand for agrarian labor was largely a demand for the labor of black men, declining cotton harvests also affected the social control of white men. Declines noticeably increased the rate at which white men were sent to prison. But they did so only rarely, when smaller harvests were coupled with the wider economic distress generated by depressions (Myers 1991). Finally, white men did not escape the consequences of economic competition with blacks. Irrelevant for black men, a narrowing of the gap between white and black wealth nonetheless increased the risk that white men would be sent to prison or placed, as a misdemeanant, on the chain gang (Myers 1993).

These results suggest that the historical punishment of whites was driven by different factors than that of blacks. As such, they call into question the findings of color-blind research, within both the stability of punishment and political economy traditions. As yet unknown is the full scope of the "dual punishment system." Did it extend to the length of prison sentences and to rates of release from the penitentiary? Chapters 6 and 7 address these questions.

Role of the State

Thus far, structural forces outside the crime control system have occupied our attention. What of forces within the system, namely, the behavior of officials who devised and administered the social control apparatus and whose alliances with private entrepreneurs have already been discussed (Sutton 1987)? Of interest here are the Progressive-era reforms of probation, parole, and indeterminate sentences. The introduction of probation, discussed in chapter 2, drastically altered judicial discretion. Its use could well have inhibited the rate at which convicts were admitted to the penitentiary. The twin innovations of indeterminate sentences and parole broadened the discretion exercised by yet another official agency: the parole board. Together, their use could dictate the speed with which convicts left the penitentiary.

Quite apart from responding to external forces, then, punishment may respond to policy changes within the system. Research has just begun to explore this possibility. In California between 1850 and 1970, probation had no effect on imprisonment rates, while parole depressed rates of prison expansion (Berk et al. 1981, 1983). Sutton's analysis of state-level data on inmates, aggregated to the national level for the period 1880 to 1923, broadens and deepens our understanding (Sutton 1987). On the surface, probation, parole, and indeterminate sentencing had no impact on incarceration rates. Upon closer inspection, it becomes apparent that the introduction of parole slowed rates of prison growth in rural states. Often beset with low revenues, these states discouraged prison growth in one of two ways. Either they used probation to restrict admissions to the penitentiary, or they used indeterminate sentences to increase rates of conditional release from the penitentiary.

The Present Study

The research summarized above has often developed parsimonious models to account for patterns in the use of the penitentiary. Researchers working within the political economy perspective, for example, limit their vision to determining whether a labor surplus intensifies punishment. Scholars who base their work on the stability of punishment perspective focus on assessing stability, and only recently have they become interested in the link between social upheavals and punishment. This research casts a broader net over the major forces of theoretical interest. The ultimate purpose is not to declare any one perspective the victor but rather to obtain the fullest understanding of the linkages between punishment and social change. To that end, the models developed in chapter 4 include cataclysmic events such as war and depressions. The political economy perspective directs our attention to the cotton economy, the agrarian labor market, and industrial production. From the interracial competition perspective flows an interest in the magnitude of racial economic inequality. Finally, the most important actions that state officials undertook during this period are included. Among these were abolition of the lease in 1909 and the institution of probation (1913), parole (1908), and indeterminate sentencing (1919).

In a second respect, this study casts a wider net—over the phenomenon of punishment itself. Of interest are three distinct dimensions of punishment. Admission to the penitentiary has already received some scholarly attention. Length of sentence and release rates have been relatively neglected. For each dimension, the analysis poses the same set of questions. Did depressed economic conditions and declines in racial inequality, for example, not only increase the rate at which blacks were admitted to the penitentiary but also increase the length of their sentences and discourage their release? Answers to such questions will identify more clearly than before the scope of each account of the punishment process.

In addition to linking each dimension of punishment with broader social forces and events, the analysis will forge links among the dimensions themselves. Of interest is the extent to which punishment was a self-regulating phenomenon. Did officials, for example, compensate for more severe sentences by decreasing the frequency with which they punished and by increasing the frequency with which they released offenders from the penitentiary? Were lower admission rates compensated for by slowing rates of release? Answers to questions like these will assess more clearly than before the merits of the stability of punishment thesis.

The analysis will consider each dimension of punishment along two axes.[2] The first, and most obvious, is race. A consideration of new dimensions of punishment enables us to elaborate on the conclusion that, despite similarities in form, the punishment of black men was driven by different forces than was the punishment of white men. The second and less obvious axis is the nature of the offense for which offenders were admitted to the penitentiary. The distinction between violent and property crime has only recently captured the attention of researchers exploring official responses to crime. Cross-sectional analysis, for example, has found that growth in the size of the minority population increases the rate at which blacks are arrested for violent crimes; it has no impact on their risk of being arrested for property crime. Income inequality generates more substantial increases in arrest rates for property crimes than it does for violent crimes. This difference is particularly pronounced for whites. As income inequality increases, the rate at which urban whites are arrested for property crimes rises. Their risk of being arrested for violent crimes remains unchanged. The same cannot be said for urban blacks. As inequality becomes more pronounced, they are more likely to be arrested for both violent and property offenses (Liska and Chamlin 1984; Sampson 1985; Chamlin and Liska 1992).

Longitudinal analysis of arrest rates confirms the importance of distinguishing offenses against the person from offenses against property. Between 1957 and 1990, improvements in economic well-being, an index based on unemployment and income levels, reduced the rate at which whites were arrested for burglary; it had no bearing on their risk of being arrested for homicide (LaFree and Drass 1996). Changes in economic well-being operated differently for blacks. Improvements in family income and reductions in black male unemployment actually increased arrest rates for homicide; they had no bearing on arrests for burglary (LaFree, Drass, and O'Day 1992). Rather, racial differences in income were relevant to burglary arrests. As differences declined, blacks ran a greater risk of being arrested for burglary; their risk of being arrested for homicide was unaffected (LaFree and Drass 1996).

In research on criminal punishment, the importance of considering the distinction between violence and theft has yet to surface. Longitudinal research has typically failed to disaggregate the punishment of violent offenders from the punishment of their property offense counterparts. Cross-sectional analysis indicates that, at least in contemporary contexts, the distinction between violent crime and property crime has clear implications for punishment. Today, the most vigorous prosecution and harshest penalties are often reserved for blacks who perpetrate violence against whites, with lenience extended to blacks who victimize fellow blacks (see, e.g., Hawkins 1987; Paternoster 1991). At the base of such differences are notions about the relative value of victims, assessed on the basis of their race. Also relevant are notions about the differential threat posed by blacks who victimize members of socially advantaged groups. If current patterns have historical roots, then one would expect black property offenders to be punished more severely than either black violent offenders or white property offenders. This is so because blacks were more likely to cross racial lines when committing property crimes (Smith 1975, 1982). As is the case today, violent crimes were more likely to be intraracial.

The nature of the crime has broader implications, however. It shapes punishment not only directly but also indirectly by determining which social factors play a role in the punishment process (Myers and Talarico 1987). In contemporary Georgia, for example, urbanization, racial inequality, and a large minority population are tightly linked with the punishment of certain property offenders. Their role during the punishment of violent offenders is correspondingly less pronounced. Together with earlier research on imprisonment rates (Jacobs 1978), these results suggest that the political economy and intergroup competition exert a profound influence on the punishment of offenders who threaten property. They could well be tangential to the punishments imposed on violent offenders.

Conclusion

Central to this study, then, is the presumption that punishment in Georgia in the late nineteenth and early twentieth centuries was, in a sense, no different than punishment today. It encompassed a complex set of processes that differed for black and white men, for property and violent offenders, and for the various aspects of punishment itself. Drawing on the literature reviewed above, chapter 4 lays the descriptive foundation for an exploration of these processes.

4

Modeling Use of the
Penitentiary in Georgia

DRAWING ON THE PERSPECTIVES PRESENTED IN CHAPTER 3, THIS CHAP-
ter develops a model of punishment in Georgia between 1870 and 1940. It first
describes the data that form the basis for an examination of patterns in the use of
the penitentiary. Next identified are social changes and events that had implications for penitentiary admissions, terms of imprisonment, and release from the
penitentiary. Concluding the chapter is a description of the analytic strategy, which
enables us to estimate the independent contribution that each social change and
event made to punishment.

Data Sources and Sampling Procedure

Two sources provided information about offenders sentenced to Georgia's penitentiary. The first source consists of the published reports of administrators responsible for managing the penitentiary. Between 1870 and 1897, the principal
keeper issued reports on an annual or biennial basis. Included in each report was a
roster of all inmates in the penitentiary at the end of the reporting period. In
addition to the convict's name, race, and age were recorded his offense, date and
county of conviction, and sentence imposed. Principal keeper reports also listed
offenders who had left the system during the period between reports, whether
through discharge, parole or pardon, escape or death.

In 1897, the legislature placed control of the penitentiary in the hands of an elected Prison Commission. Unfortunately, its biennial reports included only aggregate statistics. As a result, I obtained data from a second source, the Central Register of Convicts, a microfilmed series of manuscript inventories on file at the Georgia Department of Archives and History. The Georgia Department of Corrections granted access to volumes that listed felons convicted between 1817 and 1942.[1]

From each source, I gathered information on all offenders convicted of a violent crime between January 1870 and December 1940. Among the most common forms of violence were homicide (n = 5,650), manslaughter (n = 5,452), assault with intent to murder (n = 3,091), attempted murder (n = 2,232), rape (n = 1,168), and attempted rape or assault with intent to rape (n = 1,123). Less frequently encountered were minor assaults such as stabbing and shooting at another and miscellaneous sex offenses such as sodomy. I also recorded information about all offenders convicted of both a violent and a property crime. Fewer than 1 percent of the sample (n = 239) fell into this category, and they are classified as violent offenders.

Each data source also provided information about offenders convicted of burglary and larceny, the two most common property crimes.[2] All white men in both data sources were included. For the black penitentiary population, which outnumbered the white population eight to one, I used a different sampling procedure. I drew the entire population of black burglary and larceny offenders from the principal keeper reports (1870–97) and from the two manuscript inventories of inmates who received a term of life imprisonment. From the remaining inventories, I drew a one-third random sample of black property offenders. This sample was weighted by its sampling percentage in the descriptions and analysis that follow. The sampling procedure yielded 17,791 black offenders convicted of burglary, 8,789 convicted of larceny, and 268 convicted of committing both offenses.

Table 4.1 provides a general description of the sample. Forty-three percent were violent offenders, and the rest were convicted of one or more property crimes. More than three-quarters were black, and these offenders differed in most respects from their white counterparts. Significantly younger than whites, black offenders were also more likely to have been convicted of violent offenses and of more serious crimes. Consistent with this greater seriousness, they faced more severe punishment. Black men were significantly more likely than white men to receive either the death penalty or life imprisonment. Among those who received neither life nor death sentences, black offenders received longer sentences, on average, than did white offenders. Not surprisingly, they served significantly more time in the penitentiary. While this difference may have been a result of longer sentences, it could also reflect the tendency for fewer blacks to obtain early release through parole, pardon, or commutation of their sentence. Finally, a larger percentage of blacks than whites escaped or died while in prison.

45

Table 4.1 Description of the sample, by race

Variable	Total ($n = 46,566$)	Black ($n = 36,400$)	White ($n = 10,166$)
Offense[a]			
Homicide	12.2	12.3	11.8
Manslaughter	11.7	11.6	12.4
Sexual assault	5.0	5.0	5.0
Other violent crime	13.5	14.9	8.5
Burglary	38.8	40.9	31.4
Theft or property damage	18.9	15.5	30.9
Mean Age	26.4	25.9	28.0*
Mean Offense Seriousness	14.7	14.8	14.2*
Disposition[b]			
Discharge	33.6	37.6	20.5
Pardon	6.5	4.0	15.0
Conditional release	39.0	36.6	47.4
Escape	11.2	11.9	9.0
Death	6.6	7.5	3.3
No time served	1.0	.4	2.7
Release to others	.5	.4	.8
Execution	1.5	1.7	1.1
% Death Penalty	1.7	2.0	1.0*
% Life Imprisonment	10.6	11.0	10.0*
Mean Sentence (Years)	10.6	10.8	9.5*
Mean Time Served (Years)	4.0	4.3	3.0*

[a]$\chi^2 = 1425, p < .0001$; Gamma = .15.

[b]$\chi^2 = 2944, p < .0001$; Gamma = .10.

*Race difference significant at $p \leq .01$.

Punishment Time Series

The sample of offenders described above provided the raw material for three aggregate measures of punishment, calculated by race and type of offense. The first measure is the annual rate of admission into the penitentiary. It refers to the number of males sentenced to the penitentiary, per 10,000 males in the general population. Figure 4.1 presents trends in the admission of black and white men and reveals several patterns. First, black men were consistently admitted at a substantially

Figure 4.1. Admissions to the penitentiary

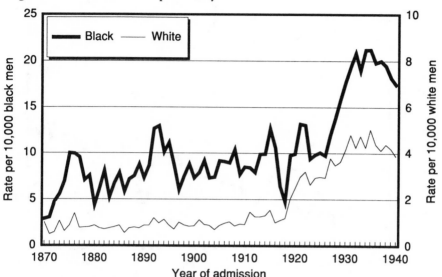

higher rate than were white men. Second, the admission rate for white men appears to have been more stable than its black counterpart, much like trends in the South as a whole (Myers and Sabol 1986). Only after World War I did white male admission rates increase noticeably. Black admission rates, in contrast, experienced sharp temporary growth during the depressions of the 1870s and 1890s, and they declined during World War I. Finally, although both black and white rates rose sharply after World War I, white admissions rose earlier and more dramatically than black admissions. For black men, the largest growth occurred between 1926 and 1935, when admission rates increased by 119 percent (from 9.7 to 21.2). For white men, growth began in 1918 and, by 1935, had entailed a 317 percent increase (from 1.2 to 5.0).

The same race differences surface in admission rates for violent and property offenders. To highlight important offense differences, figures 4.2 and 4.3 present the trends for black and white admissions separately. Two features of these trends merit emphasis. First, the rate at which black men were admitted to the penitentiary for violence rose steadily during the period under consideration. Their rates of admission for property offenses, in contrast, exhibited many of the peaks and valleys noted earlier. Furthermore, while both rates rose dramatically after World War I, the magnitude of the increase was much greater for property offenses. Between 1926 and 1937, admissions for violent crimes rose by nearly 90 percent (from 4.7 to 8.8). In the shorter space of five years (1926–32), admissions for property crimes increased by 165 percent (5.1 to 13.5).

Figure 4.2. Black admissions for violent and property crime

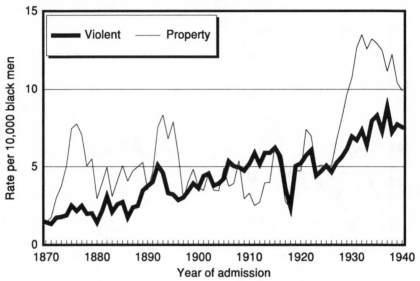

Figure 4.3. White admissions for violent and property crime

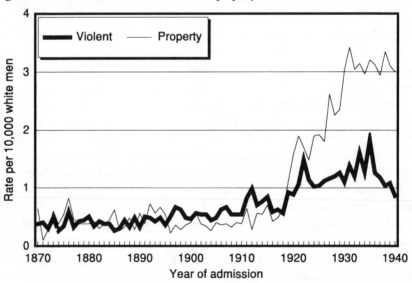

Figure 4.4. Average prison sentence

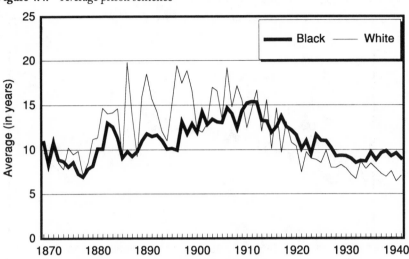

The second noteworthy feature applies to the rate at which white men were admitted to the penitentiary. Like its black counterpart, the admission of white men experienced the same postwar increase. As noted above, this increase began earlier and was more pronounced. Admissions for property crime account in part for this pattern (fig. 4.3). Between 1918 and 1935, the rate at which white men were admitted to the penitentiary for violent crimes increased by 200 percent (from .6 to 1.8). In a slightly shorter period (1918–31), admissions for property crimes rose by 467 percent (from .6 to 3.4).

The second measure of punishment provides an indication of trends in its severity over time. It is the average sentence imposed on convicted offenders, in years.[3] The sentences imposed on both black and white offenders lengthened until about 1910, after which they became shorter (fig. 4.4). Until the early twentieth century, black offenders received *shorter* sentences on average than did white offenders. Thereafter, they were likely to receive longer sentences. A comparison of the sentences imposed on property and violent offenders sheds light on this shift in severity. The sentences imposed on white violent offenders fluctuated more widely and were significantly *longer* than those imposed on black violent offenders (fig. 4.5). This was particularly the case between 1880 and 1910, precisely when the general trend indicated that white offenders were punished more severely than black offenders.

A second and quite different pattern applies to offenders convicted of property crimes (fig. 4.6). During an exceptional period (1883–92), white property offenders

Figure 4.5. Average prison sentence for violent offenders

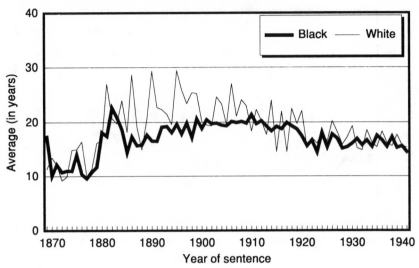

Figure 4.6. Average prison sentence for property offenders

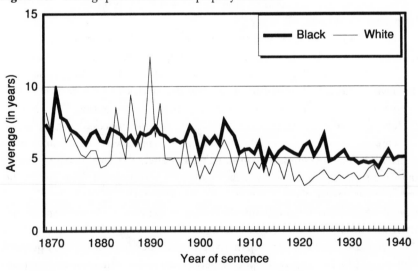

Figure 4.7. Release from the penitentiary

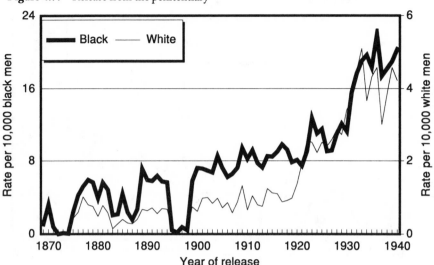

received longer sentences on average than black property offenders. This exception doubtless contributed to the general tendency toward more severe punishment for nineteenth-century white offenders. In the twentieth century, this trend reversed, and white offenders received shorter sentences on average than black offenders. In part, this reversal is due to a change in the composition of the inmate population. Recall that between 1918 and 1931, white men were admitted to the penitentiary for property offenses at a much higher rate than were black men. These were precisely the offenses for which white men received less severe punishment.

The final measure of punishment captures trends in release from the penitentiary. It is based on offenders who left the system for whatever reason, whether because of death, escape, legal execution, or actual discharge. This global measure of release is based on the rationale developed by Berk et al. (1983). From an institutional viewpoint, any convict who left the system had been "released," and he was neither a drain on existing resources nor a laborer capable of being exploited.

Given higher admission rates, it is not surprising that black offenders were released from the penitentiary at substantially higher rates than were white offenders (fig. 4.7). This difference aside, both release rates followed similar trajectories. Sharp declines coincided with the onset of nineteenth-century economic crises. Sharp increases occurred in the twentieth century, particularly after World War I. A major source of this rapid growth was the availability of conditional release from the penitentiary after 1908 (figs. 4.8 and 4.9). Parole was particularly important for black offenders. In the twentieth century, their unconditional release rates fell,

51

Figure 4.8. Black release from the penitentiary

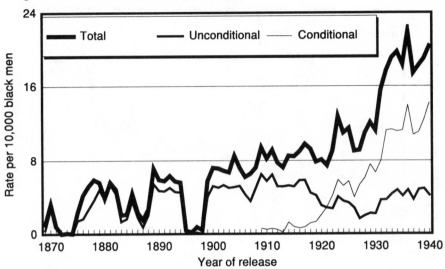

Figure 4.9. White release from the penitentiary

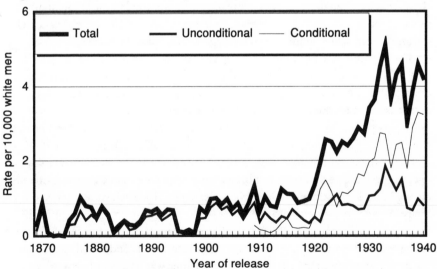

rising only slightly during the Great Depression. Their conditional release rates, in contrast, rose precipitously. White offenders benefited from the advent of parole to a lesser extent. Twentieth-century growth in their release from the penitentiary reflected not only increases in conditional release but also increases in unconditional release.

A comparison of the release process for property and violent offenders in no way alters the general description provided above (figures not presented). Black offenders, whether convicted of property or violent crimes, were released at substantially higher rates than were comparable white offenders. Black and white release rates, for violent and property offenders alike, followed similar trajectories. Sharp declines coincided with the onset of nineteenth-century economic crises. Sharp increases occurred in the twentieth century, particularly after World War I. Not surprisingly, property offenders, whose rates of admission to the penitentiary rose sharply in the twentieth century, were more likely to be released than were comparable violent offenders.

Accounting for Punishment

The following sections identify a set of social forces and events that help account for trends in the dimensions of punishment described above. Two features of the agrarian political economy figure most prominently: cotton, with its dramatic price fluctuations, and the state of the labor market. Against the backdrop of the cotton economy are placed the related processes of industrialization and urbanization, a series of economic crises, changes in the relative economic position of blacks and whites, and World War I and its aftermath. Specific policy changes concern us next. At the state level, these include the introduction of probation and parole and abolition of the lease. At the federal level, significant policies include passage of the Federal Aid Road Act in 1916 and the Agricultural Adjustment Act in 1933. The section concludes with a discussion of factors that, while of no direct theoretical relevance, may nonetheless have implications for punishment.

The Cotton Economy

The economy of the postbellum South was predominantly agrarian and remained so for most of the period considered here. Until the Great Depression, its centerpiece was cotton, which had two unique qualities. First, cultivation required an intensive and continuous use of labor. Nearly five times more field hands were needed, over nearly ten months, to produce cotton than were needed to produce corn (Scott 1920). Preharvest operations did not become mechanized to any appreciable degree until the federal government offered economic incentives in the 1930s

(Wright 1986). Harvest operations were even more labor-intensive, and they did not become mechanized until after World War II.

Without mechanization and the large stable labor force once provided by slavery, landowners considered tractable and inexpensive labor a rare commodity (Baron 1971; Bloom 1987). The specter of scarce labor became even more haunting as cotton production expanded and intensified. This growing dependence on cotton, with its voracious appetite for dependable labor, was an outgrowth of its second attribute. More than any other crop, cotton was currency and could generate the cash income so scarce after the Civil War (Clark and Kirwan 1967; Wright 1986). Yet like many "ruthless dictators," King Cotton was untrustworthy (Coulter 1947: 202). One could depend on neither its amount nor its price. The size of the harvest was vulnerable to drought, excessive rain, disease, and pests. The best-known pest was the boll weevil, which at one time was the "world's largest consumer of raw cotton" (Vance 1929: 89). The weevil reached Texas in 1892 and southeast Georgia in 1913 (Tindall 1967; Coleman 1991). By 1921, all cotton-producing areas had been affected, and the harvest fell by 30 percent. The boll weevil left more than ruined cotton in its wake. Farms foreclosed because their tenants were unable to repay debts with a small crop that grew ever more dependent on increasingly expensive fertilizers and insecticides (Raper 1936; Coleman 1991).

A generous cotton harvest meant gainful employment, but it did not guarantee prosperity. The price that a harvest could bring at market depended in part on world demand for cotton, which fluctuated dramatically and which America could not control (Hawk 1934; Mann 1990). Price also depended on the world supply of cotton, another factor over which farmers could exercise little control. Large yields in Egypt, Brazil, and India depressed the price of cotton, just as did overproduction and a badly deteriorated product in America (Saloutos 1960; Wynne 1986). Only intermittently, then, was the production of cotton a profitable enterprise (Tindall 1967; DeCanio 1974; Wright 1986). Sharp fluctuations in its price are evident in figure 4.10, which plots the annual wholesale price of cotton, in constant 1900 cents per pound (U.S. Bureau of the Census 1975).

Despite uncertain yields and prices, farmers seldom sought alternatives to the production of cotton. Their preference for cotton, even in the face of declining prices, derived from its greater profitability than any other crop (Mann 1990). Moreover, few farmers were in a financial position to consider planting alternatives. Capital was so scarce in the postbellum South that credit was an absolute necessity (Hammond 1897; Arnett [1922] 1967; Ransom and Sutch 1977; Wynne 1986). While planters and merchants could prevail on northern banks for capital, small farmers and tenants could not. Instead, they had to rely on local banking facilities. Hardest hit by the Civil War defeat, such facilities were few and far between (Thompson 1915). While even the Far West provided one banking facility

Figure 4.10. Price of cotton

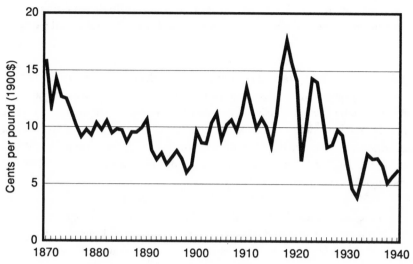

for every 5,452 residents in 1880, the South could provide only one facility for every 22,603 inhabitants (Saloutos 1960). As late as 1895, 123 of Georgia's 137 counties had no banks at all (Hammond 1897). Even if available, a local bank was seldom the solution to a farmer's credit problem. Many banks were reluctant to extend personal loans or loans on real estate or anticipated crop production (Ransom and Sutch 1972). Of necessity, smaller farmers and tenants turned to local planters and merchants, who often were one and the same person (Bloom 1987).

To receive the credit and the supplies they needed over the course of a long production cycle, tenants and sharecroppers[4] pledged part of their unplanted crops as well as any personal or real property they owned. Through crop-lien agreements, permitted by law in 1866, farmers became bound to the production of cotton. Merchant-planters would simply extend credit for no other crop. This was so because cotton afforded the best security on the loans that creditors offered. It was readily sold on an organized market, easily stored, not perishable, and, barring natural disasters, produced a fairly predictable yield (Ransom and Sutch 1977).

Inextricably linked with cotton production, then, was the lien system, which, in the eyes of the South's leading historian, "spread like Jimson weed, a curse to the soil" (Woodward 1971: 180). Indebtedness deepened because lien agreements often required that tenants and sharecroppers purchase their supplies only from creditors:

Every mouthful of food he purchases, every implement that he requires on the farm, his mules, cattle, the clothing for himself and family, the fertilizers for his land, must

55

all be bought of the merchant who holds the crop lien, and in such amounts as the latter is willing to allow. Except for cash no other merchant will sell him anything, for the first merchant holds the lien on his property and prospective crops, and the second merchant would have nothing as a guarantee of payment. (Hammond 1897: 149)

Creditors not only provided inferior goods (Clark and Kirwan 1967). They also charged an implicit interest rate that could average nearly 60 percent a year (Ransom and Sutch 1977; Kirby 1987). If cotton prices were low, farmers slipped deeper into debt and dependency on cotton and credit, because contracts required defaulting farmers to renew the lien with the same merchant the following year (Woodward 1971). Higher cotton prices brought more cash ready to hand, but self-sufficiency was extremely difficult to maintain or to achieve. For to

sever the relationship with the provisioning merchant, a farmer would have to alter his crop mix. The crop decisions could be made only at the beginning of a new season. If he had not produced sufficient food in the previous season to meet the needs of the farm for a full year, the typical farmer would not have sufficient stocks of foodstuffs to supply his farm over the coming season. Unless he had these stocks, or the cash to purchase them, he would be forced to borrow to cover the first year of his program of self-sufficiency. But this need for credit inexorably drove him back to the very merchant he sought to escape. (Ransom and Sutch 1977: 162)

In short, the price that cotton could bring at market strongly affected the well-being of blacks and whites alike (Ransom and Sutch 1977; Fligstein 1981; Johnson and Campbell 1981; Marks 1985; Grossman 1989). With high cotton prices, farmers achieved or retained financial independence and could, at least in theory, cross the line from landless tenancy to landownership. With falling cotton prices, in contrast, farmers became less able to pay for staples and to purchase or retain land. Debt became unavoidable.

As noted earlier, the previous literature has established a link between declining cotton prices and increasingly coercive social control. The expectation here is that as cotton prices fall, punishment should become more severe. Rates of admission to the penitentiary should rise, sentences lengthen, and release become more difficult to achieve. While present for both black and white men, these tendencies should be more pronounced for the economically more vulnerable population of black men. They should also be more robust for property than for violent offenders. Finally, the link between cotton prices and punishment should weaken with time, as cotton became less central to Georgia's economy.

The second feature of the cotton economy is its labor market, in particular, the demand for agrarian labor and its supply. The size of the cotton harvest captures

Figure 4.11. Size of the cotton harvest

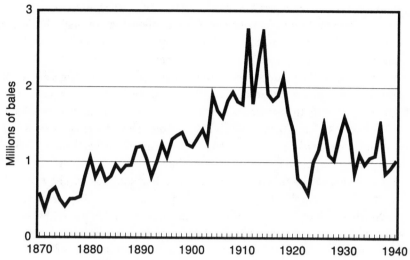

the demand for agrarian labor. Its link with punishment departs from that examined in earlier work, because the analysis relies on a different measure of harvest. Previous research used the number of acres of cotton harvested, and in so doing provided an indication of the extensiveness of the cotton economy (e.g., Myers, 1993). The expectation was that expansion of the cotton economy would, in turn, expand the forceful expropriation of black labor through the convict lease. This expansion would occur because of the synchronicity between convict labor and the cotton political economy (Myers and Massey 1991). In a very real sense, black convicts helped lay the foundation for the successful expansion of cotton production (Lichtenstein 1996). They repaired and constructed railroads, mined the coal that fueled textile mills, and built and maintained public-access roads on which cotton bales were transported to market.

The measure of harvest used here differs, as does its expected relationship with punishment (fig. 4.11). Cotton harvest refers to the number of bales, in millions, of harvested cotton (U.S. Department of Agriculture 1951–52). An increase in the number of bales harvested implied growth in the demand for labor in the fields. To the extent that large harvests kept men at home working in the fields, they reduced the demand for formal social control. Small harvests, in contrast, dispersed family members to neighboring farms, villages, and towns in search of work, increasing their vulnerability to formal control. If this argument has merit, then as cotton harvests grow smaller, punishment should intensify. More men should be admitted to the penitentiary. Those admitted should receive longer sentences. Release from

57

the penitentiary should become more difficult to achieve. Since the demand for agrarian labor was in large part a demand for black labor, the punishment of black men should bear the brunt of smaller harvests and intensify accordingly. Further, as cotton became less central to the state's economy, the size of the harvest should become increasingly peripheral to punishment over time.

As noted above, the production of cotton demanded a large and constant supply of labor. Planters preferred that this labor force be subordinate, as slaves once were (Royce 1993). Hence, the demand for agrarian labor was, foremost, a demand for the labor of black men, women, and children. Although such demands were quite consistent (Baron 1971), the available labor force, particularly black men, declined steadily during the period under study. The solution to the problem of scarce labor was not to be found in southern European or Chinese immigrants. The American West offered these immigrants more land than planters were willing to sell (Royce 1993). Northern factories, mills, and shops offered them higher wages than planters were willing to pay (Saloutos 1960). Not surprisingly, native northerners were unwilling to migrate South to perform work that had traditionally been the province of slaves.

Landowners were therefore left with an indigenous labor force. Yet blacks slowly migrated out of the South after Emancipation, pushed and pulled to other regions of the country by a multiplicity of social, economic, and cultural factors (Fligstein 1981). Much has been made of the Great Migration of 1916–18, in which nearly half a million blacks left the South. Stimulated by northern demands for labor made scarce by World War I and by the depredations of the boll weevil (Marks 1985), this particular migration intensified white concerns about the adequacy of the labor supply (Scott 1920; Woofter 1920). Georgia's net out-migration between 1910 and 1920 was 7 percent of the average black population for the decade (Eldridge and Thomas 1964). This percentage pales in comparison with the next decade, when nearly 30 percent of the average black population left the state. Particularly crucial were the years 1922–24, when economic recovery and restrictive immigration laws stimulated migration north (Baron 1971). When coupled with declines in black fertility (Tolnay 1985, 1987), the consequences of out-migration were clear. In 1870, blacks constituted 46 percent of Georgia's population. By 1940, they were less than 35 percent of the state's population. Comparable figures for the population of black men were 22.6 percent in 1870 and 16.6 percent in 1940.

Previous work suggests that declines in the size of the black male population generated compensatory increases in the rate at which black men were incarcerated in the penitentiary and their labor forcefully expropriated (Myers 1993). Indeed, a shrinking supply of black labor increased the rate at which *white* men were admitted to the penitentiary and sent as misdemeanants to chain gangs (Myers 1993, 1995a). These findings provide the basis for expecting that punishment should intensify with a decline in the relative size of the black population. Admission rates should rise, sentences lengthen, and release rates fall. These relationships should be more pronounced for black than white offenders and for property more than for violent offenders. Finally, the tightest linkages should be present immediately after the Civil War, when planters could no longer rely on slave labor and were in the throes of developing alternative ways of obtaining the reliable labor force that cotton demanded. To explore these possibilities, the analysis includes census figures for percentage black male in the population. Linear interpolation completes the data for intercensal years.

The Industrial Economy

While predominant, agriculture was hardly the only element of the southern political economy. The South was in transition from feudal agrarianism to capitalism, with its emphasis on market relations, industrial production, and population concentration (Fields 1983). Of all workers ten years or older, for example, three-quarters were employed in the agrarian sector in 1880. By 1940, only one-third were so employed. Much has been written of the transition to capitalism, particularly about the relationship between planters and industrialists (Cobb 1988). Whether comrades or antagonists, planters and industrialists alike exploited the South's strengths: abundant unskilled and cheap labor in conjunction with abundant natural resources (Goldfield 1982; Cobb 1984; Wood 1986). For a few southern states, iron ore, coal, and limestone were the central resources. For many more states of the former Confederacy, including Georgia, the chief resource was locally produced cotton, which the textile industry used to produce yarn and coarse cloth for export to northern finishing factories.

The common theoretical supposition is that industrialization profoundly affected the exercise of formal social control (Gurr, Brabosky, and Hula 1977; Gatrell 1980; Hay 1980; Monkkonen 1981; Feeley and Little 1991). Work in industrial factories constrained behavior through close supervision, sustained attention to tasks, and regulations governing arrival, departure, and comportment while working (Levasseur 1900; Pollard 1963). Under stable economic conditions, long work days integrated urban residents into this new social order and countered its potential dislocations. Thus, industrialization contributed to a decline in criminality, an increase in informal social control, and a decline in the exercise of formal social control such as punishment.

How well does this argument apply to the industrializing South? Industrial workplaces did indeed enforce a new discipline on southern men, whose former work as farmers or tenants gave them more autonomy and independence (Janiewski 1985; Hall et al. 1987; McHugh 1988). Boys joined their parents at the mill as soon as they were physically able. By the age of ten or twelve, boys earned wages, often under parental supervision. In addition to the family labor system, which required the employment of all fit members of the family, southern mill owners embellished the paternalistic system pioneered in the Northeast (Kessler-Harris 1982; Freeze 1991; Schulman and Leiter 1991; Flamming 1992). As a management style, paternalism emphasized personal involvement in the lives of workers. Private lives were still public property. Thus, southern industrialization not only brought more men into structured workplaces but also intensified the informal control of their behavior outside factory walls.

The "civilizing" influences of industrial workplaces weighed more heavily on white men than on black men, however. Sharply bifurcated racial roles accompanied the shift to a market economy, ensuring that white men were placed in industrial factories while black men were limited to manual labor in farming and extractive enterprises (Wood 1986; Wright 1986). In 1890, for example, one-fifth of Georgia's cotton mill operatives were black. Ten years later, after white workers in several mills initiated walkouts to protest the presence of black coworkers, only 3 percent of all mill operatives were black (Dittmer 1977). If industrial labor had a "civilizing" influence, then whites more so than blacks were subject to that influence. As a result, the industrialization process should have an impact on the punishment of white men but few implications for the social control of black men. Specifically, with growth in industrialization, white male admission rates should fall, prison sentences should become more lenient, and release rates should rise. Since industrialization surged in the twentieth century, its link with punishment should be relatively weak in the nineteenth century and should grow stronger over time.

As Georgia became industrialized, it became progressively more urban. In 1870, slightly more than 8 percent of its population resided in urban areas. Seventy years later, more than a third were urban residents. Southern urbanization was distinctive, because it did not entail the growth of large urban areas noted for heavy industry (Vance and Demerath 1954; Brownell 1975; Biles 1988; Larsen 1990). Instead, it involved growth in the number of towns under ten thousand, whose commercial and transportation enterprises served agricultural production. Whether they involved textiles, furniture, or fertilizer, southern industries usually located in small towns to avail themselves of surplus agrarian workers. Town populations ebbed and flowed with the seasons and with the profitability of cotton production. Rural norms that emphasized honor, family, and religion followed migrants to towns and cities (Woodward 1971; Goldfield 1982). Migrants saw familiar faces in towns and cities: whites and blacks from neighboring counties dispossessed of land by debt, unable to afford farmland, or faced with a family incapable of farm work (Larsen 1990). Southern towns, then, lacked the cultural heterogeneity, loosened informal controls, and overcrowding that presumably generated crime and unrest in northern cities (Gurr, Brabosky, and Hula 1977; Bursik 1988).

Southern towns were different and more hostile places for black men, however. Whites defined the "proper" place for blacks as not only in the South but also on southern farms, where they would be supervised and "uplifted" by paternalistic whites (Wade 1964; Newby 1965; Rabinowitz 1976). Abandonment of their "proper" place and relocation to cities purportedly put blacks in contact with the worst social elements, both black and white. The conventional wisdom was that this contact made blacks dissatisfied and unwilling to work. Whites also feared that the concentration of blacks in urban areas would generate better organized and more constant "trouble" than their dispersion in rural areas. From the late nineteenth century onward, blacks were blamed for the high crime rate in Atlanta (Crowe 1968; Watts 1973). Further confirmation of the urban black "troublemaker" found expression in the Atlanta riot of 1906 and in earlier incidents of resistance to the police in Atlanta and Savannah (Baker 1908; Rudwick and Meier 1966; Rabinowitz 1976). Residential and public segregation, whether by custom or explicit ordinance, failed to alter the perception that urban blacks threatened public safety. It only resulted in the loss of white supervision and knowledge about black behavior (Frederickson 1971).

Unwelcome in urban areas, then, black men were often perceived as idle and as sources of urban unrest and rural labor shortages (Miller 1975; Doyle 1980; Evans 1989). They were restricted from all but the most menial employment. In 1880, for example, 80 percent of all unskilled and 70 percent of all semiskilled workers in Atlanta were black (Russell 1988). Indeed, as more whites migrated to urban areas, blacks found themselves excluded from the few unskilled jobs (e.g., messengers and sanitation workers) that traditionally had been theirs (Dittmer 1977). Periodic depressions and recessions intensified demands to substitute black workers for whites in even the most menial positions.

The precarious state of employment generated a more transient black population, which flocked to cities when opportunities presented themselves and fled when opportunities withered. Black urban dwellers tended to locate farther away from the central city than whites (Russell 1988). As a result, they were the last to receive municipal services such as police or fire protection, sanitation, street repair, poor relief, or education.

In short, urbanization was a more disruptive process for black men and should increase their risk of being subject to coercive social controls. As urbanization increased, then, black men should be admitted to the penitentiary at an increasing rate; their sentences should become more severe; and release should be less likely. Unlike industrialization, urbanization should exert its strongest influence in the nineteenth century, when concerns about the reliability of black agrarian labor were at their height.

For white men, who experienced greater continuity between rural and urban

Figure 4.12. Value added by manufacturing

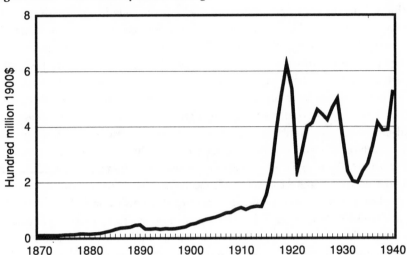

experiences, urbanization could have one of two implications. It may have no effect on their punishment. Alternatively, the combination of informal controls in the urban workforce and other supervisory institutions may shape behavior so intensively that formal coercive controls are less necessary (Lane 1970, 1974, 1979, 1980; Gillis 1996). As a result, growth in urbanization should reduce their risk of being admitted to the penitentiary, moderate the sentences of those so admitted, and make release from the penitentiary less difficult to achieve.

The only exceptions to this rule should be violent offenders. The rural legacy of feuds, vigilantism, and backwoods fighting was quite at odds with the image that elites wish to project of the "New South," a region that was sober and rational in its pursuit of wealth (Woodward 1971; Gorn 1985; Wyatt-Brown 1986). As the state became urbanized, then, intolerance for unpredictable outbursts of violence grew. This intolerance should stimulate white admissions for violence, prompt longer sentences for white violent offenders, and inhibit their release from the penitentiary.

A potentially threatening aspect of urbanization, the concentration of blacks in places where they did not "belong," should also have implications for the punishment of black men. During its early stage, urbanization encouraged the concentration of blacks in urban areas. The percentage of the urban population that was black rose slowly between 1870 and 1900 (from 45.4 to 48.1 percent). Albeit minor, this increase in the concentration of blacks in urban areas should intensify concerns that blacks were a threat to public safety. As a result, black rates of admission to the penitentiary should rise, terms of imprisonment should lengthen, and release rates should fall.

As the pace of urbanization increased, however, urban areas grew progressively whiter. Between 1900 and 1940, the percentage black in urban areas declined by more than 10 percent. This decline should have alleviated concerns that blacks were a threat to public safety. As a result, black rates of admission to the penitentiary should decline, terms of imprisonment should shorten, and release rates should rise.

Following Monkkonen (1975), the measure of industrialization used in the analysis taps the magnitude and profitability of manufacturing enterprises. It is the value added by manufacturing, in millions of 1900 dollars. Obtained from perennially issued Census of Manufactures reports and interpolated for missing years, value added by manufacturing gradually increased until the first decade of the twentieth century (fig. 4.12). Thereafter, surges followed precipitous declines. The census also provided data about percentage urban and percentage black urban. To complete the data set, census figures were linearly interpolated for intercensal years.

Economic Crises

Southerners were forced to contend not just with the chronic uncertainties of the cotton and industrial economies. They were also confronted with equally unexpected, often acute recessions and depressions, again not of their own making (table 4.2). Panics in European and northeastern markets radiated southward, affecting cotton prices, the availability of credit, levels of industrial production, the financial solvency of banks, commodity prices, and employment prospects (Flamant and Singer-Kerel 1968). Many economic downturns were short-lived and not particularly severe. Not all affected levels of employment (Lebergott 1964, 1984). But being brief was no guarantee that a depression would be mild. The "heartbreaking Nineties" (Arnett [1922] 1967: 156) included four economic declines. The most severe, the depression of 1893–94, lasted only seventeen months but generated an average 31 percent decline in business activity, industrial production, and trade. Its effects lasted longer and were felt more deeply in the South than in other regions of the country (Woodward 1971). Georgia, in particular, exceeded the national average in firm failures and indebtedness (Arnett [1922] 1967). A decade earlier the country had suffered the longest depression in its history. So severe and protracted was the 1873–79 Depression, with its "utter lack of enterprise" (Thorp 1926: 132), that it was referred to as the Great Depression for decades afterwards.

What we now call the Great Depression underscores how sharply race filtered the experience of economic downturns. Urban blacks suffered higher unemployment than whites because they were segregated in unskilled, unorganized, and unprotected jobs, precisely those most vulnerable to economic downturns and to social pressure for displacing blacks in favor of whites seeking work (Ross 1940; Wolters 1970). Yet the Great Depression marks the advent of concerted federal and state efforts to provide relief and employment for those rendered homeless and

Table 4.2 Economic crises, 1870–1940

Years	Duration (Months)	Average Decline in Indexes	% Increase in Unemployed	Rank
1873–1879 (1876)	65	26.9	10.0	15.0
1882–1884 (1884)	38	27.9	4.0	16.0
1887–1888	13	11.2	*	3.0
1890–1891	10	17.0	*	9.0
1893–1894 (1894)	17	30.7	6.7	18.0
1895–1897	18	24.3	*	14.0
1899–1900	18	14.4	*	7.5
1902–1904	23	14.4	*	7.5
1907–1908 (1908)	13	29.5	5.2	17.0
1910–1912	24	12.0	*	5.0
1913–1914	23	23.2	3.6	13.0
1918–1919	7	22.0	*	12.0
1920–1921 (1921)	18	34.7	6.5	19.0
1923–1924	14	21.8	2.6	11.0
1926–1927	13	9.3	*	2.0
1929–1933 (1931–33)	43	75.1	22.0	20.0
1937–1938	13	a	4.8	a

Sources: Gordon (1986: 750, 761–62); Lebergott (1984: 396).

Note: Depressions are italicized, their worst years noted in parentheses. Asterisked entries denote a value of less than 2 percent. The average decline in indexes is based on three indexes tapping business activity, industrial production, and trade. The mildest downturns are ranked 1–5, the most vigorous or severe, 16–20.

[a]Information not available.

jobless (Stern 1940–41). In other contexts, such efforts reduced admissions to the penitentiary, since public employment increased the demand for labor (Berk et al. 1981). Southern states, in contrast, were never known for their generosity in providing social services (Russell 1988). During the Great Depression, they provided less relief than the national average, resisted federal relief policies, and channeled relief to whites rather than to blacks (Daniel 1985; Biles 1990). Indeed, federal policies aggravated the displacement of southern black workers from the labor force. Of greatest consequence in urban areas was federal insistence on racial equality in wages, which removed the financial incentive to hire cheaper black labor.

Economic crises should have several implications for punishment. To the extent that they generated a labor surplus, depressions and recessions should intensify punishment. Admission rates should rise, prison sentences lengthen, and release rates fall. Second, the more severe the downturn, the more pronounced its impact on each aspect of punishment. Thus, depressions should exert stronger and more consistent influences than should recessions. Third, during protracted depressions, punishment should moderate somewhat as the state, counties, and entrepreneurs reach the limits of their capacity to address social control concerns (Lichtenstein 1996). Admissions to the penitentiary should fall, sentences shorten, and release rates increase, all in an attempt to relieve the strain caused by earlier punitiveness.

The remaining expectations apply to the two axes around which our examination of punishment revolves. The first is the distinction between black and white punishment. The greater economic vulnerability of black men generates the expectation that their punishment will be linked more tightly with depressions and recessions than the punishment of white men. The second axis is the distinction between property and violent offenders. To the extent that economic crises raise concerns about the loss of existing property and lower tolerance levels for theft, they should have clearer relevance for the punishment of property offenders than of violent offenders. Their impacts should be stronger and should occur more frequently and consistently.

Interracial Competition

Emancipation gave blacks freedom, but little else. The anticipated receipt of "40 acres and a mule" failed to materialize, and freed slaves, 99 percent of all Georgia's blacks, were left essentially penniless (Higgs 1982; Royce 1993). Particularly in cotton-producing areas, whites resisted black efforts to purchase land, to rent land, and to obtain loans for both purposes. The only viable option left to many freedmen, then, was to return to work for their former masters. Planters preferred the traditional gang form of labor. For obvious reasons, blacks did not. Although preferred by neither landowners nor blacks, both parties entered into sharecropping agreements. Landowners divided their plantations into plots of thirty to fifty acres and leased them to families. Black men, women, and children provided labor and their own food and clothing. They received between one-half and two-thirds of the crop. The planter provided farm implements and animals, decided the crop mix, and took between one-third and one-half of the crop.

Given their impoverished position, blacks more so than whites were vulnerable to sharecropping arrangements and to the indebtedness they entailed. Indeed, cotton producers preferred black, rather than white, sharecroppers and day laborers (Baker 1908; Dollard 1937; Davis, Gardner, and Gardner 1941; Baron 1971; Higgs 1977a; Flynn 1983; Corzine, Huff-Corzine, and Creech 1988). This preference stemmed from the subordinate caste status of blacks, which made them more tractable, ostensibly more productive, and more easily defrauded and intimidated than whites. As late as 1939, a North Carolina planter drew sharp distinctions between black and white tenants: "A white tenant has his notions of running a farm

65

and is less amenable to suggestion. . . . I can say, 'Go hitch up the horse,' when I want a horse hitched . . . to a negro . . . and I can't to a white man. . . . Negroes are more loyal" (quoted in Kirby 1984: 413).

Despite white resistance and limited capital, a small minority of blacks was able to accumulate land in the years after Emancipation (Oubre 1978). They met with greater success in counties with extensive plantation agriculture and cotton cultivation, relatively cheap farmland, and relatively low levels of black tenancy (Higgs 1982). In Georgia, blacks owned one of every eighty-five acres of improved land in 1875 and one of every twenty-five acres by 1903 (Banks 1905). With the exception of the 1890s, accumulation surged until World War I. Sharp declines in 1916 and 1917 represent the impact of the Great Migration (Higgs 1982). Despite these gains, blacks as a group remained less likely than whites to own their own land and more likely than whites to be tenants (Higgs 1973). Whether as tenants or sharecroppers, their holdings were smaller, less capitalized, and less prosperous than the holdings of similarly placed whites (Higgs 1973; Flynn 1983; Wright 1986).

Just as a few plantation-area blacks were becoming "made," many white farmers in the Piedmont or Upcountry were being undone (Hahn 1985). Formerly self-sufficient and unlikely to have owned slaves, these farmers sought to recover or to build their fortunes in cotton. Like their Black Belt brethren, they found it increasingly difficult to achieve or maintain financial solvency: "The acquisition of credit demanded the expansion of cotton production; the expansion of cotton production meant proportionately shorter food crops; and shorter food crops sent the farmer back to the merchant's door for provisions" (Hahn 1985: 190). An increasing number of independent farmers slid into the ranks of landless tenants, ensnared in the lien system. In 1900, for example, 47 percent of all tenants in Georgia were white; by 1940, the figure had increased to more than 60 percent. The volatility of cotton prices was not the only culprit here. Southern fertility rates were the highest in the nation. They aggravated pressure for land, some of which had already been ravaged by decades of cotton production (Wright 1986). Despite the prospect of employment in textile mills, nonagricultural opportunities were limited (Hahn 1985).

As the nineteenth century wore on, then, competition increased between whites and freedmen for land, tenancies, wage labor, and other scarce resources (Higgs 1977a; Wright 1986). The sharp caste boundaries that had previously separated the races became blurred. In pursuit of cheap labor, planters and industrialists did not automatically confer an advantage on white labor. No longer did the color of one's skin guarantee more favorable tenantry arrangements or higher wages (Higgs 1974, 1977a, 1977b). Nor could whites rely on economic segregation to maintain their competitive advantage. Within the same occupation, for example, whites working in segregated workforces were on average paid no differently than their colleagues in integrated workforces (Higgs 1977b). Competition intensified

Figure 4.13. Racial inequality

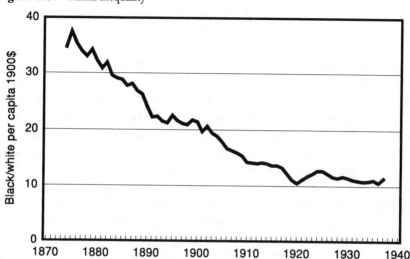

during frequent depressions and recessions, as whites clamored for jobs traditionally staffed by blacks (Raper and Reid 1941).

In short, the once broad economic divide between blacks and whites narrowed after the turn of the century (fig. 4.13). Measured as the per capita value of white-owned property divided by its black equivalent, in constant 1900 dollars, inequality steadily declined throughout the period.[5] Blalock (1967) suggests that such a decline should generate and intensify interracial economic competition, in turn fostering interracial tension and punitive actions against blacks. Empirical work on criminal punishment (Myers 1991, 1993) offers a second possibility. An erosion of their economic position vis-à-vis blacks put at least some *white* men at greater risk of being punished. Thus, declines in racial inequality should affect the punishment of both blacks and whites, but should be more salient for the economically more vulnerable of the two groups. Declining inequality should also be more relevant for property offenders, whose crimes threaten the economic order most directly. Finally, relationships between inequality and punishment should be more pronounced in the nineteenth century, when race relations were undergoing profound changes and the caste distinction was experiencing its initial challenge.

World War I and Its Aftermath

Although seldom spared economic hardship, the South was for the most part spared the dislocations of a major global conflict. The only—and a particularly significant exception—was World War I. The onset of the war closed cotton exchanges and triggered a price collapse. Within two years, however, the demand

67

for cotton, lumber, and textiles rebounded, making the war "one great blessing to all of Dixie" (quoted in Tindall 1967: 60). Strong cotton prices enabled farm owners and tenants to pay off debts. Black tenants could buy land in greater quantities than ever before (Dittmer 1977). The war closed immigration channels as well, and in so doing provided yet another impetus for the Great Migration of 1916–18 (Scott 1919). Workers who remained found higher wages and landlords who were willing to negotiate contracts more beneficial to tenants (Dittmer 1977).

America's entry into the war in April 1917 ushered in conscription, and nearly one million southerners joined the war effort (Tindall 1967). In Georgia, nearly 113,000 blacks registered for the draft. Slightly more than 30 percent were inducted into the armed services (Murray 1972). In general, black men who were called for military service were more likely than white men to be classified as fit for service and were less likely to win deferments (Murray 1972). The most egregious example of discriminatory treatment was the Fulton County draft board, which exempted 85 percent of registered whites but drafted 97 percent of registered blacks. In the state as a whole, 43 percent of those registered for the draft were black, while 51 percent of those actually inducted were black. Most black soldiers never saw combat, however, and worked behind the lines as stevedores (Dittmer 1977). Even those drilled for service at the front were excused and placed in Reserve Labor Battalions (Scott 1919).

America's entry into the war should moderate punishment for several reasons (Berk et al. 1981, 1983; Archer and Gartner 1984). At least part of the civilian population most at risk for being punished, namely, young men, were removed from the general population, and they no longer had the opportunity to engage in crime. For those left behind, economic opportunities reduced the motivation to commit crimes that tended to result in imprisonment. From sheriffs to judges, social control agents may have been reluctant to enforce the law zealously, for fear of depriving the armed forces or local industry of needed labor. America's entry into the war, then, should prompt less intense punishment. To accommodate demands for conscripts and civilian workers, admission rates should fall, penitentiary terms shorten, and release rates rise. Since the burden of conscription fell more heavily on black shoulders, any moderation in punishment should be more evident for the punishment of black than of white men.

The war and the economic revitalization it encouraged ended with the Armistice, signed on November 11, 1918. Accompanying demobilization in 1919 were sharp declines in the demand for commodities and growing labor unrest and militancy (Waskow 1966). Unemployed black men flooded into urban areas, where rumors of racial discontent became rife (Scott 1919; Grantham 1983). During the summer of 1919, twenty-five racial riots and disturbances in both the North and South signaled the advent of a profound change in race relations (Waskow 1966;

Tindall 1967; Williams 1991). Among the disturbances capturing national attention were a four-day riot in Washington, D.C. (July 19–22), and an even longer series of riots in Chicago (July 27-August 8), which left thirty-eight dead and more than five hundred injured. Between February 28 and August 29, 1919, Georgia experienced four "minor" disturbances, which claimed the lives of seven blacks and seven whites.

Some contemporaries blamed outside agitators (e.g., Bolsheviks) for the upsurge in racial unrest. Others blamed black veterans, whose experiences in the European theater brought them from a "sequestered vale into the broad light of modern times" (Scott 1919: 402), less willing to tolerate the unequal treatment that had been their lot at home and in the army (Waskow 1966; Dittmer 1977). But just as speculations about the sources of racial unrest reached no consensus, neither did the response. Some argued for a return to racial hierarchies; black spokesmen and organizations such as the NAACP called for greater accommodation, if not equality. The return to law and order figured prominently, however. To achieve this goal, observers argued for greater social control in the form of more and better trained police (Waskow 1966).

Demobilization, then, generated acute but different crises for black and white men. It brought fewer jobs for whites and the prospect of fewer jobs and greater white hostility for blacks. The expectation, then, is that in this climate of unrest and threat punishment should become more severe, with blacks bearing the brunt of increased severity. Admission rates should rise, prison sentences grow longer, and release rates decline.

Policies

Chapter 3 emphasized the potential impact of several state policies on punishment. Of interest here are the introduction of parole in 1908, abolition of the lease in 1909, and the institution of probation in 1913. The impact of indeterminate sentencing in 1919 could not be estimated because it coincided with, and was overshadowed by, the demobilization following World War I. The preceding discussion suggested that federal policies should have implications for punishment as well. Of particular significance are the Federal Aid Road Act and the Agricultural Adjustment Act.

Previous research leads us to expect that parole, introduced in 1908, should slow penitentiary growth rates by increasing the release of offenders, particularly whites. The stability of punishment thesis suggests other possibilities. To compensate for the "early" loss of convict labor through conditional release and maintain a steady level of punishment, the advent of parole may also increase admission rates and lengthen sentences.

The expiration of the last lease on March 31, 1909, heralded a return to county-administered punishment. This return occurred at an opportune moment, for long-standing public interest in new and improved roads had not diminished. Nor had the public or the press rescinded their preference for the use of convicts to build and maintain these roads. Thus, abolition of the lease may have been a seamless transition, having no implications for punishment at all. It is equally possible that abolition stimulated the admission of potential road laborers and the imposition of longer sentences on those so admitted. Likewise, it may have discouraged release from the penitentiary, again to serve the prevailing demand for convict labor on public roads.

As an alternative to incarceration, the advent of probation in 1913 should precipitate a decline in the rate at which men, particularly whites, were imprisoned. Its relevance to other dimensions of punishment is less clear. There is no reason to expect a direct link between probation and sentence length. On the surface, any link would be mediated by offense seriousness. That is, if probation were reserved for less serious offenders, then only more serious offenders would be admitted to the penitentiary, thereby lengthening prison terms. Finally, to the extent that the availability of adult probation raised concerns about a possible shortage of convict labor, it may encourage a short-term decline in releases.

In addition to demands for convict labor by private entrepreneurs, chapter 2 outlined a vigorous and long-lived demand in the public sector for the use of convict labor on roads. This demand escalated with passage of the Federal Aid Road Act in 1916. As interpreted by Georgia, the act allowed counties to qualify for federal assistance if they "paid" their share in convict labor. Previous work (e.g., Myers 1991) provided evidence that federal legislation had a delayed impact on the rate at which white men were incarcerated. The expectation is that federal legislation will operate the same here. To maximize the inmate pool available for use on public roads, admission rates should rise, sentences lengthen, and release rates fall with passage of the act. These tendencies should be more pronounced for white men, who were a relatively untapped source of convict labor for a task that traditionally had been their province.

Of greater and more sustained importance was a federal response to the Great Depression. Designed to raise farm prices by lowering production, the Agricultural Adjustment Act (AAA), passed in 1933, authorized payments to planters who agreed to rent a certain amount of acreage to the secretary of agriculture, who chose not to plant cotton. Only owners, landlords, cash tenants, or managing share tenants could enter into contracts. Landlords of sharecroppers or share tenants thus received the entire subsidy (Whatley 1983). While they were instructed to give sharecroppers and tenants an appropriate portion, most landlords expropriated the lion's share of the payments, in part as collection on debts owed them. More so than comparable whites, black sharecroppers relinquished their share of payments, a substantial minority being forced to do so (Wolters 1970). Although locally administered, the program offered few opportunities for redressing grievances of this kind, since white landowners dominated county committees.

As early as 1934, the first full crop year after passage of the act, landlords did more than simply expropriate tenant and sharecropper subsidies. They began to evict unneeded sharecroppers and to change the status of others to wage laborers, who were entitled to neither subsidies nor housing. Both races suffered, but blacks were displaced earlier than whites (Johnson, Embree, and Alexander 1935). Evictions accelerated between 1935 and 1940, as contracts provided no mechanism to prevent them and incentives to engage in them. Later contracts, for example, increased the share of the subsidy to which sharecroppers were entitled from one-quarter in 1936–37 contracts to half in 1938–39 contracts (Whatley 1983). This modification simply gave landlords more incentive to reduce the number of tenants (Wolters 1970). Moreover, since contracts were negotiated before planting, landlords could adjust the tenure status of tenants in such a way that their own interests were served (Whatley 1983). For the South, then, the most influential government response to the depression, the AAA and its policies, served only to deprive more tenants and sharecroppers of a home and a job (Hoffsommer 1935; Johnson, Embree, and Alexander 1935; Conrad 1965; Daniel 1985, 1994). Thus, the AAA operated much like the depression that had generated it. Given the length of time its policies operated, the AAA should have the same consequences on punishment as a protracted depression: initially intensifying punishment, then ameliorating it in response to strain on capacities to punish.

Confounding Factors

Thus far, the discussion has examined factors identified by theoretical perspectives as central for the exercise of social control in general and of punishment in particular. Of concern in this section are factors that might otherwise obscure the relationships described above. Adverse economic conditions most likely affected levels of criminality. Thus, levels of black and white criminal behavior must be held constant. Similarly, both the age of offenders and the seriousness of their offenses most likely affected the severity of their punishment and the likelihood of release from the penitentiary. Thus, changes in the cohort of admitted offenders must be held constant. The following sections examine each of these factors.

Black and White Criminality

Although levels of criminality undoubtedly affected the punishment of both whites and blacks, historical records fail to provide reliable information about them. The analysis conducted here requires state-level data on black and white

71

criminality, and these do not exist. County-level data on indictments exist, but they are not available for all counties. Nor do they consistently specify the race of the accused (Smith 1975, 1982). Indeed, indictments are weak measures of criminality, since they may also be shaped by social and economic changes. Studies of selected courts, undertaken in the early twentieth century (Georgia Department of Public Welfare 1925, 1937; Fuller 1929), provide a sound foundation for county comparisons of the volume and distribution of crime. Unfortunately, none include the race of the accused or a majority of Georgia's counties.

The historical record thus severely restricts our choice to an approximate but ambiguous measure of criminality. The most obvious candidate is the relative size of the male population most likely to be accused of crime, namely, those between twenty and twenty-nine years of age (Georgia Department of Public Welfare 1937). This measure is ambiguous because it includes a group of men who were more likely to be both accused of crime and useful as laborers. Earlier research found that a decline in the population of young black men did not produce the anticipated reduction in incarceration rates. Instead, declines operated much as did reductions in the black male population more generally. They *increased* the rate at which black men were incarcerated in the penitentiary (Myers 1993). To the extent, then, that a smaller population of young black men raised concerns about a shortage of labor, the punishment of black men should intensify. Admission rates should rise, prison sentences grow longer, and release rates fall, all in an effort to expropriate forcefully as much black labor as possible.

A decline in the population of young white men should operate differently, in part because it is a less ambiguous measure of white criminality. Although this group of men was more likely to be accused of crime, they were not particularly useful as manual laborers, at least not until most convicts were used to maintain roads. To the extent that it indicates a drop in white criminality, a decline in the population of young white men should reduce the admission of white men to the penitentiary, moderate the sentences imposed on those so admitted, and encourage their release.

Changing Convict Population

A clear understanding of prison sentences and release rates requires that we consider changes in the population of felons. Clearly, prison sentences should lengthen consistently over time in response to the admission of more serious offenders. Release rates should fall for two reasons. First, the admission of a larger proportion of serious offenders with long sentences should reduce the number of convicts eligible for release. The second and more speculative reason posits that officials limit release from the penitentiary to convey a message of general deterrence. The admission of noticeably more serious offenders may introduce a note of urgency to this message and precipitate an immediate decline in releases.

To control for these possibilities, the analysis includes an aggregate measure of offense seriousness. To create such a measure, each offender received an offense seriousness score. Its value was the average of the minimum and maximum statutory penalty of each offense at the time of conviction. To maintain a sense of scale, a ceiling of forty-two was put on the seriousness of noncapital multiple offenses. Offenses for which life imprisonment was an option received a score of forty-two, while offenses carrying the death penalty received a score of sixty.

An example will make the derivation of offense seriousness clear. In 1870, burglary carried a minimum penalty of five years and a maximum of twenty years. An offender convicted of burglary in 1870 received a legal seriousness score of 12.5 [(5 + 20)/2]. Had he been convicted of two burglaries, his score would be 25 (12.5 × 2). Statutory revisions enacted in 1879 reduced the minimum sentence to one year in the penitentiary. An offender convicted of burglary between 1880 and 1895 therefore received a slightly lower seriousness score of 10.5 [(1 + 20)/2]. After 1895, offenders convicted of many felonies, including burglary, became eligible for punishment as misdemeanants. Under this provision, offenders could receive a minimum of six months imprisonment. As a result, an offender convicted of burglary between 1896 and 1940 received a legal seriousness score of 10.25 [(.5 + 20)/2]. Conviction of two burglaries would double the score. As these examples make clear, offense seriousness incorporates both changes in penalties that occurred over time and the particular constellation of crimes of which each offender was convicted.

To create the seriousness time series, individual scores were summed and averaged, by year of admission to the penitentiary (fig. 4.14). Until the first decade of the twentieth century, offenders admitted to the penitentiary had, on average, been convicted of increasingly more serious offenses. The seriousness of both black and white offenders declined after 1910. Note as well that until abolition of the lease in 1909, white offenders admitted to the penitentiary tended to be much more serious than black offenders. Afterwards, there was little discernible difference. Racial differences in seriousness are more complicated than figure 4.14 suggests, however. Focusing solely on violent offenders (fig. 4.15), it is clear that the average white violent offender had been convicted of more serious violence than had the average black violent offender. This was the case throughout the period under consideration. The reverse was the case for property offenders (fig. 4.16). Here, the average white offender had often been convicted of less serious property crimes than comparable black offenders. This difference became more consistent and pronounced after World War I.

In addition to seriousness, sentences should depend on the age of felons admitted to the penitentiary. Young felons were undoubtedly more useful as laborers than older offenders. For this reason, the admission of a younger cohort of offenders should prompt the imposition of longer sentences. This relationship should

73

Figure 4.14. Seriousness of admissions to the penitentiary

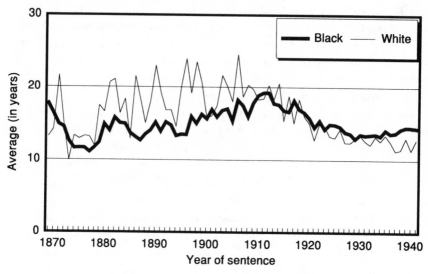

Figure 4.15. Seriousness of violent admissions to the penitentiary

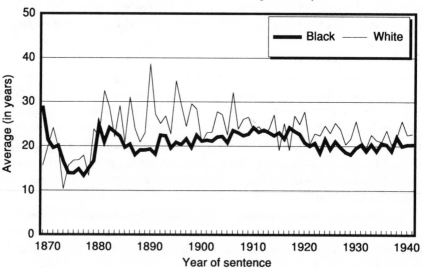

Figure 4.16. Seriousness of property admissions to the penitentiary

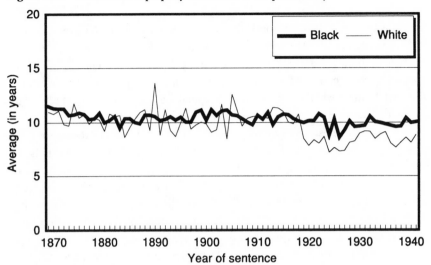

hold for black offenders, who were generally thought to be less amenable to reformation and more amenable to hard labor. The opposite relationship should appear for white offenders. The admission of younger white men, with greater prospects of rehabilitation (Prison Commission 1906–7) and less value as laborers, should stimulate shorter sentences. As for release rates, the admission of a younger cohort of offenders may introduce a note of urgency to a general deterrent message and discourage release from the penitentiary.

As noted earlier, the average white offender was significantly older than his black counterpart. This was consistently the case over time and true for both property and violent offenders (figures not presented). Indeed, the age of the admitted cohorts—black and white, violent and property alike—varied only in the short term.

Relationship among Punishment Series

Of final interest is the extent to which admissions, sentences, and releases were linked. If the stability of punishment thesis has merit, then each facet of punishment should compensate for changes in other aspects of punishment. Higher admission rates should be offset by shorter sentences and/or higher release rates. Conversely, declines in admission rates should precipitate longer sentences and/or lower release rates. Longer sentences should be offset by more expeditious release. Should release rates fall precipitously, admission rates should rise and/or sentences grow longer.

75

Analytic Methods

To assess the arguments developed in previous sections, the analysis of each punishment series used ARIMA modeling procedures.[6] These procedures allow us to estimate both the impact of specific events and policies and the dynamic effect that each social change, in the form of an input series, had on punishment. We will be able to determine whether effects were instantaneous or delayed and whether they occurred all at once or were felt over a given length of time.

The chief diagnostic tool for locating and identifying these relationships is the cross-correlation function. This function is a standardized measure, ranging between -1 and $+1$, of the association between two time series: the input or causor series and the past, present, and future values of an output time series. The cross-correlation function provides an indication of the strength of the relationship, when it began, and how long it lasted. Before discussing cross-correlation functions in detail, it is important to note that their accuracy requires that three conditions be met. First, input and output series must be stationary. Second, input series must have no autocorrelated errors. Third, each input series must be unrelated to other input series.

Accurate cross-correlation functions require that the input and output series exhibit no trend or drift in mean or variance.[7] Otherwise, a correlation between the two series would always be present. It would nevertheless be spurious, because the series share common patterns of drift or trend. To determine whether instability in the variance was a problem, I used the power transformation strategy, which compares the error sum of squares for maximum likelihood estimates of various transformations of the series (Wei 1990). In many cases, an estimate of the natural logarithm of the series yielded the lowest error sum of squares.[8]

To determine whether instability in the mean was a problem, I estimated an autocorrelation function for each series. This function describes the association between values of the same time series at different times. The persistence of large autocorrelations at long lags indicates that the series has a nonstationary mean. A nonstationary series is typically stabilized by creating a new time series that consists of differences between observations at successive periods. The first observation of the series is subtracted from the second observation, the second observation from the third, the third observation from the fourth, and so on ($X_t - X_{t-1}$, $X_{t-1} - X_{t-2}$, . . .). The new series will have one less observation and will be stationary if the trend in the original data is linear. The autocorrelation function of the first-differenced data should drop to near zero after the second or third lag. If the trend in the original data is nonlinear (e.g., exponential), then stationarity can be achieved by second-order differencing, that is, by taking the first difference of the first-differenced series. This proved to be the case with the demographic series, each of which needed second-order differencing. These exceptions aside, all series were nonstationary and required only first-order differencing.

Second, accurate cross-correlations require that patterns in the input series, whether due to drift or trend, be removed. In the language of time series analysis, the input series must approximate white noise. The process that generated the time series must consist of a series of random shocks, each of which is distributed normally and independently around a mean of zero with constant variance. If this were not the case, the correlation between the two series would be contaminated by the presence of correlations *within* the input series and, for this reason, would be misleading.

Autocorrelations within the input series were removed by modeling the underlying process that generated the series. These processes took two of three forms. The first form was a moving average process, that is, a random shock that disturbs the series for a fixed number of periods before dying out. The order (q) of a moving average model refers to the number of earlier disturbances that significantly affect the input series at time t. For example, a first-order moving average process ($q = 1$) indicates that the value of the time series in any given year is influenced by the current error term and by the error term or random shock the preceding year.

The second process involved built-in inertia, where the current value of the series was affected by its previous value. The order (p) of this autoregressive process refers to the number of earlier values upon which the current value depends. A first-order autoregressive process ($p = 1$), for example, describes a situation in which the value of the time series in any given year is influenced by the current error term and by the value of the time series the preceding year.[9]

To satisfy the second requirement, namely, that the correlation between the series be uncontaminated by within-series correlation, I used Box-Jenkins (1976) techniques to model the underlying process that generated each input series. As the first step, I estimated two functions for each series, once it had been rendered stationary. The first was the autocorrelation function, described above; the second was the partial autocorrelation function. Unlike the autocorrelation function, the partial autocorrelation function identifies the relationship between the current values of a series and its own earlier values, after holding constant correlations at intermediate lags.

Together, these functions enable us to determine the kind and order of the process that generated the time series. In the case of a first-order moving average process, for example, the autocorrelations fall abruptly to zero for all lags greater than one. The partial autocorrelation function is nonzero, and successive lags grow smaller in absolute value. A first-order autoregressive process generates quite different functions. The autocorrelation function decays exponentially from lag to lag, while the partial autocorrelation function has a nonzero function at the first lag with all successive lags being zero.

After tentatively identifying the model, I used maximum likelihood techniques to estimate the parameters, that is, to estimate the weight attached to preceding values of the series (if an autoregressive process) or to the previous error term (if a moving average process). Acceptable models met two criteria. First, the parameter estimates were statistically significant ($p < .05$) and lay within the bounds of stationarity or invertibility.[10] Second, the residuals of the model contained no significant autocorrelation. The input series was then "prewhitened" by inverting its ARIMA model and, to preserve the integrity of the functional relationship between the two series, the prewhitening transformation was applied to the output series as well.

The final requirement for estimating accurate cross-correlation functions is that input series must be unrelated to one another. The literature suggests that the exact opposite is more plausible. Contemporary observers often claimed that the over-production of cotton depressed its price (Woodman 1968), and previous research (Myers 1991) substantiates this observation. Rising cotton prices led farmers to consolidate gains made during times of prosperity (Fligstein 1981) and stimulated growth in the size of the cotton harvest (Myers 1991). Cotton prices also affected the relative economic position of whites vis-à-vis blacks. The already precarious position of blacks made them more vulnerable than whites to shifts in cotton prices. Falling prices tended to widen the racial gap in economic position. Finally, unstable or depressed economic conditions initiated black migration from rural to urban areas and from southern to northern cities (Woodson 1918; Scott 1920; Johnson and Campbell 1981; Marks 1985; Grossman 1989). As a result, the relative size of the black male population declined as cotton prices fell (Myers 1991).

In short, cotton prices, cotton harvest, racial inequality, and various population measures were linked, and these linkages must be estimated and removed before the analysis of punishment can proceed.[11] Appendix A describes the procedures in detail. Here, I need only note that interrelated series were rendered independent of each other by modeling each series as a dual function of its noise component and of a transfer function or functions representing the effect of the remaining input series. For example, racial inequality responded to growth in the urban and black urban populations. After modeling these impacts, the resulting residuals were a white noise process, which needed the addition of neither a moving average nor an autoregressive parameter. The residuals of this model constitute a series that has been purged both of correlations among its residuals and of the effects of other input series. All subsequent analysis, including the calculation of cross-correlation functions, uses series that have been "residualized" in this manner.

As noted above, cross-correlations provide evidence of the direction, magnitude, and delay in the influence exerted by an input series. A single significant cross-correlation at the first lag, for example, suggests that the input series produced a temporary change in the output series one year later. To estimate this kind of impact, the model predicting punishment includes a zero-order transfer function, ωX_{t-1}. The parameter ω indicates the magnitude and direction of the impact that series X had on punishment a year later. Significant cross-correlations that decay over several lags indicate the presence of an impact that was distributed slowly over time. In these cases, models include a more complicated first-order transfer function, $[\omega/(1 - \delta B)]X_{t-n}$. The parameter ω measures change in level; the parameter δ captures the rate at which that change is realized. As δ approaches unity, its effect is distributed slowly through time.

Thus far, the discussion has focused on relationships between punishment and factors that take the form of time series (e.g., cotton price). A similar strategy was appropriate when estimating the impact of events and polices. After being rendered stationary, each punishment series was inspected for the impact of economic crises, state and federal policies, World War I, and demobilization. Cross-correlation functions corroborated visual evidence of an impact. The most common impact was temporary and indicated by a single significant cross-correlation. A zero-order transfer function, ωX_{t-n}, captures this impact. The "series" X in this case is a binary pulse variable. Taking the introduction of parole as an example, the series takes the value of one in 1908 and zero in all remaining years. Less frequently encountered were permanent impacts, realized slowly over time. Cross-correlations that decayed slowly suggested the appropriateness of estimating a first-order transfer function, $[\omega/(1 - \delta B)X_{t-n}]$. Once again, ω indicates change in level and δ, the rate at which change is realized. In this case, the "series" X is a binary *step* variable, in which all years before the event are coded zero and the years including and after the event are coded one. Using the introduction of parole as an example, the series has a value of zero before 1908 and a value of one in 1908 and all subsequent years.[12]

Analytic Strategy

The analysis of trends in punishment proceeds in three stages. The first stage, intervention analysis, explores the relationship between punishment and events such as war and depressions. Separate estimation of each transfer function allows us to assess the relative contribution that each event or policy makes to our understanding of punishment. The second stage, multivariate analysis, explores the relationship between punishment and social change. It uses as data the residuals from the intervention analysis, which in essence is a series from which the influence of events and policies has been removed. Multivariate analysis begins with the calculation of cross-correlation functions, which guide the selection of transfer functions to estimate significant relationships. To compare the relative importance of each social change series, I estimate transfer functions separately. The final model includes all significant social change series. It is judged adequate if estimates are significant and if the residuals are a white noise process. For both intervention and multivariate analysis, the statistical significance of estimates is a necessary but not sufficient consideration. Of greater importance is the relative contribution of an event or series, and this is assessed by comparing reductions in the residual (or error) sum of squares (SSE).

The final stage of the analysis examines changes over time in the relationship between punishment and social changes (Isaac and Griffin 1989). It uses a moving average strategy, in which the punishment time series is subdivided into a set of series twenty years in duration (e.g., 1870–89, 1871–90, . . . 1929–40). For each subseries, I estimated a transfer function for the relevant input series (e.g., cotton price). I then plotted the estimates to assess changes in either the strength of the relationship or its direction over time. To conserve space, the body of the text discusses all results but presents the graphs for nontrivial predictors only.[13]

Conclusion

From the data and techniques described above, attention now turns to the results of the analysis. Considered first are admission rates, which indicate the frequency with which black and white men were punished for violent and property crimes over time. Chapter 5 is devoted to the severity of imposed punishment, and chapter 6 considers the rate at which black and white men left the penitentiary. The final analytic chapter estimates the relationship that remains among the three dimensions of punishment after the impact of interventions and social changes has been removed.

5

Admissions to
the Penitentiary

IN THE PREVIOUS CHAPTER, WE SAW THAT INCARCERATION WAS HARDLY
an uncommon event in the lives of Georgia's black men. Indeed, they were consistently admitted to the penitentiary at a markedly higher rate than were white men.
Nevertheless, their risk of laboring under the convict lease and, later, on the
chain gang fluctuated dramatically over time. Admissions rose during nineteenth-
century depressions, fell during World War I, and rose again during the 1920s and
1930s. For white men, in contrast, admission to prison was a rare event, and it
remained so until the end of World War I. Thereafter, it became a more distinct
possibility, rising at a faster rate than black admission rates.

Our understanding of these trends begins with an exploration of the influence
exerted by important events. Prominent among these is a series of economic crises,
World War I and its aftermath, and the introduction of several state and federal
policies. Considered next are the consequences of social changes such as fluctuations in the price of cotton and in the size of the cotton harvest. The focus then
narrows to assess more specific models, designed to shed light on admissions for
violent and property crimes. The chapter concludes with a summary of the findings and a discussion of their theoretical implications.

Theoretical Expectations

Before proceeding with the analysis, the expectations that informed the analysis
should be brought once more to the fore. The first set involves economic crises. In

81

general, the onset of depressions and recessions should increase the rate at which both black and white offenders were imprisoned. More intense economic crises such as depressions should exert stronger effects than milder recessions. At some point during protracted depressions, admission rates should fall, as a deepening of the fiscal crisis jeopardizes public and/or private capacities to punish. As the more vulnerable group, black offenders should bear the brunt of these impacts. Their admission rates should respond more quickly, consistently, and forcibly to economic crises than white admission rates. Finally, changes in the business cycle should have more intense impacts on rates of admission for property crimes than for violence.

The second set of expectations revolves around World War I and its aftermath. America's entry into the war should precipitate a decline in the rate at which offenders were sent to prison. This decline should be more pronounced for black men because they experienced greater conscription. The acute crises that demobilization generated in 1919 should have the opposite effect of increasing admission rates. Once again, black men experienced greater dislocations and hostility after the war. Thus, their rates of admission should be more tightly linked with demobilization than white rates of admission.

The third set of hypotheses addresses the implications of policy changes for punishment. Of interest are the advent of parole in 1908, abolition of the lease in 1909, the institution of probation in 1913, and passage of the Federal Aid Road Act in 1916 and Agricultural Adjustment Act (AAA) in 1933. As noted in chapter 4, expiration of the last lease heralded a return to county-administered punishment at a time of strong public demand for new and improved roads. Thus, abolition per se may have had no impact on admissions. Alternatively, it may have stimulated growth in the rate at which potential road laborers, both black and white, were admitted to the penitentiary.

The stability of punishment thesis suggests an expectation about the impact of parole. To compensate for the "early" loss of convict labor through conditional release and to maintain a steady level of punishment, admission rates should rise with the introduction of parole. As an alternative to incarceration, the advent of probation in 1913 should have the opposite impact, triggering declines in the admission rate. White offenders should be the primary, if not the only, beneficiaries of such lenience.

To the extent that the Federal Aid Road Act stimulated the demand for convict labor to build and maintain roads, rates of admission to the penitentiary should rise shortly after its passage. Since white men were a relatively untapped resource for convict labor, their rates of admission should react more strongly than black rates of admission. Finally, passage of the AAA, a consequence of the Great Depression, should initially increase admissions to the penitentiary. Like a lengthy depression, its impact should alter as the dispossession of tenants strained social control capacities. At some point, admissions should decline.

Additional expectations inform the multivariate stage of the analysis, which focuses on the link between social change and punishment. The rate at which black men were sent to prison should rise as the price of cotton falls, the size of the cotton harvest declines, and the supply of black labor (i.e., percentage black male) shrinks. The cotton economy should exercise its most vigorous influence in the nineteenth century, when cotton's hegemony was clear. Growth in urbanization and in the black component of the urban population should also increase black admission rates. Again, their impact should be clearest in the nineteenth century, when concerns about the proper role of blacks in the cotton economy were at their height. Because blacks were excluded from the industrialization process, rates of admission should be unresponsive to growth in the value added by manufacturing. Declines in racial inequality should foster higher admission rates, particularly in the nineteenth century, when the threat posed by Emancipation to caste distinctions was the sharpest. Finally, a decline in the size of the young black male population should raise admission rates, in an attempt to expropriate forcefully as much black labor as possible.

Similar, though not identical, expectations inform the admission of white men to the penitentiary. Admissions should rise in response to falling cotton prices, shrinking cotton harvests, declines in the size of the black male population, reductions in the magnitude of racial inequality, and growth in the size of the young white male population. In contrast, the intensified informal controls implied by industrialization suggest that white men should face a declining risk of imprisonment as industrialization proceeded. Since industrialization increased most dramatically in the twentieth century, its link with admissions should be relatively weak in the nineteenth century and should gradually strengthen during the twentieth century. Finally, the continuities between rural and urban experiences, outlined earlier, suggest that urbanization should have little, if any, impact on the rate at which white men were imprisoned. Only admissions for violent crimes should rise with urbanization, in response to urban intolerance of the rural tradition of backwoods feuding. Moreover, this relationship should characterize the nineteenth and early twentieth centuries, when the rural-urban boundary was less clear and concerns about inappropriate violence were more prominent.

The analysis begins with a determination of events and social changes that affected the admission of black men to the penitentiary. Considered next is the admission process for white men. As will become apparent, the admission of black and white men depended on a variety of events and social changes. None exerted an overwhelming influence, and few affected black and white punishment in precisely the same way.

General Admission Process

Admission of Black Men

Table 5.1 presents the results of the intervention analysis, performed on the black male admission rate. Expectations about the role of economic crises received mixed support. Only one economic crisis, the prolonged depression of 1873–79, prompted growth in admissions, and it did so two years after the onset of the crisis. More often than not, economic crises *reduced* the likelihood that black men would be sent to prison. This tendency was expected of intense and long-lived depressions. Indeed, it did occur a year after the onset of the depression of 1882–84. Yet black admissions also fell during less intense downturns. With the deepening of an eighteen-month recession that began in 1895, fewer black men were admitted to the penitentiary. The briefer and less intense recession of 1923–24 had a similar impact. In this case, the onset of the recession coincided with an immediate fall in the rate at which black men were admitted to the penitentiary. In short, economic crises tended to reduce black admissions. This tendency was neither limited to the most severe depressions nor necessarily a delayed reaction to an economic crisis.

Table 5.1 Impact of events on black admission rate

Event	Transfer Function	Model 1	2	3	4	5	6	7
Economic Crises								
1873–79 depression	ω_2	.36						.36
		(1.62)						(1.92)
1882–84 depression	ω_1		−.43					−.43
			(−1.95)					(−2.29)
1895–97 recession	ω_2			−.37				−.37
				(−1.66)				(−1.96)
1923–24 recession	ω_0				−.33			−.33
					(−1.47)			(−1.74)
War								
World War I	ω_3					−.50		−.50
						(−2.26)		(−2.65)
Demobilization	ω_0						.73	.73
							(3.47)	(3.87)
Original SSE		3.60	3.60	3.60	3.60	3.60	3.60	3.60
Model SSE		3.43	3.41	3.43	3.49	3.31	3.07	2.23
% reduction in SSE		4.72	5.28	4.72	3.06	8.06	14.72	38.06

Note: T-ratio of estimate in parentheses. SSE denotes error sum of squares.

Table 5.2 Cross-correlations for black admission rate

Social Change	Cross-Correlation at Lag				
	0	1	2	3	p
Cotton Economy					
Cotton price	−.34*	.15	−.09	.04	.11
Cotton harvest	−.20	−.20	.09	.09	.31
Percentage black male	−.03	.05	−.15	.10	.75
Industrial Economy					
Value added by manufacturing	.01	−.02	−.08	.10	.93
Percentage urban	.21	.22	−.15	.01	.11
Percentage black urban	.15	−.01	−.08	.10	.81
Inequality					
Racial inequality	.09	−.34*	.08	.09	.13
Control Series					
Percentage young	.12	−.09	.07	.12	.72

Note: The impacts of events were removed before estimation. Series were made independent of one another and prewhitened. See Appendix A for details.

*$p \leq .05$

While significant, the findings for economic crises must be placed within the context of the remaining impacts. As expected, the admission of black men declined with America's entry into the war in 1917 and rose with demobilization in 1919. More important, World War I and demobilization had the strongest impacts on the admission rate. No single economic crisis reduced the unexplained variance in black admissions by more than 5 percent. In contrast, World War I reduced the error sum of squares by 8 percent and demobilization reduced it by nearly twice as much.

The final events of interest are policy changes. Each proved to be singularly irrelevant to black admission rates. Neither the institution of parole in 1908, abolition of the lease a year later, nor federal legislation in 1916 and 1933 stimulated a rise in admission rates. The advent of probation in 1913 precipitated no decline. Thus, only selected economic crises and World War I affected the admission of black men to the penitentiary. Together these factors reduced the unexplained variance in admissions by a respectable 38 percent.

The multivariate stage of the analysis uses the residuals from the intervention analysis to evaluate hypotheses that link prison admissions to a variety of social changes. It begins with an estimation of cross-correlation functions between the black male admission rate and each input series (table 5.2). Although no function attained significance, several individual cross-correlations approached or exceeded

85

Table 5.3 Impact of social change on black admission rate

Social Change	Transfer Function	Model 1	Model 2	Model 3	Model 4
Cotton Economy					
Cotton price	ω_0	−4.73			−5.48
		(−2.82)			(−3.64)
Industrial Economy					
Percentage urban	$\omega_0 - \omega_1$		14.05		12.68
			(1.92)		(1.96)
			−18.87		−13.30
			(−2.85)		(−2.01)
Inequality					
Racial inequality	ω_1			−1.93	−1.67
				(−3.19)	(−2.99)
χ^2 of residuals					4.08
(p)					(.67)
Original SSE		1.96	2.23	1.95	1.95
Model SSE		1.74	1.90	1.68	1.27
% reduction in SSE		11.22	14.80	13.85	34.87

Note: T-ratio of estimate in parentheses. SSE denotes error sum of squares. Variation in original SSE is due to variation in time span of the residualized input series. See Appendix A for details.

statistical significance, and they merit further exploration. They suggest that black men were more likely to be admitted as the price of cotton fell, urbanization grew, and racial inequality declined. The pattern of cross-correlations suggests the appropriateness of estimating zero-order transfer functions, which test for abrupt temporary impacts. As expected, industrialization had no implications for the black male admission rate. Notably absent, however, are hypothesized links between admissions and changes in the composition of the black population.

Considered in the multivariate analysis, then, are the price of cotton, percentage urban, and racial inequality (table 5.3). Each proved to be equally important as determinants of the admission rate and, as a group, they reduced the error sum of squares a further 35 percent. As expected, a decline in the price of cotton generated an immediate increase in admissions. The moving average strategy described earlier shows that the *direction* of influence barely altered: depressed cotton prices consistently increased rates of admission (fig. 5.1). In contrast, the *magnitude* of impact

Figure 5.1. Impact of cotton price on black admission rate

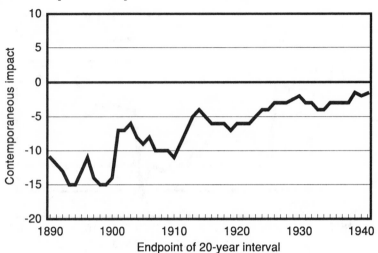

Endpoint of 20-year interval

varied dramatically. The link between the price of cotton and the admission rate tightened during two of the most serious nineteenth-century depressions (1873–79, 1893–94). Only after the depression of 1907–8 did the relationship weaken. As expected, the impact of cotton price on admission rates was negligible by 1940.

In addition to the price of cotton, black admissions to the penitentiary responded to growth in Georgia's urban population. Urbanization yielded a more sustained increase in admissions, as its impact occurred both contemporaneously and a year later. The trajectory of these influences over time suggests that their direction was consistent (fig. 5.2). Note, however, that the lagged impact of urbanization diminished with time, and by 1940 it was irrelevant. The contemporaneous impact began a similar attenuation, but showed clear signs of strengthening after World War I. Thus, even as World War II approached, urbanization quickly intensified the punishment of black men.

The final influence on black admission rates was racial inequality. The year after a decline in the economic gap between blacks and whites, black men were more likely to be imprisoned. Once again, this relationship was remarkably consistent in direction over time (fig. 5.3). Nevertheless, just as the price of cotton became less relevant to black punishment, so too did racial inequality. As expected, the link between inequality and black admissions loosened over time, never regaining the strength it had enjoyed in the late nineteenth century.

The following section examines the admission process for white men. The theoretical arguments developed earlier suggest that this process should differ in

Figure 5.2. Impact of urbanization on black admission rate

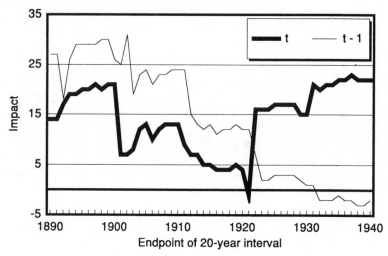

Figure 5.3. Impact of racial inequality on black admission rate

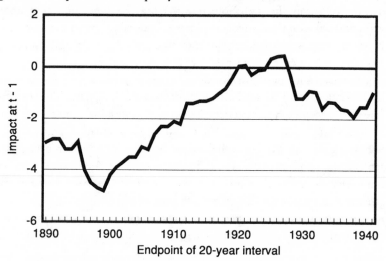

both degree and kind from its black counterpart. Simply put, the admission of white men should be less responsive to economic crises and urbanization, and more responsive to industrialization and policy changes. As we will see, the analysis provides some support for this expectation.

Admission of White Men

Our examination of the admission process for white men begins with intervention analysis, which estimates the impact of economic downturns, World War I and demobilization, and policies at the state and federal levels. As expected, economic crises increased the rate at which white men were admitted to the penitentiary (table 5.4). Among the more influential, not surprisingly, were the serious depressions of 1873–79 and 1929–1933. In neither case did a deepening of the depression alter the tendency toward punitiveness. White men were also more likely to be admitted in 1911, the most serious year of the 1910–12 recession, and again in the latter half of the 1926–27 recession. Thus, growth in white admissions was not usually an immediate consequence of an economic downturn. Typically, a year or more elapsed before admission rates rose.

The only exception to this pattern was the 1923–24 recession. Fourteen months in duration and moderate in severity, its onset coincided with a decline in the white male admission rate. While significant, this impact was modest when compared with the more pervasive tendency toward punitiveness during times of economic distress.

Unlike the admission process for black men, the process for white men was unaffected by America's entry into World War I. Demobilization did, however, stimulate the expected growth in admission rates. Its impact was no greater than that exerted by several economic downturns, accounting for an 8 percent reduction in unexplained variance. War and demobilization, then, were clearly more prominent for the admission of black men to the penitentiary.

Of final interest are federal legislation and policy changes that involved probation, parole, and the convict lease. Recall that black admissions were unaffected by these changes. The same was true for white admissions. Neither abolition of the lease nor the introduction of parole increased the rate at which white men were imprisoned. The availability of probation failed to lower white admission rates. The only policies of relevance involved federal legislation. Passage of the Federal Aid Road Act triggered an unexpected fall in white admissions. Despite its statistical significance, the act exerted a minor influence on the rate at which white men were admitted, accounting for less than 4 percent of the unexplained variance. It nevertheless raises doubts that federal aid stimulated interest in enhancing the forceful expropriation of white labor on roads. Considerably more important was passage of the Agricultural Adjustment Act in 1933. Tenant evictions escalated two

89

Table 5.4 Impact of events on white admission rate

Event	Transfer Function	Model								
		1	2	3	4	5	6	7	8	9
Economic Crises										
1873–79 depression	ω_3	.54 (1.60)								.54 (2.06)
1910–12 recession	ω_1		.54 (1.60)							.54 (2.06)
1923–24 recession	ω_0			−.58 (−1.72)						−.58 (−2.21)
1926–27 recession	ω_1				.86 (2.62)					.86 (3.28)
1929–33 depression	ω_2					.66 (1.97)				.66 (2.51)
War										
Demobilization	ω_0						.82 (2.49)			.82 (3.12)
Policies										
Federal Aid Road Act	ω_0							−.54 (−1.60)		−.54 (−2.06)
Agricultural Adjustment Act	ω_2								.78 (2.36)	.78 (2.97)
Original SSE		8.26	8.26	8.26	8.26	8.26	8.26	8.26	8.26	8.26
Model SSE		7.58	7.97	7.92	7.52	7.71	7.59	7.97	7.54	4.21
% reduction in SSE		8.23	3.51	4.12	8.96	6.66	8.11	3.51	8.72	49.03

Note: T-ratio of estimate in parentheses. SSE denotes error sum of squares.

Table 5.5 Cross-correlations for white admission rate

Social Change	Cross-Correlation at Lag				
	0	1	2	3	p
Cotton Economy					
Cotton price	−.10	−.01	.06	−.06	.98
Cotton harvest	−.11	−.11	−.19	.09	.40
Percentage black male	−.09	−.18	.20	−.25*	.05
Industrial Economy					
Value added by manufacturing	−.24*	.02	.19	−.16	.17
Percentage urban	.12	.12	−.07	.06	.71
Inequality					
Racial inequality	.04	.09	−.11	.02	.70
Control Series					
Percentage young	.05	.12	−.01	.04	.90

Note: The effects of events were removed before estimation. Series were made independent of one another and prewhitened. See Appendix A for details.

*$p \leq .05$

years after passage, and white men were more likely to be admitted to the penitentiary during that year. As was the case with economic crises, there was no evidence that admission rates fell in response to strains on the capacity to punish.

The analysis next assesses the role played by cotton price, cotton harvest, urbanization and industrialization, population changes, and racial inequality. A single cross-correlation function reached significance, and only one individual cross-correlation deserves closer inspection (table 5.5). Both cross-correlations suggest the appropriateness of including zero-order transfer functions, which test for the presence of abrupt temporary impacts. Contrary to expectation, there was no evidence that white admissions responded in any way to the price of cotton, size of the harvest, levels of racial inequality, or the size of the young white male population.

Multivariate analysis estimates, then, the influence exerted by percentage black male and value added by manufacturing (table 5.6). Three years after a decline in the size of the black male population, more white men were sent to prison. Declines consistently intensified the punishment of white men (fig. 5.4). Although the magnitude of this impact varied substantially over time, there was no clear tendency for the relationship to strengthen or weaken over time. Using the transfer function estimate ($\omega_3 = -40$) as a general point of reference, the relationship was stronger than average both during the nineteenth century and after the Great Depression.

Table 5.6   Impact of social change on white admission rate

Social Change	Transfer Function	Model 1	Model 2	Model 3	Model 4
Cotton Economy					
Percentage black male	ω_3	−41.32		−38.27	−46.23
		(−2.18)		(−2.03)	(−2.51)
Industrial Economy					
Value added by	ω_0		−.43	−.38	−.39
manufacturing			(−1.70)	(−1.57)	(−1.55)
Noise component	θ_4				−.24
					(−1.75)
χ^2 of residuals				7.54	3.84
(p)				(.27)	(.57)
Original SSE		3.74	4.21	3.74	3.74
Model SSE		3.11	4.03	2.99	2.80
% reduction in SSE		16.84	4.28	20.05	25.13

Note: T-ratio of estimate in parentheses. SSE denotes error sum of squares. Variation in original SSE is due to variation in time span of residualized input series. See Appendix A for details.

Figure 5.4.   Impact of percentage black male on white admission rate

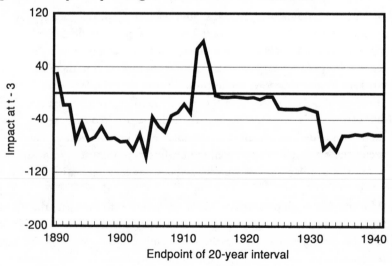

Unlike changes in the population of black men, growth in industrialization had an immediate impact on admissions. As expected, it prompted a decline in the rate at which white men were sent to prison. Nevertheless, value added by manufacturing exerted an unimpressive influence, reducing the error sum of squares by only 4 percent. There were only two exceptional periods when its inhibiting influence on punishment predominated (results not presented).[1] The first period appeared to be precipitated by the 1882–84 depression. Once that depression ended, the link between industrialization and admissions attenuated. In this instance, an economic crisis appears to have shaped punishment not only directly but also indirectly by conditioning its relationship with levels of industrialization. The second period saw a sharper and more sustained strengthening of the relationship. As anticipated, it was a twentieth-century phenomenon, coinciding with World War I and the Great Depression.

Summary

Several conclusions flow from the analysis of general admission rates. First, both specific events and more general social changes dramatically enhance our ability to predict the rate at which men were admitted to the penitentiary. For black and white men, models reduced unexplained variance by nearly two-thirds (from 3.60 to 1.27 for black men, and from 8.26 to 2.80 for white men). Second, no single event or social change provides the key to understanding rates of admission to the penitentiary. Instead, several factors, in varying degrees, shed light on this facet of punishment.

Third, the analysis supports the argument that the admission of black men differed both in degree and in kind from its white corollary. For black men, admissions were swayed most by economic crises, the price of cotton, World War I and its aftermath, the urbanization process, and changes in racial inequality. More often than not, economic crises *lowered* their risk of being imprisoned. For white men, admissions were driven less by World War I and not at all by urbanization, racial inequality, and changes in the price of cotton. Instead, the admission of white men depended on a succession of economic crises, federal policies, shifts in the black male population, and, to a lesser extent, growth in industrialization. More often than not, economic crises *increased* white admissions to the penitentiary, typically after a year or more had passed.

What unite the admission process for black and white men are factors of irrelevance, not relevance. Most depressions and recessions, as well as most policy innovations, had no impact on either admission rate. Neither did changes in the size of the young male population.

With these general conclusions as a backdrop, the analysis now considers two additional and more specific admission processes. First analyzed is the rate at which black and white men were admitted to the penitentiary for violent crime. A consideration of trends in property admissions follows. Largely exploratory in tone, each analysis begins with the impact of specific events, followed by the influence of social changes. Two expectations underlie the analysis. First, weaknesses in the cotton economy, declines in the business cycle, and reductions in racial inequality should find clearer and more immediate expression in admissions for property than for violent crimes. Second, urbanization should intensify the admission of white men for violent crimes, but should have little, if any, bearing on their admission for property crime.

Admissions to the Penitentiary for Violence

Admission of Black Men for Violence

Presented in table 5.7 are the results of the first stage of analysis: the impact of economic crises, war, and policies on the rate at which black men were admitted to the penitentiary for violent crimes. For the most part, the findings resemble those obtained for the black admission rate as a whole. Thus, the expectation that hard times would increase admissions received only partial support. Black men were more likely to be admitted to the penitentiary for violence in 1875, two years after the onset of the 1873–79 depression. They also experienced higher admissions with the onset of the 1887–88 recession. Unanticipated declines occurred at the onset of a moderately intense recession (1923–24) and during two major but short-lived depressions (1882–84, 1893–94). More often than not, then, economic crises prompted reductions in black incarceration for violence.

Like admissions in general, admissions for violence were affected most strongly by World War I and its aftermath, which generated 8 and 18 percent reductions in unexplained variance. Admissions for violence fell with America's entry into World War I (1917) and rose with subsequent demobilization. Finally, policy changes had no discernible influence on admissions for violence.

When we consider the impact of social changes, the findings also resemble those reported for the admission rate as a whole. Cross-correlation functions suggest that black men were more likely to be imprisoned for violence as Georgia became more urbanized and as racial inequality became less pronounced (table 5.8). As was the case more generally, neither the black male population nor its urban and young components had an impact. What distinguishes admissions for violence from the general admission process is the role played by the price of cotton. The significant cross-correlation at the first lag suggests an unexpected tendency for admissions to fall as cotton prices plummet. In contrast, the more immediate, though marginally significant, contemporaneous impact resembles the relationship found

Table 5.7 Impact of events on black violent admission rate

Event	Transfer Function	Model							
		1	2	3	4	5	6	7	8
Economic Crises									
1873–79 depression	ω_2	.28 (1.39)							.28 (1.72)
1882–84 depression	ω_1		−.38 (−1.90)						−.38 (−2.32)
1887–88 recession	ω_0			.31 (1.54)					.31 (1.89)
1893–94 depression	ω_1				−.33 (−1.62)				−.33 (−1.99)
1923–24 recession	ω_0					−.32 (−1.57)			−.32 (−1.93)
War									
World War I	ω_3						−.45 (−2.26)		−.45 (−2.75)
Demobilization	ω_0							.72 (3.88)	.72 (4.40)
Original SSE		2.94	2.94	2.94	2.94	2.94	2.94	2.94	2.94
Model SSE		2.84	2.80	2.85	2.84	2.85	2.71	2.42	1.67
% reduction in SSE		3.40	4.76	3.06	3.40	3.06	7.82	17.70	43.20

Note: T-ratio of estimate in parentheses. SSE denotes error sum of squares.

Table 5.8   Cross-correlations for black violent admission rate

| Social Change | Cross-Correlation at Lag | | | | |
	0	1	2	3	p
Cotton Economy					
Cotton price	−.22	.23*	−.08	.06	.24
Cotton harvest	−.06	−.17	.11	.11	.64
Percentage black male	−.10	.10	−.13	.13	.70
Industrial Economy					
Value added by manufacturing	−.06	.05	−.15	.07	.61
Percentage urban	.23*	.25*	−.17	.09	.04
Percentage black urban	.03	.11	−.07	.14	.30
Inequality					
Racial inequality	.07	−.40*	.17	.02	.05
Control Series					
Percentage young	−.01	.03	.08	.11	.66

Note: The impacts of events were removed before estimation. Series were made independent of one another and prewhitened. See Appendix A for details.

*$p \leq .05$

for the admission rate as a whole. The results reported below reflect the best fitting function among a set of estimated alternatives.[2]

Multivariate analysis focuses attention, then, on the price of cotton, percentage urban, and racial inequality (table 5.9). As the price of cotton fell, more black men were admitted to the penitentiary for violence. Given the size of the estimate ($\delta = −.69$), the impact of cotton price dissipated slowly with time. Like the general relationship, the link between the price of cotton and admissions for violence was consistently negative, but it diminished as the twentieth century progressed (results not presented).

The second influence on admissions for violence was urbanization. As expected, growth in percentage urban increased the rate at which black men were imprisoned for violent crimes. Initially, urbanization had significant contemporaneous and lagged impacts. With the addition of a noise component, the delayed impact of urbanization lost statistical significance. Thus, figure 5.5 traces only the contemporaneous relationship through time, comparing it with the relationship between urbanization and admissions as a whole. Unlike its general counterpart, admissions for violence grew increasingly *less* dependent on growth in urbanization. As expected, then, early growth in urbanization was more central than later growth to the admission of black violent offenders.

Racial inequality was the final and most influential determinant of the rate at

Table 5.9 Impact of social change on black violent admission rate

Social Change	Transfer Function	Model 1	2	3	4	5
Cotton Economy						
Cotton price	$\omega_0/(1 - \delta B)$	−3.69			−4.40	−3.60
		(−2.26)			(−3.13)	(−2.85)
		−.69			−.57	−.59
		(−3.03)			(−2.47)	(−2.79)
Industrial Economy						
Percentage urban	$\omega_0 - \omega_1$		13.33		10.20	13.74
			(2.12)		(1.76)	(2.59)
			−16.17		−11.70	a
			(−2.83)		(−1.98)	
Inequality						
Racial inequality	ω_1			−2.17	−1.98	−1.98
				(−4.19)	(−3.74)	(−4.36)
Noise component	θ_4					.38
						(2.91)
χ^2 of residuals					7.71	4.03
(p)					(.26)	(.55)
Original SSE		1.59	1.67	1.55	1.55	1.55
Model SSE		1.43	1.41	1.24	.97	.92
% reduction in SSE		10.06	15.57	20.00	38.42	40.65

Note: T-ratio of estimate in parentheses. SSE denotes error sum of squares. Variation in original SSE is due to variation in time span of residualized input series. See Appendix A for details.

[a]Estimate was nonsignificant and the model reestimated without the transfer function.

which black men were admitted to the penitentiary for violence. As was true more generally, a decline in inequality increased admissions for violence. Through time, this relationship resembles the trend presented earlier (see fig. 5.3). For that reason, the results of the moving average strategy are not presented. As expected, the link between inequality and black admissions for violence was robust in the late nineteenth century and diminished thereafter.

Admission of White Men for Violence

The analysis now turns to consider the rate at which white men were admitted to the penitentiary for violent crimes. Table 5.10 provides estimates of the impacts of

Figure 5.5. Impact of urbanization on black violent admission rate

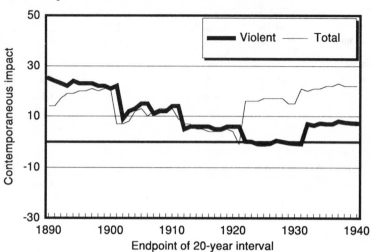

economic downturns, war, demobilization, and policies. In general, white men were more likely to be imprisoned for violence during depressions and recessions. No single crisis exercised a dominant influence. Reductions in unexplained variance ranged from a low of 2.5 percent for the 1873–79 depression to a high of 4.6 percent for the 1923–24 recession. The lengthy 1873–79 depression increased admissions even in 1876, its worst year. Similarly, the Great Depression triggered growth in admissions in 1931, the onset of its three worst years (1931–33). The recession of 1910–12 had a slightly more immediate but equally intense impact. In short, then, prolonged depressions failed to ameliorate the punishment of white men for violence. Admissions fell only once: at the onset of the recession of 1923–24.

Like the general admission rate, admissions for violence were unaffected by America's entry into World War I. Demobilization, in contrast, prompted the expected growth in admissions. Among state policy innovations, only probation was significant. As anticipated, it lowered the rate at which white men were admitted to the penitentiary for violent behavior. As for federal legislation, passage of the Federal Aid Road Act had an unexpected impact: it depressed admissions for violence. Of greater consequence was the federal response to the Great Depression. The Agricultural Adjustment Act produced both immediate and delayed increases in admissions for violence. Indeed, the AAA emerged as a dominant factor, reducing unexplained variance by 19 percent. Like economic crises, the AAA failed to ameliorate admissions, even as the dispossession of tenants strained social control capabilities.

Taken together, the events described above reduced the error sum of squares by

Table 5.10 Impact of events on white violent admission rate

Event	Transfer Function	Model								
		1	2	3	4	5	6	7	8	9
Economic Crises										
1873–79 depression	ω_3	.24 (1.30)								.24 (1.62)
1910–12 recession	ω_1		.28 (1.54)							.28 (1.89)
1923–24 recession	ω_0			−.34 (−1.89)						−.34 (−2.29)
1929–33 depression	ω_2				.28 (1.54)					.28 (1.89)
War										
Demobilization	ω_0					.36 (2.01)				.36 (2.43)
Policies										
Probation	ω_0						−.28 (−1.54)			−.28 (−1.89)
Federal Aid Road Act	ω_0							−.26 (−1.43)		−.26 (−1.75)
Agricultural Adjustment Act	$\omega_0 - \omega_2$								.40 (2.38) −.54 (3.21)	.40 (2.70) −.54 (−3.64)
Original SSE		2.38	2.38	2.38	2.38	2.38	2.38	2.38	2.38	2.38
Model SSE		2.32	2.30	2.27	2.30	2.25	2.30	2.32	1.93	1.32
% reduction in SSE		2.51	3.36	4.62	3.36	5.46	3.36	2.51	18.91	44.54

Note: T-ratio of estimate in parentheses. SSE denotes error sum of squares.

Table 5.11 Cross-correlations for white violent admission rate

Social Change	Cross-Correlation at Lag				
	0	1	2	3	p
Cotton Economy					
Cotton price	.01	−.07	−.05	−.03	.93
Cotton harvest	.06	−.11	−.00	−.05	.97
Percentage black male	−.12	−.36*	.00	−.19	.00
Industrial Economy					
Value added by manufacturing	−.05	−.07	−.05	.09	.85
Percentage urban	.06	.19	−.02	−.11	.48
Inequality					
Racial inequality	−.02	−.02	−.06	.12	.79
Control Series					
Percentage young	.21	−.03	.00	−.01	.79

Note: The effects of events were removed before estimation. Series were made independent of one another and prewhitened. See Appendix A for details.

*$p \leq .05$

Table 5.12 Impact of social change on white violent admission rate

Social Change	Transfer Function	Parameter	Estimate (t-ratio)
Cotton Economy			
Percentage black male	$\omega_1 - \omega_5$	ω_1	−30.39
			(−3.08)
		ω_5	35.49
			(3.60)
χ^2 of residuals			3.19
(p)			(.78)
Original SSE			1.22
Model SSE			.79
% reduction in SSE			35.25

Note: SSE denotes error sum of squares.

Figure 5.6. Impact of percentage black male on white violent admission rate

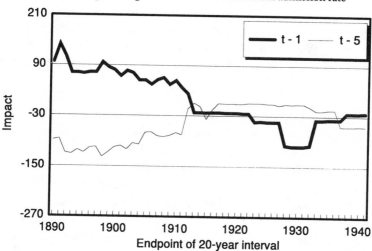

a substantial minority, nearly 45 percent. Their predictive power contrasts sharply with the ability of social changes to enhance our understanding of admissions to the penitentiary for violence. Table 5.11 makes it clear that only one cross-correlation function was significant. As expected, admissions for violence rose as the black male population declined. There is a significant cross-correlation at the first lag (CCF $+ 1 = -.36$) and an even larger correlation, not presented, at lag five (CCF $+ 5 = -.41$). Apart from percentage black male, admissions for violence failed to react to falling cotton prices, shrinking harvests, or lower racial inequality. Nor did they respond to levels of industrialization or urbanization.

The analytic model tests, then, only for the impact of percentage black male (table 5.12). As black men became a smaller component of the population, white men ran an increasingly greater risk of being admitted to the penitentiary for violence. This relationship is impressive, for it reduced the error sum of squares by 35 percent. Its trajectory over time is depicted in figure 5.6. Most noticeable is the lack of complementarity between the two impacts during the nineteenth century. The most immediate impact, after a delay of one year, is unexpected: admissions for violence fell with a decline in percentage black male. The more distant impact, after a delay of five years, is in the predicted direction: admissions for violence *rose* with a decline in the size of the black male population. This more distant—and expected—influence was a feature of the nineteenth century. As anticipated, it faded during the twentieth century. The more immediate and unanticipated impact intensified and ultimately assumed the predicted direction. In the nineteenth century, then, slight reductions in the black male population initially reduced white admissions, only to increase them four years later. Over time, admissions for violence reacted more quickly and in the expected direction. On the eve of America's entry into World War II, a decline in the size of the black male population continued to increase the risk that white men would be imprisoned for violence.

Summary

Before shifting attention to property crimes, let us consider whether the results reported above in any way alter our general understanding of the admission process for black and white men. In most respects, they do not. The same events and social changes that were relevant to black admissions in general were central to admissions for violence. Among the most crucial were selected depressions and recessions, World War I and its aftermath, the price of cotton, percentage urban, and racial inequality. The only difference of note involves economic crises, some of which affected the general rate but exerted no influence on admissions for violence.

Similar observations apply when we compare the general admission process for white men with its violence component. Both trends were driven by a variety of economic crises, postwar demobilization, federal policies, and changes in the black male population. Differences were relatively minor. The advent of probation lowered admissions of white men for violence. Yet its relevance did not surface for the admission rate as a whole. Conversely, industrialization prompted a modest decline in the admission rate as a whole. It had no discernible influence on the rate at which white men were admitted to the penitentiary for violence.

For the most part, then, the general admission process for both black and white men faithfully represents the specific process of admissions for violent crimes. As we will see below, the same cannot be said of admissions to the penitentiary for property offenses.

Admission to the Penitentiary for Property Crimes

The sections that follow consider the final set of admission rates, namely, those for theft and burglary. Once again, the admission process for black and white men undergoes separate examination. The analysis begins with the intervention of specific events, followed by an analysis of social changes and variation, if any, in their impact over time. Two crucial comparisons conclude the section. At issue in the first comparison is the extent to which a consideration of property offenders alters our general understanding of admissions to the penitentiary. The second comparison determines whether admissions for property crimes were linked more strongly to economic events and conditions than were admissions for violent crimes.

Admission of Black Men for Property Crimes

Presented in table 5.13 are the results for the first stage of the analysis, a test of the significance of several interventions. Once again, economic crises did not uniformly increase the rate at which black men were admitted to the penitentiary for property crimes. Like admissions in general, black men were more likely to be admitted for property crimes two years after the onset of the 1873–79 depression. The worst year (1921) of the brief 1920–21 depression also increased admissions for property crimes. However, economic crises were just as likely to moderate the admission process. Fewer black men were admitted for property crimes during the 1882–84 depression and the 1895–97 recession. Both tendencies surfaced earlier, in the analysis of the admission process as a whole.

The centrality of World War I and its aftermath have already been documented twice: for the general admission rate and for its violence component. Both events emerge again as important predictors of the rate at which black men were admitted to the penitentiary for property crimes. With America's entry into World War I, admissions for property crimes declined. With postwar demobilization, they rose. Each event reduced the residual sum of squares by 9 percent, rivaling in significance the most influential economic crises.

The final events of interest are the introduction of parole, abolition of the lease , the availability of adult probation, and federal legislation. Neither parole nor federal legislation raised admissions for property crimes. Probation failed to reduce admissions. Only abolition of the convict lease in 1909 was consequential. It generated an unexpected decline in the rate at which black men were imprisoned for property offenses.

Presented in table 5.14 are cross-correlations between the black property admission rate and the social change series. Although no function attained statistical significance, several individual cross-correlations merit consideration. There is support here for the previously documented roles played by the price of cotton and racial inequality. Of greater consequence is the emergence of a new relationship. Recall that urbanization generated higher admission rates in general and higher admissions for violence in particular. In contrast, a single significant cross-correlation suggests that, after a two-year lag, growth in urbanization *lowered* the rate at which black men were admitted to the penitentiary for property offenses.

Considered in the multivariate analysis, then, are the same social changes examined earlier in this chapter: the price of cotton, percentage urban, and racial inequality (table 5.15). As it did for admissions in general, the price of cotton emerges as a central determinant of admissions for property crimes. Its inclusion in the model reduced the error sum of squares by more than 10 percent. As expected, the rate at which black men were admitted to the penitentiary for property crimes rose significantly as cotton prices fell. Particularly influential during the severe

103

Table 5.13 Impact of events on black property admission rate

Event	Transfer Function	Model							
		1	2	3	4	5	6	7	8
Economic Crises									
1873–79 depression	ω_2	.39 (1.36)							.39 (1.63)
1882–84 depression	ω_1		−.47 (−1.64)						−.47 (−1.97)
1895–97 recession	ω_2			−.67 (−2.42)					−.67 (−2.82)
1920–21 depression	ω_1				.45 (1.58)				.45 (1.90)
War									
World War I	ω_3					−.56 (−1.99)			−.56 (−2.37)
Demobilization	ω_0						.72 (2.59)		.72 (3.04)
Policies									
Lease abolition	ω_0							−.61 (−2.15)	−.61 (−2.55)
Original SSE		5.98	5.98	5.98	5.98	5.98	5.98	5.98	5.98
Model SSE		5.63	5.76	5.33	5.77	5.44	5.45	5.61	3.52
% reduction in SSE		5.85	3.68	10.87	3.51	9.03	8.86	6.19	41.14

Note: T-ratio of estimate in parentheses. SSE denotes error sum of squares.

Table 5.14 Cross-correlations for black property admission rate

Social Change	Cross-Correlation at Lag				
	0	1	2	3	p
Cotton Economy					
Cotton price	−.37*	.04	−.04	−.01	.14
Cotton harvest	−.17	−.05	.16	.07	.47
Percentage black male	.13	−.01	−.11	.05	.57
Industrial Economy					
Value added by manufacturing	.01	−.04	−.09	.14	.86
Percentage urban	.09	.17	−.23*	−.00	.19
Percentage black urban	.02	−.07	−.21	.05	.71
Inequality					
Racial inequality	.03	−.25*	.01	.09	.47
Control Series					
Percentage young	.09	−.18	−.05	.08	.26

Note: The effects of events were removed before estimation. Series were made independent of one another and prewhitened. See Appendix A for details.

*p ≤ .05

depression of 1873–79, the price of cotton became increasingly less relevant to admissions involving property crimes. Thus, the findings of the moving average strategy reinforce those evident for the general admission rate and, to conserve space, are not presented.

Though less important, a decline in racial inequality also increased black admissions for property crime. The trajectory of its impact also resembles that of the overall admission rate and is not reproduced. Inequality had its clearest impact on property admissions in the late nineteenth century and, like the price of cotton, grew more tangential during the twentieth century.

Urbanization exerted the final influence on admissions for property offenses. Recall that as Georgia became more urbanized, black men experienced higher admission rates in general and higher admissions for violent crimes. The moving average strategy reveals a consistently different impact on admissions for property offenses (fig. 5.7). Indeed, the ability of urbanization to inhibit admissions for property crimes grew dramatically over time.

Admission of White Men for Property Crimes

The final analysis shifts attention to white men and their admission to the penitentiary for property crimes. Economic crises clearly had robust and consistent impacts (table 5.16). White admissions for property crimes rose with both depressions

Table 5.15   Impact of social change on black property admission rate

Social Change	Transfer Function	Model 1	2	3	4
Cotton Economy					
Cotton price	ω_0	−6.05			−5.75
		(−2.88)			(−2.79)
Industrial Economy					
Percentage urban	ω_2		−11.91		−14.36
			(−1.40)		(−1.64)
Inequality					
Racial inequality	ω_1			−1.65	−1.79
				(−2.10)	(−2.45)
χ^2 of residuals					2.94
(p)					(.82)
Original SSE		3.08	3.52	3.04	3.04
Model SSE		2.73	3.13	2.85	2.35
% reduction in SSE		11.36	11.08	6.25	22.70

Note: *T*-ratio of estimate in parentheses. SSE denotes error sum of squares. Variation in original SSE is due to variation in the time span of residualized input series. See Appendix A for details.

Figure 5.7.   Impact of urbanization on black property admission rate

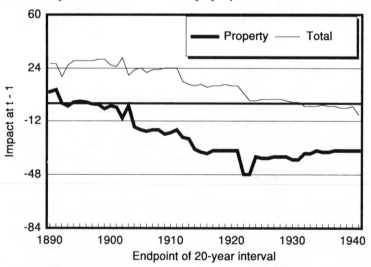

Table 5.16 Impact of events on white property admission rate

Event	Transfer Function	Model 1	Model 2	Model 3	Model 4	Model 5	Model 6	Model 7	Model 8
Economic Crises									
1873–79 depression	ω_0	.32 (1.24)							.32 (1.60)
1920–21 depression	ω_0		.48 (1.89)						.48 (2.40)
1923–24 recession	ω_1			.42 (1.65)					.42 (2.10)
1926–27 recession	ω_1				.82 (3.40)				.82 (4.10)
1929–33 depression	$\omega_1 - \omega_2$					.68 (2.79) −.38 (−1.56)			.68 (3.40) −.38 (−1.90)
1937–38 recession	ω_1						.40 (1.56)		.40 (2.00)
War									
Demobilization	ω_0							.48 (1.89)	.48 (2.40)
Original SSE		4.74	4.74	4.74	4.74	4.74	4.74	4.74	4.74
Model SSE		4.62	4.51	4.56	4.06	4.27	4.58	4.51	2.48
% reduction in SSE		2.32	4.85	3.80	14.35	9.92	3.38	4.85	47.68

Note: T-ratio of estimate in parentheses. SSE denotes error sum of squares.

Table 5.17 Cross-correlations for white property admission rate

Social Change	Cross-Correlation at Lag				
	0	1	2	3	*p*
Cotton Economy					
Cotton price	−.20	.21	−.10	.15	.16
Cotton harvest	−.02	−.02	−.21	.23*	.17
Percentage black male	−.14	−.01	.01	−.10	.84
Industrial Economy					
Value added by manufacturing	−.17	.05	.11	−.13	.59
Percentage urban	−.08	.06	−.12	−.05	.72
Inequality					
Racial inequality	.06	.17	−.08	−.01	.44
Control Series					
Percentage young	−.21	.22	−.11	−.03	.22

Note: The effects of events were removed before estimation. Series were made independent of one another and prewhitened. See Appendix A for details.

*p ≤ .05

and recessions, most typically a year after their onset. Twentieth-century crises were particularly influential. The 1926–27 recession reduced the error sum of squares by 14 percent, the Great Depression, by 10 percent. As was the case earlier, admission rates failed to decline as depressions deepened. The only other event of significance was postwar demobilization, whose influence on admissions in general and violent admissions in particular has already been documented. White admissions for property crimes also rose with demobilization. Finally, no federal or state policy affected the rate at which white men were imprisoned for property crime. Thus, their admissions were driven by economic crises and demobilization, which together reduced the error sum of squares by nearly half.

The multivariate phase of the analysis begins with cross-correlations between social changes and white admissions for property crime (table 5.17). Noticeably absent are relationships that were important for the admission rate in general, namely, percentage black male and value added by manufacturing. Instead, only a cross-correlation for cotton harvest reached significance, suggesting an unexpected though fragile tendency for admissions to fall three years after a smaller harvest. Table 5.18 confirms this weakness. Once the necessary noise component, a first-order autoregressive process, is included in the model, cotton harvest has no discernible impact. Thus, in any given year, the rate at which white men were admitted to the penitentiary for property crimes is solely a function of the rate the previous year.

Table 5.18 Impact of social change on white property admission rate

Social Change	Transfer Function	Model 1	Model 2	Model 3
Cotton Economy				
Cotton harvest	ω_3	.22	.15	a
		(1.67)	(1.30)	
Noise component	ϕ_1		−.43	−.44
			(−3.67)	(−4.08)
χ^2 of residuals		16.86	2.36	2.06
(p)		(.01)	(.80)	(.84)
Original SSE		2.16	2.16	2.48
Model SSE		1.99	1.65	2.09
% reduction in SSE		7.87	23.61	15.72

Note: T-ratio of estimate in parentheses. SSE denotes error sum of squares. Variation in original SSE is due to variation in the time span of residualized input series. See Appendix A for details.

[a]Estimate was nonsignificant and the model reestimated without the transfer function.

Summary

Before considering the theoretical relevance of the findings, it is important that we ask once again whether a consideration of admissions for property offenses alters our general understanding of the admission process. Recall that, for the most part, the overall admission process for black men faithfully reflected their admission for violent offenses. The same cannot be said for admissions involving property crimes. Were we to rely exclusively on the general findings, we would mistakenly conclude that, for black men, abolition of the lease was an irrelevant change in state policy. It was not, for it significantly *reduced* the risk that they would be admitted to the penitentiary for property offenses. We would only compound the error by continuing to rely on the general results to inform our understanding of the link between social change and penitentiary admissions for property crimes. The general analysis led us to assume that urbanization would invariably intensify the punishment of black men. In the case of violence, urbanization did indeed prompt more admissions. In the case of theft, it prompted the opposite.

The general admission process also does not faithfully reproduce the process of admitting white property offenders to the penitentiary. Clearly, economic crises and postwar demobilization affected both admissions in general and admissions for property crime. Yet several factors that figured prominently in accounting for the admission rate as a whole were useless in accounting for property admission

109

rates. Most notably, neither federal policy (i.e., Federal Aid Road Act and Agricultural Adjustment Act) affected the admission of white men to the penitentiary for property crimes. Furthermore, neither a decline in the black male population nor growing industrialization helped us understand the property admission rate. Indeed, once the impact of selected economic crises had been removed, white admissions for property crimes were driven by inertia, that is, by the previous year's admission rate.

In light of these differences, it should not surprise us that property admissions were driven by a slightly different set of considerations than were admissions for crimes involving violence. For black men, the similarities between the two outweigh the differences. Admissions for both violent and property crime rose as the 1873–79 depression deepened, as the region demobilized from World War I, as the price of cotton fell, and as the economic gap between blacks and whites narrowed. Similarly, black admissions for both violent and property crime fell a year after the onset of the 1882–84 depression and the year that the United States entered World War I.

Apart from these similarities, admissions for property crimes responded to other economic crises (1895–97, 1920–21) and to abolition of the lease, none of which affected admissions for violence. Most important, however, urbanization reduced the rate at which black men were admitted to the penitentiary for property crimes, but increased their risk of being admitted for violence.

For white men, differences between property and violent admissions outweigh the similarities. Of course, both rates were united by their insensitivity to changes in the price of cotton, levels of urbanization and industrialization, and racial inequality. Similarly, both rates responded to a series of economic crises and to postwar demobilization. Nevertheless, the crises that drove property admissions were seldom the same crises that affected admissions for violence. Even though both rates rose during two major depressions (1873–79, 1929–33), property admissions responded more quickly and, in the case of the Great Depression, for a longer period. Finally, property admissions were more insulated from broader social changes and policies than were admissions for violence. They were unaffected by the Agricultural Adjustment Act and probation. Even their response to reductions in the size of the cotton harvest paled in comparison with their reaction to admissions the previous year.

In short, then, the preceding comparisons argue for a cautious interpretation of research that focuses on a global admission measure, one that is insensitive to either race or offense. For white men in particular, the distinction between punishment for theft and punishment for violence was crucial. The following section revisits these distinctions, placing them in the context of expectations derived from a consideration of competing theoretical perspectives. At this point, it is clear that

110

theoretical perspectives face a complicated task, for they must account not simply for one admission process but, rather, for a set of processes conditioned by race and by offense.

Theoretical Implications

Our evaluation of theoretical expectations begins with the political economy, in particular, with several dimensions of the cotton and industrial economies. Examined first is the price of cotton, which provides an overall sense of the health of Georgia's agrarian economy. Two features of the agrarian labor market follow: the demand for labor, indicated by the size of the cotton harvest, and its supply, indicated by the relative size of the black male population. Constrained as they were by the cotton economy, three features of the industrial economy are relevant: industrialization, urbanization, and the size of the black urban population. Expectations for each were conditioned heavily by race. The remaining factors of economic relevance are racial inequality, a central element of the intergroup competition perspective, and a series of declines and increases in the business cycle. Differing primarily in degree, each economic downturn was expected to have some bearing on the rate at which white and black men were admitted to the penitentiary. The final events of note are World War I, demobilization, and several actions undertaken by federal and state officials. These include the introduction of parole in 1908, abolition of the lease in 1909, the advent of adult probation in 1913, and passage of the Federal Aid Road Act in 1916 and the Agricultural Adjustment Act in 1933. The final demographic change of note is the size of the young population, which should have had quite different consequences for the imprisonment of black and white men.

The Cotton Economy

One of the most enduring findings of the literature on nineteenth-century punishment is the link between repressive social control and declines in the price of cotton. The results reported in this chapter yield further, but qualified, support for this finding. Cotton price had an immediate influence on the rate at which black men were admitted to the penitentiary, for both violent and property crimes. As expected, its most vigorous impact was reserved for the incarceration of black men for theft and burglary. Not surprisingly, the price of cotton lost its centrality to the admission process as Georgia's economy diversified. Indeed, its influence waned to such an extent that by 1940 the punishment of black men was virtually independent of fluctuations in the price of cotton.

In the nineteenth century, though, cotton was king in more ways than one. Its link with the punishment of black men was particularly tight during periods characterized by a succession of recessions and depressions. But King Cotton's authority had clear limits. Its price had no discernible impact on the rate at which *white* men were admitted to the penitentiary. This was true for the admission process in general as well as for admissions involving property and violent offenders in particular.

In addition to the price of cotton, rates of admission were expected to respond to shifts in the demand for labor, indicated by cotton harvest. A smaller cotton harvest signified reduced demand for agrarian labor and raised the prospect of a labor surplus, thereby increasing both black and white admissions to the penitentiary. This did not prove to be the case. For neither race was the harvest a significant predictor of penitentiary admissions.

Shifts in the supply of agrarian labor proved to be more central to the admission process, but only for white men. As expected, a decline in the size of the black male population tended to increase the overall rate at which white men were admitted to the penitentiary. Subsequent analysis revealed that declines in the black male population affected only admissions for violent crimes. Indeed, the size of the black male population was not only the single influence but also a vigorous one. For admissions involving property crimes, in contrast, the size of the black male population was irrelevant.

In very different ways, then, the cotton economy was essential to an understanding of the punishment of both black and white men. For black men, the price of cotton immediately influenced violent and property admissions to the penitentiary. For white men, the supply of labor influenced admissions, but only for violent offenses and only after some time had elapsed.

The Industrial Economy

Profoundly shaped by the cotton economy, industrialization and urbanization should also have had implications for the incarceration of black and white men. Since industrialization and its intensification of informal social control involved whites rather than blacks, its influence should have been limited primarily to the punishment of white men. Indeed it was. Industrialization had no effect on the rate at which black men were imprisoned. It exerted the expected dampening effect on the punishment of white men and, as anticipated, was more likely to do so in the twentieth than in the nineteenth century. Nevertheless, industrialization exerted a weak influence and was clearly overshadowed by the cotton economy, particularly the demand for agrarian labor.

The urbanization process also differed by race, involving greater discontinuities and problems for blacks than for whites. Thus, growth in urbanization should, first and most pervasively, increase the admission of black men to the penitentiary. Accompanying urbanization was escalating intolerance for the rural legacy of violence among white men, however. As a result, growth in urbanization should, second, increase the imprisonment of white men for violent crimes.

Neither expectation received clear support. Urbanization did indeed increase the rate at which black men were imprisoned. But it did not do so pervasively or consistently over time. The general increase in the admission of black men to the penitentiary can be traced to the specific influence that urbanization exerted on the admission of black men for violent conduct. Urbanization did not exercise the same influence over the admission of black men for property crime. As Georgia became more urbanized, black men became *less* likely to be admitted to the penitentiary for theft and burglary. Equally unanticipated was variation in urbanization's role over time. As expected, its tendency to intensify admissions for violence grew steadily weaker. In contrast, its tendency to restrict admissions for property offenses grew unexpectedly and steadily stronger. Finally, even though urbanization was central to the admission of black men for violence, it was irrelevant for the admission of their white counterparts. The admission of white men, whether for violence or for theft, was not altered as the state became more urbanized.

The final dimension of the industrial economy was the black urban population, whose decline should have reduced perceptions of threat and lowered black admissions to the penitentiary. It did not. For none of the black admission rates was the size of the black urban population significant.

In sum, the findings support the general argument that race dictated the relevance of urbanization and industrialization for the punishment process. Urbanization had implications only for the punishment of black men, industrialization only for the punishment of white men. In its specifics, however, the argument fared less well. Though more disruptive for blacks than for whites, urbanization increased only their risk of being imprisoned for violence. At the same time, it reduced the likelihood that they would be imprisoned for property offenses. Industrialization, on the other hand, was relevant for white admissions to the penitentiary, but it ran a distant second to a more integral feature of the cotton economy.

Interracial Competition

As noted in chapter 4, racial inequality declined steadily after the Civil War, placing whites in a precarious position vis-à-vis blacks. To the extent that a narrowing of the economic racial divide increased perceptions of threat, it should have generated greater punitiveness, directed especially toward black men. This proved to be the case. Not only did black admissions overall rise. Admissions for violence and property crimes also rose in response to a decline in racial inequality. Unexpectedly, inequality played a less central role for admissions for property crimes. Its impact reduced the unexplained variance in property admissions by only 6 percent. The comparable figure for violence admissions was 20 percent. For both rates, though, inequality exercised its most vigorous influence closest to the postbellum period. During most of the twentieth century, even when declines were precipitous, racial inequality was irrelevant.

A drop in racial inequality placed whites in an increasingly vulnerable position, one which presumably rendered them less able to resist the imposition of coercive social control. Their risk of being admitted to the penitentiary should also have risen, at least marginally. This hypothesis was not supported. Racial inequality and the punishment of white men were unrelated. Even absolute changes in white wealth failed to alter the rate at which white men were admitted to the penitentiary.[3]

In short, then, declines in the magnitude of racial inequality had profound implications only for the punishment of black men. Most noticeable for admissions involving violent crime, its influence nevertheless diminished over time.

Economic Crises

Chapter 4 noted that southerners had to contend not only with volatile cotton prices and harvests but also with a series of severe depressions and less intense recessions. The first expectation guiding the analysis of these crises was that admission rates would rise with the onset of depressions and recessions. Many findings supported this expectation. For example, the 1882–84 depression increased black admissions overall, and this influence extended to admissions for both property and violent crime. Similarly, the lengthy and severe depressions of 1873–79 and 1929–33 triggered growth in white admissions, and their influence extended to admissions for both violence and property crimes.

In general, however, white admissions were more likely than black admissions to rise during economic crises. Of the fifteen significant estimates reported for white admission rates, 87 percent involved growth in admissions. Of the thirteen significant impacts reported for black admission rates, only 62 percent involved rising admission rates. It merits emphasis that, for both black and white admissions, comparatively few economic crises were influential. Recall that between 1870 and 1940, there were six major depressions and eleven downturns of more moderate intensity. Of these, only between four and six crises had measurable impacts on admission rates. Among the major depressions, only the 1873–79 crisis uniformly triggered growth in the admission of black and white men to the penitentiary. The 1882–84 depression, in contrast, was consequential for black admissions, but irrelevant for white admissions. Conversely, the 1929–33 depression increased white admissions, but had no bearing on the admission of black men to the penitentiary. Among the less intense downturns, only the 1923–24 recession consistently enhanced our understanding of black and white punishment. With the exception of

Table 5.19 Comparative impact of economic crises and other events on admission rate

Event	Total SSE	Total %	Violent SSE	Violent %	Property SSE	Property %
Black Male						
Recessions	3.3	7.8	2.8	6.5	5.3	10.9
Depressions	3.3	9.7	2.6	11.9	5.2	12.9
Economic impacts	3.0	16.7	2.4	18.4	4.8	20.4
Noneconomic impacts	2.8	22.8	2.2	25.5	4.5	23.9
White Male						
Recessions	6.9	16.6	2.2	8.0	3.7	21.3
Depressions	7.2	13.4	2.2	5.9	3.7	21.5
Economic impacts	5.8	30.0	2.1	13.9	2.7	42.8
Noneconomic impacts	7.3	11.6	2.1	11.3	4.5	4.9

Note: SSE refers to the error sum of squares, % to the percentage reduction in SSE after adding the intervention(s).

white property admissions, it tended to lower all admission rates. The remaining economic crises were only occasionally relevant. Some, for example, influenced only white admissions for property; others influenced only white admissions for violence. A few economic crises were consistently *irrelevant*, namely, the recessions of 1890–91 and 1899–1900 and the depression of 1907–8.

The second expectation was that the more intense the downturn, the stronger and more consistent its impact on admission rates. Support for this expectation was stronger for black than for white admissions. Of the thirteen significant impacts that downturns had on black admission rates, 62 percent involved depressions. Indeed, two depressions (1873–79, 1882–84) affected all three admission rates. Depressions also proved to have marginally stronger impacts than recessions. As a group, depressions reduced the unexplained variance in black admissions overall by almost 10 percent; the comparable figure for recessions was less than 8 percent (table 5.19). Similar differences characterized the role that depressions and recessions played in shaping black admissions for violence and property offenses. Depressions differed from recessions in another important respect: they were more likely than recessions to increase the admission of black men to the penitentiary. Half of all impacts involving depressions precipitated growth in admission rates, while only 20 percent of all impacts involving recessions behaved in a similar manner. For black admissions, then, depressions were both slightly more influential than recessions and more likely to generate the expected growth in admission rates.

The admission process for white men was less sensitive to the intensity of the downturn. Depressions had neither more robust nor more consistent impacts than recessions. Fewer than half of all impacts involved depressions, and their influence was as strong as or weaker than that exerted by recessions (see table 5.19). Though less sensitive to the intensity of an economic crisis, white admission rates nevertheless responded more quickly to its onset. Nearly three-quarters of all impacts occurred instantaneously or after one year. For black admissions, the comparable percentage was 61 percent. White admission rates were also more likely to respond in the expected direction. For white admissions, then, the distinction between depressions and recessions was less crucial. Each type of crisis was likely to increase admission rates quickly.

The third expectation was that admission rates would at some point fall during prolonged depressions. This was so because the longer an economic crisis lasted, the greater the likelihood that the state, counties, and/or private entrepreneurs would experience a fiscal crisis that would strain their respective capacities to punish. Since black admissions vastly outnumbered white admissions, black men should, in a sense, have reaped the benefits of strained capacities and experienced lower admission rates more often than white men. Indeed they did. Of the thirteen significant estimates reported for black admission rates, 62 percent involved falling admission rates. Of the fifteen estimates reported for white admission rates, only 13 percent involved falling admission rates. It merits emphasis that black admission rates were likely to fall not only during the depths of a serious depression (1882–84). They also fell during a brief depression (1893–94), a lengthy recession (1895–97), and a brief but moderately intense recession (1923–24). As a whole, then, a variety of economic crises, both long and short, intense and less intense, jeopardized the resources needed to maintain or expand the punishment of black men.

The fourth expectation proposed the existence of clear racial differences in the impact of economic downturns, namely, that the punishment of black men would react more intensely to changes in economic conditions. Put differently, impacts should occur more often on black than on white admission rates. When they do, impacts should account for larger amounts of the unexplained variation in black than in white punishment rates. Neither prediction received support. Black admission rates were *less* responsive than white admission rates to changes in economic conditions. With the exception of admissions for violence, economic crises produced significantly smaller reductions in unexplained variance for black than for white admissions (see table 5.19). The Great Depression is a case in point. Irrelevant when accounting for black admissions, it was essential to an understanding of the admission of white men for both violent and property offenses.

The final prediction held that economic crises would have more profound implications for admissions involving property crimes than for those involving violence. This was barely the case for the punishment of black men. All significant economic downturns reduced the error sum of squares in black property admissions by 20 percent (see table 5.19). Though more numerous, economic crises reduced the error sum of squares in violence admissions by only 18.4 percent. Support for the expectation was much clearer for admissions involving white men. Taken together, depressions and recessions reduced the error sum of squares in property admission by nearly 43 percent and in violent admissions by only 14 percent. Only for white men, then, did economic crises occupy a more central position for the punishment of property than of violent offenses.

Like the cotton economy, then, economic crises proved to be essential, in very different ways, to a complete understanding of black and white punishment. Declines in the business cycle tended to ameliorate black punishment and to intensify white punishment. A variety of economic crises, both long and short, intense and less intense, threatened the resources needed to maintain or expand the punishment of black men. Few crises had the same power to ameliorate the punishment of white men. Overall, economic crises played a more central role in the punishment of white men, consistently increasing their risk of being admitted to the penitentiary, especially for property offenses.

World War I and Its Aftermath

The findings strongly supported expectations about the role of World War I and subsequent demobilization. The punishment of black men reacted more intensely to these events than did the punishment of white men. Indeed, in concert with one another, war and demobilization exerted a stronger influence on black admissions than did the combined influence of economic crises. America's entry into the war lowered the rate at which black men were admitted to the penitentiary, especially for violence. It had no influence on the punishment of white men. Demobilization triggered an immediate rise in black admissions, again especially for violent crimes. Although demobilization increased white admissions, it accounted for less unexplained variance and, hence, was not the remarkable influence it had been for black admissions.

Policies

Between 1870 and 1940, the state legislature and the federal government instituted several policy changes. Georgia introduced parole in 1908, abolished the lease in 1909, and made adult probation available in 1913. The federal government passed the Federal Aid Road Act in 1916 and the Agricultural Adjustment Act in 1933. With varying degrees of certainty, each policy was expected to alter admissions to the penitentiary.

The lease was abolished at the height of the good-roads movement, which emphasized both expanded rural roads for economic development and the use of convicts to complete such an expansion. It is possible, then, that abolition was a seamless transition, having no implications for levels of admission to the penitentiary. Alternatively, it could have stimulated an increase in the imprisonment of potential road laborers, both black and white. The findings support the former argument. Abolition of the lease neither increased nor decreased the rate at which white men were incarcerated. Nor did it affect the rate at which black men were imprisoned for violent crimes. The end of the convict lease had implications only for black admissions for property crimes. There, its impact was unexpected, producing a contemporaneous decline. Though statistically significant, this impact was weaker than that of other events, including World War I, demobilization, and a series of economic crises. It nevertheless suggests the existence of a short-term ceiling on the number of black convicts that counties could accommodate for road-building purposes.

The stability of punishment thesis suggested a possible role for the introduction of parole in 1908. Admission rates may have risen to compensate for the "early" loss of convict labor that conditional release permitted. They did not. For neither black nor white admissions was parole a relevant consideration. As an alternative to incarceration, the advent of probation in 1913 could have had the opposite effect: reducing admissions, particularly of white men. Indeed it did, but only admissions for violent behavior. Probation was irrelevant to the admission of white men for property crime. Nor did it alter black punishment.

For different reasons, federal legislation should have intensified penitentiary admissions. The supposition was that the Federal Aid Road Act stimulated the demand for white labor to build and maintain roads. White admissions should therefore increase with passage. They did not. Instead, fewer white men were imprisoned, and this general trend can be traced to a decline in admissions for violence. The decline was slight, and the act exerted a trivial influence, reducing the unexplained variance by less than 3 percent.

The final policy, the Agricultural Adjustment Act (AAA) of 1933, was an indirect result of the Great Depression. To the extent that it impoverished many tenants, the AAA should have stimulated growth in prison admissions. This expectation received little support. The AAA had no bearing on black admissions, whether for violence or for property crimes. In sharp contrast, white admissions rose two years after the AAA was passed. When admissions for violence were distinguished from those involving property crimes, it became clear that the AAA

118

had implications only for the former. Thus, its impact was most pronounced where it was least expected: on admissions for violence rather than for theft. Moreover, there was no evidence that the AAA operated as a lengthy depression, ultimately ameliorating punishment.

Young Male Population

Of final concern is change in the size of the population of young men at risk of being punished. As a rough surrogate for white criminality, the expectation was that a decrease in the young male population would find expression in a corollary decline in white admission rates. It did not. Alternatively, as a proxy for the supply of young black laborers, the expectation was that a decline in the young male population would prompt compensatory growth in black admission rates, the better to expropriate their labor forcefully. This also did not occur. Shifts in the population of young men failed to enhance our understanding of the rate at which either black or white men were admitted to the penitentiary.

Conclusion

In essence, admission to the penitentiary encompassed a set of processes that varied by race and by offense. Economic crises loomed large for both black and white men. Nevertheless, they brought an occasional surcease of punishment levels only for black offenders. While more critical to the admission of white offenders, economic crises gave them no similar relief. As expected, the cotton economy itself proved to be more pivotal to black than to white punishment. Indeed, the admission of black offenders was dictated by several other processes related to the cotton economy. White admissions, in contrast, responded much more selectively to social changes.

The second axis of the analysis—offense—cannot be considered independently of the first. The distinction between property and violent crimes was more critical for white than for black men. Economic crises, for example, figured more prominently in the incarceration of *white* property offenders than in the admission of their violent counterparts. These sporadic economic crises aside, the admission of white property offenders was insensitive to a broad range of social changes, some of which were important to the admission of white violent offenders. In contrast, the admission of both black violent and black property offenders was driven by similar events and social forces. There was only one notable difference. Urbanization stimulated the imprisonment of black violent offenders and grew increasingly less capable of doing so over time. Urbanization *inhibited* the incarceration of black property offenders and grew increasingly *more* capable of doing so.

With chapter 6, attention shifts to the fate of those admitted to the penitentiary.

119

Of interest is the length of time convicts would labor for private entrepreneurs and county authorities. As will quickly become apparent, a single factor—seriousness of admissions—profoundly shaped the severity of punishments imposed on black and white offenders. Despite this influence, both race and offense continued to determine the precise impact exerted not only by seriousness but also by a broad array of external events and social changes.

6

Prison Sentences

JUST AS ADMISSIONS TO THE PENITENTIARY DEPENDED ON ONE'S CRIMI-
nal behavior and the color of one's skin, so too did prison sentences. Until the early
twentieth century, black offenders received the first sustained lenience we have
encountered. On average, their sentences were *shorter* than those imposed on white
offenders. In part, this pattern is the product of more intense reactions to the
violent behavior of white than of black men. In the twentieth century, the situation
was quite different, and black offenders, on average, received longer sentences than
white offenders. In part, this pattern reflects two processes: exceptional growth in
white admissions to the penitentiary for property crimes and a less intense reaction
to their property crimes than to those committed by black men.

Of concern in this chapter, then, are trends in the sentences imposed on black
and white offenders. The analysis begins with the impact of economic crises, war,
demobilization, and various policies. It then explores the influence exerted by
social changes. Considered first are prison sentences in general, followed by paral-
lel examinations of the sentences imposed on violent and property offenders. In
each case, the punishment of black offenders is of initial interest, followed by a
consideration of the sentences imposed on white offenders. Concluding the chapter is a discussion of the theoretical implications of the findings.

121

Theoretical Expectations

As was the case for admission rates, several expectations provide the basis for the intervention phase of the analysis. In general, economic crises should lengthen the average sentence, with depressions exerting stronger effects than milder recessions. Nevertheless, as depressions deepen and strain county and/or entrepreneurial capacities to punish, sentences should moderate. Black convicts should bear the brunt of these impacts. Their sentences should respond more quickly and more intensely to crises than the sentences imposed on comparable whites. The same should be true for property offenders. In comparison, economic crises should have fewer and less intense consequences for the sentences imposed on violent offenders.

In addition to economic crises, prison sentences should also respond to World War I and its aftermath. America's entry into the war should shorten the average sentence, while demobilization, with its economic dislocations and perception of black threat, should lengthen the average sentence. Once again, the burden should fall more heavily on black men, and their prison terms should respond accordingly.

Policy changes should have few implications for this aspect of punishment. While the institution of parole in 1908 probably affected the length of time served, there is no compelling reason for it to affect the original sentence. Abolition of the lease may be either irrelevant or a harbinger of longer prison terms, to serve better the demand for convict road labor. Minor though they were, the consequences of probation could well be confined to penitentiary admissions. Any alteration in sentences should be mediated by offense seriousness. That is, the use of probation for less serious offenders should increase the seriousness of offenders admitted. As appendix A makes clear, this did not occur. Thus, we expect probation to have no impact on prison sentences.

As for federal legislation, passage of the Federal Aid Road Act in 1916 should lengthen penitentiary terms, in an effort to meet the demand for convict labor that it stimulated. Passage of the Agricultural Adjustment Act (AAA) in 1933 should operate much like a major depression: initially lengthening prison terms, then moderating them in response to fiscal strain.

The multivariate stage of the analysis centers on relationships between social change and the severity of punishment. The hypotheses that inform this stage are identical to those developed to account for the admission process. The sentences imposed on black offenders should lengthen in response to lower cotton prices, smaller cotton harvests, and reductions in the size of the black male population. Each element of the cotton economy should become less relevant as Georgia's economy slowly diversified in the twentieth century. The sentences imposed on black offenders should also lengthen with growth in urbanization and in the black component of the urban population. Declines in racial inequality should have the same effect. These social changes should exert their strongest influence in the nineteenth century, when concerns about the proper role of blacks in the economy and in social life more generally were most salient. Levels of industrialization, in contrast, should have few, if any, consequences for the severity of black punishment.

Similar expectations apply to the sentences imposed on white offenders admitted to the penitentiary. Prison terms should become longer as cotton prices fall, cotton harvests decline, the size of the black male population shrinks, and the magnitude of racial inequality declines. White offenders should face shorter sentences as industrialization increases. This relationship should characterize the twentieth century, during which the pace of industrialization quickened. Finally, the continuities between rural and urban experiences, outlined in chapter 4, suggest that urbanization should have little, if any, impact. Only the sentences imposed on white violent offenders should grow more severe, in response to growing disdain for overt forms of violence. Moreover, this relationship should be stronger in the nineteenth and early twentieth centuries, when inappropriate violence directly challenged the image of a new South that elites wished to project.

Finally, trends in prison sentences should reflect changes in the young male population and in the cohort of admitted offenders. The population of young *black* men includes those who are more likely to be both accused of crime and useful as laborers. To the extent that a smaller population of young black men raises concerns about a shortage of labor, prison terms should grow longer, so as to expropriate as much black labor as possible. The population of young *white* men includes those who, while more likely than other age groups to be accused of crime, are not particularly useful as manual laborers. To the extent that it indicates a drop in criminality, a decline in the population of young white men should lower the sentences imposed on whites admitted to the penitentiary.

Terms of imprisonment should respond as well to changes in the composition of the inmate population. Clearly, the admission of a more serious cohort of offenders should lengthen the sentences black and white offenders receive. The admission of a particularly young cohort should place only black offenders at a disadvantage, however. This possibility derives from the usefulness of young black men to contractors and counties as laborers. Their admission to the penitentiary should provide an incentive for longer sentences, as a means to ensure a stable pool of relatively fit labor. The admission of youthful white offenders, in contrast, should have the opposite effect of ameliorating punishment, on the grounds that such offenders were more reformable and less useful as laborers.

The next section considers the punishment of black and white offenders in general. As we will see, there were few strong racial differences in this process.

Unlike admissions to the penitentiary, where a variety of factors were important, a single factor contributed heavily to the sentences that both black and white offenders received.

General Prison Sentences

Sentences of Black Offenders

The first stage of the analysis estimates the influence exerted by economic crises, war, and government policies on the average length of sentences imposed on black offenders admitted to the penitentiary. The most noteworthy aspect of the findings is their uniform support for the expectation that economic crises stimulated longer prison terms (table 6.1). The particularly severe depression of 1882–84 had an immediate impact. Two recessions (1895–97, 1923–24) increased sentences after a delay of a year or more. The most influential economic event was clearly the recession of 1895–97, which reduced the error sum of squares by more than 18 percent. These crises aside, no other depression or recession significantly affected the sentences imposed on black offenders. Moreover, neither war nor specific policies influenced prison terms. Thus, the sentences imposed on black offenders responded only to a selected number of economic crises. While few in number, these crises reduced the error sum of squares by nearly a third.

The multivariate stage of the analysis directs our attention to relationships between social change and the severity of black punishment. An evaluation of the hypotheses developed earlier begins with a series of cross-correlation functions

Table 6.1 Impact of events on black prison sentences

Event	Transfer Function	Model			
		1	2	3	4
Economic Crises					
1882–84 depression	ω_0	.25			.25
		(2.49)			(2.83)
1895–97 recession	ω_2		.28		.28
			(2.88)		(3.11)
1923–24 recession	ω_1			.20	.20
				(1.96)	(2.26)
Original SSE		.76	.76	.76	.76
Model SSE		.70	.62	.72	.52
% reduction in SSE		7.89	18.42	5.26	31.58

Note: *T*-ratio of estimate in parentheses. SSE denotes error sum of squares.

Table 6.2 Cross-correlations for black prison sentences

Social Change	Cross-Correlation at Lag				
	0	1	2	3	p
Cotton Economy					
Cotton price	.17	−.05	.13	−.20	.04
Cotton harvest	.02	.23*	.05	.03	.59
Percentage black male	.02	−.08	.21	−.00	.37
Industrial Economy					
Value added by manufacturing	−.07	.07	−.05	−.05	.69
Percentage urban	.06	.03	−.07	−.08	.68
Percentage black urban	−.17	.11	−.11	.03	.62
Inequality					
Racial inequality	−.04	.03	−.02	−.01	.99
Control Series					
Percentage young	−.28*	.11	−.05	.05	.27
Seriousness of admissions	.60*	−.05	.16	.01	.00
Age of admissions	.01	.00	−.04	.00	1.00

Note: The impacts of events were removed before estimation. Series were made independent of one another and prewhitened. See Appendix A for details.

*$p \leq .05$

(table 6.2). Only functions for the price of cotton and the seriousness of black admissions met an acceptable level of significance. In addition, two cross-correlations merit further exploration. The first raises the possibility that sentences grew more lenient after a smaller harvest; the second, that sentences grew more severe as the young black male population declined. The pattern of all cross-correlations indicates the appropriateness of estimating zero-order transfer functions, which test for abrupt temporary impacts.

The multivariate analysis focuses, then, on four factors: the price of cotton, size of the cotton harvest, percentage young, and seriousness of black admissions (table 6.3). Of initial interest is the reduction in unexplained variance occasioned by each estimated transfer function. Two factors were clearly more influential in predicting the sentences imposed on black offenders. The first was the price of cotton, which reduced the error sum of squares by nearly 28 percent. Even more important was the seriousness of black admissions, which reduced the error sum of squares by more than 40 percent. Of lesser significance were the cotton harvest and the young male population, each of which reduced unexplained variance by less than 10 percent. Taken together, all relevant factors accounted for over half the unexplained variance that remained in prison sentences.

Table 6.3 Impact of social change on black prison sentences

Social Change	Transfer Function	Model				
		1	2	3	4	5
Cotton Economy						
Cotton price	ω_5	−1.94				−2.14
		(−2.45)				(−3.85)
Cotton harvest	ω_1		.10			.07
			(1.60)			(1.51)
Control Series						
Percentage young	ω_0			−18.88		−12.69
				(−2.53)		(−2.45)
Seriousness of	ω_0				1.04	.94
admissions					(6.64)	(6.57)
χ^2 of residuals						1.33
(p)						(.97)
Original SSE		.47	.48	.48	.38	.38
Model SSE		.34	.46	.44	.22	.16
% reduction in SSE		27.66	4.17	8.33	42.11	57.89

Note: SSE denotes error sum of squares. Variation in original SSE is due to variation in the time span of residualized input series. See Appendix A for details.

The first determinant, the price of cotton, operated as expected. A decline in price generated the expected increase in sentences. This impact was hardly immediate, as sentences rose five years after a fall in the price of cotton. Although falling prices consistently generated longer prison terms, their power to do so slowly diminished over time (fig. 6.1). Even during the nineteenth century, the price of cotton briefly lost its relevance to sentencing. In a period that spanned the depressions of the 1880s and 1890s, fluctuations in cotton prices had virtually no measurable impact on the severity of black punishment. Once again, then, there is evidence that economic crises exerted an indirect influence on punishment by conditioning its relationship with related economic conditions.

The second determinant, size of the cotton harvest, was both less consequential and unanticipated. A smaller harvest prompted shorter sentences the following year. For the most part, harvest had this ameliorating impact during the entire period under consideration (results not presented).[1] Two qualifications are in order, however. A smaller harvest did not generate uniform reductions in prison terms. Its influence waned and did not resume its nineteenth-century position of prominence until well into the Great Depression. More important, during the

Figure 6.1. Impact of cotton price on black prison sentences

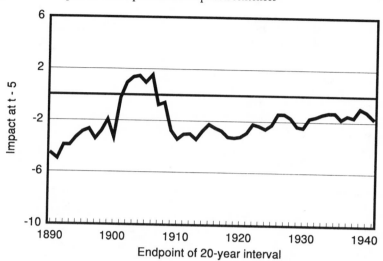

height of the good-roads movement in Georgia (1895–1914), the harvest had quite a different impact. As expected, a smaller harvest resulted in longer sentences.

The remaining impacts involve two control series: percentage young and seriousness of black admissions to the penitentiary. As expected, sentences grew longer as the population of young black men declined. This relationship was most forceful during the twentieth century, when the young population began to decline noticeably (results not presented). Between 1890 and 1900, for example, the young black male population grew from 17 to 18 percent. Its impact on sentences during this period was negligible. Between 1900 and 1920, however, the population of young black men declined from 18 percent to 16.4 percent. Its tendency to intensify punishment was particularly strong during this period.

The final and most obvious influence was also the strongest. With the admission of more serious offenders, prison sentences lengthened. This relationship was strong and stable through time, and for that reason the results of the moving average strategy are not presented.

Sentences of White Offenders

The analysis of white offenders begins with a consideration of the impact of economic crises, World War I and demobilization, and policies at the state and federal levels. Table 6.4 underscores the minor influence exerted by these events. Few were significant and, as a group, they reduced the error sum of squares by only 12 percent. The only economic crisis of note was a recession (1887–88), during

127

Table 6.4 Impact of events on white prison sentences

Event	Transfer Function	Model			
		1	2	3	4
Economic Crises					
1887–88 recession	ω_1	−.41			−.41
		(−1.75)			(−1.80)
War					
World War I	ω_1		−.43		−.43
			(−1.83)		(−1.88)
Policies					
Federal Aid Road Act	ω_0			.37	.37
				(1.56)	(1.62)
Original SSE		4.04	4.04	4.04	4.04
Model SSE		3.87	3.86	3.91	3.55
% reduction in SSE		4.21	4.46	3.21	12.13

Note: T-ratio of estimate in parentheses. SSE denotes error sum of squares.

which white offenders received unexpectedly shorter prison sentences. In 1915, well before America's entry into World War I, white offenders also received shorter prison terms. As expected, their sentences grew longer with passage of the Federal Aid Road Act.

Using the residuals from the intervention analysis, the next phase assesses the role played by cotton price and harvest, urbanization and industrialization, population changes, racial inequality, and other factors. As a whole, cross-correlation functions for cotton price, percentage young, and seriousness of white admissions reached an acceptable level of significance (table 6.5). The percentage young function owes its significance to a strong cross-correlation at the fourth lag (CCF + 4 = .32, not presented). Two additional functions, percentage urban and age of white admissions, fell slightly short of the standard. The urbanization function was marginally significant because of a strong cross-correlation at the fifth lag (CCF + 5 = .35, not presented).

For the most part, the pattern of cross-correlations argues for the existence of single, abrupt, and temporary impacts. For three series, though, the exact nature of the impact is unclear, and several alternatives are plausible. Both the price of cotton and the age of white admissions may have affected prison sentences after a lag of two or three years. Seriousness may have had two distinct impacts, one contemporaneously and another after a delay of one year. Alternatively, seriousness may have

Table 6.5 Cross-correlations for white prison sentences

Social Change	Cross-Correlation at Lag				
	0	1	2	3	p
Cotton Economy					
Cotton price	.14	−.18	.25*	−.28*	.03
Cotton harvest	.03	.16	.15	−.19	.35
Percentage black male	−.04	−.10	.18	−.14	.62
Industrial Economy					
Value added by manufacturing	.05	−.04	−.06	.09	.86
Percentage urban	−.03	−.04	.05	−.02	.08
Inequality					
Racial inequality	−.12	.02	−.03	−.12	.26
Control Series					
Percentage young	−.19	−.02	−.07	−.08	.04
Seriousness of admissions	.54*	−.35*	.13	−.11	.00
Age of admissions	−.07	−.07	.24*	−.31*	.06

Note: The impacts of events were removed before estimation. Series were made independent of one another and prewhitened. See Appendix A for details.

*$p \leq .05$

had a single contemporaneous impact that was distributed slowly over time. In each case, I estimated several transfer functions, compared the results, and selected the best-fitting function.[2]

Table 6.6 presents the results of the estimation strategy. Like the sentences imposed on black offenders, those imposed on whites responded most quickly and vigorously to the seriousness of admitted offenders. Alone, this factor accounted for nearly a 40 percent reduction in the error sum of squares. The admission of a more serious cohort produced an instantaneous effect. Given the size of the estimate ($\delta =$ −.58), its influence dissipated slowly. Even more unexpected was the tendency for seriousness to become less central to the punishment of white offenders (fig. 6.2). By the 1920s, its impact was only half as strong as it had been in the nineteenth century.

While less powerful, four other factors significantly influenced the sentences that white offenders received. First, a decline in the price of cotton generated the expected increase in prison terms. Though hardly immediate, this impact nonetheless occurred more quickly for whites than it had for black offenders. Overall, however, the price of cotton played a less pivotal role, accounting for less than 10 percent of the remaining unexplained variance. The comparable figure for blacks was 28 percent. Although the direction of cotton's impact was relatively consistent over time (fig. 6.3), its magnitude changed dramatically. As expected, cotton

129

Table 6.6 Impact of social change on white prison sentences

Social Change	Transfer Function	Model 1	2	3	4	5	6
Cotton Economy							
Cotton price	ω_3	-4.30					-3.88
		(-1.88)					(-2.54)
Industrial Economy							
Percentage urban	ω_5		26.11				33.59
			(3.14)				(5.32)
Control Series							
Percentage young	ω_4			13.34			6.64
				(2.77)			(1.98)
Seriousness of admissions	$\omega_0/ (1 - \delta B)$				.87		.73
					(5.05)		(5.12)
					$-.58$		$-.47$
					(-5.10)		(-3.54)
Age of admissions	$\omega_2 - \omega_3$					1.03	.60
						(1.77)	(1.55)
						1.34	.58
						(2.31)	(1.50)
χ^2 of residuals							5.13
(p)							(.53)
Original SSE		3.32	3.55	3.55	3.03	3.10	3.03
Model SSE		3.00	2.87	2.96	1.84	2.59	.99
% reduction in SSE		9.64	19.15	16.62	39.27	16.45	67.33

Note: SSE denotes error sum of squares. Variation in SSE is due to variation in the time span of residualized input series. See Appendix A for details.

exerted its most potent influence during the nineteenth century. Its relevance to sentencing diminished with the onset of the depression of 1882–84, and it never regained its predictive power.

The second factor to influence white sentences was urbanization. Recall that we expected industrialization to shorten prison terms and urbanization to be irrelevant. The opposite proved to be the case. Industrialization exercised no influence, while urbanization lengthened sentences after a considerable delay. As we will see, this finding reflects the impact of urbanization precisely where it was expected: on the punishment of violent offenders. Also as expected, urbanization exerted its strongest influence during the slow initial period of nineteenth-century growth

Figure 6.2. Impact of seriousness on white prison sentences

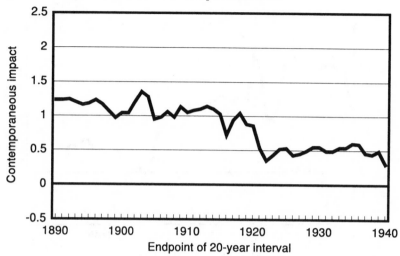

Figure 6.3. Impact of cotton price on white prison sentences

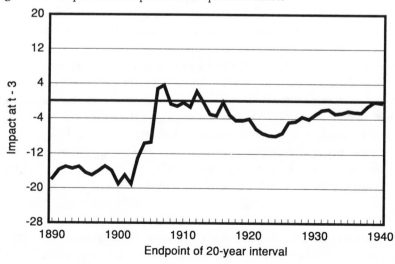

Figure 6.4. Impact of urbanization on white prison sentences

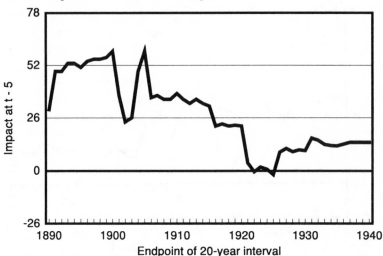

(fig. 6.4). Between 1870 and 1900, for example, Georgia's urban population grew from only 8.4 percent to 15.6 percent. Even as its pace increased, from 15.6 percent in 1900 to 30.8 percent in 1930, urbanization never regained its nineteenth-century position of strength as a determinant of prison sentences.

The third determinant of sentences was the size of the population most at risk of being incarcerated. Unlike black sentences, which reacted quickly to a decline in the young population, white sentences reacted slowly. Only after four years had passed did a decline in the population of young white men find expression in shorter prison terms. Also unlike its black equivalent, the youthful population waxed and waned in importance (results not presented). Its influence diminished after World War I and surged only toward the end of the Great Depression.

The final predictor, which accounted for a 16 percent reduction in unexplained variance, is the age of offenders admitted to the penitentiary. For white offenders, the expectation was simple: a youthful cohort would receive shorter sentences. It did not. Instead, convicts sentenced two years *after* the admission of a younger cohort were the beneficiaries of lenience, which they received throughout the period under analysis (results not presented). In contrast, convicts sentenced three years after the admission of a younger cohort suffered. They received significantly longer sentences, particularly in the nineteenth century.

Summary

The results thus far indicate quite clearly that the chief determinant of sentences was, in a sense, internal to the process itself: the seriousness of offenders admitted to the penitentiary. Alone it explained a lion's share of the unexplained variance in the prison terms that black and white offenders received. Sentences grew longer simply because more serious offenders were admitted to prison. Aside from this common point of reference, setting prison terms was in essence two separate processes: one for blacks, another for whites. As expected, the sentences imposed on blacks were swayed most by the state of the economy in general and the cotton economy in particular. The sentences of whites were more insulated from economic crises and from the state of the cotton economy. They were driven by population changes and, to a lesser degree, by World War I and federal policy. Finally, most social changes had impacts that, while consistent in direction, varied in magnitude over time. At best, then, the transfer functions reported in the tables approximate an impact that, in reality, was shifting continually during the period under consideration.

With these conclusions providing a general context, the analysis considers the more specific sentencing of violent and property offenders. Two expectations guide the analysis. Compared with their violent counterparts, the sentences imposed on property offenders should react more quickly, consistently, and forcefully to economic crises, weaknesses in the cotton economy, and declines in racial inequality. Compared with their property counterparts, the sentences imposed on white violent offenders should react more strongly to growth in the urban population.

Punishing Violent Offenders

Sentences of Black Violent Offenders

Like prison sentences in general, those imposed on black violent offenders lengthened during economic crises (table 6.7). Yet the 1895–97 recession, which figured so prominently in the general analysis, was irrelevant for violent offenders. Instead, the more intense depression of 1873–79 exerted the strongest influence, accounting for a 19 percent reduction in unexplained variance. As expected of protracted depressions, sentences rose two years after its onset and fell in 1876, its worst year. Though less influential, the 1882–84 depression and 1923–24 recession also lengthened terms of incarceration. None of the remaining economic crises had an impact. Similarly irrelevant were World War I, its aftermath, and policy innovations. Taken together, three economic downturns reduced the error sum of squares by slightly less than a third.

Using the residuals from the intervention analysis, I next consider the link between social changes and the punishment of black violent offenders. Not surprisingly, the cross-correlation function for seriousness is the most dramatic (table 6.8). Also significant is the function for the price of cotton, which suggests that declining prices generated longer sentences. Of marginal significance is the

133

Table 6.7 Impact of events on black violent prison sentences

Event	Transfer Function	Model 1	2	3	4
Economic Crises					
1873–79 depression	$\omega_2 - \omega_3$	.24			.24
		(2.21)			(2.35)
		.30			.30
		(2.70)			(2.88)
1882–84 depression	ω_0		.26		.26
			(2.22)		(2.50)
1923–24 recession	ω_1			.22	.22
				(1.89)	(2.14)
Original SSE		.99	.99	.99	.99
Model SSE		.80	.93	.94	.68
% reduction in SSE		19.19	6.06	5.05	31.31

Note: T-ratio of estimate in parentheses. SSE denotes error sum of squares.

Table 6.8 Cross-correlations for black violent prison sentences

Social Change	Cross-Correlation at Lag 0	1	2	3	p
Cotton Economy					
Cotton price	.15	−.19	.19	−.27*	.02
Cotton harvest	.03	.32*	.08	−.06	.06
Percentage black male	.13	−.12	.10	.04	.76
Industrial Economy					
Value added by manufacturing	−.20	.08	−.05	−.07	.51
Percentage urban	.00	.06	−.12	−.07	.12
Percentage black urban	−.07	.00	−.11	−.03	.31
Inequality					
Racial inequality	−.15	.16	−.00	.01	.25
Control Series					
Percentage young	−.12	−.02	−.08	.02	.63
Seriousness of admissions	.75*	−.16	−.02	−.02	.00
Age of admissions	−.03	.13	.04	.00	.85

Note: The impacts of events were removed before estimation. Series were made independent of one another and prewhitened. See Appendix A for details.

*$p \le .05$

Table 6.9   Impact of social change on black violent prison sentences

Social Change	Transfer Function	Model 1	2	3	4	5	6
Cotton Economy							
Cotton price	ω_3	−1.03				a	
		(−.97)					
Cotton harvest	ω_1		.21			.12	.10
			(2.85)			(2.20)	(2.10)
Industrial Economy							
Percentage urban	ω_4			−8.84		−6.28	−4.62
				(−2.29)		(−2.15)	(−1.72)
Control Series							
Seriousness of	ω_0				.99	.88	.86
admissions					(8.53)	(7.66)	(7.68)
Noise component	θ_1						.36
							(2.83)
χ^2 of residuals						15.58	4.60
(p)						(.02)	(.47)
Original SSE		.68	.68	.68	.65	.65	.65
Model SSE		.65	.60	.63	.29	.25	.22
% reduction in SSE		4.41	11.76	7.35	55.38	61.54	66.15

Note: SSE denotes error sum of squares. Variation in original SSE is due to variation in the time span of residualized input series. See Appendix A for details.

[a]Estimate was nonsignificant and the model reestimated without the transfer function.

counterintuitive impact of cotton harvest, encountered earlier in the general analysis. The final cross-correlation meriting attention is the delayed effect of urbanization (not presented), which failed to appear in the general analysis. With growing urbanization, black violent offenders received shorter rather than longer prison terms (CCF + 4 = −.30).

Included in the multivariate analysis, then, is the price of cotton, size of the harvest, percentage urban, and the seriousness of black violent admissions (table 6.9). Seriousness exerted by far the strongest influence, reducing the error sum of squares by over half. Like prison sentences in general, those imposed on violent offenders grew more severe in large part because more serious violent offenders were admitted to the penitentiary. Unlike general prison terms, however, seriousness did not exercise a stable influence over time (fig. 6.5). It became

Figure 6.5. Impact of seriousness on black violent prison sentences

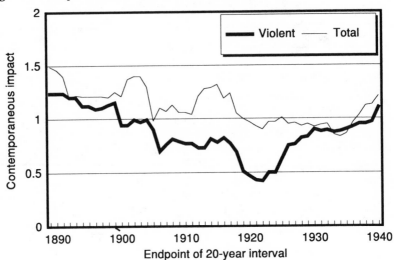

increasingly *less* critical to the sentencing of black violent offenders until the end of World War I, when it slowly resumed a central position.

In stark contrast to seriousness was the minor impact of cotton price. Alone, it reduced error sum of squares by less than 5 percent. Its transfer function failed to reach an acceptable significance level for inclusion in the full model. The remaining series had more noticeable impacts. With a decline in the harvest came an unexpected reduction in prison terms a year later, an impact that was also present for sentences in general. Results of the moving average strategy indicate that, over time, this impact was consistent in direction but variable in magnitude (results not presented). Like its general impact, the size of the harvest grew less important to the punishment of black violent offenders in the nineteenth and early twentieth centuries. Only after World War I did the relationship strengthen, and only during the Great Depression did the harvest resume its postbellum position of dominance.

The final factor of note was urbanization, which generated unexpected lenience. The earliest stages of urbanization were clearly the most consequential, tending to reduce the sentences imposed on black violent offenders precipitously (results not presented). As we will see, this was the same period during which urbanization tended to *increase* the sentences imposed on white men convicted of violence. Only briefly, at the turn of the century, did growth in urbanization lengthen the sentences imposed on black violent offenders.

Sentences of White Violent Offenders

The general analysis conveyed a clear impression about the sentencing of white offenders: it was singularly insulated from economic crises. Table 6.10 dramatizes the misleading character of this impression. The punishment of violent offenders reacted to several economic crises, each of which generated modest though significant reductions in unexplained variance. A year after the onset of the 1873–79 depression, white violent offenders received longer prison terms. Similar increases occurred with the onset of the 1890–91 and 1895–97 recessions. Economic downturns did not always intensify the punishment of white violent offenders, however. The 1887–88 recession triggered unexpected lenience, as did the more serious though brief depression of 1920–21.

The final two impacts, equally modest, mirror those found for white offenders

Table 6.10   Impact of events on white violent prison sentences

Event	Transfer Function	Model 1	2	3	4	5	6	7	8
Economic Crises									
1873–79 depression	ω_1	.41							.41
		(1.77)							(1.98)
1887–88 recession	ω_0		−.41						−.41
			(−1.76)						(−1.98)
1890–91 recession	ω_0			.35					.35
				(1.51)					(1.71)
1895–97 recession	ω_0				.41				.41
					(1.77)				(1.99)
1920–21 depression	ω_1					−.37			−.37
						(−1.60)			(−1.80)
War									
World War I	ω_1						−.50		−.50
							(−2.20)		(−2.44)
Policies									
Federal Aid Road Act	ω_0							.42	.42
								(1.80)	(2.20)
Original SSE		3.87	3.87	3.87	3.87	3.87	3.87	3.87	3.87
Model SSE		3.70	3.71	3.75	3.70	3.73	3.62	3.70	2.68
% reduction in SSE		4.39	4.13	3.10	4.39	3.62	6.46	4.39	30.75

Note: T-ratio of estimate in parentheses. SSE denotes error sum of squares.

Table 6.11   Cross-correlations for white violent prison sentences

Social Change	Cross-Correlation at Lag				
	0	1	2	3	*p*
Cotton Economy					
Cotton price	.13	−.15	.20	−.12	.33
Cotton harvest	.07	.01	.14	−.13	.82
Percentage black male	−.17	.03	.13	−.20	.44
Industrial Economy					
Value added by manufacturing	.03	−.09	.09	.03	.92
Percentage urban	.01	−.08	.05	−.01	.35
Inequality					
Racial inequality	−.04	.01	.01	−.15	.65
Control Series					
Percentage young	−.32*	.12	−.01	−.12	.03
Seriousness of admissions	.72*	−.20	.11	.10	.00
Age of admissions	−.12	−.13	−.01	−.08	.64

Note: The effects of events were removed before estimation. Series were made independent of one another and prewhitened. See Appendix A for details.

*$p \leq .05$

as a whole. White violent offenders received shorter sentences the year after World War I began and longer sentences the year the Federal Aid Road Act was passed. Taken together, the events noted above reduced the error sum of squares by nearly one-third. While not remarkable, this reduction is far greater than that obtained by the equivalent model for white prison sentences overall.

The general analysis conveyed another clear but equally misleading impression, namely, that the sentencing of white violent offenders should respond to a variety of external social changes. In reality, only three were relevant: urbanization, the size of the young white male population, and the seriousness of admissions (table 6.11). The first cross-correlation resembles earlier findings for prison terms as a whole. After a delay of five years, growth in urbanization increased the sentences imposed on white violent offenders (CCF + 5 = .26, not presented). The second function also resembles earlier findings: the sentencing of violent offenders reacted quickly and vigorously to the seriousness of offenders admitted to the penitentiary. The decay in cross-correlations suggests that this influence was distributed over time, and a first-order transfer function is therefore appropriate. The final relationship suggests that percentage young affected the sentences of violent offenders in a manner quite opposite its impact on sentences overall.

The multivariate analysis centers, then, on three possible influences: percentage

Table 6.12 Impact of social change on white violent prison sentences

Social Change	Transfer Function	Model 1	2	3	4	5
Industrial Economy						
Percentage urban	ω_5	16.94			10.64	10.30
		(2.23)			(1.99)	(1.95)
Control Series						
Percentage young	ω_0		−11.74		−1.77	a
			(−2.79)		(−.59)	
Seriousness of	$\omega_0/(1 - \delta B)$			.78	.73	.76
admissions				(8.66)	(7.26)	(8.44)
				−.37	−.37	−.36
				(−4.09)	(−3.78)	(−3.86)
χ^2 of residuals					7.53	7.43
(p)					(.28)	(.28)
Original SSE		2.59	2.68	2.32	2.32	2.32
Model SSE		2.40	2.40	.88	.82	.82
% reduction in SSE		7.34	10.45	62.07	64.66	64.66

Note: SSE denotes error sum of squares. Variation in original SSE is due to variation in the time span of residualized input series. See Appendix A for details.

[a]Estimate was nonsignificant and the model reestimated without the transfer function.

urban, seriousness, and percentage young (table 6.12). Once again, the strongest predictor is the seriousness of offenders admitted to the penitentiary. Alone, this factor reduced the error sum of squares by nearly two-thirds. As admitted violent offenders became more serious, the sentences imposed on them grew longer. Given the small size of the coefficient ($\delta = -.36$), this impact dissipated fairly quickly. Moreover, unlike its impact on sentences in general, seriousness exerted a relatively constant influence over time (results not presented).

The second noteworthy predictor was growth in urbanization. As Georgia became more urbanized, white violent offenders received longer sentences, as anticipated. Figure 6.6 depicts the trend in this impact over time. Note, first, that urbanization exerted its strongest influence during both its early and middle stages. Even on the eve of World War II, it continued to prompt longer prison terms, albeit less forcefully. Note as well that its tendency to *mitigate* the sentences imposed on black violent offenders was also most pronounced in the nineteenth century.

The final influence was the size of the youthful population. Despite its ability to reduce unexplained variance by 10 percent, percentage young exerted no significant

Figure 6.6. Impact of urbanization on white violent prison sentences

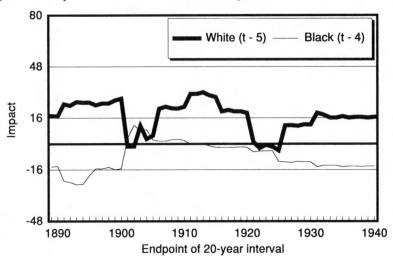

Endpoint of 20-year interval

influence when included in the multivariate model. The moving average strategy sheds light on its failure to retain significance. For reasons discussed in appendix A, the multivariate model covers a shorter time span (1879–1940) than a model that contains only percentage young (1870–1940). It therefore excludes several years during which a decline in the young population coincided with the imposition of unexpectedly longer sentences on white men convicted of violent crimes.

Summary

Before analyzing the sentences imposed on property offenders, let us consider the extent to which the sentencing of violent offenders differed from the general process described earlier. For both blacks and whites, the fundamental conclusion remains the same. At the core of the sentencing process was the seriousness of offenders admitted to the penitentiary. If anything, this factor was slightly more important for violent offenders than it was for offenders in general. Seriousness accounted for 42 percent of the unexplained variance in the sentences of black offenders overall and 55 percent of the unexplained variance in the sentences black violent offenders received. For whites, the contrast was even sharper: 39 percent overall and 62 percent for violent offenders. The reason for these differences will become apparent shortly, when we examine the punishment of property offenders.

In other respects, the general sentencing process also faithfully depicted the punishment of violent offenders. As a whole, black offenders received longer sentences at the onset of a serious depression (1882–84) and during the final year of a recession (1923–24). So, too, did black violent offenders. Overall, black offenders received lenience after a smaller harvest. So, too, did black violent offenders. Finally, World War I, its aftermath, and a wide array of policies were irrelevant for black offenders in general and for black violent offenders in particular.

These similarities aside, an exclusive reliance on the general findings conveyed four misleading impressions. First, it led us to assume that the price of cotton would be central to the sentences that black violent offenders received. It was not. Second, such a reliance conveyed the impression that a decline in the population of young black men quickly would lengthen the sentences of black violent offenders. It did not. Third, on the basis of the general model, we would assume that growth in urbanization would have no implications for the punishment of violent offenders. Clearly, it did, precipitating lenience. Finally, the general portrait of the sentencing process led us to expect that the recession of 1895–97 would have the strongest impact on the sentences that black violent offenders received. It did not.

A similar conclusion applies to the punishment of white offenders. In part, the general analysis accurately reflected the treatment of white violent offenders. Most notably, it captured the centrality of seriousness, as well as the role played by urbanization and the Federal Aid Road Act. In other respects, the general analysis was misleading. It gave the false impression that the sentencing of white violent convicts would be insulated from economic crises. Clearly, it was not. The general analysis also forged a link between sentences and variation in the price of cotton. No such link was evident for white violent offenders.

In short, sentences for offenders in general and for violent offenders in particular were outcomes of similar but not identical processes. In the next section, attention turns to the punishment of property offenders. In addition to revisiting race differences, the analysis permits us to question whether the general analysis accurately depicts the sentencing of property offenders. It also allows us to confront more directly the magnitude of the difference between violent and property offenders.

Punishing Property Offenders

The analysis begins with the intervention of specific events, followed by a multivariate analysis of social changes. The major expectations outlined in earlier sections apply, with two crucial additions. Economic events and changes should dictate the punishment of property offenders more strongly than they dictated the punishment of violent offenders. Urbanization, in contrast, should play a less central role for white property offenders than it did for white violent offenders.

Sentences of Black Property Offenders

Like sentences in general and those imposed on violent offenders, the punishment of black property offenders reacted to several economic crises (table 6.13). What

141

Table 6.13   Impact of events on black property prison sentences

Event	Transfer Function	Model					
		1	2	3	4	5	6
Economic Crises							
1899–1900 recession	ω_1	−.25					−.25
		(−2.15)					(−2.51)
1907–08 depression	ω_1		−.20				−.20
			(−1.67)				(−1.98)
1926–27 recession	ω_0			−.32			−.32
				(−2.77)			(−3.16)
War							
World War I	ω_0				.23		.23
					(1.94)		(2.28)
Policies							
Probation	ω_0					−.32	−.32
						(−2.74)	(−3.13)
Original SSE		1.02	1.02	1.02	1.02	1.02	1.02
Model SSE		.96	.98	.92	.97	.92	.66
% reduction in SSE		5.88	3.92	11.80	4.90	11.80	35.29

Note: T-ratio of estimate in parentheses. SSE denotes error sum of squares.

differs is the *nature* of this reaction. Rather than lengthen sentences, economic crises uniformly *shortened* them. In addition to economic crises, the onset of World War I also influenced the treatment of property offenders, unexpectedly lengthening their terms of incarceration. The final impact involved probation, hitherto irrelevant to sentencing. As an alternative to incarceration, probation prompted contemporaneous lenience in the sentences that black property offenders received. Indeed, it accounted for nearly a 12 percent reduction in unexplained variance. As a whole, selected economic crises, World War I, and probation reduced the error sum of squares by slightly more than a third.

Recall that the seriousness of offenders admitted to the penitentiary was the dominant predictor of the sentences imposed on blacks in general and on black violent offenders in particular. It did not exert the same influence on property offenders (table 6.14). Of equal, if not greater, significance were cross-correlations for percentage urban, percentage black urban, racial inequality, and age of black property admissions.

Table 6.14 Cross-correlations for black property prison sentences

	Cross-Correlation at Lag				
Social Change	0	1	2	3	p
Cotton Economy					
Cotton price	−.13	.08	.12	−.00	.25
Cotton harvest	−.03	.06	−.11	.11	.84
Percentage black male	−.04	−.13	.13	−.03	.72
Industrial Economy					
Value added by manufacturing	.12	.00	−.07	.20	.60
Percentage urban	.40*	−.10	−.09	−.10	.01
Percentage black urban	−.28*	.24*	−.10	.17	.04
Inequality					
Racial inequality	−.00	.02	−.12	.31*	.22
Control Series					
Percentage young	−.13	.10	−.14	.15	.40
Seriousness of admissions	.32*	−.08	.10	−.05	.27
Age of admissions	.10	.03	−.25*	.13	.48

Note: The effects of events were removed before estimation. Series were made independent of one another and prewhitened. See Appendix A for details.

*p ≤ .05

The sentencing of black property offenders reacted most strongly to growth in urbanization and changes in the composition of admitted convicts, namely, their age and seriousness (table 6.15). As expected, punishment became more severe as Georgia became more urbanized. Figure 6.7 depicts the trajectory of this influence over time, as well as the comparable trend for black violent offenders. Despite superficial similarities, the impacts were quite different. First, urbanization consistently intensified the sentences imposed on black property offenders. Just as consistently, it *ameliorated* the sentences imposed on black violent offenders. Second, the link between urbanization and the punishment of black property offenders was weakest in the nineteenth century, precisely when the link between urbanization and the punishment of black *violent* offenders was the strongest. Finally, the twentieth-century impact of urbanization on black property offenders was relatively constant. In contrast, its impact on the punishment of black violent offenders gradually became more pronounced.

The next two influences involve attributes of offenders. Sentences predictably lengthened as more serious and younger offenders were admitted to the penitentiary. While the impact of seriousness was relatively stable over time (results not

Table 6.15 Impact of social change on black property prison sentences

Social Change	Transfer Function	Model							
		1	2	3	4	5	6	7	8
Industrial Economy									
Percentage urban	ω_0	12.85					12.92	12.51	9.50
		(3.65)					(3.03)	(3.17)	(2.69)
Percentage black urban	ω_0		−13.63				−4.00	[a]	[a]
			(−2.52)				(−.60)		
Inequality									
Racial inequality	ω_3			.72			.40	[a]	
				(2.39)			(1.19)		
Control Series									
Seriousness of admissions	ω_0				.68		.50	.51	.67
					(2.73)		(2.14)	(2.18)	(3.25)
Age of admissions	ω_2					−.71	−.69	−.71	−.57
						(−1.85)	(−1.93)	(−1.99)	(−1.68)
Noise component	θ_1								.41
									(2.87)
χ^2 of residuals							11.56	12.51	6.12
(p)							(.07)	(.05)	(.30)
Original SSE		.66	.66	.44	.43	.44	.42	.42	.42
Model SSE		.56	.61	.42	.38	.39	.28	.29	.25
% reduction in SSE		15.15	7.58	4.55	11.63	11.36	33.33	30.95	40.48

Note: *T*-ratio of estimate in parentheses. SSE denotes error sum of squares. Variation in original SSE is due to variation in the time span of residualized input series. See Appendix A for details.

[a] Estimate was nonsignificant and the model reestimated without the transfer function.

144

Figure 6.7. Impact of urbanization on black property prison sentences

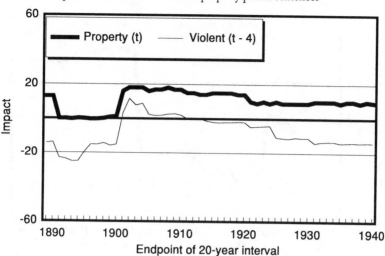

presented), the impact of age was not. Uniformly negative, its ability to influence prison sentences nevertheless diminished over time (results not presented).

The black urban population and racial inequality contributed less to our understanding of the sentences imposed on black property offenders. In the multivariate model, neither retained statistical significance. Once again, the moving average strategy helps us understand why this occurred. The multivariate model covers the period for which its shortest series or combination of series is available. In this case, it encompasses the period between 1882 and 1938. Percentage black urban lost significance because the multivariate model excludes the 1870s. As figure 6.8 shows, nineteenth-century shifts in the black urban population were tightly linked with the punishment of black property offenders. As the black urban population grew, from 45.4 percent in 1870 to 48.1 percent in 1890, black property offenders received unexpectedly shorter sentences. Only during the twentieth century did the steady exodus of blacks from urban areas, from 46.5 percent in 1900 to 35.4 percent in 1940, foster the expected lenience.

Racial inequality lost statistical significance for the same reason. The multivariate model excluded several years during which reductions in racial inequality triggered unexpectedly shorter sentences. Overall, however, inequality exerted by far the weakest influence on prison sentences, reducing unexplained variance by less than 5 percent. Moreover, its influence was unstable through time (results not presented). Contrary to expectation, inequality was intermittently linked with both nineteenth- and twentieth-century punishment.

145

Figure 6.8. Impact of percentage black urban on black property prison sentences

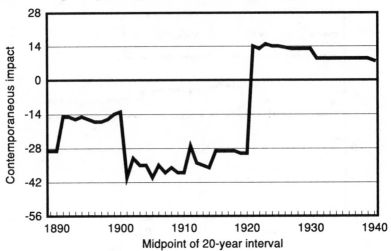

Sentences of White Property Offenders

The final analysis focuses on the sentences imposed on white property offenders admitted to the penitentiary. Two features of the intervention analysis are striking (table 6.16). Recall that the sentencing of white offenders as a whole was unaffected by economic crises. The sentencing of white property offenders, in contrast, reacted sharply to a series of economic upheavals. White property offenders received more punitive sentences during the 1882–84 depression, at the onset of the 1890–91 recession, and toward the end of the 1895–97 recession. Other economic crises stimulated lenience. This was the case at the onset of a depression (1893–94) and during two recessions (1890–91, 1910–12). Contrary to expectation, then, crises did not uniformly generate more punitive reactions. Nor was lenience a reaction to the fiscal crisis generated by lengthy depressions.

The second striking feature of the results is the role played by World War I and its aftermath. Earlier we saw that, shortly after it began, World War I restrained the sentences of whites in general and of white violent offenders in particular. For property offenders, however, the war itself was incidental. Instead, demobilization affected their sentences, prompting an unexpected reduction in prison terms.

The multivariate phase of the analysis examines the relationship between social changes and the sentences imposed on white property offenders. Only two cross-correlations reached significance (table 6.17). They suggest that the strongest influences were endemic to the pool of admitted offenders itself. In addition, a modest

146

Table 6.16 Impact of events on white property prison sentences

Event	Transfer Function	Model 1	2	3	4	5	6	7
Economic Crises								
1882–84 depression	ω_1	.55						.55
		(2.29)						(2.75)
1890–91 recession	$\omega_0 - \omega_1$		.49					.49
			(2.08)					(2.41)
			.63					.63
			(2.68)					(3.12)
1893–94 depression	ω_0			−.58				−.58
				(−2.40)				(−2.88)
1895–97 recession	ω_2				.42			.42
					(1.73)			(2.10)
1910–12 recession	ω_0					−.38		−.38
						(−1.53)		(−1.88)
War								
Demobilization	ω_0						−.38	−.38
							(−1.53)	(−1.88)
Original SSE		4.35	4.35	4.35	4.35	4.35	4.35	4.35
Model SSE		4.05	3.73	4.02	4.07	4.21	4.21	2.51
% reduction in SSE		6.90	14.26	7.59	6.44	3.22	3.22	42.30

Note: *T*-ratio of estimate in parentheses. SSE denotes error sum of squares.

cross-correlation (CCF + 5 = −.32, not presented) contributes to the marginal significance of a third factor, percentage young white male.

The multivariate analysis, then, considers percentage young, seriousness of white property admissions, and age of white property admissions (table 6.18).[3] In sharp contrast to its role elsewhere, seriousness played a minor role in the sentencing of white property offenders. It accounted for less than 7 percent of the unexplained variance. Not surprisingly, the admission of more serious property offenders initiated longer prison sentences. The link between seriousness and sentences grew stronger until the end of World War I and weaker thereafter (results not presented).

Of greater significance were changes in the young male population and in the age of offenders admitted to the penitentiary. Contrary to expectation, a decline in the population of young white men intensified the punishment of white property offenders. Its impact was both slow to be realized and inconsistent over time

Table 6.17 Cross-correlations for white property prison sentences

Social Change	Cross-Correlation at Lag 0	1	2	3	p
Cotton Economy					
Cotton price	−.02	−.01	.20	−.22	.41
Cotton harvest	−.16	.02	.07	−.20	.49
Percentage black male	−.00	−.01	−.12	.15	.81
Industrial Economy					
Value added by manufacturing	−.02	.10	−.06	−.00	.94
Percentage urban	.01	.10	.05	.02	.87
Inequality					
Racial inequality	−.05	−.04	.04	−.15	.82
Control Series					
Percentage young	−.08	.14	−.02	−.15	.07
Seriousness of admissions	.26*	.03	−.12	−.04	.04
Age of admissions	−.04	−.23*	.34*	.13	.04

Note: The effects of events were removed before estimation. Series were made independent of one another and prewhitened. See Appendix A for details.

*p ≤ .05

(fig. 6.9). During the last decade of the nineteenth century and early decades of the twentieth, changes in the young male population exercised the expected influence. The population of young men grew noticeably, from 15.6 percent in 1890 to 17.2 percent in 1910. This period of growth, which coincided with both economic crises and the good-roads movement, prompted the anticipated severity in sentencing.

The final, and strongest, influence was the average age of white property offenders admitted to the penitentiary. Once again the admission of a younger cohort failed to trigger an immediate reduction in their sentences. At some point, the admission of younger convicts did indeed moderate sentences, but the youthful cohort was not the beneficiary of this lenience. Instead, convicts sentenced three years *after* the admission of a younger cohort received shorter sentences. In contrast, convicts sentenced two years after the admission of a younger cohort suffered: they received significantly longer sentences. These opposing tendencies were hallmarks of the nineteenth century and became more muted in the twentieth century (results not presented).

Summary

Before considering the implications of the findings for theoretical perspectives, we must examine two related issues. The first is the extent to which a consideration of

148

Table 6.18 Impact of social change on white property prison sentences

Social Change	Transfer Function	Model 1	2	3	4	5
Control Series						
Percentage young	ω_5	−11.71			−10.99	−7.96
		(−2.86)			(−2.84)	(−2.38)
Seriousness of	ω_0		.53		.36	.33
admissions			(2.20)		(1.45)	(1.46)
Age of admissions	$\omega_1 - \omega_2$			−1.11	−.92	−.88
				(−2.17)	(−1.86)	(−1.93)
				−1.66	−1.39	−1.49
				(−3.12)	(−2.73)	(−3.18)
Noise component	θ_1					.41
						(3.13)
χ^2 of residuals					12.09	5.95
(p)					(.06)	(.31)
Original SSE		2.51	2.40	2.35	2.35	2.35
Model SSE		2.10	2.24	1.85	1.57	1.33
% reduction in SSE		16.33	6.67	21.28	33.19	43.40

Note: *T*-ratio of estimate in parentheses. SSE denotes error sum of squares. Variation in error sum of squares is due to variation in the time span of residualized input series. See Appendix A for details.

Figure 6.9. Impact of percentage young on white property prison sentences

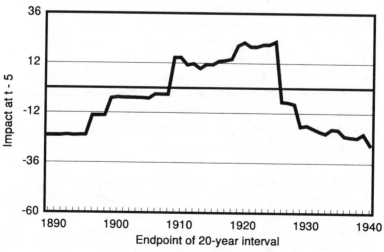

property offenders forces us to reconsider the wisdom of examining a global measure of sentence severity. The second issue is the extent to which there are two sentencing processes: one for property offenders, another for violent offenders. Underlying this comparison are two expectations. First, economic conditions in general and economic crises in particular should have stronger implications for the punishment of property than of violent offenders. Second, urbanization should play a greater role during the sentencing of white violent offenders than of their property counterparts.

In one major respect, a consideration of property offenders does indeed alter our understanding of the general process by which the severity of punishment was determined. For black and white convicts overall, the seriousness of offenders admitted to the penitentiary was indispensable to our understanding of sentencing. It was much less central to the punishment of property offenders, especially white property offenders.

In several other respects, the general analysis fell short of capturing the sentencing of property offenders. First, for black offenders overall, sentences responded to nineteenth-century economic crises. For black property offenders, in contrast, sentences reacted sharply to twentieth-century crises. Second, for black offenders overall, sentences lengthened during economic crises. For black property offenders, in contrast, sentences shortened. Third, both the price of cotton and the size of the young black population clearly predicted the sentences that black offenders as a whole received. Neither affected the sentences imposed on black property offenders. Finally, percentage urban and the age of black admissions were noticeably irrelevant for prison sentences in general. Each was critical to an understanding of the sentences imposed on black property offenders.

The general analysis also fell short of describing the sentencing of white property offenders. First, the sentences imposed on white offenders overall failed to react to most economic crises. The sentences imposed on white property offenders, in contrast, responded to a variety of economic downturns. Second, World War I and urbanization enhanced our understanding of the general sentencing process. Neither was relevant for the sentencing of white property offenders. Finally, demobilization exerted no influence on general prison sentences. It nevertheless benefited white property offenders by stimulating shorter sentences.

Not surprisingly, then, there were two sentencing processes: one for offenders convicted of violence and another for those convicted of theft. First, the sentences imposed on black property offenders were no more attuned to economic conditions than were those imposed on violent offenders. What distinguished the two groups were the economic crises of significance and the nature of their influence. Nineteenth-century downturns tended to intensify the sentences that black violent offenders received. Twentieth-century crises tended to ameliorate the sentences

150

that black property offenders received. Second, the terms imposed on black property offenders reacted to World War I and to the advent of probation. The terms of black violent offenders did not. Urbanization tempered the punishment of black violent offenders, but exacerbated the punishment of black property offenders. Finally, the sentencing of black property offenders reacted less vigorously to the seriousness of offenders admitted to the penitentiary than did the sentencing of black violent offenders.

There were two white sentencing processes as well. Few economic crises had identical implications for the punishment of property and violent offenders. The sentences imposed on white violent offenders reacted to World War I, the Federal Aid Road Act, and urbanization. Those imposed on white property offenders did not. As alluded to above, seriousness literally drove most changes in the prison terms that white violent offenders received. It was much less important for white property offenders.

Thus far, then, the analysis reveals sharp differences both in the punishment of black and white offenders and in the punishment of violent and property offenders. The sections that follow cast these findings in a different light, to determine the extent to which they support theoretical expectations about the role of events and social changes in punishment. As will quickly become apparent, many expectations received at best only partial support.

Theoretical Implications

As noted in chapter 4, the political economy perspective posits the importance of the economy to an understanding of punishment. Three facets of the cotton economy concern us in the following section: the price of cotton, the demand for agrarian labor, and changes in the supply of labor. From a general consideration of the cotton economy, the discussion turns to examine the role played by the industrial economy, racial inequality, and a series of specific depressions and recessions. As we have already seen, economic events were crucial, but not always in precisely the ways we had come to expect. Considered next are the more specific consequences of World War I, its aftermath, and actions taken by federal and state officials. The discussion concludes with the influence of control series, each of which exerts an important influence on prison sentences.

The Cotton Economy

Underlying the analysis were three presumptions about the agrarian component of Georgia's economy. The first focused on the price of cotton and predicted that declines in price would prompt longer prison sentences, particularly for black offenders. Falling prices did indeed generate longer sentences, but only after a considerable delay. Also as expected, alterations in price had greater repercussions for black than for white offenders, accounting for nearly three times the unexplained variation in their sentences. Finally, the price of cotton became less important as Georgia's economy diversified.

The second expectation focused on the demand for labor, indicated by the size of the cotton harvest. To the extent that smaller harvests presaged a labor surplus, punishment should also become harsher, with black offenders bearing a disproportionate share of the severity. The findings supported the general form of the argument, namely, that the harvest was more central to black than to white punishment. On the other hand, the findings provided fragile support for the substance of the argument. For black offenders overall and violent offenders in particular, smaller harvests precipitated *shorter* rather than longer penitentiary terms. Only during the good-roads movement, with its public demand for convict labor to build roads, did smaller harvests result in longer prison terms. This was true for black offenders overall; it did not extend to black men convicted of violence.

The final expectation focused on the supply of agrarian labor, indicated by the size of the black male population. To the extent that a decline in the relative supply of black labor signaled a possible labor shortage, sentences should become more severe in an attempt to expropriate forcefully as much labor as possible in the service of the cotton economy. They did not. Shifts in the size of the black male population played no discernible role in setting prison sentences.

In sum, the cotton economy was more central to the punishment of black offenders than of white offenders. Nevertheless, weaknesses in the economy were neither invariably nor quickly translated into more severe punishment. Unlike the admission process, sentences responded slowly to declining cotton prices. Smaller harvests, irrelevant for admissions, triggered more lenient terms of imprisonment for black offenders. Finally, shifts in the supply of agrarian labor, especially relevant to white admissions, were irrelevant to decisions about the length of time they and their black counterparts would labor in the penitentiary.

The Industrial Economy

Three straightforward predictions framed our consideration of the twin processes of industrialization and urbanization. First, growth in industrialization should moderate the punishment of those participating in the process, namely, white men. For those excluded from the stringent informal controls the process entailed, namely, black men, industrialization should have no implications for punishment. We saw in chapter 5 that this reasoning applied fairly well to the first dimension of punishment. Industrialization tended to lower white admissions to the penitentiary, but had no effect on black admissions. The argument applied only half as well to the second dimension of punishment. As expected, industrialization was irrelevant to the penitentiary terms imposed on black offenders. Yet it was also unexpectedly irrelevant to the terms imposed on white offenders.

The second prediction argued that growth in urbanization should intensify punishment, especially for black offenders. For white men, who experienced fewer rural-urban discontinuities, urbanization should be less relevant. Only white violent offenders should suffer, their sentences becoming more severe in reaction to intolerance for violent behaviors common in rural settings.

This argument fared somewhat better than the argument for industrialization. As Georgia became more urbanized, black property offenders received significantly longer sentences, as expected. Black violent offenders, in contrast, received significantly shorter sentences. Thus, while urbanization lowered the risk that black men would be admitted to the penitentiary for theft and burglary, it fostered severity toward offenders admitted for these offenses. This severity was most obvious in the twentieth century. Further, while urbanization enhanced the risk that black men would be admitted to the penitentiary for violence, it triggered lenience toward those so admitted. This lenience was most obvious in the nineteenth century. Yet it, too, persisted.

As expected, urbanization did not affect the sentences imposed on white property offenders. It nevertheless intensified the punishment of whites imprisoned for violence. While this severity was most noticeable early in the urbanization process, it persisted, if at diminished strength.

The final aspect of the southern industrial economy was change in the racial composition of Georgia's urban areas. In 1870, 45 percent of all urban residents were black. Seven decades later, only 35 percent were black. The progressive "whitening" of urban areas suggested a gradual reduction in perceptions of racial threat and a moderation of punishment directed toward black offenders. Recall from chapter 5 that this argument received no support for initial admissions to the penitentiary. It met virtually the same fate in this chapter. The size of the black urban population played only a minor role in the sentencing of black property offenders. Unexpectedly shorter sentences accompanied slight nineteenth-century growth in the black urban population. In the twentieth century, however, declines in the black urban population stimulated the expected lenience.

Only occasionally, then, did the industrial economy operate as expected. There was no evidence that industrialization prompted the imposition of more lenient sentences on white offenders. Although urbanization escalated the sentences imposed on black property and white violent offenders, it also mitigated the punishment of black violent offenders. Finally, shifts in the black urban population played a circumscribed role. Only in the twentieth century and only for black property offenders did declines in the black urban population precipitate shorter sentences.

Interracial Competition

Underlying the analysis was a presumption that a narrowing of the economic racial divide would increase perceptions of threat and generate punitiveness aimed primarily, but not exclusively, at black offenders. In the final analysis, the sentences imposed on blacks were unaffected by changes in the magnitude of racial inequality. There was only faint evidence that black property offenders actually benefited from a decline in racial inequality. Upon further analysis, the reason behind this lenience becomes clear. As the absolute wealth of blacks grew, black property offenders received shorter sentences (see appendix table C-1). In the final analysis, the sentences imposed on white offenders were also unaltered by changes in racial inequality. Even the absolute economic position of white men failed to influence the sentences imposed on whites admitted to the penitentiary.[4]

Economic Crises

Previous chapters have emphasized that southerners faced a series of severe depressions and less intense recessions. The first expectation was that prison terms would lengthen during depressions and recessions. Usually they did. For example, the 1882–84 depression lengthened the sentences imposed on black felons in general, black violent offenders, and white property offenders. Similarly, the 1895–97 recession lengthened the sentences imposed on black and white offenders. Though less frequently the case, short-lived depressions and milder recessions triggered lenience for some groups of offenders. In no instance, however, did the majority of economic upheavals affect sentencing. Between 1870 and 1940, there were seventeen depressions and recessions. Of these, between one and five had measurable impacts on the severity of punishment. Thus, the majority of economic crises had no implications for this aspect of punishment.

The second expectation was that depressions would exert stronger impacts than recessions on the severity of punishment. They did not. In general, the sentencing of both blacks and whites reacted more forcefully to recessions than to depressions (table 6.19). For example, depressions reduced the error sum of squares in black sentences by 8 percent. Recessions, in contrast, reduced the error sum of squares by nearly 24 percent. Only the sentencing of black violent offenders reacted more forcefully to depressions than recessions. Two nineteenth-century depressions were pivotal (1873–79, 1882–84). Together, they reduced unexplained variance by 26 percent. In contrast, recessions reduced unexplained variance by only 5 percent.

The third expectation was that, at some point during prolonged depressions, sentences should fall in response to a growing fiscal crisis. A single instance of this phenomenon surfaced. Two years after the onset of the 1873–79 depression, black violent offenders received longer sentences; the following year, their sentences

154

Table 6.19 Comparative impact of economic crises and other events on prison sentences

| | Prison Sentence | | | | | |
| | Total | | Violent | | Property | |
Event	SSE	%	SSE	%	SSE	%
Black Offenders						
Recessions	.58	23.7	.94	5.1	.86	15.7
Depressions	.70	7.9	.73	26.3	.98	3.9
Economic impacts	.52	31.6	.68	31.3	.82	19.6
Noneconomic impacts	—		—		.87	14.7
White Offenders						
Recessions	3.87	4.2	3.41	11.9	3.29	24.4
Depressions	—		3.57	7.8	3.71	14.7
Economic impacts	3.87	4.2	3.11	19.6	2.65	39.1
Noneconomic impacts	3.72	7.9	3.45	10.9	4.21	3.2

Note: SSE refers to the error sum of squares, while % refers to the percentage reduction in error sum of squares after adding the intervention(s).

became more lenient. For some offenders, sentences shortened toward the end of relatively short depressions and recessions. This was the case for whites sentenced in 1888, white property offenders sentenced in 1891, and white violent offenders sentenced in 1921. Other offenders benefited at the very onset of an economic downturn: white violent offenders sentenced in 1887 and white property offenders sentenced in 1893 and 1910. In short, neither the length nor the severity of a crisis consistently guaranteed more lenient treatment.

The fourth expectation proposed that race would shape the impact of economic downturns. The sentences imposed on black offenders should react more consistently and forcefully to changes in economic conditions. Support for this expectation was mixed. For violent offenders, the sentences imposed on blacks did indeed react more forcefully than the sentences imposed on whites (see table 6.19). As a whole, economic downturns reduced the unexplained variance in the former by 31 percent and in the latter by only 20 percent. For property offenders, in contrast, the sentences imposed on blacks reacted *less* sharply to economic downturns than did the sentences imposed on comparable whites. Economic crises were only half as successful in predicting the sentences imposed on black property offenders as they were in predicting white property sentences.

In concert with offense, then, race dictated the role that economic crises would play during sentencing. Race also shaped the substance of that role. As noted above, shorter sentences followed closely on the heels of many economic downturns. Not surprisingly, blacks were slightly less likely than whites to be the beneficiaries of such lenience. Forty percent of all significant impacts on black sentences indicated lenience. The comparable figure for white offenders was 50 percent.

The final expectation predicted that the link between economic crises and prison sentences would be tighter for property than for violent offenders. Once again, support was contingent on race, and only for whites was this the case. All significant economic downturns reduced the error sum of squares by 39 percent for white property offenders (see table 6.19). The comparable figure for white violent offenders was much lower (20 percent). For blacks, economic crises had more profound implications for the sentences imposed on *violent* offenders. Taken together, economic downturns reduced the error sum of squares by 31 percent. The comparable percentage for black property offenders was only 20 percent.

In sum, economic crises clearly affected the severity with which offenders—black and white, violent and property—were treated. Relatively few downturns were critical, however. Many, but hardly all, lengthened prison sentences, as expected. The severity of the crisis was no guarantee that it would exert an especially strong impact on sentences. It did so, but only for black violent offenders. The length of the crisis was no guarantee that punishment would, at some point, become more lenient. Especially for whites, sentences grew lenient during relatively short depressions and several recessions. The punishment of black offenders did not uniformly react more vigorously than white punishment to downturns in the business cycle. This was true only for violent offenders. Finally, the punishment of property offenders did not always react more forcefully than the punishment of violent offenders to economic crises. This was true only for whites. In concert with one another, then, race and offense determined the precise impact that economic crises had on prison sentences.

World War I and Its Aftermath

Two straightforward expectations characterized the role of World War I and demobilization. America's entry into the war should lessen punishment; its aftermath should have the opposite effect. Race should dictate the magnitude of each impact, with black offenders benefiting from the war and suffering from demobilization more than comparable whites. Neither expectation was supported. America's entry into the war had no bearing on the sentencing of either black or white offenders. The expected lenience toward blacks simply failed to materialize. In its stead was unexpected severity, directed toward black property offenders convicted in 1914, the year the war began. While the war benefited whites, especially violent offenders, its largesse arrived earlier than expected: one year after the onset of the war but well before America's entry. Moreover, the lenience generated by the war did not extend to white property offenders, whose sentences remained the same.

The reasoning underlying the proposed impact for demobilization also received virtually no support. Black offenders did not bear the brunt of the threat associated with postwar demobilization. Regardless of offense, their sentences remained the same. Similarly unresponsive to demobilization were the sentences of whites in general and of white violent offenders in particular. Much like the recession of 1910–12, demobilization in 1919 shortened the sentences imposed on white property offenders.

In sum, the role played by World War I and its aftermath was complicated by race and offense. America's entry into the war did not alter the sentences of black or white offenders. The very onset of the war triggered more severe sentences for black property offenders. A year later, white violent offenders received more lenient treatment. Demobilization's impact was even more circumscribed, surfacing only for white property offenders, who received unexpected lenience.

Policies

As noted earlier in the chapter, most policy changes should have had no impact on prison sentences. As expected, parole, instituted in 1908, did not alter terms of incarceration. Abolition of the lease a year later should either have been irrelevant or have stimulated longer prison terms. The former proved to be the more accurate prediction. There was no reason to expect a direct link between probation, instituted in 1913, and the length of sentences. Nevertheless, one relationship did surface. Probation generated shorter prison terms for black property offenders.

As for federal legislation, passage of the Federal Aid Road Act should have lengthened prison terms, in an effort to meet the demand for convict labor that it stimulated. Indeed it did, but only for whites in general and white violent offenders in particular. Finally, the Agricultural Adjustment Act failed to act like a protracted depression. It neither stimulated more severe sentences nor generated lenience later in the process. The AAA was simply irrelevant.

For the most part, then, federal and state policies were tangential to the sentencing process. This was true even of those policies, such as the AAA, Federal Aid Road Act, and lease abolition, for which some impact was reasonably expected.

Control Series

This section addresses the relevance of three series: the size of the young male population and the age and seriousness of offenders sent to prison. The expectation was that a decline in the population of young black men would find expression in longer sentences, presumably designed to extract as much labor from convicts as possible. The findings support this expectation. Particularly in the twentieth century, when the young population began to decline noticeably, black offenders received longer sentences.

Different reasoning informed the role that the youthful population would play in the sentencing of white offenders. To the extent that a decline in the young population indicates more clearly a drop in white criminality, prison sentences should shorten. In general, they did, but neither quickly nor precipitously over time. Moreover, the partitioning of violent from property offenders revealed unexpected influences. Declines in the youthful population immediately triggered harsher terms of imprisonment for white violent offenders. They prompted similar though much more delayed harshness toward white property offenders. Only during the late nineteenth and early twentieth centuries, when noticeable growth in the youthful population coincided with economic crises, the good-roads movement, and black outmigration, did an increase in the size of the young population stimulate longer prison sentences for property offenders.

The final determinants of punishment were attributes of offenders. First, sentences should become proportionately longer simply because a larger proportion of offenders were convicted of serious offenses. This was the case, especially for blacks and whites convicted of violence. Seriousness exerted a much weaker influence on the sentences imposed on property offenders, particularly those who were white.

The second relevant aspect of the convict population was the average age of offenders. For blacks, sentences should become proportionately longer with the admission of a youthful cohort of offenders. Underlying this argument was the usefulness of young black offenders as laborers. The findings failed to support this logic. A young cohort never suffered adverse consequences for their youthfulness. Instead, property offenders admitted two years after a younger cohort suffered by receiving longer sentences. Most probably the logic underlying the original hypothesis is faulty. A youthful group of offenders may simply have been less capable of performing difficult manual labor than older offenders. To compensate for the loss of labor, judges may have imposed longer sentences on later incoming cohorts. A second interpretation raises the possibility that judges imposed longer sentences on later cohorts to convey a general deterrent message.

A different expectation informed the sentencing of whites: younger cohorts should receive shorter sentences. The findings also failed to support this logic. Young incoming cohorts received neither lenience nor severity. Rather, subsequent cohorts were placed at either an advantage or a disadvantage, depending on their year of incarceration. Whites convicted of violence *two* years after the admission of a younger cohort received shorter sentences. They could rely on this lenience throughout the period under analysis. Whites convicted of violence *three* years after the admission of a younger cohort suffered. Especially in the nineteenth century, they received significantly longer sentences. The reverse was true for whites convicted of theft. Those sentenced two years after a younger cohort suffered; those sentenced three years after a younger cohort benefited by receiving shorter sentences. These opposing tendencies were most obvious during the nine-teenth century and became less pronounced over time.

Conclusion

In large part, the sentences imposed on black and white offenders were constrained by the type of offenders admitted to the penitentiary: the more serious, the longer the time offenders labored under the convict lease and, later, under county authori-ties in chain gangs. Yet sentences were by no means independent of broader social events and changes. Most notably, they responded to economic crises, the cotton economy, and urbanization. The twin axes of race and offense dictated which events and social changes would be meaningful during sentencing. Economic crises and the cotton economy were more crucial for the punishment of black offenders than they were for the punishment of white offenders. In contrast, the age of the white population in general and of the cohort of admitted offenders shaped the sentencing of whites more so than of blacks.

The distinction between property and violent offenders was both crucial and, once again, tempered by race. Economic conditions were implicated in the punish-ment of both property and violent offenders. Nevertheless, the crises of signifi-cance and the nature of their impact varied. Similarly, the seriousness of the admitted cohort was more critical to the sentencing of violent than of property offenders. Thus, the punishment of property offenders tended to be slightly more open to outside influences. For whites, economic crises were the most influential of these outside influences. For blacks, the most relevant outside influences were urbanization and the age of the admitted cohort.

The next chapter examines the third and final dimension of punishment: the rate at which offenders were released from the penitentiary. For a quite different context, it raises the same set of issues. First, to what extent did release depend on broader events and social forces? Second, to what extent did race and offense shape this dependence?

7

Release from
the Penitentiary

ADMITTED TO THE PENITENTIARY MORE OFTEN THAN WHITES, BLACK men were also released at considerably higher rates. Nevertheless, as we saw in chapter 4, the release of both white and black offenders followed similar trajectories over time. In the nineteenth century, release rates were relatively low and sometimes plummeted during major economic crises. In the twentieth century, particularly after the introduction of parole, black and white offenders found release easier to achieve, even during the Great Depression.

This chapter examines more directly the extent to which release from prison depended on economic crises as well as on a series of other events and more general social, economic, and demographic changes. It begins with a review of the major predictions, which guide the analysis of general and specific release rates. An exploration of conditional release completes the analysis. The chapter concludes with an assessment of the theoretical implications of the findings.

Theoretical Expectations

As was the case for previous facets of punishment, several expectations inform the intervention analysis. The first set posits several impacts for economic downturns. Depressions and recessions should discourage the release of offenders from prison. Given their greater intensity, depressions should exert stronger effects on release rates than milder recessions. At some point during lengthy depressions, however, release rates should rise, in response to strain on entrepreneurial and state capacities to punish. Changes in the business cycle should produce greater and more consistent impacts on the release of black than white convicts. Similarly, they should be more critical to the release of property offenders than of violent offenders.

The second set of predictions involves World War I and its aftermath. To meet the demand for conscripts, America's entry into World War I should increase the rate at which offenders, especially black men, were released. Demobilization, with its economic dislocations and unsettled race relations, should have the opposite effect and inhibit releases, once again especially of black offenders.

The third set of expectations involves the role played by policy changes. The institution of parole in 1908 gave officials an opportunity to increase the rate at which offenders were released from the penitentiary. We expect that whites received this opportunity more often than blacks. Abolition of the lease a year later should lower release rates, to serve better the demand for convict road labor. To the extent that the advent of probation, an alternative to incarceration, raised concerns about the supply of prisoners, it should trigger a short-term reduction in release rates. As for federal legislation, passage of the Federal Aid Road Act in 1916 should have an impact not unlike that of lease abolition: discouraging release to meet the demand for convict road labor. Passage of the Agricultural Adjustment Act (AAA), a consequence of the Great Depression, should operate much like a protracted depression. Initially, release rates should fall. Then, as the AAA's ramifications for tenants become more serious, release should become easier to obtain.

The final set of expectations informs the multivariate stage of the analysis. A weak economy (i.e., falling cotton prices, smaller harvests, or declines in available field labor) should inhibit the release, particularly of blacks and property offenders. Its inhibiting influence should wane over time, as cotton's grip on the agrarian economy slowly eased in the twentieth century. Industrialization should have implications only for white offenders. Especially in the twentieth century, increases in the profitability of manufacturing should trigger growth in their release from the penitentiary. In contrast, urbanization and the black component of the urban population should have stronger implications for blacks than for whites. Growth in urbanization should inhibit the release of black offenders, while declines in the black urban population should encourage their release. Urbanization should play a similar but more limited role for whites, discouraging the release only of offenders convicted of violent crimes. Like the cotton economy, urbanization should dictate release more powerfully in the nineteenth than in the twentieth century. Finally, as racial inequality declines, so too should the release of both blacks and whites. Nineteenth-century declines should be more consequential than those of the twentieth century.

In addition to events and social changes, release from the penitentiary should reflect changes in the size of the young male population and in the composition of felons admitted to the penitentiary. With a decrease in the population of young black men, who were most useful as laborers, black convicts should find release more difficult to achieve. Assuming that the population of young *white* men reflects more accurately the magnitude of the white crime problem, declines should *increase* the release of white offenders.

Two attributes of convicts should affect release rates: their overall seriousness and average age. The admission of a more serious cohort of offenders should depress release rates for two reasons. First, with the admission of a higher proportion of serious offenders, who receive longer sentences, fewer convicts are eligible for release. Second, officials may limit release to convey a message of general deterrence. The admission of noticeably more serious offenders may introduce a note of urgency to this message and prompt an immediate decline in releases. The admission of a younger cohort of offenders may operate in a similar manner: intensifying concerns about crime, enhancing the salience of the deterrent function of punishment, and discouraging release from the penitentiary.

The analysis assesses these arguments for release rates in general and then for the release of violent and property offenders. As will become apparent, the release of black and white offenders alike reacted most strongly to economic downturns. Other events and social changes were considerably less important.

General Release Rates

Release of Black Offenders

The findings from the intervention analysis confirm our earlier assessment that the release of black offenders depended on a series of economic crises (table 7.1). No single crisis overshadowed the others in significance. Instead, it was the cumulative effect, particularly of twentieth-century events, that reduced the unexplained variance in black release rates by over half. World War I and demobilization, in contrast, had no impact. Nor did abolition of the lease and the institution of parole and probation.

Despite their importance, economic crises did not invariably make release from prison more difficult to achieve. Release rates fell during the major depression of 1882–84 and at the onset of two recessions (1895–97, 1937–38). Yet black convicts were *more* likely to be released at the onset of two other moderately intense recessions (1899–1900, 1923–24). Neither finding was anticipated. Instead, we expected rates to rise only as depressions deepened and strained private and public capacities to punish criminals. Such increases occurred, but only in response to twentieth-century crises and their consequences. Well after the Great Depression began and well after passage of the AAA, black offenders found release easier to achieve.

Table 7.1 Impact of events on black release rate

Event	Transfer Function	Model 1	2	3	4	5	6	7	8
Economic Crises									
1882–84 depression	ω_1	−2.78 (−1.53)							−2.78 (−2.16)
1895–97 recession	ω_0		−5.22 (−3.00)						−5.22 (−4.06)
1899–1900 recession	ω_0			5.38 (3.11)					5.38 (4.19)
1923–24 recession	ω_0				3.62 (2.01)				3.62 (2.82)
1929–33 depression	ω_2					4.34 (2.46)			4.34 (3.38)
1937–38 recession	ω_0						−4.48 (−2.53)		−4.48 (−3.49)
Policies									
Agricultural Adjustment Act	ω_3							3.56 (1.98)	3.56 (2.77)
Original SSE		235.8	235.8	235.8	235.8	235.8	235.8	235.8	235.8
Model SSE		228.1	208.6	206.9	222.7	211.1	215.7	216.6	101.7
% reduction in SSE		3.3	11.5	12.3	5.6	10.5	8.5	8.1	56.9

Note: T-ratio of estimate in parentheses. SSE denotes error sum of squares.

Table 7.2 Cross-correlations for black release rate

| | Cross-Correlation at Lag | | | | |
Social Change	0	1	2	3	p
Cotton Economy					
Cotton price	−.14	.08	−.23*	−.21	.07
Cotton harvest	.03	−.15	.02	.14	.81
Percentage black male	−.02	.16	.09	.03	.87
Industrial Economy					
Value added by manufacturing	.18	−.28*	.08	−.09	.06
Percentage urban	−.03	.05	−.06	−.08	.10
Percentage black urban	−.05	.22	.05	−.19	.07
Inequality					
Racial inequality	.01	−.12	.02	−.08	.72
Control Series					
Percentage young	−.03	.18	.10	−.17	.36
Seriousness of admissions	.20	.09	−.14	.03	.13
Age of admissions	.22	.04	−.04	−.11	.47

Note: The impacts of events were removed before estimation. Series were made independent of one another and prewhitened. See Appendix A for details.

*$p \le .05$

More often than not, then, hard times and their consequences benefited black offenders by enhancing their chances of being released.

The next stage of the analysis explores the impact of several social changes. Among general indicators of the cotton economy, only the price of cotton was cross-correlated with the release of black convicts (table 7.2). The direction of the relationship suggests that, after a lag of two years, falling prices precipitated unexpected growth in release rates. Also associated with the release of black convicts were indicators of the industrial economy. With growth in both the value added by manufacturing and urbanization (CCF + 5 = −.37, not shown), fewer black offenders were released. Declines in the black urban population appear to have had the same result.

The multivariate analysis centers, then, on four factors: the price of cotton, value added by manufacturing, percentage urban, and percentage black urban. Value added by manufacturing merits no further attention because its estimate was nonsignificant (ω_1 = −1.17, *t*-ratio = −.87). The most influential determinant of release rates was clearly the price of cotton, which reduced the remaining unexplained variance by 23 percent (table 7.3). Percentage black urban, in contrast, was the least important, contributing only a 4 percent reduction in unexplained

Table 7.3 Impact of social change on black release rate

Social Change	Transfer Function	Model 1	2	3	4	5
Cotton Economy						
Cotton price	$\omega_2 - \omega_3$	−23.44			−20.31	−29.67
		(−2.03)			(−1.82)	(−2.87)
		31.53			23.22	22.50
		(2.72)			(2.05)	(2.16)
Industrial Economy						
Percentage urban	ω_5		−100.39		−136.50	−121.95
			(−2.17)		(−2.94)	(−2.94)
Percentage black urban	ω_1			158.89	98.80	a
				(1.67)	(1.14)	
Noise component	θ_1					.45
						(3.56)
χ^2 of residuals					9.75	5.14
(p)					(.14)	(.40)
Original SSE		95.3	100.7	100.7	95.3	95.3
Model SSE		73.7	88.8	96.7	63.2	56.7
% reduction in SSE		22.7	11.8	4.0	33.7	40.5

Note: T-ratio of estimate in parentheses. SSE denotes error sum of squares. Variation in original SSE is due to variation in the time span of residualized input series. See Appendix A for details.

variance. Not surprisingly, its estimate ultimately failed to achieve statistical signif-icance in the multivariate model, which is based on a slightly shorter time span (1876–1940). Thus, the rate at which black offenders were released was a function of error, the price of cotton, and urbanization.

The best fitting transfer function[1] indicates that release rates fell two and three years after a decline in the price of cotton. Both impacts were for the most part consistently negative over time (fig. 7.1). Only for a brief period, which encom-passed several depressions and recessions (1883–1904), did falling prices prompt the expected, albeit delayed, reduction in release rates. As the nineteenth century drew to a close, the more immediate impact (lag 2) weakened, while the more distant impact, three years after a price decline, strengthened. Though never as pivotal as it had been in the nineteenth century, the price of cotton thus continued to affect the release of black offenders well into the twentieth century.

The second predictor operated quite differently. As expected, urbanization

Figure 7.1.   Impact of cotton price on black release rate

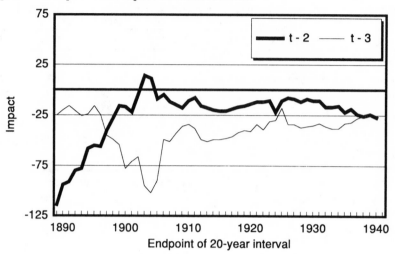

Figure 7.2.   Impact of urbanization on black release rate

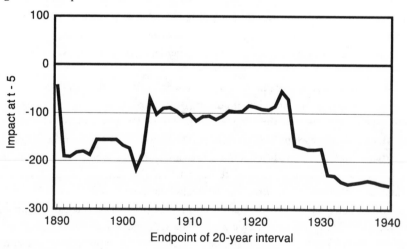

inhibited the release of black offenders. Its power to do so was especially strong at two points in time (fig. 7.2). The first was during the nineteenth century, when concerns about the influx of blacks into urban areas were most salient. The second period of intensity was understandable but unanticipated. It encompassed the late 1920s and 1930s, when the considerably larger urban population was growing more quickly. In the space of twenty years, for example, those residing in urban areas rose from 25 percent of the 1920 population to 34 percent of the 1940 population.

In sum, the release of black convicts responded to selected economic crises and to changes in general economic conditions and growth in urbanization. As the next section indicates, the release of white offenders was also dictated by economic crises, though not always in precisely the same manner.

Release of White Offenders

As was the case for black convicts, World War I, demobilization, and most policies played no role in the release of white offenders from prison (table 7.4). Instead, selected twentieth-century economic crises and the AAA were critical. In their

Table 7.4 Impact of events on white release rate

Event	Transfer Function	Model				
		1	2	3	4	5
Economic Crises						
1910–12 recession	ω_0	−.66				−.66
		(−1.53)				(−2.19)
1929–33 depression	$\omega_1 - \omega_3$		.70			.70
			(1.68)			(2.32)
			−.88			−.88
			(−2.13)			(−2.91)
1937–38 recession	$\omega_0 - \omega_1$			−1.58		−1.58
				(−4.12)		(−5.23)
				−.86		−.86
				(−2.24)		(−2.85)
Policies						
Agricultural	ω_1				−1.44	−1.44
Adjustment Act					(−3.58)	(−4.77)
Original SSE		13.25	13.25	13.25	13.25	13.25
Model SSE		12.81	11.40	10.01	11.18	5.65
% reduction in SSE		3.32	13.96	24.45	15.62	57.36

Note: T-ratio of estimate in parentheses. SSE denotes error sum of squares.

Table 7.5 Cross-correlations for white release rate

Social Change	Cross-Correlation at Lag				
	0	1	2	3	p
Cotton Economy					
Cotton price	.02	−.06	.08	−.11	.93
Cotton harvest	−.04	−.19	−.07	−.03	.64
Percentage black male	−.13	.02	.21	−.06	.12
Industrial Economy					
Value added by manufacturing	−.09	−.18	.16	−.04	.26
Percentage urban	.18	.11	−.19	−.11	.34
Inequality					
Racial inequality	.02	−.03	.22	−.14	.17
Control Series					
Percentage young	−.07	.06	.22	−.11	.50
Seriousness of admissions	.10	−.07	−.19	.15	.38
Age of admissions	.05	−.13	.06	−.07	.80

Note: The impacts of events were removed before estimation. Series were made independent of one another and prewhitened. See Appendix A for details.

*$p \leq .05$

Table 7.6 Impact of social change on white release rate

Social Change	Transfer Function	Estimate (t-ratio)
Cotton Economy		
Percentage black male	ω_4	47.58
		(2.00)
χ^2 of residuals		6.19
(p)		(.40)
Original SSE		5.44
Model SSE		4.81
% reduction in SSE		11.58

Note: SSE denotes error sum of squares.

Figure 7.3. Impact of percentage black male on white release rate

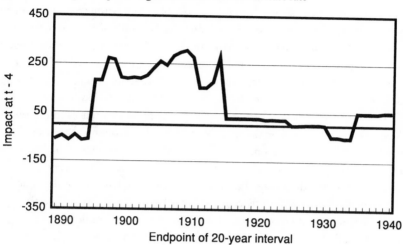

entirety, these events accounted for over half the error sum of squares. Unlike their black counterparts, however, white offenders found release uniformly more difficult to achieve at the onset of depressions and recessions. Release rates fell at the beginning of the 1910–12 and 1937–38 recessions and the year after the AAA was enacted. Release rates rose only when we expected them to do so, as the Great Depression and subsequent recession deepened.

Using residuals from the intervention analysis, the next phase of the analysis examines the role played by the cotton economy, urbanization and industrialization, population changes, racial inequality, and other factors. No cross-correlation function attained statistical significance, and only one cross-correlation was substantial enough to merit further analysis (table 7.5). Percentage black male and white release rates were significantly cross-correlated at the fourth lag (CCF + 4 = .29, not presented). Unlike black offenders, then, the release of white offenders was insulated from most social changes. With a decline in the black male population, fewer white convicts were released (table 7.6). Both delayed and weak, this relationship coincided with the good-roads movement (fig. 7.3). By World War I, changes in the size of the black male population had become considerably less important to the release of white men.

Summary

Thus far, the analysis supports several conclusions about the release of convicts from Georgia's penitentiary. First, the release of both blacks and whites was a creature of economic crises, which accounted for fully half the remaining unexplained

169

variance. Second, the release of both blacks and whites was insulated from most major events and many social changes. Neither black nor white convicts benefited from America's entry into World War I, and neither suffered in the aftermath of the war. Criminal justice innovations had no discernible relevance for the release of either black or white offenders. Similarly irrelevant were a variety of social changes including falling cotton harvests, growth in industrialization, changes in the young male population, and the incarceration of younger or more serious felons.

These similarities aside, there were two major racial differences in the release process. The first centered on the specific role played by economic crises. For black convicts, the onset of an economic crisis could either encourage or discourage release from the penitentiary. For white convicts, the onset of an economic downturn more uniformly discouraged release. For black offenders, release depended on both nineteenth- and twentieth-century downturns. For whites, only twentieth-century depressions and recessions had repercussions for their release.

The second difference centered on the role played by social changes. The release of white offenders was clearly less sensitive to social changes than was the release of black offenders. Fewer changes had an impact and, where present, their impact was less pronounced. For whites, release depended only on the size of the black male population, which reduced unexplained variance by less than 12 percent. The release of black offenders, in contrast, depended on the price of cotton and growth in the urban population, which together reduced unexplained variance by a third.

Against this general background, the analysis now considers specific release rates. At issue is whether the general results provide an accurate account of the rate at which violent offenders were released. As we will see, the general findings convey an impression that, while often accurate, misses important factors that affected only the treatment of violent offenders.

Release of Violent Offenders

Release of Black Violent Offenders

Like black offenders overall, the release of black violent offenders depended only on economic crises and on a federal policy deriving from the Great Depression (table 7.7). World War I, its aftermath, and policy innovations had no discernible impact. Again, the expectation that hard times would inhibit release received only partial support. Like blacks in general, those convicted of violence were less likely to be released at the onset of two recessions (1895–97, 1937–38). Yet the onset of a less severe recession in 1899 had the opposite effect: it triggered release from the penitentiary. So, too, did the deepening of the Great Depression. Finally, passage of the AAA operated as expected. First, it generated a relatively quick decline in

Table 7.7 Impact of events on black violent release rate

Event	Transfer Function	Model 1	2	3	4	5	6
Economic Crises							
1895–97 recession	ω_0	−2.00					−2.00
		(−2.72)					(−3.36)
1899–1900 recession	ω_0		2.08				2.08
			(2.84)				(3.50)
1929–33 depression	ω_2			1.90			1.90
				(2.57)			(3.20)
1937–38 recession	ω_0				−1.68		−1.68
					(−2.25)		(−2.83)
Policies							
Agricultural Adjustment Act	$\omega_1 - \omega_2$					−1.52	−1.52
						(−2.05)	(−2.56)
						−1.24	−1.24
						(−1.67)	(−2.09)
Original SSE		41.38	41.38	41.38	41.38	41.38	41.38
Model SSE		37.38	37.05	37.25	38.56	37.01	22.26
% reduction in SSE		9.67	10.46	9.98	6.81	10.56	46.21

Note: *T*-ratio of estimate in parentheses. SSE denotes error sum of squares.

release rates, then prompted an increase two years after implementation. Together, economic downturns and the AAA were quite influential, reducing the error sum of squares by 46 percent.

Table 7.8 reports cross-correlations for several social changes. Although no function met an acceptable level of significance, several individual cross-correlations warrant further consideration. As indicators of the cotton economy, both the price of cotton and size of the harvest exerted an unexpected influence. Declines in the price and size of the harvest appear to have encouraged the release of black violent offenders. The final indicator of the cotton economy behaved as expected. A decline in the black male population discouraged release, if only after a considerable delay (CCF + 5 = .27, not shown). Finally, industrialization appears to have inhibited the rate at which black violent offenders were released from prison. Recall that arguments outlined earlier posited no link between the two series.

Examined in the multivariate analysis, then, is the price of cotton, size of the harvest, the black male population, and value added by manufacturing. Once again, industrialization exerted a trivial influence ($\omega_3 = -.15$, *t*-ratio $= -.23$) and

Table 7.8 Cross-correlations for black violent release rate

| Social Change | Cross-Correlation at Lag | | | | |
	0	1	2	3	p
Cotton Economy					
Cotton price	.06	.00	.04	−.25*	.17
Cotton harvest	.18	−.25*	.17	.02	.14
Percentage black male	−.04	.16	−.05	−.12	.16
Industrial Economy					
Value added by manufacturing	−.02	−.01	.12	−.26*	.19
Percentage urban	−.18	.09	−.06	.04	.46
Percentage black urban	−.14	.06	.20	−.04	.44
Inequality					
Racial inequality	.06	−.04	.01	−.13	.84
Control Series					
Percentage young	−.06	.01	.12	−.09	.90
Seriousness of admissions	−.10	.10	−.13	.06	.22
Age of admissions	.13	−.09	−.04	.12	.69

Note: The impacts of events were removed before estimation. Series were made independent of one another and prewhitened. See Appendix A for details.

*$p \le .05$

Table 7.9 Impact of social change on black violent release rate

| Social Change | Transfer Function | Model | | | |
		1	2	3	4
Cotton Economy					
Cotton price	ω_3	−19.97			−20.12
		(−3.60)			(−3.64)
Cotton harvest	ω_1		−.85		−.76
			(−2.01)		(−1.71)
Percentage black male	ω_5			90.80	83.66
				(1.85)	(1.90)
χ^2 of residuals					5.42
(p)					(.49)
Original SSE		21.66	22.18	21.30	21.30
Model SSE		17.56	20.89	20.08	15.48
% reduction in SSE		18.93	5.82	5.73	27.32

Note: T-ratio of estimate in parentheses. SSE denotes error sum of squares. Variation in original SSE is due to variation in the time span of residualized input series. See Appendix A for details.

Figure 7.4. Impact of percentage black male on black violent release rate

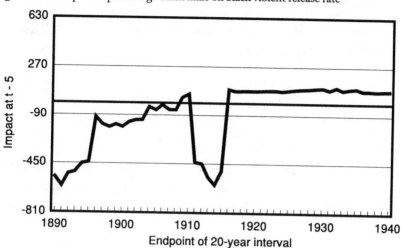

Endpoint of 20-year interval

was excluded from further consideration. Thus, the release of black violent offenders depended solely on the state of the cotton economy (table 7.9).

The most important determinant was the price of cotton. A price decline triggered delayed increases in the release of black violent offenders. Its influence was both steadier and weaker for violent offenders than it was for black offenders overall (results not presented). Moreover, its ability to stimulate the release of black violent offenders faded as the nineteenth century drew to a close and remained limited until a slight upsurge in the 1920s and 1930s.

In addition to the price of cotton, the release of black violent offenders also responded to changes in the size of the harvest. A smaller harvest triggered unexpected growth in prison releases. Considerably less influential than the price of cotton, the harvest reduced the unexplained variance by less than 6 percent. Though weaker, its impact was more immediate. A decline encouraged releases the following year. Moreover, the size of the harvest exerted an impact that grew more powerful over time (results not presented). Indeed, its ability to encourage release was strongest between World War I and the Great Depression.

The final predictor was the black male population. As expected, a decline in the population of black men inhibited the release of black violent offenders. Its ability to do so, however, was limited to the postwar era, during which the black population declined most precipitously (fig. 7.4). Before World War I, changes in the black male population had quite different consequences for black violent offenders. Prewar declines were comparatively small. Between 1890 and 1910, for example, the black male population fell by only 1 percent. In the two preceding decades, the

173

black male population had actually grown slightly, by almost 1 percent. Even these minor alterations affected the treatment of black violent offenders. The slight prewar decline unexpectedly encouraged release, while the equally slight increase unexpectedly discouraged release.

In general, then, the release of black violent offenders hinged on the state of the economy in general and of the cotton economy in particular. The next section, which focuses on comparable white offenders, highlights the importance not only of the economy but also of a wider array of social changes.

Release of White Violent Offenders

In large measure, the findings for white violent offenders mirror those reported for white offenders overall (table 7.10). Release depended primarily on a series of twentieth-century economic crises and on the AAA, passed in 1933. As expected,

Table 7.10 Impact of events on white violent release rate

Event	Transfer Function	Model 1	2	3	4	5	6
Economic Crises							
1910–12 recession	$\omega_0 - \omega_1$	−.40					−.40
		(−2.00)					(−2.75)
		−.36					−.36
		(−1.80)					(−2.48)
1929–33 depression	ω_3		.34				.34
			(1.65)				(2.34)
1937–38 recession	ω_0			−.72			−.72
				(−3.79)			(−4.96)
War							
World War I	ω_0				.52		.52
					(2.61)		(3.58)
Policies							
Agricultural	$\omega_1 - \omega_2$					−.50	−.50
Adjustment Act						(−2.60)	(−3.44)
						−.48	−.48
						(−2.49)	(−3.30)
Original SSE		3.01	3.01	3.01	3.01	3.01	3.01
Model SSE		2.72	2.85	2.50	2.74	2.48	1.29
% reduction in SSE		9.63	5.32	16.94	8.97	17.61	57.14

Note: T-ratio of estimate in parentheses. SSE denotes error sum of squares.

Table 7.11 Cross-correlations for white violent release rate

Social Change	Cross-Correlation at Lag				
	0	1	2	3	p
Cotton Economy					
Cotton price	−.12	−.03	.02	−.06	.92
Cotton harvest	−.19	−.20	−.22	−.02	.20
Percentage black male	−.03	.18	.24*	.01	.24
Industrial Economy					
Value added by manufacturing	−.19	−.08	.26*	−.11	.06
Percentage urban	.29*	.06	−.13	.00	.29
Inequality					
Racial inequality	.00	−.13	.21	−.26*	.16
Control Series					
Percentage young	−.17	.09	.23*	−.09	.30
Seriousness of admissions	.05	−.16	−.07	.14	.70
Age of admissions	.08	.12	−.16	.10	.74

Note: The effects of events were removed before estimation. Series were made independent of one another and prewhitened. See Appendix A for details.

*p ≤ .05

fewer white violent offenders were released at the onset of recessions (1910–12, 1937–38) and soon after the AAA was passed. Also as expected, white violent offenders found release easier to obtain as two economic crises deepened (1910–12 recession, 1929–33 depression) and as the AAA dispossessed larger numbers of tenants (1935). The release of white violent offenders was clearly dominated by the AAA and 1937–38 recession. The former reduced the unexplained variance by nearly 18 percent; the latter, by 17 percent.

The final influence on the treatment of white violent offenders was World War I. Contrary to expectation, America's entry into the war was irrelevant. Rather, the declaration of war itself stimulated their release from prison. Its impact was comparable to that exerted by a prewar recession (1910–12), but it was much less pronounced than the economic dislocations of the 1930s.

Table 7.11 begins an assessment of the impact of social changes. Only the cross-correlation function for value added by manufacturing reached a marginal level of significance. As expected, it suggests that growth in industrialization encouraged release from the penitentiary. Several individual cross-correlations also achieved statistical significance and, for that reason, merit further attention. The multivariate analysis centers, then, on five series: percentage black male, value added by manufacturing, percentage urban, racial inequality, and percentage young

Table 7.12 Impact of social change on white violent release rate

Social Change	Transfer Function	Model 1	2	3	4	5	6
Cotton Economy							
Percentage black male	ω_2	21.31					20.89
		(1.93)					(2.19)
Industrial Economy							
Value added by	ω_2		.34				.25
manufacturing			(2.33)				(1.84)
Percentage urban	ω_0			13.93			13.66
				(2.42)			(2.74)
Inequality							
Racial inequality	ω_3				−1.27		−1.09
					(−2.65)		(−2.31)
Control Series							
Percentage young	ω_2					5.84	6.75
						(1.92)	(2.62)
χ^2 of residuals							6.52
(*p*)							(.37)
Original SSE		1.23	1.29	1.29	1.14	1.29	1.08
Model SSE		1.07	1.19	1.18	1.06	1.22	.74
% reduction in SSE		13.01	7.75	8.53	7.02	5.43	31.48

Note: *T*-ratio of estimate in parentheses. SSE denotes error sum of squares. Variation in original SSE is due to variation in the time span of residualized input series. See Appendix A for details.

(table 7.12). As a group, these social changes were much less central to the release of white violent offenders than were the economic crises discussed earlier. They were able to reduce the error sum of squares by only 31 percent.

As the size of the black male population declined, fewer white violent offenders were released. This inhibitory influence was unstable over time, however (fig. 7.5). Indeed, the overall transfer function accurately captures only the influence that the black male population exerted on releases at the turn of the century and beyond. During the nineteenth century, a different relationship emerged, one which we encountered before for black violent offenders. Slight nineteenth-century declines in the black male population *encouraged* the release of white violent offenders. Slight nineteenth-century growth *inhibited* their release. Despite

Figure 7.5. Impact of percentage black male on white violent release rate

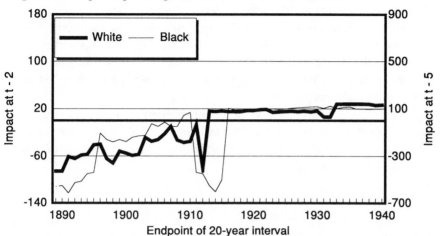

differences in magnitude and length of delay, the trajectory of demographic influences was quite similar for black and white violent offenders.

In two respects, the remaining results are unexpected. First, they did not surface earlier for the release of white offenders overall. Thus, they provide clear evidence that the general analysis distorts rather than clarifies the treatment of violent offenders. Second, only occasionally do the remaining results support theoretical predictions about the relationship between social change and punishment. The first predictor, value added by manufacturing, operated as expected. As Georgia became more industrialized, white violent offenders found release easier to achieve. As the pace of industrialization quickened, its ability to stimulate the release of white violent offenders grew stronger (results not presented). The link between industrialization and release only began to attenuate in the 1920s and 1930s, as the profitability of manufacturing peaked and experienced sharp declines and slow recoveries.

The second factor, urbanization, exercised an unexpected influence. As Georgia became more urbanized, white violent offenders found release from prison easier, rather than more difficult, to achieve. This was true throughout the period under analysis (results not presented). Indeed, the tendency for urbanization to stimulate the release of white violent offenders gradually grew stronger.

Racial inequality, the third factor, exercised a similarly unexpected influence, encouraging rather than discouraging the release of white violent offenders. Its ability to do so grew stronger during the first decade of the twentieth century, precisely when white property values were rising (results not presented). Despite

177

some variation, the relationship remained strong even during the 1920s and 1930s, when declines in white wealth narrowed the racial economic divide.

The final influence was change in the size of the young white male population. Contrary to expectation, a decline in the youthful population discouraged the release of white violent offenders. The young population was especially significant for a brief period after World War I and for a more extended period after the Great Depression (results not presented).

In general, then, the release of white violent offenders reacted most forcefully to twentieth-century economic crises and their consequences. To a lesser extent, a variety of social changes were also important, most typically playing roles not anticipated by previous research and theorizing.

Summary

Before considering property offenders, it is instructive to compare once again the general process with its more specific violent component. In a global sense, the general release process accurately depicted the release of black violent offenders from the penitentiary. Economic downturns and the AAA were the only events of significance for both trends. Neither World War I and its aftermath nor state and federal policies exerted a measurable impact on either release rate. Moreover, the price of cotton was the most important predictor of the release of black offenders overall and of black violent offenders in particular.

Nevertheless, the general analysis conveyed several misleading impressions. First, it led us to expect that urbanization would make it more difficult for black violent offenders to gain their release from the penitentiary. It did not. Urbanization was simply immaterial to the treatment of black violent offenders. Second, the general analysis led us to expect that the agrarian labor market would have no bearing on the release of black violent offenders. Instead, both the demand for labor and its supply dictated the rate at which black violent offenders would be released. Third, the general analysis led us to expect that fewer black violent convicts would be released during the 1882–84 depression and that more would be released at the onset of the 1923–24 recession. Neither expectation was met. Finally, the general analysis suggested that the AAA would play a simple role: encouraging release three years after passage. For black violent offenders, the act exerted an influence that occurred earlier and was more complicated. Its most immediate consequence was to *inhibit* their release. Its more extended impact, occurring *two* rather than three years after passage, was to *stimulate* the release of black violent offenders.

To a similar extent, the general results shed light on, as well as distort, our understanding of the process whereby white violent offenders were released from prison. For white offenders overall and white violent offenders in particular, release depended on twentieth-century economic crises, the AAA, and alterations in the black male population. Neither process reacted to policy changes, the price of cotton, the size of the harvest, or attributes of convicts admitted to the penitentiary.

Nevertheless, the release of white violent offenders diverged in several respects from the release process in general. Clearly, it did not respond to the same economic events in precisely the same manner. Three examples best illustrate this point. First, the 1910–12 recession triggered a short-lived, modest fall in general release rates. Its influence on the release of white violent offenders was more substantial and enduring. Second, the Great Depression twice increased general release rates, once in 1930 and once again in 1932. Its influence on the release of white violent offenders occurred late and only once, in 1932. Finally, the AAA discouraged the release of white offenders overall. At least initially, it also discouraged the release of white violent offenders. Two years after the act was passed, however, white violent offenders found release easier to obtain.

The release of white violent offenders also did not respond to social changes in precisely the same manner. The general results conveyed the impression that most changes would have no implications for the release of white violent offenders. Clearly they did. The release of white violent offenders reacted not only to shifts in the black male population but also to growth in industrialization and urbanization, to declines in racial inequality, and to fluctuations in the population of young white men.

Thus, the general results, based as they are on global release rates, provide only a rough approximation of the events and the changes that shaped the release of violent offenders from prison. The sections that follow indicate that the same conclusion applies to the release of property offenders.

Release of Property Offenders

The analysis begins with an evaluation of the extent to which the release of property offenders depended on economic, political, and criminal justice events. Multivariate time series analysis follows, and it estimates the influence of a variety of social changes. With two exceptions, the major expectations outlined earlier apply. First, economic events, general economic conditions, and racial inequality should figure more prominently in the release of property than of violent offenders. Second, urbanization should figure less prominently for white property offenders than it did for their violent counterparts.

Release of Black Property Offenders

Table 7.13 reports the results for the first stage of analysis, a test of the significance of several interventions. In two major respects, the results resemble earlier

179

Table 7.13 Impact of events on black property release rate

| | Transfer | | | | Model | | | | |
Event	Function	1	2	3	4	5	6	7	8
Economic Crises									
1895–97 recession	ω_0	-3.22 (-2.50)							-3.22 (-3.16)
1899–1900 recession	ω_0		3.30 (2.57)						3.30 (3.24)
1923–24 recession	ω_0			2.38 (1.81)					2.38 (2.34)
1926–27 recession	ω_0				-2.06 (-1.56)				-2.06 (-2.02)
1929–33 depression	ω_2					2.46 (1.88)			2.46 (2.41)
1937–38 recession	ω_0						-2.80 (-2.15)		-2.80 (-2.75)
Policies									
Agricultural Adjustment Act	$\omega_2 - \omega_3$							-2.58 (-2.02) −2.78 (-2.18)	-2.58 (-2.53) -2.78 (-2.73)
Original SSE		124.9	124.9	124.9	124.9	124.9	124.9	124.9	124.9
Model SSE		114.5	114.0	119.2	120.6	115.9	117.0	107.4	62.3
% reduction in SSE		8.3	8.7	4.6	3.4	7.2	6.3	14.0	50.1

Note: T-ratio of estimate in parentheses. SSE denotes error sum of squares.

Table 7.14 Cross-correlations for black property release rate

Social Change	Cross-Correlation at Lag				
	0	1	2	3	p
Cotton Economy					
Cotton price	−.08	.09	−.24*	−.18	.29
Cotton harvest	.03	−.11	−.03	−.02	.88
Percentage black male	.02	.11	.08	.26*	.39
Industrial Economy					
Value added by manufacturing	.24*	−.25*	−.15	.12	.01
Percentage urban	.08	.03	−.18	−.14	.07
Percentage black urban	.04	.27*	−.03	−.14	.07
Inequality					
Racial inequality	.06	−.10	.14	−.01	.80
Control Series					
Percentage young	−.00	.19	.04	−.07	.43
Seriousness of admissions	.30*	.04	−.01	.06	.39
Age of admissions	−.02	.08	−.18	−.12	.30

Note: The effects of events were removed before estimation. Series were made independent of one another and prewhitened. See Appendix A for details.

*$p \leq .05$

findings. First, only economic downturns and the AAA significantly affected the release of black property offenders from the penitentiary. World War I and its aftermath, as well as the policy innovations of probation, parole, and lease abolition, were irrelevant. Second, economic downturns did not always inhibit release. This was true of three recessions (1895–97, 1926–27, 1937–38). Yet release became more likely at the onset of two other moderately intense recessions (1899–1900, 1923–24). As expected, a deepening of the Great Depression in 1931 encouraged releases. The AAA, which exerted the strongest impact, also operated as expected. It generated an initial reduction in release rates two years after passage and a subsequent increase three years after passage.

Considered next are cross-correlations involving social change series (table 7.14). While industrialization produced the only function of statistical significance, two other functions narrowly missed significance and deserve further analysis. They suggest that growth in urbanization (CCF + 5 = −.26, not presented) and a decline in the black urban population discouraged release from the penitentiary. Finally, significant individual cross-correlations raise the possibility that the price of cotton, percentage black male, and seriousness of black property admissions also affected the release of black property offenders.

181

Table 7.15 Impact of social change on black property release rate

Social Change	Transfer Function	1	2	3	4	5	6	7	8
						Model			
Cotton Economy									
Cotton price	ω_2	-22.21 (-2.38)					-16.17 (-1.65)	-21.30 (-2.29)	-25.19 (-2.66)
Percentage black male	ω_3		150.59 (1.92)				114.04 (1.51)	136.34 (1.84)	152.93 (2.23)
Industrial Economy									
Value added by manufacturing	$\omega_0 - \omega_1$			2.80 (2.60)			1.40 (1.19)	a	a
				2.57 (2.26)			1.85 (1.59)	-1.20 (-1.21)	
Percentage black urban	ω_1				158.95 (2.16)		81.78 (1.14)	a	
Control Series									
Seriousness of admissions	ω_0					7.24 (2.52)	7.61 (2.72)	8.99 (3.36)	7.67 (3.11)
Noise component	θ_2								.29 (2.10)
χ^2 of residuals (p)							13.24 (.04)	15.96 (.01)	7.83 (.17)
Original SSE		59.72	58.08	62.30	62.30	56.30	56.30	56.30	56.30
Model SSE		52.24	53.12	55.39	58.26	50.73	38.75	40.70	38.16
% reduction in SSE		12.53	8.54	11.09	6.48	9.89	31.17	27.71	32.22

Note: T-ratio of estimate in parentheses. SSE denotes error sum of squares. Variation in original SSE is due to variation in the time span of residualized input series. See Appendix A for details.

Figure 7.6. Impact of percentage black male on black property release rate

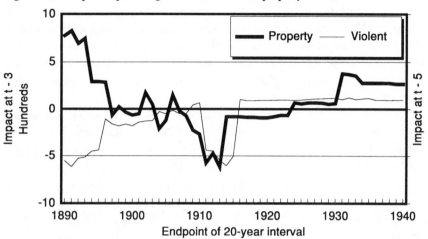

Endpoint of 20-year interval

Included in the multivariate analysis, then, are cotton price, percentage black male, the three indicators of the industrial economy, and seriousness of black property admissions (table 7.15). Because its initial estimate was nonsignificant (ω_5 = −53.24, t-ratio = −1.43), urbanization merits no further attention. Industrialization and percentage black urban were both significant during the period of the original estimation (1870–1940). For reasons that will become apparent later, neither retained significance during the shorter period represented in the multivariate model (1880–1938).[2] In the final analysis, then, only three factors significantly influenced the rate at which black property offenders were released from prison: the price of cotton, percentage black male, and seriousness of black property admissions. Nearly equal in significance, these factors reduced the error sum of squares by almost a third.

The first factor, cotton price, operated in part as it did for the release of black offenders in general. Two years after a price decline, black property offenders found release from the penitentiary easier to achieve. Uniformly negative, the trend in this relationship over time mirrors the general trend and, to conserve space, is not presented. As cotton's hegemony over the economy gradually declined, its ability to influence the release of black property offenders attenuated, remaining at a stable and weak level during the twentieth century.

The second influence was change in the size of the black male population. Recall that postwar declines hindered the release of black violent offenders, while prewar declines encouraged release. Black property offenders faced a different situation (fig. 7.6). The overall transfer function accurately reflects a relationship that characterized two periods: the early years of the convict lease and the Great

183

Depression era. As expected, slight growth in the black male population, which occurred during the 1870s and 1880s, encouraged the release of black property offenders. Also as expected, depression-era declines in the black male population discouraged their release. Absent from the general estimate is any indication of a quite different and unexpected impact, however. During the good-roads movement (1895–1914), a declining black male population stimulated the release of black property offenders.

The final result marks the first appearance of seriousness, which had been so prominent in the analysis of prison sentences. The admission of a more serious cohort of black property offenders precipitated growth, rather than the expected decline, in release rates. Consistently positive, the relationship nevertheless diminished over time and began to regain some of its former strength only with the approach of the Great Depression (results not presented).

The following section reports the results for the release of white property offenders. Once again, quite different processes were at work, and the release of these offenders was indeed as isolated from social changes as the general analysis led us to expect.

Release of White Property Offenders

As has been the case thus far, economic crises had the strongest and most consistent impacts on the treatment of white property offenders (table 7.16). As expected, release rates fell with the onset of the 1937–38 recession and one year after passage of the AAA. With the Great Depression and the deepening of the recession that followed it, release rates rose. Taken together, economic events reduced the error sum of squares by over half. Note, however, that no nineteenth-century depression or recession affected the release of white property offenders. Neither did World War I, its aftermath, or criminal justice innovations.

The second phase of the analysis estimates cross-correlations involving social changes (table 7.17). The only significant functions suggest that the strongest influences were endemic to the cohort of admitted offenders, namely, its seriousness and age. As expected, two years after the admission of more serious offenders, white property offenders found release more difficult to achieve (table 7.18). This relationship was stable over time, and in the interests of space, the results of the moving average strategy are not presented. The admission of a youthful cohort operated in a similar manner. Consistent in direction, its tendency to inhibit release nevertheless grew more robust with time (results not presented).

In the following section, the results for black and white property offenders are placed in two related contexts. The first draws a comparison between the general release process and that experienced by property offenders. At issue, once again, is

Table 7.16 Impact of events on white property release rate

Event	Transfer Function	Model			
		1	2	3	4
Economic Crises					
1929–33 depression	$\omega_1 - \omega_2$	.70			.70
		(2.73)			(3.57)
		−.54			−.54
		(−2.11)			(−2.75)
1937–38 recession	$\omega_0 - \omega_1$		−.84		−.84
			(−3.31)		(−4.28)
			−.56		−.56
			(−2.21)		(−2.86)
Policies					
Agricultural Adjustment Act	ω_1			−.94	−.94
				(−3.67)	(−4.75)
Original SSE		5.40	5.40	5.40	5.40
Model SSE		4.33	4.38	4.52	2.42
% reduction in SSE		19.81	18.89	16.30	55.19

Note: T-ratio of estimate in parentheses. SSE denotes error sum of squares.

the extent to which a global consideration of the release process hinders or facilitates our understanding of the release of property offenders. The second context compares property and violent offenders. At issue is whether the release of property offenders depended more heavily on economic events and changes than did the release of violent offenders.

Summary

For black convicts overall, the results conveyed a clear impression. Central to our understanding of their release from the penitentiary were economic crises, the price of cotton, and growth in urbanization. In most major respects, the situation was no different for black property offenders. Economic crises and the price of cotton were key factors in their release. Nevertheless, economic crises operated differently. For example, a major nineteenth-century depression (1882–84) affected the release of black offenders overall, but had no discernible impact on the release of black property offenders. The AAA had a simple impact on the release of black offenders overall. Three years after passage, they found release from prison easier to obtain. Its impact on black property offenders arrived earlier and was

Table 7.17 Cross-correlations for white property release rate

| Social Change | Cross-Correlation at Lag | | | | |
	0	1	2	3	p
Cotton Economy					
Cotton price	.13	−.20	.06	−.02	.54
Cotton harvest	−.04	−.21	.06	−.18	.32
Percentage black male	−.07	−.12	.14	.11	.50
Industrial Economy					
Value added by manufacturing	.02	−.21	.03	.15	.46
Percentage urban	.13	.14	−.18	−.04	.56
Inequality					
Racial inequality	−.04	−.02	.13	−.02	.31
Control Series					
Percentage young	.06	.04	.14	−.05	.75
Seriousness of admissions	−.16	.04	−.39*	.03	.03
Age of admissions	.26*	.15	−.18	−.08	.26

Note: The effects of events were removed before estimation. Series were made independent of one another and prewhitened. See Appendix A for details.

*$p \le .05$

Table 7.18 Impact of seriousness and age on white property release rate

| Social Change | Transfer Function | Model | | |
		1	2	3
Control Series				
Seriousness of admissions	ω_2	−.82		−.73
		(−3.54)		(−3.18)
Age of admissions	ω_0		.99	.99
			(1.97)	(2.12)
χ^2 of residuals				7.24
(p)				(.30)
Original SSE		2.42	1.98	1.98
Model SSE		1.98	1.86	1.58
% reduction in SSE		18.18	6.06	20.20

Note: T-ratio of estimate in parentheses. SSE denotes error sum of squares. Variation in original SSE is due to variation in the time span of residualized input series. See Appendix A for details.

more complicated. Initially, the AAA discouraged their release; later, it stimulated the higher release rates evidenced in the general analysis.

Urbanization operated differently as well. Clearly important to the release process overall, it had no bearing on the release of black property offenders. Finally, the general analysis conveyed the impression that both the black male population and the seriousness of admitted offenders were irrelevant to the release process. Both factors were considerably more central to an understanding of the release of black property offenders.

In light of these differences, it is not surprising that the release of black property offenders was driven, in part, by a different set of factors than was the release of black violent offenders. The economy in general and the cotton economy in particular were indeed more relevant to property offenders. In comparison with violent offenders, the release of property offenders reacted more quickly to changes in the state of the cotton economy; it also reacted more often to economic downturns. Finally, the seriousness of violent offenders admitted to the penitentiary had no implications for the release of black violent offenders. In contrast, the admission of more serious property offenders quickly encouraged the release of black property offenders.

For white convicts, the general analysis also conveyed a clear impression. Release depended on economic crises and was insulated from most social changes considered relevant in the literature. The analysis of white property offenders conveyed a slightly different impression. Though also influenced by twentieth-century economic events, it proved to be even more insulated than general releases from outside social, economic, and demographic changes.

Once again, then, offense was a critical distinction, and the release of white property and violent offenders reacted differently to the same influences. As expected, economic crises had more immediate and more sustained impacts on white property offenders than they had on white violent offenders. Moreover, a variety of other events and changes—World War I, percentage black male, urbanization, and racial inequality—affected white violent offenders. None exerted a discernible influence on the release of white property offenders.

As the foregoing comparisons indicate, the analysis of general release rates provides a composite portrait, one that lacks the precision of an analysis that focuses specifically on property and violent offenders. With more precise analysis, it quickly becomes apparent that economic crises dictated the release, though often in different ways, of blacks and whites, property and violent offenders alike. A broad range of social changes and events were only intermittently relevant for some groups of offenders. Before discussing the extent to which the findings support theoretical expectations, we must determine whether they are artifacts of a reliance on a global measure of release. The next section explores this possibility.

Conditional Release from the Penitentiary

Offenders obtained their release in various ways. A small percentage obtained "release" through escape, death, or legal execution. In the nineteenth century, most convicts received unconditional discharges, which involved completion of a court-imposed sentence minus any time deducted for good behavior. The introduction of parole in 1908 enlarged the scope of discretionary decision making. The parole board could entertain the conditional release of convicts long before the expiration of court-imposed sentences. In the process, its members could consider not only attributes of the convict before them but also broader social changes and events. It is entirely possible, then, that *conditional* release rates were more responsive to social changes and events than the global measure of release led us to expect.

To explore this possibility, I used the data and procedures described in chapter 4 to create and analyze two additional rates. The first was the rate at which blacks and whites were discharged or unconditionally released; the second was their rate of conditional release (i.e., parole). Appendix B presents the results of the intervention and multivariate analysis. This section highlights the major findings.

As expected, parole did increase the opportunity for social changes and events to shape the conditional release of offenders from the penitentiary. In general, events and changes accounted for significantly more of the unexplained variation in *conditional* than in unconditional release rates. In part, this was due to the enhanced role that economic crises played during the conditional release process. Twentieth-century crises were relevant to the global release rate precisely because they had strong impacts on conditional release. Their impact on unconditional release rates was intermittent, becoming noteworthy only for white property offenders.

Once convicts could be released conditionally, the cotton economy also became more salient. A decline in the price of cotton encouraged the conditional release of black offenders in general and black property offenders in particular. Its impact on their unconditional release either was absent or considerably delayed. A decline in the black male population discouraged the conditional release of black violent offenders. It had no bearing on their unconditional release.

The availability of parole also expanded the influence exerted by the industrial economy, often in unexpected ways. Recall that growth in the value added by manufacturing ultimately had no impact on the release of black convicts. Once conditional release from the penitentiary became possible, industrialization grew more relevant to the treatment of black offenders. Contrary to expectation, industrialization encouraged their conditional release. In fact, for black property offenders, it initially encouraged conditional releases, and then inhibited them the following year. None of these results can be dismissed as trivial. Each was as strong as other determinants of conditional release rates. For example, value added reduced

188

the unexplained variance in black conditional release rates by 16 percent. Its role was even more critical to the release of black property offenders, where it accounted for 37 percent of the error sum of squares. Moreover, industrialization seldom lost its ability to affect the release of black offenders. Indeed, it grew increasingly capable of doing so over time.

Equally unexpected was the role that the industrial economy played in the conditional release of white offenders. Growth in the profitability of manufacturing discouraged the release of white violent offenders, especially in the early twentieth century. Though with less alacrity, urbanization also discouraged the conditional release of white offenders from prison. From 1920 onwards, it grew increasingly more capable of doing so.

Finally, the availability of parole allowed parole boards to respond more often, and unpredictably, to changes in the cohort of offenders admitted to the penitentiary. As expected, conditional release rates fell shortly after the admission of a more serious cohort of black offenders. Yet black property offenders faced a different situation. They found conditional release *easier* to achieve after a more serious cohort of black property offenders had been incarcerated. For whites, the age of the admitted cohort was important. With the admission of a younger cohort, both property and violent offenders found conditional release more difficult to achieve.

Although the unconditional release process was less open to outside influences, it was hardly a closed process. Selected nineteenth-century depressions and recessions, for example, were crucial for the discharge of black and white offenders. Growth in urbanization inhibited the discharge of black offenders in general and of black property offenders in particular. The next section revisits the distinction between conditional and unconditional release, as it assesses the implications of all the findings for the theoretical predictions that guided the analysis.

Theoretical Implications

As noted earlier, the political economy perspective draws attention to the agrarian economy, especially the price of cotton, the demand for agrarian labor, and changes in the supply of labor. After considering the cotton economy in detail, the discussion turns to the role played by the industrial economy and a series of specific depressions and recessions. As we have already seen, these changes and events were often crucial, though not always in ways we had come to expect. Considered next is the decline in racial inequality, followed by World War I and its aftermath, and the actions of state officials. None of these factors played a major role in the release of offenders from prison. The section concludes with the influence of the control series: the size of the population of young males and the composition of the inmate pool, namely, the seriousness and average age of those admitted to the penitentiary. Once again, these factors played a circumscribed role, influencing the release of some, but not all, groups of offenders.

The Cotton Economy

Underlying the analysis was the assumption that three aspects of the cotton economy would determine the extent to which black and white convicts were released from prison. The first aspect is the price of cotton, and the prediction was that as prices fall, so too should releases from prison, especially the release of black and property offenders. They did not. Although the price of cotton was more central to the release of black than of white offenders, it did not exert the expected influence. Typically, a fall in price encouraged release. Only during a difficult period of depressions and recessions (1883–1904) did lower prices operate as expected. A comparison of violent and property offenders yielded evidence that black property offenders benefited from a fall in price much more quickly than did black violent offenders. An examination of conditional release indicated that parole enhanced the salience of cotton prices, triggering the conditional release of black offenders more quickly than their unconditional discharge.

The second prediction focused on the demand for labor, indicated by the size of the cotton harvest. To the extent that smaller harvests presage a labor surplus, release rates should fall, once again especially for black and property offenders. The findings supported only the general *form* of the argument, namely, that the harvest was more central to the release of black than of white offenders. Support was weak, however, because the harvest was irrelevant for black property offenders. Moreover, it exercised only a minor influence on the release of their violent counterparts. Evidence supporting the *content* of the argument was noticeably absent. Smaller harvests, like declining cotton prices, encouraged release from the penitentiary, and their moderating influence grew stronger over time.

The final expectation focused on the supply of agrarian labor, indicated by the size of the black male population. To the extent that a decline in the supply of black labor also signals a labor shortage, fewer black and white offenders should be released, in an attempt to maximize the expropriation of labor. Recall that declines in the black male population affected only the admission of white men to prison. Here, it exercised a broader influence, affecting the release of both black and white convicts.

With a decline in the population of black men, fewer black violent and black property offenders were indeed released. Similarly, declines discouraged the release of white convicts in general and of white violent offenders in particular. In each case, alterations in the black male population exerted an influence that was neither quickly nor strongly felt. Moreover, the black male population had a dramatically different impact during some periods. The relatively small declines that occurred before World War I actually encouraged the release of black and white violent offenders from the penitentiary. In contrast, the more precipitous postwar declines operated as expected and *discouraged* their release. For black property offenders, changes in the black male population operated quite differently. During the early years of the lease, slight population *growth* encouraged the release of black property offenders. In contrast, at the height of the good-roads movement and subsequent black out-migration, *declines* encouraged their release.

In general, then, the cotton economy proved to be more central to the punishment of black offenders than of white offenders. Yet weaknesses in the economy were neither invariably nor quickly translated into a reluctance to release convicts. Indeed, weaknesses benefited some offenders. Despite a considerable delay, lower cotton prices and smaller harvests prompted the release of black violent offenders from the penitentiary. Declines in the supply of agrarian labor exercised a broader and more complicated influence. Their overall tendency to inhibit the release of both black and white offenders obscures exceptional periods during which slight declines stimulated the release of certain offenders.

The Industrial Economy

Three predictions guided our consideration of industrialization and urbanization. First, growth in industrialization should encourage the release of those with some potential for participating in the process, namely, white offenders. For those excluded from the process, namely, blacks, industrialization should have no relevance for their release. Earlier we saw that this reasoning applied fairly well to prison admissions. It fared less well here. First, industrialization did not have an impact where it was expected, on the release of white offenders. Only for whites convicted of violence was there evidence that growth in industrialization, after a short delay, stimulated release. Closer inspection of the release process after the introduction of parole requires us to qualify this general conclusion. Industrialization had another more immediate and unexpected impact on the treatment of white violent offenders. It discouraged their *conditional* release.

Second, industrialization appeared to operate as expected, playing no discernible role in the release of black offenders. Yet once conditional release from the penitentiary became possible, industrialization grew important to both black property and violent offenders. Even as it discouraged the conditional release of white violent offenders, growth in the profitability of manufacturing *encouraged* the conditional release of their black counterparts. For black property offenders, industrialization initially encouraged conditional releases, only to inhibit them the following year. None of these findings can be dismissed as trivial, because industrialization was as important as, if not more important than, other social changes.

The second prediction held that growth in urbanization should inhibit the release of black offenders and of white violent offenders. As expected, urbanization discouraged the release of black offenders. At the same time, however, it *encouraged* the release of white violent offenders. Urbanization continued to behave unexpectedly once the analysis focused solely on conditional release. It assumed a role not unlike the one it played in the general release of black offenders as a whole. As the state became more urbanized, white offenders overall were less likely to be conditionally released. Indeed, urbanization was the only determinant of the conditional release of whites, accounting for fully 17 percent of the unexplained variation (see appendix table B-4).

The final aspect of the industrial economy was change in the racial composition of Georgia's urban areas. The gradual "whitening" of urban areas suggested a decline in perceived racial threat and moderation in the punishment of black offenders. Recall from earlier chapters that this argument received no support for initial admissions or for the severity of prison sentences. It met the same fate here. There was only trace evidence that the black urban population played an unexpected role. A decline in percentage black urban had the unanticipated effect of *lowering* the rate at which black offenders, particularly those convicted of property crimes, were released from prison. Weak as it was, this tendency grew no stronger with the availability of parole after 1908. Alterations in the black urban population simply had no implications for either conditional or unconditional release.

In general, then, the industrial economy seldom operated as expected. Industrialization was indeed more important in the twentieth than in the nineteenth century. Yet its role was, in one sense, broader than anticipated, determining the release of both black and white offenders. In another sense, its role was more circumscribed than expected, shaping only conditional release from the penitentiary. There, industrialization benefited an unexpected group of offenders: black men convicted of violent crime. At the same time, it placed at a distinct disadvantage another equally unexpected group of offenders: whites convicted of violent crimes. Urbanization also seldom conformed to expectations. Even as it discouraged the release of black offenders, it unexpectedly stimulated the release of white violent offenders. The availability of parole enlarged and further complicated its role. As the state grew more urbanized, white offenders in the aggregate found conditional release more difficult to obtain. Even the weakest influence, shifts in the black urban population, induced harshness where lenience was anticipated.

Interracial Competition

As noted earlier, racial inequality declined steadily after the Civil War, placing whites in a more ambiguous economic position vis-à-vis blacks. A narrowing of the traditional economic divide should provide the basis for greater punitiveness, directed primarily at black offenders. For admissions to the penitentiary, this expectation received some support. Black admissions as a whole rose, as did their property and violent crime components. But racial inequality had no further bearing on the punishment of black men. Changes in its magnitude did not alter the extent to which they were released from prison. Indeed, additional analysis indicated that changes in the absolute economic position of neither blacks nor whites affected the release of black offenders.[3] The same was true for whites. Neither declines in their relative position vis-à-vis blacks nor fluctuations in their absolute economic position inhibited release from the penitentiary. Instead, only one group of whites, those convicted of violence, benefited from declining inequality and found release easier to achieve. Moreover, it was clearly their relative position vis-à-vis blacks that generated lenience. Considered alone, changes in white property values had no impact on white release rates, nor did changes in black property values.

Economic Crises

A variety of expectations guided the analysis of economic downturns in the nineteenth and twentieth centuries. The first predicted that fewer convicts would be released at the onset of depressions and recessions. The majority of findings, particularly for white offenders, supported this expectation. The 1937–38 recession, for example, discouraged the release of all offenders, black and white, property and violent alike. A late nineteenth-century recession (1895–97) had the same effect on the release of black property and violent offenders. It merits emphasis that, while some crises operated as expected, most had no impact on the release process. Of the seventeen economic downturns included in the analysis, between one and six had measurable impacts on release rates. The most influential economic crises occurred during the twentieth century, where they figured prominently in the *conditional* release of offenders.

The second expectation was that severe crises would have stronger impacts than recessions. They did not. Only one depression (1929–33) consistently affected release rates, and for the most part it was less influential than a variety of recessions (table 7.19). As a whole, for example, depressions reduced the unexplained variance in black releases by 14 percent. Recessions, in contrast, reduced the error sum of squares by nearly 38 percent. Only for white property offenders did the Great Depression and several recessions play equivalent roles.

The third prediction was that, during prolonged depressions, release rates would rise in response to a growing fiscal crisis. This occurred only during the Great Depression, which consistently encouraged release from the penitentiary. No other depression exerted a similar influence. Instead, some moderate downturns encouraged releases. For example, with the onset of the 1899–1900 recession, black property and violent offenders found release easier to obtain. White convicts

Table 7.19   Comparative impact of economic crises and other events on release rates

| | Release Rate | | | | | |
| | Total | | Violent | | Property | |
Event	SSE	%	SSE	%	SSE	%
Black Offenders						
Recessions	146.4	37.9	30.2	27.0	85.9	31.2
Depressions	203.4	13.7	37.3	10.0	115.9	7.2
Economic impacts	114.0	51.6	26.1	36.9	76.9	38.4
Noneconomic impacts	216.6	8.1	37.0	10.5	107.4	14.0
White Offenders						
Recessions	9.6	27.7	2.2	26.6	4.4	18.9
Depressions	11.4	14.0	2.9	5.3	4.3	20.0
Economic impacts	7.7	41.7	2.0	32.2	3.3	38.7
Noneconomic impacts	11.2	15.6	2.2	26.6	4.5	16.3

Note: SSE refers to the error sum of squares, while % refers to the percentage reduction in SSE after adding the intervention(s).

were the beneficiaries of higher release rates during the 1937–38 recession. Thus, higher release rates, for both black and white convicts, were not only the result of major depressions. They were also the unanticipated outcome of less intense crises.

The fourth expectation proposed the presence of clear racial differences. The release of black offenders should respond more strongly to changes in economic conditions. Put concretely, impacts should occur more often and, where present, should account for larger amounts of unexplained variation. To a certain extent, this was the case. For white convicts in general, economic crises reduced the unexplained variance by 42 percent. The comparable figure for black convicts was 52 percent. Of greater significance were race differences in the nature of the influence exerted by economic crises. While all offenders benefited from the Great Depression, whites benefited more quickly and for longer periods. The reverse was true for recessions. While all offenders benefited from an occasional recession, blacks benefited more often than whites. White offenders, in contrast, benefited less often and typically only after experiencing fewer releases the previous year.

The final expectation predicted that economic downturns would have more profound implications for the treatment of property than of violent offenders. They did, but only marginally. Economic crises generated slightly greater reductions in unexplained variance for property offenders (table 7.19). For whites, the reduction was 38 percent for property offenders and 37 percent for violent offenders. The comparable figures for blacks were 39 and 32 percent.

In sum, economic crises clearly affected the rate at which both black and white violent and property offenders were released from the penitentiary. Relatively few downturns were critical, however. Many, though not all, reduced release rates, as expected. The severity of the crisis was no guarantee that it would exert an especially strong impact. The Great Depression, for example, was not overwhelmingly important. Nevertheless, it behaved consistently and increased the rate at which all offenders—black and white, property and violent—were released. Yet neither the length nor the severity of a crisis guaranteed that release would eventually become more likely. Even relatively minor recessions were capable of triggering releases. Race conditioned the role that both depressions and recessions played in the release process. More so than whites, blacks found release easier to obtain with the onset of a number of recessions. More so than blacks, white offenders found release easier to obtain during the Great Depression. Offense occupied a less critical position. The same economic downturns tended to exercise the same general influence on the release of both property and violent offenders from prison.

World War I and Its Aftermath

Arguments developed earlier posited that America's entry into World War I should encourage release from the penitentiary. Postwar demobilization should exert the opposite influence and make release more difficult to obtain. Race should figure prominently in the magnitude of each impact, with black offenders benefiting from the war and suffering from demobilization more than white offenders. These expectations fared well when admissions to the penitentiary were the focus of the inquiry. They fared poorly here. Neither America's entry into the war nor subsequent demobilization affected the rate at which black or white offenders were released. Instead, the onset of war, which coincided with the worst year of the 1913–14 recession, prompted the release of white violent offenders.

Policies

Policy changes had few clear implications for the release process. Parole, instituted in 1908, gave officials an opportunity to increase rates of release from prison, particularly for white offenders. The analysis uncovered no evidence that this actually occurred, however. Instead, parole operated indirectly, providing an opportunity for officials to consider a variety of external events and changes when determining whether conditional release was warranted.

Abolition of the lease a year after parole was instituted should have had the opposite effect of lowering release rates, to serve better the demand for convict road labor. Similar reasoning applied to the advent of probation in 1913 and passage of the Federal Aid Road Act in 1916. Again, there was no evidence to support these arguments.

The final expectation proposed an indirect effect of the Great Depression,

195

operating through a major federal policy. To the extent that the AAA impoverished many tenants, it should, at least initially, curb release from the penitentiary. As it impoverished more tenants, the AAA should encourage release to avoid a fiscal crisis. In general, the results support the argument. For black violent and property offenders, the AAA initially lowered release rates, only to increase them the following year. Judging from the greater reduction in unexplained variation, the AAA was slightly more pivotal to the release of whites. Initially, the AAA inhibited the release of white property and violent offenders. It later stimulated only the release of white violent offenders. Thus, while the AAA was more relevant to the release of white offenders, it benefited them less than it did black offenders.

Control Series

Three final factors concern us in this section. The first is change in the population of young offenders at risk of being punished. Declines in the young black male population should discourage the release of black offenders from prison. This did not prove to be the case. Similarly, I expected declines in the young white population to encourage the release of white offenders. This also was not the case. After a short delay, a decline in the youthful population tended to inhibit the release of white violent offenders. This was particularly the case shortly after World War I and after the Great Depression.

The second factor is the seriousness of admitted offenders, which was critical to the sentences imposed on most offenders. Here, the expectation was that the admission of more serious offenders would inhibit release from the penitentiary. For black and white offenders overall, there was no evidence that this occurred. Instead, the admission of a more serious cohort of black property offenders had the opposite effect of *encouraging* their release. Only upon examination of the conditional release process did support for the argument surface. Conditional release rates fell two years after the admission of more serious black offenders.

The final factor is the average age of offenders admitted to the penitentiary. The admission of younger offenders should discourage prison release. It did, but only white offenders were affected. The admission of younger white property offenders discouraged the release of white property offenders already in prison. Indeed, after parole was introduced, the admission of younger offenders made the *conditional* release of white violent and property offenders more difficult to achieve.

Conclusion

The release of offenders from Georgia's penitentiary was clearly a creature of economic crises, correspondingly isolated from many long-term social changes. Yet indispensable to our understanding of prison releases were the twin axes of the analysis. Race and offense dictated the precise role that economic events and social changes would play during the release process. Whites, for example, clearly benefited more than blacks from the Great Depression, while black offenders benefited more than whites from selected recessions. The release of black offenders was deeply imbedded in outside social changes, while the release of white offenders was not. For both blacks and whites, however, economic events and changes were more pivotal to the treatment of property than of violent offenders. The release of black property offenders, for example, reacted more often and more sharply than the release of their violent counterparts to changes in the economic arena. Similarly, economic crises had more immediate and more sustained impacts on the release of white property offenders than they had on the release of white violent offenders.

The next chapter moves the analysis to a much different realm. It addresses two issues. First, once the influence of social changes and events has been removed, are the three manifestations of punishment linked? Second, how central are race and offense to our understanding of these links?

8

The Self-Regulation
of Punishment

THE PUNISHMENTS IMPOSED ON BLACK AND WHITE MEN RESPONDED, often sharply, to a variety of external events and social forces. This chapter examines the extent to which they responded to one another. Underlying the analysis is the presumption, derived from the stability of punishment thesis, that growth in one aspect of punishment is counterbalanced by a constriction in other aspects of punishment. Put concretely, should admissions to the penitentiary rise, the sentences imposed on admitted offenders will become more lenient and/or incarcerated offenders will find release easier to obtain. Should prison sentences lengthen, rates of release will rise and/or admissions will fall. Finally, to compensate for growth in rates of release, admission rates will rise and/or prison sentences will lengthen. The stability of punishment literature provides no compelling reason for either race or offense to alter these relationships.

An accurate exploration of the linkages among punishments requires that, in essence, we strip each punishment series of any outside influences that might create the appearance of a relationship where none, in fact, exists. The analysis uses, then, the residuals from the multivariate analysis. These series represent punishments from which the significant impacts of events and changes have been removed. The analysis occurs in two stages. The first focuses on within-race relationships among punishments. It examines, for example, whether changes in white admission rates altered the sentences imposed on white offenders. After removing these impacts, the analysis then explores linkages that crossed racial boundaries. It considers, for example, whether black admissions to the penitentiary had implications for the admission of white men. The two-stage strategy is applied first to punishment in general, then to the punishment of violent and property offenders.

Punishments of Black and White Offenders

The analysis begins with a series of cross-correlation functions between each dimension of black and white punishment. For black men, these functions suggest only three significant relationships (table 8.1). Black admissions responded to changes in both the length of prison sentences and rates of release. Admissions rose as sentences grew shorter and, after a lengthy delay (CCF + 5 = −.33, not presented), as release rates fell. Sentences and release rates are also linked (CCF + 1 = .23). As a result, the impact of sentences and releases on the admission of black men to the penitentiary could be spurious. For this reason, the analysis must first identify and, if necessary, remove the impact that the release rate had on prison sentences. This stage yielded only nonsignificant results. The release rate had no measurable impact on prison sentence (ω_1 = .01, t-ratio = 1.08) and generated no discernible reduction in unexplained variance. Hence, the impact of releases on subsequent sentences need not be removed, as it was trivial. We are now free to estimate the influence exerted by the release rate and sentences on black admissions to the penitentiary. Of the two punishments, the release rate was the more influential (table 8.2). Alone, it reduced the error sum of squares in admissions by 36 percent. Much weaker by comparison, prison sentences reduced the error sum of squares by only 8 percent.

First, then, black admissions rose after a decline in the release of black men. This relationship was both unexpected and slow to be realized. Five years elapsed before admissions reacted to a change in release rates. Over time, admissions

Table 8.1 Cross-correlations for black punishment series

| Punishment Series | Input Series | Cross-Correlation at Lag | | | | |
		0	1	2	3	p
Black Admission Rate	Prison sentence	−.29*	.09	.02	.03	.47
	Release rate	.15	.05	.19	.10	.09
Black Prison Sentence	Admission rate	−.29*	.09	−.10	−.21	.12
	Release rate	.18	.23*	−.00	−.06	.41
Black Release Rate	Admission rate	.03	.10	−.05	−.16	.65
	Prison sentence	−.01	−.08	−.03	.14	.50

Note: The effects of events and social changes were removed before estimation. As an input series, black release rate was prewhitened, its noise component modeled as a first-order moving average process.

*$p \leq .05$

199

Table 8.2 Impact of other punishments on black admission rate

Input Series	Transfer Function	Model 1	Model 2	Model 3
Prison Sentence	ω_0	−.73		−.63
		(−2.27)		(−2.16)
Release Rate	ω_5		−.07	−.06
			(−4.49)	(−4.36)
χ^2 of residuals				5.87
(*p*)				(.44)
Original SSE		1.01	1.14	1.01
Model SSE		.93	.73	.67
% reduction in SSE		7.92	35.96	33.66

Note: *T*-ratio of estimate in parentheses. SSE denotes error sum of squares. Variation in original SSE is due to variation in the time span of the residualized punishment series: prison sentence (1881–1940) and release rate (1879–1940).

Figure 8.1. Impact of black punishments on black admission rate

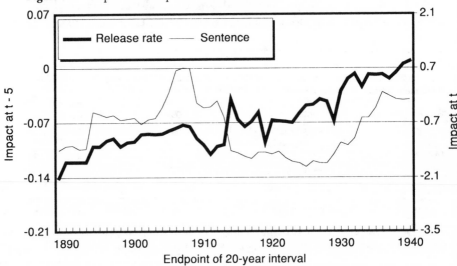

Table 8.3 Cross-correlations for white punishment series

| Punishment Series | Input Series | Cross-Correlation at Lag | | | | |
		0	1	2	3	p
White Admission Rate	Prison sentence	−.11	.01	.17	−.17	.44
	Release rate	.12	−.05	.09	−.07	.88
White Prison Sentence	Admission rate	−.12	−.16	.01	−.05	.81
	Release rate	.18	−.09	−.09	.07	.68
White Release Rate	Admission rate	.12	.16	.02	−.08	.73
	Prison sentence	.18	−.30*	.04	.11	.03

Note: The effects of events and social changes were removed before estimation. As an input series, the admission rate was prewhitened, its noise component being modeled as a moving average process [$q = (0,4)$].

*$p \leq .05$

grew even less responsive to release rates (fig. 8.1). On the eve of World War II, the two dimensions of punishment were independent of one another.

Second, black admissions rose as prison sentences grew shorter. This impact was expected and realized quickly. Strongest during the early years of the lease, the ability of sentences to influence admissions weakened dramatically with the onset of the economic crises of the 1890s (see fig. 8.1). It strengthened again during a period that encompassed the good-roads movement (1895–1914), World War I, and the 1920s. Yet once the Great Depression deepened, sentences lost most of their ability to affect admissions to the penitentiary.

In sum, only black rates of admission reacted to changes in other punishments. As expected, they rose quickly though slightly in response to shorter prison sentences. Contrary to expectation, they reacted more forcefully albeit slowly to release rates, rising after the release of fewer black offenders. By 1940, the link between admissions and other punishments had been severed. Prison sentences and release rates no longer dictated the level at which black men were admitted to the penitentiary.

For white offenders, rates of admission never responded to other punishments (table 8.3). Similarly, prison sentences were insensitive to changes in admissions and releases. The only relationship of note was inconsistent with stability of punishment notions. Fewer whites were released one and four years after white offenders received longer sentences (CCF + 4 = −.33, not presented). Together, these two effects were powerful, generating a 31 percent reduction in unexplained variance (table 8.4). Over time, they tracked one another closely, with the more immediate influence dominating the more distant (fig. 8.2). During the nineteenth century, prison sentences grew increasingly more important to white release rates. Their influence persisted and stabilized in the twentieth century. Even during the Great

Table 8.4 Impact of white prison sentence on white release rate

Input Series	Transfer Function	Parameter	Estimate (*t*-ratio)
Prison Sentence	$\omega_1 - \omega_4$	ω_1	−.85
			(−3.16)
		ω_4	.78
			(3.11)
χ^2 of residuals			4.67
(*p*)			(.59)
Original SSE			4.66
Model SSE			3.22
% reduction in SSE			30.90

Note: SSE denotes error sum of squares.

Figure 8.2. Impact of white prison sentence on white release rate

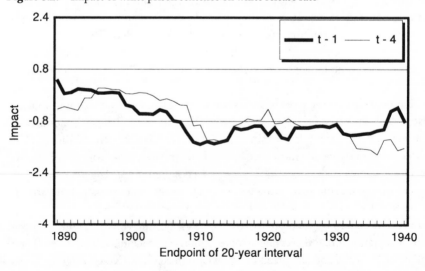

202

Table 8.5 Impact of white punishment on black punishment, all offenders

Input Series	Transfer Function	Black Admission Rate			Black Release Rate	
		1	2	3	1	2
White Offenders						
Admission rate	ω_2	−.15		−.13		
		(−2.27)		(−2.02)		
Release rate	ω_3		−.17	−.15		
			(−2.76)	(−2.50)		
Prison sentence	ω_0				2.64	2.39
					(2.77)	(2.51)
Noise Component	θ_1					.35
						(2.70)
χ^2 of residuals				8.28	10.03	5.24
(p)				(.24)	(.12)	(.39)
Original SSE		.64	.67	.67	58.38	58.38
Model SSE		.61	.51	.47	51.47	46.42
% reduction in SSE		4.69	23.88	29.85	11.84	20.49

Note: T-ratio of estimate in parentheses. SSE denotes error sum of squares. The effects of events, social changes, and within-race punishments were removed before estimation. White admission rate was prewhitened, its noise component modeled as a first-order moving average process.

Depression, the release of white offenders continued to be affected, albeit more slowly, by the prison terms imposed on previous cohorts of white offenders.

Within each race, then, punishments were infrequently and inconsistently intertwined with one another. The same conclusion holds for relationships that transcended racial boundaries. Only four links surfaced and, taken together, they indicate that black punishments were more sensitive to shifts in white punishment than the reverse.[1] The first relationship involved black prison sentences and white admission rates. A significant cross-correlation (CCF + 1 = .24) suggests that the imposition of more severe sentences on black offenders prompted unexpected growth in white admissions the following year. While significant, black sentences exercised a weak influence (ω_1 = .91, t-ratio = 1.64) and reduced the unexplained variance in white admissions by less than 5 percent.

Of greater import was the extent to which black punishment *reacted* to alterations in white punishment. Black admissions responded to both the admission of white offenders to the penitentiary and their release. Growth in white admissions generated the expected decline in black admissions two years later (table 8.5). Although this relationship fluctuated over time, it exhibited no clear propensity to

Figure 8.3. Impact of white punishment on black admission rate

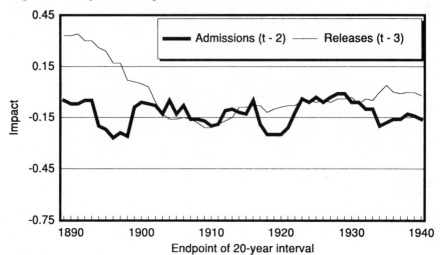

strengthen or weaken (fig. 8.3). Instead, it was stronger than average during the economic crises of the 1890s and immediately after World War I.

Black admissions also reacted to shifts in white releases. As fewer whites were released, more blacks were admitted. Though more potent than admissions, white release rates exercised their influence slowly. Three years elapsed before fewer releases prompted the admission of more black offenders. Although the overall relationship is inconsistent with stability of punishment notions, it masks a period during which the relationship was indeed regulatory (see fig. 8.3). During the nineteenth century, the release of more whites triggered the admission of more blacks. Only in the twentieth century, then, was there a marked and stable tendency for the release of white offenders to operate in tandem with the admission of black offenders.

Admissions were not the only black punishments to respond to shifts in white punishment. Black releases also reacted to the sentences imposed on white offenders (table 8.5). Contrary to expectation, the imposition of longer sentences coincided with the release of more black offenders from the penitentiary. Though less pronounced than the link between black and white admissions, the relationship between black releases and white sentences was more stable and consistent over time. It declined only after the onset of the Great Depression (results not presented).

Summary

In one fundamental respect, the punishments of both black and white offenders were similar. Rarely were they linked with one another and, when interrelated, only occasionally did they regulate one another. Aside from this similarity, race played a major role in shaping the precise nature of the relationships among punishments. For blacks, the core process was admission to the penitentiary; it responded to shifts in other black and white punishments. For whites, *release* was the central process, reacting only to changes in other white punishments. Second, as time passed, black punishments became more independent of one another; white punishments, more dependent on one another. Third, cross-race linkages were far more consequential for black offenders. Their punishment was more likely to be influenced by white punishments than the reverse. Finally, black punishments weakly and inconsistently regulated one other. Just as weakly, they regulated white punishment. In contrast, white punishments never regulated one another. Nor were they ever regulated by black punishments. Instead, they regulated some, though not all, black punishments. Their performance of this task was weak and inconsistent over time.

The following sections expand the racial comparison to include the offenses for which black and white men were convicted. We shall see that, once again, support for the stability of punishment surfaced sporadically and that race and offense, operating together, conditioned its appearance. The analysis begins with a consideration of the punishments imposed on violent offenders, then continues to explore the same issues for property offenders.

Punishments Imposed on Violent Offenders

As was the case in general, the punishments imposed on black violent offenders rarely depended on one another (table 8.6). Release from the penitentiary affected

Table 8.6 Cross-correlations for black violent punishment series

Punishment Series	Input Series	Cross-Correlation at Lag				
		0	1	2	3	*p*
Black Violent Admission Rate	Prison sentence	−.22	−.00	−.05	.02	.44
	Release rate	.18	−.11	.07	−.11	.20
Black Violent Prison Sentence	Admission rate	−.09	−.13	.05	−.08	.78
	Release rate	.03	−.09	.12	.03	.94
Black Violent Release Rate	Admission rate	.25*	.16	−.17	.12	.27
	Prison sentence	−.01	−.06	−.06	−.01	.99

Note: The effects of events and social changes were removed before estimation. As input series, admission rate and prison sentence were prewhitened, their noise components modeled as moving average processes [$q = (0,4)$ and $q = 1$, respectively].

*$p \leq .05$

205

Table 8.7 Impact of release rate on admission rate, black violent offenders

Input Series	Transfer Function	Estimate (t-ratio)
Release Rate	ω_5	−.07
		(−2.50)
χ^2 of residuals		4.84
(p)		(.56)
Original SSE		.86
Model SSE		.57
% reduction in SSE		33.72

Note: SSE denotes error sum of squares.

admissions five years later (CCF + 5 = −.28, not presented). It also appeared to depend on contemporaneous levels of admission [CCF + 0 = .25]. The analysis must first estimate and, if necessary, remove the contemporaneous impact of admissions on release before it can examine the impact of release rates on admissions five years later.

The first stage of the analysis indicated that the instantaneous impact of admissions on release was nonsignificant (ω_0 = .72, t-ratio = 1.37) and trivial. It reduced the unexplained variance by only 3 percent. There is no need, then, to remove the contemporaneous relationship between admissions and releases before estimating the delayed impact of release on admissions.

The results of the second stage indicate that five years after the release of fewer black violent offenders, more black violent offenders were admitted to the penitentiary (table 8.7). Again, this relationship was strong, accounting for a 34 percent reduction in unexplained variance. Unlike the general association, which weakened over time, the link between the release and admission of black violent offenders grew stronger as the nineteenth century drew to a close (fig. 8.4). Indeed, release affected subsequent admissions most strongly between 1890 and 1909. Thereafter, release rates gradually lost their ability to affect the admission of black violent offenders. The two punishments had become virtually independent of one another by the Great Depression.

For the most part, then, the punishments imposed on black violent offenders varied independently of one another. Release dictated admissions, but only after a considerable delay and primarily during the nineteenth and early twentieth centuries. In contrast, the punishments imposed on white violent offenders were linked with each other more often if less tightly. Cross-correlations suggest that the admission of white violent offenders responded to both the length

Figure 8.4. Impact of release rate on black violent admission rate

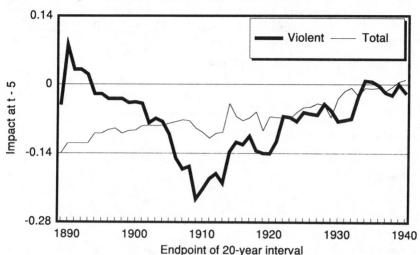

Table 8.8 Cross-correlations for white violent punishment series

Punishment Series	Input Series	Cross-Correlation at Lag				
		0	1	2	3	*p*
White Violent Admission Rate	Prison sentence	.13	−.06	−.06	.28*	.33
	Release rate	.09	.07	−.01	−.24*	.15
White Violent Prison Sentence	Admission rate	.13	.13	−.04	.06	.39
	Release rate	.05	.26*	−.19	.06	.11
White Violent Release Rate	Admission rate	.09	−.03	−.10	.11	.43
	Prison sentence	.05	−.13	.02	.03	.56

Note: The effects of events and social changes were removed before estimation. As an input series, prison sentence was prewhitened, its noise component modeled as a first-order moving average process.

*$p \leq .05$

of sentences and their release (table 8.8). Moreover, sentences responded, after a short delay, to fluctuations in the release rate.

To assess the true impact of other punishments on white admissions, we must first estimate and remove the relationship between sentences and the release rate. The first stage of the analysis accomplishes this task (table 8.9, col. 1). The release of fewer white violent offenders triggered lenience toward white violent offenders sentenced the following year. While both significant and expected, this relationship was fragile indeed. It reduced the unexplained variance in prison sentence by a trivial

Table 8.9 Relationships between white violent punishment series

Input Series	Transfer Function	Prison Sentence	Admission Rate		
			1	2	3
Release Rate	ω_1	.26			
		(1.98)			
	ω_3		−.26		−.29
			(−1.89)		(−2.14)
Prison Sentence[a]	ω_3			.23	.27
				(1.77)	(2.09)
χ^2 of residuals		6.38			1.57
(p)		(.38)			(.96)
Original SSE		.79	.79	.79	.79
Model SSE		.77	.75	.75	.69
% reduction in SSE		2.53	5.06	5.06	12.66

Note: T-ratio of estimate in parentheses. SSE denotes error sum of squares.
[a]Series was purged of the influence of release rate.

amount (less than 3 percent). Not surprisingly, the link was highly unstable over time (results not presented). Release rates grew more tangential to sentences during the nineteenth and early twentieth centuries, reaching the nadir of their influence between 1892 and 1911. Thereafter, they grew more capable of affecting prison sentences, reaching maximum strength during the early 1930s. Once the Great Depression deepened, release rates and prison sentences were no longer related.

The next stage of the analysis uses the residuals of the first model to estimate the independent impact of sentences and release rates on the admission of white violent offenders to the penitentiary (see table 8.9, models 1–3). Neither punishment was especially influential and, together, they reduced unexplained variation by less than 13 percent. Furthermore, neither influence supported expectations derived from the stability of punishment literature. Admission rates rose three years after white violent offenders experienced lower release rates and longer prison sentences. In both cases, admissions adjusted ever more certainly to fluctuations in other punishments (results not presented). The link between longer sentences and higher admission rates strengthened over time. To a lesser extent, so did the link between lower release rates and higher admission rates.

Only two relationships crossed racial boundaries. Unlike those reported earlier, they suggest that the punishment of white violent offenders reacted more forcefully to the punishment of their black counterparts than the reverse. White

Table 8.10 Impact of black punishment on white punishment, violent offenders

Input Series	Transfer Function	White Violent Offenders Admission Rate	White Violent Offenders Release Rate
Black Violent Offenders			
Admission rate	ω_4	−.30	
		(−2.17)	
Release rate	ω_3		−.07
			(−2.26)
χ^2 of residuals		2.80	5.38
(*p*)		(.83)	(.50)
Original SSE		.61	.77
Model SSE		.52	.70
% reduction in SSE		14.75	9.09

Note: T-ratio of estimate in parentheses. SSE denotes error sum of squares. The effects of events, social changes, and within-race punishments were removed before estimation.

Figure 8.5. Impact of black violent admissions on white violent admissions

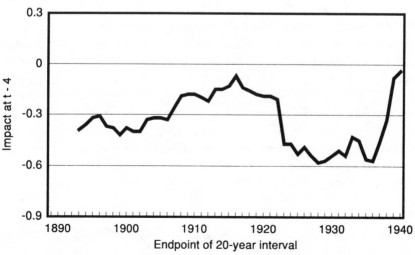

Figure 8.6. Impact of black violent release rate on white violent release rate

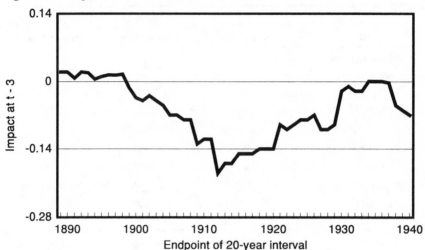

admissions for violence fell after more black violent offenders were admitted to the penitentiary (table 8.10). Delayed by four years, this relationship generated a modest 15 percent reduction in unexplained variation. Its direction was uniform over time, providing consistent support for the stability of punishment thesis (fig. 8.5). Nevertheless, the strength of the bond varied: gradually diminishing until World War I, then tightening and remaining robust until the end of the Great Depression. On the eve of World War II, though, the admission of white men for violence no longer dictated the extent to which their black counterparts would be admitted.

The second relationship between the punishment of black and white violent offenders involved release from the penitentiary (see table 8.10). Whites found release more difficult to achieve after the release of more black violent offenders. Like black admissions, black releases exerted an influence that was delayed and modest, accounting for only 9 percent of the unexplained variation in white releases. Uniform in direction over time, the finding also provides consistent support for the stability of punishment thesis (fig. 8.6). Once again, the link between black and white releases fluctuated in magnitude. Over the course of the nineteenth century, it grew more pronounced, reaching maximum strength during the height of the good-roads movement. Thereafter, black releases became less capable of determining the release of white violent offenders from the penitentiary.

Summary

Linkages among the punishments imposed on violent offenders were also the exception rather than the rule. Once again, race shaped their nature. As evidenced by greater reductions in unexplained variation, black punishments were more tightly linked with one another than were white punishments. Yet the punishments of black violent offenders also grew more independent. The punishment of comparable whites, in contrast, grew more intertwined. Cross-race linkages were more consequential for white violent offenders. Their punishment was more likely to be influenced by black punishments than the reverse. Finally, the punishments imposed on white violent offenders loosely regulated each other and were more strongly regulated by black punishments. The punishment of black violent offenders, in contrast, was regulated by neither black nor white punishment.

In the following section, the punishment of property offenders occupies the analytic stage. As will become apparent, the stability of punishment hypothesis fares slightly better for these offenders than for those convicted of violence.

Punishments of Property Offenders

The analysis begins with a consideration of the interdependence among punishments imposed on black property offenders. Cross-correlations yielded two major relationships (table 8.11). Encountered before, the first association provides evidence that admission rates fell five years after an increase in release rates (CCF + 5 = −.30, not presented). The second relationship, not encountered before, involves admissions and prison sentences. In the general analysis, the relationship was a contemporaneous one: longer sentences coincided with lower admission rates. For black property offenders, the relationship was delayed (CCF + 5 = −.26, not presented). More important, longer sentences were a *consequence* of lower admission rates.

The first stage of the analysis estimates and removes the impact of release on

Table 8.11 Cross-correlations for black property punishment series

Punishment Series	Input Series	Cross-Correlation at Lag				
		0	1	2	3	p
Black Property Admission Rate	Prison sentence	−.09	.08	.12	.18	.55
	Release rate	.07	−.10	−.03	−.01	.17
Black Property Prison Sentence	Admission rate	−.04	−.20	.01	.10	.36
	Release rate	−.05	.14	−.05	.05	.95
Black Property Release Rate	Admission rate	.07	.14	−.06	−.05	.74
	Prison sentence	.01	−.12	−.16	.08	.76

Note: The effects of events and social changes were removed before estimation. As input series, release rate and prison sentence were prewhitened, their noise components modeled as moving average processes [$q =$ (0,2) and $q = 1$, respectively].

211

Table 8.12 Relationships between black property punishment series

Input Series	Transfer Function	Admission Rate	Prison Sentence 1	Prison Sentence 2
Release Rate	ω_5	−.06 (−2.08)		
Admission Rate[a]	ω_5		−.12 (−2.19)	−.12 (−2.11)
Noise Component	θ_1			.29 (1.98)
χ^2 of residuals (*p*)		5.54 (.48)	13.01 (.04)	4.34 (.50)
Original SSE		2.14	.28	.28
Model SSE		1.72	.25	.23
% reduction in SSE		19.63	10.71	17.86

Note: T-ratio in parentheses. SSE denotes error sum of squares.

[a]Series was purged of the influence of release rate.

Figure 8.7. Impact of release rate on black property admission rate

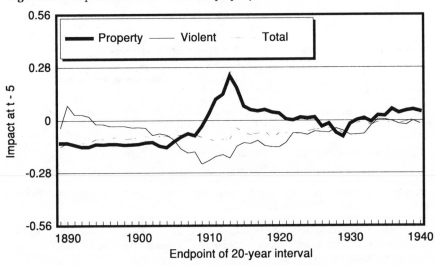

Figure 8.8. Impact of admission rate on black property prison sentence

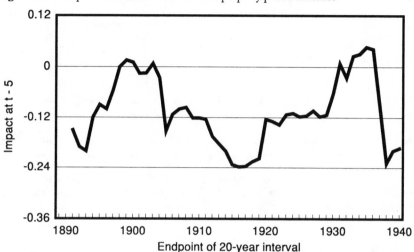

admissions (table 8.12, col. 1). Contrary to expectation, a decline in release rates triggered an increase in admission rates. While accounting for nearly a fifth of the unexplained variation, this tendency was not as powerful as that encountered for black violent offenders. In addition, the relationship varied more over time (fig. 8.7). Until the end of the nineteenth century, the link between lower release rates and higher rates of admission was robust and stable. Shortly after the lease was abolished, the relationship reversed direction and provided support for the stability of punishment thesis. The release of more black property offenders triggered the admission of more black men for property crimes. This relationship proved to be a short-lived feature of the good-roads movement. Soon after, the release rate quickly lost its ability to affect the admission of black property offenders to the penitentiary.

Using residuals from this model, the analysis next estimates the impact of admissions on prison sentences (see table 8.12, cols. 2 and 3). As expected, rising admission rates triggered shorter terms of incarceration. They exerted this impact inconsistently over time, however (fig. 8.8). During the nineteenth century, the relationship gradually diminished, until admissions and prison sentences were unrelated. This situation was only temporary, as the relationship strengthened during the early twentieth century. Support for the stability of punishment thesis was strongest during the good-roads movement, World War I, and its aftermath. The link between sentences and admissions attenuated once again, becoming virtually nonexistent by the onset of the Great Depression. Only after the worst years of the depression had passed did admissions regain their ability to moderate terms of imprisonment.

213

Table 8.13 Cross-correlations for white property punishment series

Punishment Series	Input Series	Cross-Correlation at Lag				
		0	1	2	3	*p*
White Property Admission Rate	Prison sentence	.01	.02	.15	−.13	.34
	Release rate	−.12	−.03	−.04	.15	.77
White Property Prison Sentence	Admission rate	−.03	.03	.13	−.14	.30
	Release rate	.15	−.22	.19	.12	.31
White Property Release Rate	Admission rate	−.08	.31*	−.01	−.30*	.05
	Prison sentence	.12	−.18	−.01	.09	.77

Note: The effects of events and social changes were removed before estimation. As input series, admission rate, prison sentence, and release rate were prewhitened, their noise components modeled as first-order autoregressive, first-order moving average, and third-order moving average [$q = (0,3)$] processes, respectively.

*$p \le .05$

Table 8.14 Relationships between white property punishment series

Input Series	Transfer Function	Release Rate	Prison Sentence	
			1	2
Admission Rate	$\omega_1 - \omega_3$	.30		
		(2.60)		
		.26		
		(2.33)		
Release Rate[a]	ω_2		.31	.30
			(2.24)	(2.53)
Noise Component	θ_1			.43
				(3.51)
χ^2 of residuals		6.43	11.73	8.42
(*p*)		(.38)	(.07)	(.13)
Original SSE		1.58	1.56	1.56
Model SSE		1.34	1.45	1.22
% reduction in SSE		15.19	7.05	21.79

Note: *T*-ratio of estimate in parentheses. SSE denotes error sum of squares.

[a]Series was purged of the influence of admission rate.

Figure 8.9.   Impact of admission rate on white property release rate

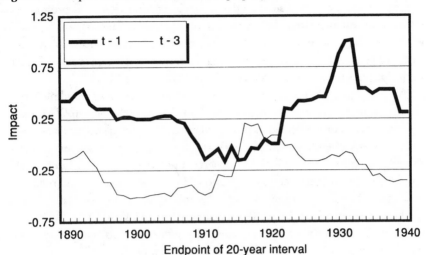

For black property offenders, then, release from prison affected subsequent admissions, which, in turn, determined the length of prison sentences. In contrast, the admission of white property offenders depended on neither release nor the severity of punishments imposed on previous cohorts of white property offenders (table 8.13). Prison sentences, at least on the surface, responded to neither admissions nor releases. Only release rates reacted to changes in other dimensions of punishment. As more white property offenders were admitted, more were released the following year and fewer three years later (table 8.14, col. 1). These relationships cannot be dismissed as trivial, because they accounted for a 15 percent reduction in error sum of squares. Their trajectories over time are complicated (fig. 8.9). The most immediate impact is consistent with the stability of punishment argument: rising admissions were quickly compensated for by higher rates of release from the penitentiary. During the nineteenth century, this relationship gradually diminished, and admissions and releases were unrelated until the 1920s. During the nineteenth century, however, the more distant and unexpected tendency for rising admissions to depress rates of release gradually strengthened and remained more influential than the opposing tendency. In the nineteenth century, then, the dominant relationship between the release and admission of white property offenders was complementary rather than regulatory. After some delay, lenience in the admission process found expression in lenience during the release process.

During the 1920s and especially at the onset of the Great Depression, the quick and expected tendency for rising admissions to foster more releases regained

215

strength. Yet it was never the sole or dominant influence on release rates. Beginning slightly earlier, the more distant tendency for rising admissions to depress rates of release also regained strength. On the eve of World War II, then, an increase in admissions had two different but equally important consequences. In the short term, it operated as expected, encouraging the release of white property offenders. In the longer term, it *discouraged* their release.

After purging the release rate of the complicated influence of admissions, a routine recalculation of cross-correlations yielded a final relationship.[2] The release of fewer white property offenders prompted the imposition of shorter sentences on white property offenders admitted two years later. While significant and expected, this relationship accounted for only a 7 percent reduction in error sum of squares. Until the early twentieth century, the relationship was stable and weak (results not presented). The bond between release rates and prison sentences then tightened, reaching its apex during the good-roads movement and World War I. This, too, was short-lived. By the end of the 1930s, release rates were as irrelevant to prison sentences as they had been during the nineteenth century.

In sum, the release of black property offenders affected subsequent admissions, which, in turn, altered prison sentences. For whites, the *admission* of property offenders to the penitentiary affected subsequent release, which, in turn, altered sentences. The punishments of black and white property offenders were linked as well. Table 8.15 presents the first set of cross-race relationships. White prison sentences had implications for two dimensions of black punishment: the sentences imposed on black property offenders and the rate at which they were released. Two years after white property offenders received longer sentences, the sentences imposed on black property offenders shortened appreciably. Consistent in direction and relatively stable in magnitude over time (results not presented), this relationship provides clear support for the stability of punishment thesis. Three years after white property offenders received longer sentences, black property offenders found release from the penitentiary more difficult to achieve. Despite the longer delay, black release rates responded twice as forcefully as black sentences to changes in white punishment. White prison sentences accounted for 25 percent of the unexplained variation in black property release rates, but only 12 percent of the unexplained variation in black prison sentences. Also consistent in direction, this relationship weakened somewhat after World War I (results not presented).

The remaining cross-race relationships involve the influence exerted by black punishments on the release of white property offenders (table 8.16). Taken together, black punishments were quite influential; they reduced the unexplained variation in white property release rates by 38 percent. Black admissions exerted the weakest influence, reducing unexplained variance by only 10 percent. Contrary

Table 8.15 Impact of white punishment on black punishment, property offenders

Input Series	Transfer Function	Black Property Offenders			
		Prison Sentence		Release Rate	
		1	2	1	2
White Property	ω_n	−.15	−.14	−1.98	−2.00
Prison Sentence[a]		(−2.52)	(−2.27)	(−3.24)	(−3.51)
Noise Component	ϕ_1		−.26		
			(−1.79)		
	θ_1				.41
					(3.26)
χ^2 of residuals		8.59	2.82	10.06	4.55
(p)		(.20)	(.73)	(.12)	(.47)
Original SSE		.25	.25	38.68	38.68
Model SSE		.22	.20	28.89	25.62
% reduction in SSE		12.00	20.00	25.31	33.76

Note: T-ratio of estimate in parentheses. SSE denotes error sum of squares. The effects of interventions, social changes, and within-race punishments were removed before estimation.

[a]For black property prison sentence, $n = 3$; for release rate, $n = 2$.

to expectation, the admission of more black property offenders to the penitentiary triggered the release of fewer white property offenders. In general, black admissions became more tightly linked to the release of white property offenders over time (results not presented).

Of greater significance to the release of white property offenders were the sentences imposed on black property offenders. Also contrary to expectation, as black property offenders received longer terms of incarceration, white property offenders found release more difficult to obtain. This relationship was especially strong in the nineteenth century and, after a slight attenuation, remained stable (results not presented).

The final predictor of the release of white property offenders was the release of their black counterparts, which had two contrasting consequences. Initially, it triggered a complementary decline in the release of white property offenders. Relatively stable over time, this tendency did not grow stronger until the Great Depression. One year after fewer black property offenders were released, however, white property offenders found release easier to obtain. Until the Great Depression, this relationship, which supports the stability of punishment thesis, grew

Table 8.16 Impact of black punishment on white property release rate

Input Series	Transfer Function	Model 1	2	3	4	5
Black Property Offenders						
Admission rate	ω_2	−.25			−.34	−.35
		(−2.17)			(−2.96)	(−3.42)
Prison sentence	ω_5		−.86		−.57	−.65
			(−2.47)		(−1.76)	(−2.35)
Release rate	$\omega_0 - \omega_1$			.06	.08	.09
				(2.12)	(2.25)	(2.61)
				.06	a	
				(2.49)		
Noise Component	θ_3					−.32
						(−2.00)
χ^2 of residuals					11.70	8.05
(p)					(.07)	(.15)
Original SSE		1.22	1.16	1.22	1.16	1.16
Model SSE		1.10	.93	.96	.72	.64
% reduction in SSE		9.84	19.83	21.31	37.93	44.83

Note: T-ratio of estimate in parentheses. SSE denotes error sum of squares. The effects of events, social changes, and within-race punishments were removed before estimation.
[a]Estimate was nonsignificant in earlier estimation and excluded from the model.

Figure 8.10. Impact of black property releases on white property releases

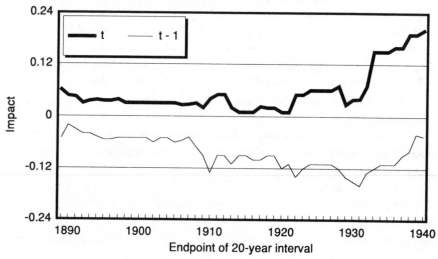

stronger (fig. 8.10). With the Great Depression, however, the dominant relationship between the release of black and white property offenders entailed not regulation but complementary declines.

Summary

The ties that bound together the punishments of property offenders were both tighter and more numerous than those we discovered earlier for violent offenders. Also more prominent were racial similarities in the role that punishments played for property offenders. First, the admission of both black and white men for property crimes was an active process. Black admissions affected the sentences that black property offenders received. White admissions affected the rate at which white property offenders were released. Second, cross-race linkages were common for both black and white property offenders. The punishments of black property offenders, especially their sentences, were influenced, if not regulated, by both black and white punishments. The punishments of white property offenders, especially their release from prison, were also influenced, if not regulated, by white and black punishments.

In comparison with the punishments of violent offenders, then, those imposed on property offenders—whether black or white—were linked more often with each other. These links were likely to be both internal (within race) and external (across race). The substance of the linkages also differed for property and violent offenders. For black offenders, the most consistent relationship was between the release and the admission of property and violent offenders to the penitentiary. Yet this relationship was clearly less robust and less stable over time for property than for violent offenders. Most important, the punishment of black property offenders occasionally supported the stability of punishment thesis. During the good-roads movement, the release of more black property offenders triggered the admission of more black property offenders. During this period, black violent offenders experienced just the opposite treatment. The release of more black violent offenders prompted the admission of fewer black violent offenders.

Offense thus conditioned the strength and direction of the internal links among black punishments. It also conditioned external links between black and white punishment. The punishment of black violent offenders was unequivocally an active process. Their admission to the penitentiary altered the admission of comparable whites; their release altered the release of comparable whites. In both instances, the relationship was regulatory: as the punishment of black violent offenders intensified, the punishment of white violent offenders moderated. In contrast, the punishment of black property offenders was alternately an active and a passive process. Evidence of regulation was equivocal. Each punishment imposed on black property offenders affected the release of white property offenders.

219

Two punishments—sentences and releases—were also subject to the influence of white punishment, namely, the sentences imposed on white property offenders. While not present in every instance, support for the stability of punishment nevertheless surfaced in both directions. As fewer black property offenders were released, more white property offenders were released. As white property offenders received longer sentences, black property offenders received shorter sentences.

Punishments involving black violent offenders, then, were active processes, likely to regulate white punishments. Punishments involving black property offenders played more diverse roles. At times, they affected white punishments, regulating some while acting in concert with others. At other times, they were affected by white punishments, sometimes but not always subjected to a regulatory influence.

For whites, the relationships among punishments also varied by offense. The only finding common to property and violent offenders was the relatively weak tendency for the release of more offenders to stimulate longer prison sentences. This similarity aside, offense shaped the number, strength, and direction of links among white punishments. As noted earlier, the punishments of white property offenders were intertwined more often with one another and with black punishments. The punishments of white violent offenders were, in a sense, more self-contained. Either they affected one another or they were affected by black punishments. Like their black counterparts, the punishments imposed on white property offenders played more multifaceted roles. Most notably, they were more likely than the punishments imposed on violent offenders to cross racial boundaries and affect the punishments that black property offenders received. The punishments of white violent offenders seldom regulated other white punishments and never regulated black punishments. Though not uniformly, the punishments of white property offenders regulated each other as well as the punishment of comparable black offenders.

Finally, the core punishment process for white violent offenders, involved in many relationships, was a passive one. The admission of white men to the penitentiary for violence reacted to changes in the release of white violent offenders, the length of their sentences, and the rate at which black men were admitted for violence. Though similarly passive, the core process for white property offenders was release from prison, which was strongly dictated by alterations in an array of black and white punishments. Moreover, the sentences imposed on white property offenders were also pivotal. They dictated not only the sentences that black property offenders received but also the rate at which they would achieve release.

The next section returns to the theoretical underpinnings of this investigation and summarizes whether and to what extent punishments regulated one another. As we shall see, no conclusion about the stability of punishment is possible without considering race, offense, and the element of time.

Theoretical Implications

Like all linkages, the regulatory force of punishments varied dramatically over time and was conditioned strongly by race and offense. Of the eleven instances where white punishment affected either other white or black punishments, six (54 percent) provided at least partial support for the stability of punishment thesis. In three instances, white punishments regulated one another. The admission of more white property offenders was compensated for by the release of more white property offenders the following year. The release of fewer white violent and property offenders triggered shorter sentences. The remaining instances involved the regulation of black punishment by white punishment. The admission of more whites to the penitentiary was compensated for by the admission of fewer blacks. As whites received longer sentences, more black offenders were released. Finally, as white property offenders received longer sentences, their black counterparts received shorter sentences.

In none of the above instances was the regulatory force of white punishment especially strong. Reductions in unexplained variation averaged around 10 percent. Further, in no instance was the regulatory influence of white punishment stable over time. In general, tight regulation was fleeting. White releases, for example, barely regulated white sentences during much of the nineteenth and early twentieth centuries. For white violent offenders, the strongest support for the thesis occurred at the onset of the Great Depression; it diminished thereafter. For white property offenders, the most vigorous support occurred earlier, during the good-roads movement. For violent and property offenders alike, the two punishments ended the period of study as they had begun, ineffectually linked with one another.

Finally, a stabilizing influence was not always the only effect operating on subsequent punishment. The admission and release of white property offenders was regulatory in the short term (after a one-year lag) but destabilizing in the longer term (after a three-year lag). Moreover, the regulatory force of white admissions to the penitentiary weakened during the nineteenth century and remained essentially irrelevant until the 1920s. The dominant relationship during the nineteenth century was therefore destabilizing: rising admissions discouraged release. In the twentieth century, both impacts grew stronger. The immediate stabilizing influence, wherein rising admissions encouraged release, was undercut two years later by an equally robust destabilizing tendency.

While hardly uncommon, then, evidence of self-regulation was a relatively weak and inconsistent feature of white punishments. In terms of their ability to reduce unexplained variance, destabilizing relationships were often more substantial. Three examples best illustrate this point. First, longer sentences discouraged the release of white offenders from the penitentiary and continued to do so four years after they were imposed; sentences reduced the unexplained variance in releases by over 30 percent. Second, as fewer whites were released, more blacks were admitted; white release rates reduced the unexplained variance in black admissions by 24 percent. Third, as white property offenders received longer sentences, fewer black property offenders were released; white sentences reduced the unexplained variance in black releases by one-quarter.

Of the eleven relationships where black punishment affected other sanctions, five (45 percent) provided at least partial support for the stability of punishment thesis. As black offenders received longer sentences, fewer blacks were admitted to the penitentiary. With the admission of more black property offenders, the sentences imposed on them grew shorter. Black punishments also regulated the punishment of white men and did so more frequently. The admission of fewer blacks for violence encouraged the admission of more whites for violence. The release of more black violent offenders from the penitentiary was compensated for by the release of fewer white violent offenders. Finally, an increase in the release of black property offenders inhibited the release of white property offenders the following year.

Once again, support for the thesis was neither strong nor consistent over time. Reductions in unexplained variance averaged around 13 percent. In many instances, there were periods during which the two dimensions of punishment were barely related to one other. Black property admissions regulated the sentences imposed on black property offenders during the good-roads movement, World War I, and its aftermath. They lost their regulatory capacity at the onset of the Great Depression, only to regain it after the Great Depression had ended. In contrast, the ability of black admissions to regulate white admissions was a postwar phenomenon that did not survive the Great Depression. The link between the release of black and white violent offenders was strongest during the good-roads movement and weaker afterwards.

Destabilization was present alongside a stabilizing influence as well. As noted earlier, the release of more black property offenders discouraged the release of white property offenders the following year. Its first impulse, however, was to trigger the release of more white property offenders from the penitentiary. Finally, the more impressive and consistent relationships indicated that black punishments acted in concert with, rather than in opposition to, one another. Lenience was met with lenience: growth in release rates fostered declines in the admission of black property and violent offenders. Of the relationships reported thus far, this tendency was the strongest: it accounted for a third of the unexplained variance.

Self-regulation, then, was slightly stronger for white than for black punishment. Yet it was the dominant feature of neither punishment. Support for the stability of punishment hypothesis also varied by offense. Of the six relationships where the punishments imposed on violent offenders affected other sanctions, half supported the thesis. Only the punishment of white violent offenders was regulated by other punishments, however. Regulation came from both sources: internal (other white punishments) and external (black punishments). Indeed, external regulation tended to be stronger than internal, clearly accounting for greater proportions of unexplained variation.

Of the nine relationships involving the punishment of property offenders, five (or 56 percent) supported the stability of punishment thesis. Here, the racial distinction was less crucial, and the punishments imposed on both black and white property offenders were subject to regulation. Again, the sources for the regulation were internal and external. For example, black property offenders received more lenient sentences in response to the admission of more black property offenders and in response to the imposition of longer sentences on white property offenders. White property offenders found release easier to achieve after more white property offenders were admitted and fewer black property offenders were released. Unlike punishments involving violent offenders, external regulations were no more influential than internal regulations.

The element of time is the final critical consideration. As noted, support for the stability of punishment thesis varied over time. It was often clearest during the good-roads movement, which emphasized the use of convict labor on roads. Economic crises were also a staple feature of this period, which began with the 1893–94 depression and ended with consecutive recessions (1910–12, 1913–14). In the interim were an additional depression (1907–8) and three more recessions. Elsewhere we have seen how economic crises shaped the relationship between social changes and punishment. These findings suggest yet another instance where economic crises operated in the same manner, by conditioning the extent to which punishments regulated one another.

Conclusion

More often than not, the punishments of white and black offenders varied independently of one another. In those instances where punishments were linked, self-regulation was common. Nevertheless, it was never strong or constant over time. The regulatory force of some sanctions was undercut by earlier or later impacts that destabilized punishment. Indeed, destabilizing influences surfaced with equal frequency and often with greater force.

Alone and in concert, race and offense shaped the extent to which punishments were related and the precise nature of their relationship over time. The punishments imposed on white offenders were slightly more likely than those imposed on black offenders to act in a regulatory capacity. Their regulatory force extended beyond the boundaries of other white punishments to include selected black punishments as well. The punishments imposed on property offenders played more multifaceted roles than their violent counterparts. Intertwined more often and more tightly, they were slightly more likely to regulate one another. Moreover, the influence exerted by the punishments of property offenders crossed racial boundaries more often, encompassing selected punishments imposed on the other racial group. Finally, regulatory ties between sanctions were seldom stable over time. Often though not always, they strengthened during a period that combined a demand for convict labor and a series of intense depressions and recessions.

9

Understanding Punishment
in Georgia

JUST AS LITTLE UNITED THE SOCIAL AND ECONOMIC POSITIONS OF BLACK
and white men in postbellum society, so too did little unite their punishment
for criminal behavior. This chapter summarizes the results presented in previous
chapters and identifies the ways in which our understanding of punishment hinges
on the twin dimensions of race and offense. It then returns to the theoretical
foundations of the analysis and assesses the extent to which the findings support
specific expectations about social changes and events. Suggestions for further research and theorizing conclude the chapter.

Race and Punishment

The process of punishing black and white offenders differed in both degree and
kind. Factors that loomed large for the sanctions imposed on black men often
dictated with considerably less force the sanctions imposed on their white counterparts. The reverse was true as well. At times, the same event or social change had
equal but opposite repercussions on the punishment of white and black men. Thus,
racial differences were common features of postbellum punishment. They were not
constant, however. The sharpest racial contrasts were present for admissions to the
penitentiary, while the most muted characterized the decision to release offenders.

Only two economic crises, for example, affected the admission of both black
and white men to prison. The lengthiest nineteenth-century depression (1873–79)
increased all admissions, whereas a much shorter postwar recession (1923–24)

lowered all admissions. Since neither event exerted more than a trivial influence, incarceration was the outcome of two distinct processes: one for black men and another for white men. The admission of black men to the penitentiary reacted most forcefully to changes in other punishments, especially the rate at which black offenders were released. The admission of white men, in contrast, was independent of other punishments. Black admissions also responded to a variety of social and economic changes, including World War I, demobilization, depressions, recessions, urbanization, changes in racial inequality, and weaknesses in the cotton economy. The admission of white men to the penitentiary, in contrast, was more selectively driven. It responded with considerably less force to World War I and not at all to urbanization and racial inequality. Whether white men would be admitted depended, instead, on a different aspect of the cotton economy, different economic crises, and a federal policy of no consequence for black admissions. Indeed, white admissions responded not only to a distinct set of economic downturns. They also responded in a distinct manner. More central to white admissions, depressions and recessions placed white men at a comparative disadvantage. More often than not, downturns *encouraged* imprisonment. Economic crises generally exerted less force on the incarceration of black men. When influential, they often benefited black men by *discouraging* imprisonment.

In sum, then, the admissions of black and white men to the penitentiary had little in common. Black admissions were more open than white admissions to other punishments and to external social events and changes. White admissions responded more selectively, if more intensely, to the social context and quite differently to economic downturns.

Only upon admission to the penitentiary did the punishments imposed on black and white offenders find common ground. Black and white prison sentences grew more severe primarily because more serious offenders were imprisoned. Aside from this similarity, sentences were also outcomes of processes that varied by race. The sentences imposed on black offenders were clear creatures of the economy: its general health, reflected in depressions and recessions, and the specific health of the cotton economy, reflected in the price of cotton and the size of its harvest. The sentences imposed on white offenders, in contrast, were more insulated from the economy and responded, if modestly, to social and demographic changes. Despite their greater sensitivity to the economy, the sentences imposed on black offenders were weakly involved with other punishments. They triggered only slight alterations in black admissions. Although less sensitive to the economy, the sentences imposed on white offenders took an active and prominent role in determining the release of both white and black offenders.

Black and white offenders found the most common ground during release from the penitentiary, which depended heavily on the economy and little, if at all, on other events and social changes. Even here, however, there were noticeable racial contrasts. The economy was more central to black offenders, accounting for a greater proportion of the unexplained variance in their release. Once again, depressions and recessions played distinctive roles. The onset of a crisis was an unpredictable event for black offenders. Like admissions, an economic downturn could either encourage or discourage their release. Economic crises had more uniform repercussions for white offenders, discouraging their release. Thus, at two crucial points in the punishment process—admissions and releases—white offenders bore a disproportionate share of the harshness associated with economic downturns.

The release of black offenders was not only a more open process but also a more active one. It sharply altered the extent to which black men were imprisoned. To a lesser extent, the release of black offenders was a passive process, mildly regulated by the sentences imposed on white property offenders. In contrast, the release of white offenders was more deeply implicated in other punishments, taking both an active and a passive role. It reacted forcefully to the prison sentences imposed on white offenders. At the same time, the release of white convicts was a strong determinant of the admission of black men. Overall, then, the rate at which black convicts were released was more tightly linked than its white counterpart to the economic and social context. Although less tethered to this context, the release of white offenders was more deeply enmeshed with other black and white punishments.

In sum, race shaped the strength and direction of the links between punishment and its context. The punishment of black men, especially their sentences and release, was more firmly linked than comparable white punishments to economic events and conditions. Greater sensitivity to the economy did not always place black offenders at a comparative disadvantage, however. Black men benefited during some economic crises, which both discouraged their admission to and encouraged their release from the penitentiary. White men did not receive these benefits with the same regularity. In general, the punishment of white men, especially their sentences and release, was less firmly linked than comparable black punishments to the broader context. At the same time, white punishment was often more heavily implicated in other punishments imposed on both black and white offenders.

The differences identified thus far apply to all black and white offenders, irrespective of whether they were convicted of violent or property crimes. The introduction of offense into the analysis complicates our understanding of punishment. Whether alone or in concert with race, offense just as forcefully shaped the strength and direction of the links between social context and punishment.

Offense and Punishment

During most of the analysis, a consideration of the offense often required us to refine or qualify general accounts of the punishment process. Indeed, since race and offense were often inextricably linked, no single account of the punishments imposed on either violent or property offenders was possible. Like racial contrasts, offense differences were common but not stable features of postbellum punishment. They surfaced with greater regularity among white offenders and among the sentences imposed on offenders admitted to the penitentiary.

The distinction between crimes of violence and crimes of property was least crucial for the admission of black men to the penitentiary. Admissions for both violent and property crime, for example, rose as the 1873–79 depression deepened, the region demobilized from World War I, the price of cotton fell, and racial inequality declined. Fewer property and violent offenders were admitted to the penitentiary during the 1882–84 depression and the year that America declared war on Germany. Although fundamentally similar, the admission of black men for violence nonetheless differed in three respects from their admission for property crimes. First, admissions for violent crimes responded more forcefully to many of the factors noted above. This was even true of economic changes, which were expected to be more pivotal for admissions that involved theft and burglary. Racial inequality, for example, accounted for three times the unexplained variance in admissions for violence than in admissions for property crimes. The second difference is qualitative, and it centers on the influence exercised by growth in the urban population. Admissions for violent crimes rose with urbanization, while admissions for property crimes fell. The final difference, also qualitative, is the extent to which admissions reacted to or were shaped by other punishments. The admission of black men for violent conduct was a passive, self-contained sanction. It affected no other punishment and was affected only by the rate at which black offenders were released from prison. The admission of black men for property crime was a more active and open process. Less sensitive to the release of black property offenders, admissions for property crime regulated the sentences imposed on black property offenders and exercised a destabilizing influence on the release of white property offenders.

In general, then, the admission of black men to the penitentiary for violence differed from its property crime counterpart primarily in degree and secondarily in kind. In declining order of importance, admissions for violence were shaped by the release of black violent offenders, World War I, racial inequality, economic crises, urbanization, and the cotton economy. Admissions for theft and burglary, in contrast, reacted to economic crises, the release of black property offenders, World War I, the cotton economy, urbanization, and racial inequality. Qualitative differences revolved around the precise role played by urbanization and other punishments.

The distinction between crimes of theft and crimes of violence was more critical for the admission of white men to the penitentiary. In general, admissions for both crimes were united by their insensitivity to a variety of social changes and their responsiveness to economic crises and postwar demobilization. Nevertheless, admissions for violence were less tightly linked than admissions for property crime to economic downturns. Fewer crises affected admissions for violence, and as a result depressions and recessions accounted for considerably less of the unexplained variance. Although less sensitive to economic crises, admissions for violence reacted strongly to policy changes and to weaknesses in the cotton economy. Admissions for theft and burglary did not. Finally, the admission of white men to the penitentiary for violence was a passive process, reacting weakly to other white sanctions and more forcefully to black sanctions. Like its black counterpart, the admission of white men for theft and burglary more actively dictated other punishments, in particular, the rate at which white property offenders would be released. In sum, then, the admission of white men for violence depended on the health of the cotton economy, policies, other punishments, and economic crises. Their admission for property offenses depended heavily on economic crises and little else of substance.

After admission to the penitentiary, the distinction between theft and violence grew more critical for the treatment of both black and white offenders. Three key offense differences surfaced during the sentencing of black offenders. First, economic crises had quite different implications for the punishment of violent and property offenders. Contrary to expectation, they were more central to the sentences imposed on violent offenders, accounting for 10 percent more of the unexplained variance. Different crises were important as well. Nineteenth-century downturns were central for the sentences imposed on violent offenders; twentieth-century downturns were key determinants of the sentences imposed on property offenders. Finally, economic crises had markedly different impacts. They put black violent offenders at a disadvantage by lengthening prison sentences. In contrast, depressions and recessions put black property offenders at a distinct *advantage* by shortening their terms of imprisonment. For black offenders, then, the first offense difference centers on the very different roles that economic crises played during the sentencing of violent and property offenders.

The second offense difference, one of degree rather than kind, involves the relative contribution that seriousness made to sentencing outcomes. As more serious offenders were imprisoned, sentences grew longer. While true for violent and property offenders alike, seriousness played a dramatically enhanced role during the sentencing of black violent offenders. It accounted for nearly five times the unexplained variance in their sentences.

The penitentiary terms imposed on black violent offenders, then, were more sensitive both to economic crises and to the character of offenders admitted to the penitentiary. At the same time, they were remarkably independent of other black and white punishments. In contrast, the sentences imposed on black property offenders, thus far less open to other influences, were more deeply enmeshed in other sanctions. They played two important roles. First, they were subject to regulation by both black and white punishments. Sentences grew shorter as more black property offenders were admitted to the penitentiary and as white property offenders received longer sentences. Second, the sentences imposed on black property offenders exercised a moderate destabilizing influence on white punishments. As their sentences grew more severe, fewer white property offenders were able to achieve release. In general, then, the sentencing of black violent offenders reacted forcefully to economic crises and seriousness. The sentencing of their property counterparts reacted with less force to both phenomena and was more deeply implicated in other punishments.

Similar offense differences surfaced during the sentencing of white offenders. As noted above, economic crises were more central for the sentences imposed on black violent offenders than on black property offenders. The opposite was the case for whites. As expected, economic crises played a smaller role during the sentencing of violent offenders. They played a qualitatively different role as well. Just as economic crises disadvantaged black violent offenders, so too did they put white violent offenders at a disadvantage, subjecting them to longer sentences. Economic crises played a far less predictable role for white property offenders. Some triggered more severe sentences; others, no less severe or protracted, prompted more lenient sentences. The first offense difference, then, is a reprise of that encountered for black offenders. Depressions and recessions had quite different repercussions for the sentences imposed on property and violent offenders.

The second offense difference was also present for black offenders. Just as seriousness and the sentences imposed on black violent offenders were tightly linked, so too were seriousness and the sentences imposed on white violent offenders. This single factor accounted for nearly ten times the unexplained variance in white violent sentences than in white property sentences. Indeed, for white property offenders, seriousness accounted for little more than a trivial amount of the unexplained variance. The third offense difference is also a familiar one. Just as the sentences of black violent offenders were independent of other punishments, so too were the sentences imposed on their white counterparts. The sentences imposed on white property offenders, in contrast, were deeply implicated in the punishment of black offenders, affecting their sentences and subsequent release. The final difference centers on the relative importance of social changes. The sentences imposed on white violent offenders were more open not only to seriousness but also to other social changes (e.g., urbanization) and events (e.g., World War I). Fewer outside factors influenced the sentences imposed on white property offenders.

In short, the sentencing of white violent offenders was driven less by economic conditions and more by the seriousness of admitted cohorts and a selective array of general social events and changes. The sentencing of their property counterparts, in contrast, responded more to economic crises and less to seriousness and other social events and changes. Furthermore, the sentences imposed on white property offenders dictated other punishments, a role not played by the sentences imposed on white violent offenders.

During sentencing, then, the races were united by the sharpness of the distinction between crimes of violence and those of theft. For both black and white offenders, events, social changes, and other punishments exerted contrasting influences on the sentences that violent and property offenders received. This racial unification all but disappears when we focus on release from prison. Once again, race shaped the significance of the offense, and the distinction between violent and property offenders was more relevant for white than for black men.

As noted earlier, sending black men to prison for violence and theft involved fundamentally similar processes. So did their subsequent release. Indeed, the only noteworthy offense difference was one of degree. As expected, the economy in general and the cotton economy in particular figured more prominently for black property offenders. Their release reacted more quickly to changes in the cotton economy and responded more often to economic downturns than did the release of black violent offenders.

Offense differences were more pivotal for white offenders seeking release from prison. As expected, economic crises had fewer and less sustained ramifications for violent offenders. Instead, a variety of events and social changes, including industrialization, urbanization, and racial inequality, dictated the release of white violent offenders. These changes were irrelevant to the release of white property offenders. While more open to events and social changes, the release of white violent offenders failed to adjust to changes in other punishments. In contrast, the release of white property offenders was sharply dictated, at times even regulated, by the punishments imposed on black offenders.

For white violent offenders, then, release depended on economic crises, the cohort of admitted offenders, policies, industrialization, and urbanization. For white property offenders, release hinged primarily on the punishment of black property offenders. Only secondarily were economic crises significant, with policies taking third place.

As the foregoing comparisons indicate, an examination of general punishment rates, even one sensitive to race, lacks the precision of an analysis that distinguishes between property and violent offenders. Like racial differences, those based on offense were matters not only of degree but also of kind. Social changes that were central to the punishment of violent offenders were peripheral for property offenders, and vice versa. As we saw in the case of urbanization and economic crises, factors that disadvantaged violent offenders placed property offenders at an advantage. The sections that follow address the findings more directly, placing racial and offense differences within the context of theoretical perspectives. It will quickly become apparent that no social change or event exercised an influence that was felt across all three dimensions of punishment and all groups of offenders. The central task of each section, then, is to assess the extent and precise location of support for theoretical expectations.

Theoretical Implications

The discussion begins with the agrarian economy and its central features: the price of cotton and the state of its labor market. As will become clear, the cotton economy was central to punishment but seldom its dominant determinant. Features of the industrial economy, shaped by cotton production, concern us next. Their influence on punishment was intermittent and often unexpected. From broad changes in the political economy, attention focuses more narrowly on specific changes in racial economic inequality and on the depressions and recessions that buffeted the economy between 1870 and 1940. As we will see, economic downturns, in the aggregate, typically exercised the most consistent and powerful influences on punishment. The final set of events includes World War I, its aftermath, and a set of federal and state policies. Each event played some role during punishment, if only a narrowly circumscribed one. The section concludes with an examination of the remaining time series: the size of the young male population and attributes of incarcerated offenders. As the findings will show, each warrants more sustained theoretical attention than it has received in the past.

The Cotton Economy

Several expectations informed our interest in the cotton economy. At their core was the argument that a weak economy will trigger harsher punishments and that black and property offenders will bear the brunt of any increase in harshness. In particular,

1. Punishment will become more severe as cotton prices fall.

More often than not, declines in the price of cotton precipitated more severe punishment. A fall in price increased admissions and lengthened terms of imprisonment. Unexpectedly, however, declining prices moderated a third punishment: release from prison. Regardless of its impact, the price of cotton rarely acted swiftly to affect punishment. Only admissions to the penitentiary responded quickly to a fall in prices. Release reacted more slowly after a minimum two-year delay; sentences, only after a delay of three to five years. In short, then, falling cotton prices were a mixed blessing. They fostered harshness toward offenders being admitted to prison but slowly benefited offenders already serving time. In neither case did the price of cotton dominate punishment. Changes in price, for example, ranked well behind other punishments, economic crises, urbanization, and racial inequality in their ability to affect the admission of black men to the penitentiary. They exercised less influence than seriousness and economic downturns on sentences, and they ranked well behind economic crises in determining release.

The next hypothesis focuses on the supply of agrarian labor. Its underlying presumption is that a smaller cotton harvest raises the prospect of a labor surplus, which intensifies formal social control. Thus,

2. Punishment will become more severe as cotton harvests grow smaller.

There was virtually no support for this expectation. A smaller harvest uniformly moderated punishment by lowering admissions, reducing sentences, and encouraging release from the penitentiary. Only during the good-roads movement (1895–1914) did a decline in the size of the harvest have the anticipated effect of lengthening the prison sentences imposed on black offenders. Overall, though, the size of the harvest was a facet of the cotton economy that was most tangential to punishment. Only sporadically relevant, its impact was usually weak, reducing unexplained variance by less than 10 percent.

The final dimension of the cotton economy was the supply of agrarian labor. In 1870, black men constituted 22.6 percent of the state's population. Seventy years later, they constituted only 16.6 percent. Previous work provided grounds for expecting that this decline would generate compensatory increases in punishment to ensure the lengthy expropriation of convict labor in service of the cotton economy. In short,

3. Punishment will become more severe as the size of the black male population declines.

In general, declines in the black male population had the anticipated effect. They increased admission rates and discouraged release from prison. Nevertheless, there were exceptional periods during which demographic declines operated quite differently. For example, the relatively small prewar drop in the black male population sharply encouraged the release of black and white violent offenders. This finding suggests that during mild labor shortages, the release of serious offenders could be used to counteract, if only marginally, the shortfall in labor. During the more

233

acute postwar labor shortage, the forceful expropriation of labor did increase as expected, but only selectively. Sharp declines in the black male population discouraged the release of offenders whose violent criminality and long prison terms made retention in the penitentiary more attractive than their release into the civilian population. These same declines in the black male population had opposite repercussions for black property offenders. Their rates of release rose. Evidently, nonviolent criminality coupled with comparatively short prison terms made retention less attractive than a quick return to revive a seriously depleted labor force.

Thus far, hypotheses have proposed general relationships between punishment and the cotton economy. Both race and offense should alter the strength of these relationships. Their economic subordination generates the expectation that black offenders will suffer disproportionately when the cotton economy is weak. Thus,

4. The link between the cotton economy and punishment will be stronger for blacks than for whites.

Support for this expectation depended on the dimension of the cotton economy under consideration. The price of cotton clearly had stronger implications for the punishment of black men. Declines in price increased their admission to the penitentiary for property and violent crimes, but had no effect on the admission of white men. Falling prices encouraged the release of black offenders, but were irrelevant to the release of whites. In fact, the price of cotton influenced the punishment of white men only once. A fall in price lengthened their terms of incarceration. Although expected, this influence was delayed, modest, and far less pronounced than that exerted by other social changes.

The size of the cotton harvest was also more consequential for the punishment of blacks than of whites. Although never forcefully, it affected the sentences imposed on black violent offenders as well as their release from prison. Only once did the punishment of whites respond to fluctuations in the harvest. A smaller harvest inhibited the imprisonment of white property offenders. Its ability to do so was delayed, weak, and ultimately nonsignificant.

Both the price of cotton and the size of its harvest were more central, then, to the punishment of black offenders. The opposite is true for the final dimension of the cotton economy: the size of the black male population. A decline in the supply of black agrarian labor triggered the admission of more white men to the penitentiary, largely for violent crimes. Indeed, the black male population was the strongest predictor of white admissions for violence, accounting for more than a third of the unexplained variance. In contrast, declines in the black male population were irrelevant to the incarceration of black men. A declining black male population also inhibited the release of whites, particularly violent offenders. Its impact on the

234

release of black offenders was neither as quick nor as forceful. Thus, the cotton economy was equally relevant to the punishment of black and white offenders. Black punishments responded more to the price of cotton and size of the harvest, and white punishments responded more to the state of the labor market, in particular, the supply of agrarian labor.

Underlying the following expectation is the supposition that a weak economy also intensifies concerns about the safety of property and lowers tolerance levels for theft. As a result,

> 5. The link between the cotton economy and punishment will be stronger for property than for violent offenders.

There was no evidence that this was the case. If anything, problems in the economy focused attention on violent offenders. As noted above, lower cotton prices encouraged the release of black property and violent offenders. The release of violent offenders reacted to price declines with greater force, albeit more slowly. A smaller harvest benefited black violent offenders by shortening their sentences and increasing their rate of release. In contrast, the harvest exerted no influence on the sentences that black property offenders received. Nor was it relevant to their release. The final indicator of the cotton economy, percentage black male, exercised its central influence on white punishments. There, too, its impacts were reserved for violent offenders. As the black male population declined, white admissions for violence rose and fewer white violent offenders were released. Admissions for property crimes and the release of property offenders remained unchanged.

In general, then, the cotton economy was not implicated more deeply in the punishment of property offenders. Black violent offenders benefited from a weak economy, while black property offenders benefited less, if at all. White violent offenders, in contrast, suffered from weaknesses in the cotton economy; their property counterparts did not.

The final hypothesis addresses change over time in the relationship between the cotton economy and punishment. Since Georgia's economy diversified in the twentieth century, the expectation was that

> 6. The link between the cotton economy and punishment will weaken with time.

As expected, the price of cotton became more tangential to punishment. Indeed, its influence waned to such an extent that, by 1940, black admissions and sentences were virtually independent of fluctuations in the price of cotton. In contrast, the size of the cotton harvest never lost its relevance to punishment. Although weak, its influence on prison sentences strengthened after World War I.

By the Great Depression, the harvest had regained its postbellum position of importance. The final dimension of the cotton economy, the black male population, also exhibited no consistent tendency to become more peripheral to punishment. Even on the eve of America's entry into World War II, a decline in the size of the black male population continued to increase the risk that white men would be imprisoned for violence. Though still relevant for prison admissions, the black male population did grow less salient to release from the penitentiary. For violent offenders in particular, the relationship was both stronger and qualitatively different in the nineteenth century. As noted earlier, slight nineteenth-century declines in the black male population sharply *encouraged* the release of white and black violent offenders. At the turn of the century and beyond, the black male population noticeably declined, but this only mildly inhibited the release of white and black violent offenders.

The cotton economy, then, did not fade quietly and completely into the background of the punishment process. While true of the price of cotton, it was not true of the agrarian labor market. The demand for agrarian labor, never a particularly strong factor, continued to affect the length of prison sentences. The supply of agrarian labor lost much of its ability to dictate release, but it continued to affect the rate at which whites were admitted to prison.

In sum, weaknesses in the agrarian economy did not intensify all aspects of punishment. Instead, they appear to have introduced a measure of fluidity into the sanctioning process. Release rates often rose when the cotton economy was weak, thereby offsetting the higher admissions and longer sentences that also accompanied an unsettled agrarian economy. Neither black nor property offenders received a disproportionate share of the burdens or, in the case of higher release rates, the benefits that a weak agrarian economy generated. In quite different ways, the cotton economy was equally important to the punishment of black and white offenders. More surprising, it proved to be more central to the sanctions imposed on violent offenders. Black violent offenders benefited more from a weak economy than did black property offenders, largely by securing release more easily. White violent offenders, in contrast, suffered more than did white property offenders, largely through higher admissions and more restrictions on their release from prison. As the state's economy diversified, some features of the cotton economy lost their ability to affect punishment. Others did not. Overall, then, the cotton economy was essential to an understanding of postbellum punishment. As we will soon see, it was only one of several important influences.

The Industrial Economy

Agriculture was the core of Georgia's political economy, but not its only element. As noted in chapter 4, the state was in transition from feudal agrarianism to

236

capitalism, with its emphasis on industrial production and population concentration. The transition posed different challenges to black and white men. Black men were excluded from employment in the industrial sector and hence were less likely to be subject to the informal controls that white men experienced both at home and in the workplace. This difference provided grounds to expect that

1. Growth in industrialization will moderate the punishment of whites and have no effect on the punishment of blacks.

As expected, industrialization inhibited the incarceration of white men. Nevertheless, it acted with considerably less force than the cotton economy and so was never a major influence on the probability that white men would be subject to punishment. Moreover, industrialization had few implications for the treatment of white men after admission to the penitentiary. It prompted no alteration in their sentences and affected the release of only one group of whites, those convicted of violence. After a short delay, industrialization stimulated mild growth in their release. The introduction of parole requires us to qualify this general conclusion, however. Once parole was available, the first impulse of industrialization was stronger and qualitatively different: it inhibited the conditional release of white violent offenders. Thus, intolerance of violent conduct was not necessarily limited to the nineteenth century. Indeed, it may have grown as a larger proportion of the workforce held industrial jobs. If so, its expression in punishment awaited the advent of parole, which introduced the exercise of broad discretion into the release process.

Industrialization was more weakly linked to the punishment of black men. It played no discernible role in their admission to the penitentiary, the sentences imposed on black offenders, and their release. The introduction of parole, once again, forged an unanticipated link between industrialization and punishment. As manufacturing became more profitable, black violent offenders found conditional release *easier* to achieve. At least initially, so did their property counterparts. Whether intentional or not, the release of more black offenders increased the supply of labor available for the agrarian and extractive enterprises that underpinned industrial growth. Although this interpretation may account for immediate growth in the release of black offenders, it cannot explain why the initial tendency to release black property offenders was offset the following year by a drop in their release rates.

Industrialization was an evolutionary process, but its pace nonetheless quickened in the twentieth century. This situation generated the expectation that

2. The link between industrialization and punishment will strengthen with time.

237

As expected, industrialization grew more capable of affecting punishment. Thus, while its overall influence on white admissions was weak, it nevertheless strengthened and grew more sustained in the twentieth century. The same was true of industrialization's impact on the conditional release of both white and black offenders.

In sum, industrialization was more relevant to the punishment of white than of black offenders. Yet even for whites, its influence was generally weak and circumscribed. Only for one specific sanction were its ramifications both broad and unanticipated. Industrialization affected conditional release. In so doing, it placed selected white offenders at a comparative disadvantage and black offenders at a comparative advantage.

Just as black and white men experienced industrialization differently, so too did their urban experiences differ. Unwelcome in the city and confined to the most menial jobs, black men led more precarious lives in urban places. This precariousness enhanced their risk of being subject to formal social controls. Thus,

3. The punishment of black offenders will intensify with growth in urbanization.

Urbanization did indeed increase the severity of punishments imposed on black men. It encouraged their admission to the penitentiary, lengthened their sentences, and discouraged their release. Yet urbanization did not exert these influences on all black offenders equally. The increase in general admissions was due solely to the role that urbanization played in stimulating the admission of black men to the penitentiary for violent crimes. Its role for admissions involving theft and burglary was different: as urbanization increased, admissions for property crime fell. The longer sentences that accompanied urbanization were also imposed on only one group of black offenders, those convicted of property crimes. Black violent offenders, in contrast, benefited because their sentences grew more lenient. Urbanization, then, generated no consistent tendency for black men to receive harsher treatment. It simply tended to make the punishment of black violent offenders more selective, restricting admissions to fewer offenders, who were then treated more harshly. At the same time, urbanization made the punishment of black property offenders less selective, expanding admissions to include more offenders. Although wider, the net cast over black property offenders grew more shallow since, once admitted to the penitentiary, offenders were treated more leniently. This pattern of selective harshness and more indiscriminate lenience resurfaces as we consider racial differences in the influence exerted by declines in the business cycle.

In comparison with blacks, white men experienced more continuity between rural and urban life. One continuity, the transplantation of rural violence into urban areas, was especially unwelcome, however. As a result,

4. The punishment of white violent offenders will intensify with growth in urbanization.

Only once did urbanization place white violent offenders at a comparative disadvantage. As the state became more urbanized, white violent offenders received longer sentences. They did not experience this treatment immediately, however. Longer sentences were a delayed reaction to growth in urbanization. The more immediate response to urbanization was a surprising lenience, namely, the swift release of white violent offenders from prison. Once again, then, urbanization generated two contrasting impulses. Its initial impulse to encourage the release of white violent offenders raises doubts about the extent of intolerance toward white violence in urban areas. Its delayed impulse to encourage more punitive sentences could stem less from altered tolerance levels and more from the unanticipated consequences of releasing more white violent offenders into the general population.

The advent of parole was a watershed event because it allowed parole authorities to forge a link between urbanization and the release of white offenders. This link involved a more general severity. After some delay, urbanization *discouraged* the conditional release of both white violent and white property offenders. From 1920 onwards, it grew increasingly more capable of doing so. Like industrialization, then, the rapid pace of twentieth-century urbanization could well have lowered tolerance levels for white misconduct. The expression of this intolerance awaited the appearance of a mechanism, conditional release, which allowed officials to treat white offenders in a more discretionary fashion.

The next expectation posits temporal shifts in the link between urbanization and punishment. Its underlying presumption is that urbanization will alter punishment more profoundly when two concerns are more salient: the supply and reliability of black agrarian labor and the persistence, in urban areas, of the rural legacy of white violence. Thus,

5. The link between urbanization and punishment will be stronger in the nineteenth century than in the twentieth century.

Rarely was this true. For black violent offenders, slow nineteenth-century growth in urbanization was more pivotal than its rapid twentieth-century counterpart. It fostered more indiscriminate, albeit more lenient, punishment. More black men were imprisoned for violence, but they received shorter sentences. For most offenders, however, twentieth-century growth in urbanization exerted equal if not stronger impacts on their punishment. It fostered selective harshness toward black property offenders. Fewer black men were incarcerated for theft and burglary, but they received longer sentences. Urbanization lengthened the terms of imprisonment imposed on white violent offenders in both the nineteenth and the twentieth centuries. Its ability to encourage the release of white violent offenders grew over time. Once parole was possible, urbanization grew more capable of inhibiting the conditional release of white offenders. In short, the bond between urbanization and punishment varied over time in a complex manner. There was no sustained evidence that concerns about the proper place of blacks and the proper comportment of whites in urban areas were confined to the nineteenth century. Indeed, the findings suggest that these and related concerns were heightened by the pace of urbanization and could be expressed more easily once parole became available.

The final element of the southern industrial economy was the racial composition of urban areas. In the nineteenth century, the black urban population grew slightly; in the twentieth, it declined sharply. Nineteenth-century increases threatened the supply of agrarian labor and public safety in urban areas. Presumably, twentieth-century declines alleviated both concerns. Thus,

6. The punishment of black men will intensify with nineteenth-century increases in the size of the black urban population. Their punishment will moderate with twentieth-century declines in the black urban population.

The black urban population played a role that was both circumscribed and unexpected. Its impacts were confined to the punishment of the most numerous black offenders, those convicted of property crimes. Contrary to expectation, nineteenth-century growth in the black urban population failed to intensify punishment. Instead, it prompted the imposition of unexpectedly shorter sentences. It is possible that nineteenth-century growth in the black urban population was simply too slight (under 3 percent) and localized to find expression in the sanctions imposed on all black offenders. The source of lenience remains a puzzle, however. Most felons convicted in the nineteenth century came from rural counties, some of which lost population to urban areas. In the heaviest cotton-producing areas, then, agrarian labor shortages could well have been acute enough to prompt lenience toward nonviolent offenders.

Twentieth-century declines in the black urban population did not invariably prompt greater lenience in the treatment of black men. Newly admitted property offenders quickly benefited; they received slightly shorter sentences. But declines in the black urban population had delayed implications for black property offenders already in prison: they found release more difficult to obtain. Even as the sharp

240

exodus of blacks from urban areas alleviated fears about public safety, it could well have generated other concerns. What if newly released offenders returned to urban places seeking employment? What if more convict labor was needed for urban public works? Restricting release could allay both concerns by lengthening the forceful expropriation of black convict labor. What remains unknown, however, is why restrictions on release rather than higher admissions or longer sentences were the preferred mechanism for addressing these concerns.

Although shifts in the black urban population seldom operated as expected, it merits emphasis that they were even more peripheral to punishment than were other dimensions of the industrial economy. As noted earlier, only the punishments imposed on black property offenders reacted to changes in the black urban population. They did so neither quickly nor forcefully.

In sum, the southern industrial economy, like its agrarian counterpart, shaped the punishment of black and white offenders selectively and inconsistently. Industrialization was more firmly implicated in the punishment of white men; urbanization, in the punishment of black men. Yet neither facet of the industrial economy exercised a simple, straightforward influence. The advent of parole dramatically altered their role in punishment, expanding it to include a wider range of offenders, whose punishments were often taken in unexpected directions.

Interracial Competition

The economic chasm that divided blacks and whites gradually closed during the period under study. This narrowing of racial inequality generated three expectations about the link between punishment and changes in the magnitude of racial inequality. Overall,

1. Punishment will grow more severe as racial inequality declines.

Racial inequality played a major though limited role in punishment. As expected, declining inequality increased admissions to the penitentiary. The strength of its impact rivaled that exerted by other economically related factors, such as the cotton economy and economic crises. Yet its influence ended with admissions. Inequality had virtually no impact on sentences or release.

The literature suggested that the general relationship between inequality and punishment should vary in strength as a dual function of race and offense. To the extent that reductions in racial inequality threaten white hegemony, repressive actions disproportionately targeting blacks should ensue. To the extent that declines in inequality imply that the economic position of at least some whites has weakened, whites too should become more vulnerable to the exercise of formal social control. Much like more general economic conditions and events, then,

241

declines in racial inequality should affect the punishment of blacks and whites, but they should be more salient for the more vulnerable of the two groups. Declining inequality should also be more salient for property offenders, whose crimes threaten the economic order most directly. Thus,

2. The link between racial inequality and punishment will be stronger for blacks and for property offenders.

Only part of this expectation was supported. Inequality was clearly more central to the punishment of black men than of white men. Declines in inequality altered neither the admission of white men to the penitentiary nor the terms imposed on whites sentenced to serve time. In fact, inequality influenced the punishment of whites only once, encouraging the release of white violent offenders. This influence was weak, however, and lagged well behind general economic conditions and the cotton economy. Thus, there was no evidence that whites grew increasingly subject to formal social control as their relative economic position worsened.

Contrary to expectation, racial inequality was not more central to the punishment of property offenders. In fact, declines in racial inequality accounted for more of the unexplained variation in the incarceration of black men for violence than for theft or burglary. Its single impact on the punishment of whites also specifically targeted violent offenders. Like weaknesses in the cotton economy, then, inequality had greater repercussions for the punishment of violent offenders.

The final expectation addresses changes in the relationship between inequality and punishment over time. The underlying supposition is that nineteenth-century declines in racial inequality were more threatening because they constituted an initial challenge to traditional caste distinctions. Thus,

3. The link between inequality and punishment will be stronger in the nineteenth century than in the twentieth century.

As expected, inequality exerted its most vigorous influence closest to the postbellum period. During most of the twentieth century, when declines in inequality were precipitous, racial inequality was irrelevant.

In sum, reductions in the magnitude of racial inequality tended to intensify punishment, especially in the nineteenth century. Yet only one punishment, admission to the penitentiary, responded to changes in inequality. Black men did indeed bear the brunt of declining inequality; whites experienced no disadvantage. Property offenders, however, did not bear a disproportionate share of the harshness associated with lower racial inequality. Like the cotton economy, racial inequality exercised its strongest influence on the treatment of violent offenders. Once again, race dictated the nature of that influence. In this instance, white violent offenders were at a slight advantage, and black violent offenders were at a clear disadvantage.

Economic Crises

In the aggregate, economic downturns had pervasive and strong consequences for each dimension of punishment and for all offenders. Yet their precise role varied by race, offense, and the facet of punishment under consideration. Economic crises exercised their weakest influence on black admissions to the penitentiary and their strongest influence on the release of black and white offenders. Nineteenth-century crises were more pivotal to the admission of black men and to the sentences imposed on both black and white offenders. Twentieth-century crises, in contrast, were more central to the admission of white men and to their subsequent release.

Although each punishment responded to a slightly different set of depressions and recessions, none reacted to more than a selected few downturns. As a result, no single depression or recession played a pivotal role across all three punishments. Of the six depressions, for example, three exerted consistent influences. Yet even here, their influence never encompassed both races and all dimensions of punishment. The severe depression of 1873–79 triggered the admission of more black and white men to prison for both violent and property offenses. Its role in setting prison sentences was limited; its role in determining release was nonexistent. The depression of 1882–84 was relevant only for black men. While it discouraged their admission to the penitentiary, it lengthened the sentences imposed on those blacks who were admitted to prison. The same depression held no significance for the release of black offenders. Finally, the Great Depression was more relevant for white men, encouraging their admission to and release from prison. In contrast, it had no implications for the prison terms imposed on white offenders.

Many recessions were also linked with punishment, but none exercised a pervasive influence. Like the depression of 1882–84, the recession of 1895–97 was more critical to the punishment of black men. On the one hand, it put them at an advantage by lowering their risk of being imprisoned. On the other hand, the recession disadvantaged incarcerated black offenders by lengthening sentences and discouraging release. Though less forceful, the recession of 1923–24 was also more important for blacks than for whites. It too discouraged admissions and lengthened the terms of those imprisoned. Yet, unlike its nineteenth-century counterpart, the 1923–24 recession benefited black offenders in a second sense by stimulating their release.

As noted above, white punishments reacted more strongly, if selectively, to twentieth-century recessions. The 1910–12 recession, for example, placed whites at a disadvantage in two respects: it simulated their admission to the penitentiary and discouraged their release. It was of little consequence for the length of time that white offenders were sentenced to serve. Of all recessions, the downturn between 1937 and 1938 exerted the strongest influence on white punishment. At the same time, its impact was restricted to the release of white offenders.

The remaining recessions affected punishment even more sporadically. The recession of 1899–1900, for example, encouraged the release of black offenders, but did little else. The recession of 1926–27 triggered lenient sentences and discouraged release from prison, but operated this way only for black property offenders. Other recessions (1902–4, 1913–14, 1918–19) were totally irrelevant to punishment. In sum, then, no single recession or depression exercised a pervasive influence on punishment. Impacts were invariably limited to a subset of offenders and to one or two facets of punishment. The rest of this section focuses attention on the substance of these impacts and their support for expectations about the precise relationship between economic crises and punishment.

The first expectation is the most straightforward. It argues that

1. Depressions and recessions will intensify punishment.

Support for this expectation was complicated by race, which sharply dictated whether a crisis would trigger the expected harshness. Declines in the business cycle tended to make the punishment of black men more selective, restricting it to fewer offenders, who were treated more harshly than before. In contrast, economic declines made the punishment of white men more indiscriminate, expanding it to include more whites than had been the case during more settled economic conditions. Though wider, the net cast over whites was also more shallow than before: whites admitted to the penitentiary were treated more leniently.

Economic downturns had more ambiguous implications for the subsequent release of both white and black offenders. Some downturns discouraged release. The recession of 1895–97, for example, inhibited the release of black offenders, whereas the recession of 1937–38 performed the same role for white offenders. Other crises encouraged release. Most notably, the Great Depression encouraged the release of both black and white offenders. The recession of 1899–1900, in contrast, benefited only black offenders. In sum, then, economic crises did not uniformly intensify punishment. Their precise role depended on the race of the offender and the sanction under consideration.

Underlying the next hypothesis is the supposition that depressions and recessions differ primarily in degree rather than in kind. As the more intense of the two downturns, depressions will have more pronounced repercussions on punishment than will recessions. In short,

244

2. Depressions will exert stronger and more consistent influences on punishment than recessions.

Support for this hypothesis was weak. Depressions seldom exerted a more dominant influence than recessions over punishment. For example, depressions were only slightly more influential than recessions in predicting the rate at which black men were admitted to the penitentiary. In contrast, each type of crisis was likely to encourage the admission of white men. The severity of the downturn also did not guarantee that it would exert an especially forceful impact on prison sentences. Only the terms imposed on black violent offenders reacted more sharply to depressions than to milder recessions. Finally, only one depression (1929–33) consistently affected release from prison, and for the most part it was less influential than a variety of recessions. In short, then, the severity of a downturn was no guarantee that punishment would react either consistently or sharply.

The next expectation focuses on intense downturns and their duration. The underlying presumption is that, at some point, lengthy depressions strain social control capabilities. Thus,

3. Punishment will moderate during protracted depressions.

Again, there was little evidence to support this hypothesis. Rarely did a lengthy depression generate more lenient punishment. In fact, only once did admissions fall in the midst of a long depression. Fewer black men were imprisoned during the 1882–84 depression. Similarly, only once did sentences shorten in response to a growing fiscal crisis. Two years after the onset of the 1873–79 depression, black violent offenders received longer sentences; the following year, their sentences became more lenient. Finally, only the Great Depression consistently encouraged the release of black and white offenders. Race determined who would receive more of its benefits. All offenders benefited from the Great Depression, but whites benefited more quickly and for longer periods.

Not limited to depressions, the potential for lenience was to be found in many downturns of varying duration and intensities. Whether that potential became a reality depended on race, offense, and the punishment involved. Fewer blacks were admitted to the penitentiary not only during the depths of the 1882–84 depression but also during a brief albeit severe depression and two moderately intense recessions. A variety of serious crises, varying primarily in duration, had the capability to jeopardize the resources needed to maintain or expand the punishment of black men. In contrast, none inhibited the admission of white men to the penitentiary. Instead, several economic crises, whose intensity and duration varied dramatically, moderated the sentences imposed on incarcerated white men. Some white

245

offenders benefited toward the end of short depressions and recessions. This was the case for white offenders sentenced in 1888, white property offenders sentenced in 1891, and white violent offenders sentenced in 1921. Other white offenders benefited quickly at the very onset of an economic downturn. This was the case for white violent offenders sentenced in 1887 and white property offenders sentenced in 1893 and 1910. Fewer downturns moderated the sentences imposed on black offenders, and they extended lenience only to blacks convicted of property offenses. Nevertheless, these crises were just as diverse as those that prompted the lenient treatment of white offenders.

Finally, the business declines that stimulated the release of black and white offenders ranged widely from a mild recession to a brief, intense depression. For example, with the onset of the 1899–1900 recession, black property and violent offenders found release easier to obtain. White convicts were the beneficiaries of higher release rates during the 1937–38 recession. Once again, race determined who would receive more of the benefits bestowed by a decline in the business cycle. All offenders benefited from an occasional recession, but black convicts benefited more often than white convicts. White offenders, in contrast, benefited less often and typically only after experiencing fewer releases the previous year. In short, the severity of a crisis seldom predicted the appearance of lenient treatment. Instead, lenience was a consequence of a selective though wide array of milder crises, where it was not always reserved for white offenders.

The next two hypotheses focus on the ways in which race and offense alter the relationship between economic crises and punishment. The greater economic vulnerability of black men generated the expectation that

4. Economic crises will have stronger and more consistent impacts on black punishment than on white punishment.

In general, neither the burdens nor the benefits of economic crises fell disproportionately on the shoulders of black offenders. For the admissions process, whites bore more of the burdens associated with economic crises than did blacks. Depressions and recessions generated significantly greater reductions in unexplained variance for white admissions in general and white property admissions in particular. This put whites at a comparative disadvantage because economic crises prompted higher admissions more consistently for whites than for blacks.

The sentences imposed on black offenders also did not react more consistently and forcefully to changes in economic conditions. This was true only for black violent offenders, who bore a disproportionate amount of the harshness associated with economic downturns. Among property offenders, whites suffered disproportionately. Economic crises affected their sentences more forcefully and tended to trigger more severe terms of imprisonment. The sentences imposed on black property offenders reacted less sharply to economic downturns but tended to become more lenient.

Finally, the release of black offenders from the penitentiary reacted more forcefully to declines in the business cycle than did the release of white offenders. Again, however, black offenders were not always at a disadvantage. As noted above, all offenders benefited from the Great Depression, but white convicts, especially those convicted of property crimes, benefited more quickly and for longer periods. All offenders benefited from an occasional recession, but black convicts, especially those convicted of violence, benefited more than comparable white convicts.

In concert with offense, then, race determined the magnitude and substance of the role played by economic crises in determining punishment. In general, declines in the business cycle had greater repercussions for the punishment imposed on two groups of offenders: blacks convicted of violence and whites convicted of theft and burglary. Neither group was consistently harmed during downturns in the business cycle, however. Newly admitted offenders tended to receive longer sentences, but their counterparts already in prison benefited by achieving release more easily. Like the political economy, then, economic crises induced harshness in one punishment only to offset it by lenience in another.

Underlying the next hypothesis, which addresses offense differences in role of economic downturns, is the supposition that economic crises lower tolerance levels for theft and burglary, thereby strengthening their ability to affect the punishment of property offenders. Thus,

5. Economic crises will have stronger and more consistent impacts on the punishment of property than of violent offenders.

Support for this expectation was confined to punishments imposed on white men. The imprisonment of white men for property offenses responded to economic crises more often and more forcefully than their imprisonment for violence. The same was true for prison sentences and release. It merits emphasis that the stronger link between economic downturns and punishment did not invariably put white property offenders at a comparative disadvantage. Indeed, selected economic crises benefited white property offenders more than white violent offenders, by inducing shorter sentences and release. The 1890–91 recession, for example, lengthened the sentences imposed on white property and violent offenders. Ultimately, white property offenders benefited because only they received shorter sentences the year after the recession began. The Great Depression triggered the release of both property and violent offenders. Yet it did so more quickly and sharply for white property offenders. The ensuing recession (1937–38) initially inhibited the release of both property and violent offenders. Once again, white property offenders ultimately benefited because more were released the year after the recession began.

For whites, then, the distinction between property and violent crime was essential to an understanding of the role that economic crises played during punishment. For blacks, the distinction was less central. That is, economic crises were equally important and played similar roles in the punishment of property and violent offenders. Only for prison sentences did offense differences emerge. Economic crises played an expanded and qualitatively different role for the sentences imposed on violent offenders. They tended to lengthen the sentences imposed on black violent offenders. In contrast, economic crises benefited black property offenders by shortening their sentences.

In sum, economic downturns had widespread consequences for each facet of punishment and each group of offenders. They did not uniformly intensify punishment, however. Severe crises were not invariably more crucial than milder downturns. This was the case only for one sanction imposed on one group of offenders, namely, the sentences imposed on black violent offenders. Economic crises that were both severe and prolonged did not always prompt lenience. It was more often the case that lenience surfaced during economic downturns that varied in both severity and duration. Finally, neither blacks nor property offenders consistently bore a disproportionate share of the severity that depressions and recessions often (though not always) precipitated.

Apart from a direct influence, there is evidence to indicate that declines in the business cycle influenced punishment indirectly as well. Economic crises sharply affected the operation of the political economy, which, as we have already seen, determined the amount and severity of punishment (see appendix A). Economic crises also appear to have influenced the strength and direction of the relationship between social changes and punishment. For example, the tendency for falling cotton prices to trigger the admission of more black men to the penitentiary grew stronger during two of the most serious nineteenth-century depressions. At the same time, the tendency for lower prices to lengthen prison sentences grew weaker during the depressions of the 1880s and 1890s. A smaller harvest had the anticipated effect of generating longer sentences for black offenders only during the good-roads movement (1895–1914). Punishments also tended to regulate each other more often during this period. Noted for its public support for convict labor to improve the state's infrastructure, this period also encompassed two severe depressions and five recessions. In addition to direct impacts, then, the findings indicate that declines in the business cycle exercised less visible but equally crucial influences on punishment.

World War I and Its Aftermath

Previous research guided the development of three expectations about the role that war would play during punishment. For reasons outlined in chapter 4,

1. Punishment will grow less severe with America's entry into World War I.

There was clear support for this expectation. America's entry into the war generated lenience by selectively lowering admissions to the penitentiary. Nevertheless, its role in punishment was narrow. The declaration of war prompted no lenience during sentencing nor any increase in releases. For these outcomes, the onset of the war itself was relevant, if only for some offenders. World War I put black property offenders at an immediate disadvantage by lengthening their prison sentences. At the same time, the war benefited white violent offenders because it encouraged shorter sentences and their release.

The next hypothesis focuses on the end of the war and subsequent demobilization. Unsettled economic conditions and problematic race and labor relations generated the expectation that

2. Punishment will grow more severe with postwar demobilization.

There was support for this expectation as well. Yet, like the war itself, demobilization played a narrow role in punishment. Only admissions to the penitentiary rose with demobilization. Sentences reacted unexpectedly; release from prison reacted not at all. Whites convicted of theft and burglary received unexpectedly shorter sentences in 1919, but the precise source of this lenience is unknown. A brief, moderate recession accompanied demobilization. Like its prewar (1910–12) equivalent, the recession of 1918–19 could have been responsible for the lenience that white property offenders received.

The final hypothesis addresses the salience of race, which shaped one's position in the war and its aftermath. Black men were at greater risk of being conscripted and more likely to suffer the social and economic dislocations that followed the war. For this reason,

3. World War I and demobilization will have stronger and more consistent impacts on the punishment of blacks than of whites.

The punishment of black men did indeed react more powerfully to America's involvement in the war and the aftermath of its participation. America's entry into the war had no implications for the admission of white men to the penitentiary, the

249

sentences imposed on those admitted, or the release of white offenders already in prison. As noted earlier, the war itself was relevant for the punishment of white men. Although less forceful than other social changes and events, its impact was unexpected in two respects. First, repercussions were confined to the most serious offenders: white men convicted of violence. Second, they actually redounded to the benefit of these offenders. The onset of war triggered an immediate increase in their release and a delayed reduction in their sentences. Although unexpected, the war's influence was comparatively slight, reducing unexplained variance by less than 10 percent. Thus, each impact lagged well behind virtually all other social changes and events.

Overall, then, expectations about America's involvement in World War I and its aftermath were supported. As anticipated, America's entry into the war was more central to black than to white punishment, where it placed blacks at a comparative advantage. Also as expected, postwar demobilization was more central to black than to white punishment, where it placed blacks at a comparative disadvantage. Yet each event—America's entry into the war and demobilization—exercised an extremely limited influence on punishment, confining its role to penitentiary admissions. Other dimensions of punishment reacted, if only mildly and intermittently, to the onset of the war itself. The declaration of war placed the most numerous black offenders, those convicted of property crimes, at a comparative disadvantage. At the same time, it placed the most serious white offenders, those convicted of violence, at a comparative advantage.

Policies

The literature provided comparatively little guidance about the relevance of state and federal actions to punishment. Of interest in this study were five policy changes for which reasonable expectations could be developed: the introduction of parole in 1908, abolition of the lease in 1909, the advent of adult probation in 1913, and passage of two federal acts, the Federal Aid Road Act in 1916 and the Agricultural Adjustment Act in 1933. As we will see, policies rarely exerted the influence that characterized broader social changes and events.

The previous literature suggested that parole could be a useful tool for curbing prison expansion in rural states with low revenues (Sutton 1987). Yet the state of Georgia, with its generally robust demand for convict labor, could well have feared prison expansion less than a shortage of convict labor. The use of parole had the potential to destabilize punishment by prompting the release of too many offenders. This reasoning underlies the expectation that

1. Parole will increase admission rates and lengthen prison sentences.

There was no direct support for this hypothesis. Parole had no implications for admissions to the penitentiary, nor did it alter the sentences imposed on black and white offenders. Instead, parole played an indirect role in the release process by giving officials an opportunity to consider external events and changes when determining whether conditional release was warranted. Inadvertently, then, parole limited expansion of the black inmate population by enhancing the role of cotton price, whose decline increased the conditional release of black offenders in general and black property offenders in particular. Parole placed similar limits on expansion by increasing the weight attached to industrialization, which encouraged the conditional release of black violent offenders. Just as inadvertently, however, parole encouraged expansion of the white inmate population. It did so by enhancing the role of industrialization, urbanization, and age of the admitted cohort, each of which discouraged the conditional release of some, if not all, white offenders from prison. Indirectly, then, parole curbed the expansion of the black inmate population, while encouraging growth in its much smaller white counterpart.

The second policy was abolition of the lease, which occurred at the height of the good-roads movement in 1909. An integral component of this movement, which encouraged the expansion of rural roads for economic development, was the use of convicts as the primary source of road labor. The implications of abolition were therefore unclear: it could either continue or escalate the forceful expropriation of convict labor. As a result,

2. Abolition of the lease either will be irrelevant to punishment or will intensify the sanctions imposed on black and white offenders.

The findings support the notion of a seamless transition from private to public exploitation of convict labor. Abolition of the lease exerted but a single influence, prompting a slight decline in the admission of black men to the penitentiary for property offenses. While not strong, the finding nevertheless suggests the presence of a short-term ceiling on the number of black convicts that counties could accommodate for road-building purposes.

The third policy change was the availability of adult probation, instituted in 1913. Its implications for punishment were limited and straightforward:

3. Probation will lower admissions to the penitentiary, especially the admission of white men.

4. To the extent that probation, as an alternative to incarceration, raised concerns about the supply of able-bodied prisoners, it should trigger a short-term reduction in release rates.

Support for these expectations was weak. Probation reduced white admissions to the penitentiary; it exercised no influence on the admission of black men. Yet its inhibitory influence on white admissions was both trivial and limited to admissions for violence. Moreover, probation had no consequences for the release of white offenders. Its only substantial effect was limited to the punishment of black property offenders, who received shorter sentences in the year that probation was instituted. As noted in chapter 4, no direct link between probation and sentences was expected. The general context of the results yields an alternative, more plausible explanation of the finding. Twentieth-century depressions and recessions uniformly triggered the imposition of shorter sentences on black property offenders. The advent of probation coincided with a moderately intense recession, which lasted nearly two years and led to a 23 percent reduction in business activity. This recession, rather than probation per se, probably accounts for the lenience that black property offenders suddenly experienced in 1913.

Underlying our interest in the fourth policy, the Federal Aid Road Act, is the supposition that it stimulated the demand for convict labor, especially the untapped source of white labor, to build and maintain roads. This supposition generated two hypotheses:

5. Punishment will grow more severe with passage of the Federal Aid Road Act.
6. The link between the Federal Aid Road Act and punishment will be stronger for white than for black offenders.

As expected, the Federal Aid Road Act was more significant for the punishment of white than of black men. Nevertheless, it did not consistently induce harsh punishment. Rather, it induced punishments that were selectively harsh. With passage, fewer white men were admitted to the penitentiary, but those who were admitted received longer terms of imprisonment. Releases remained the same. Overall, then, the Federal Aid Road Act played a narrow role during punishment. More important, its role was barely noticeable because it never produced more than a 5 percent reduction in unexplained variance.

The final policy, the Agricultural Adjustment Act (AAA), was the most influential. Designed to raise farm prices by lowering production, the AAA ultimately displaced tenants and sharecroppers. In this respect, the AAA behaved much like the lengthy depression that spawned it. Hence, expectations about its impact mirror those developed for protracted depressions:

7. Punishment will initially grow more severe, then more lenient, with passage of the Agricultural Adjustment Act.

8. The AAA will have stronger and more consistent impacts on the punishment of blacks and of property offenders.

Overall, there was support for the expectation that passage of the AAA would initially intensify punishment, only to moderate it later. Like most policies, however, the AAA tended to affect a single dimension of punishment. Its most notable influence was confined to prison releases, which thus far had been insensitive to state and federal policies. Contrary to expectation, black men did not bear the brunt of the act's impact on punishment. Two years after passage, more white men were admitted to the penitentiary for violence. The admission of black men, in contrast, remained unchanged. Based on its ability to reduce more unexplained variation, the AAA also exercised a stronger influence on the release of whites than of blacks.

Contrary to expectation, property offenders did not bear the brunt of the AAA's impact on punishment. More white men were incarcerated for violence, but admissions for property crimes were unaltered. The AAA put white property offenders at a comparative disadvantage only by withholding the benefits it extended to white violent offenders. One year after passage, fewer white property and violent offenders were released from the penitentiary. Two years after passage, the AAA triggered the release only of white violent offenders. The act put black property offenders at a comparative disadvantage only by delaying both its burdens (viz., lower release rates) and its benefits (viz., higher release rates).

In sum, then, the actions taken by state and federal officials usually exercised minor and sporadic influences on punishment. Even the most consequential, the Agricultural Adjustment Act, was relevant primarily to a single aspect of punishment: release from the penitentiary. There was scant support for the expectation that race and offense would shape the role that policies played during punishment. Probation and the Federal Aid Road Act were more consequential for the punishment of white than of black men. Yet their influence was either trivial or coincidental. Contrary to expectation, the AAA was more relevant to the punishment of white and violent offenders than to their black and property counterparts.

Young Male Population

Inherently ambiguous, the size of the youthful male population measures two discrete if related phenomena: the potential pool of manual laborers and levels of criminal behavior. Thus, a decline in the population of young black men could signify a shortage of agrarian labor or a reduction in criminality. Underlying the following hypothesis is the presumption that the more salient information concerns a possible labor shortage, which intensifies efforts to expropriate black labor forcefully:

1. The punishment of black offenders will grow more severe as the population of young black men declines.

Although present, support for this expectation was modest. As the size of the young black population fell, black offenders received longer sentences. Overall, the relationship was tenuous. Reducing unexplained variance by only 8 percent, the youthful black population lagged well behind other factors in significance. Changes in the youthful black population, then, were more tangential to the punishment of black men than originally expected.

A decline in the population of young white men raised fewer concerns about the supply of field labor. Underlying the following hypothesis, then, is the presumption that the most salient information contained in a declining population of young white men is a reduction in white criminality. As a result,

2. The punishment of white offenders will grow less severe as the population of young white men declines.

A decline in the youthful population did indeed moderate the sentences imposed on white offenders as a whole. Considerably delayed, this impact grew weaker over time and regained its influence only toward the end of the Great Depression. Once violent and property offenders were separated, more immediate and unanticipated relationships emerged. Slight declines in the youthful population coincided, first, with the immediate imposition of unexpectedly *longer* sentences on white violent offenders. Second, they triggered a delayed increase in the sentences imposed on white property offenders. Recall that these tendencies surfaced for black offenders. Their presence for white offenders casts doubt on the argument that the most salient information conveyed by the youthful white population pertained to levels of their criminality.

Only during the late nineteenth and early twentieth centuries did one group of white offenders, those convicted of property offenses, receive the longer sentences that I had originally expected. This period was exceptional because it included not only noticeable growth in the youthful population (from 15.6 percent in 1890 to 17.2 percent in 1910). It also encompassed a series of depressions and recessions, the good-roads movement, and black outmigration. In and of itself, then, an increase in the youthful white population did not intensify punishment. It behaved as expected only when the increase exceeded a certain threshold and dovetailed with events that both enhanced the potential for youthful criminality and allowed, if not encouraged, the penitentiary to absorb growth in white criminality.

Absent these circumstances, it remains unclear why slight growth in the youthful white population should moderate punishment. Demographic changes clearly affected the age and seriousness of offenders incarcerated. As the size of the young white male population grew larger, for example, younger and less serious white property offenders were imprisoned. Presumably, these offenders would have received shorter sentences. Preliminary analysis, reported in appendix A, incorporated these indirect influences, however. Moreover, we will soon see that a youthful cohort did not receive shorter sentences. Thus, the logic underlying the findings remains obscure. Interpretation is hampered by the inherent defects of age as a measure of white criminality. While it may reflect an increase in crime, the age composition of the male population conveys no information about the size of the increase or the types of crimes involved. Interpretation is also hampered by the imprecision inherent in census data on shifts in the population. In essence, change in the size of the youthful population is based on eight figures, each taken at ten-year intervals. To an unknown degree, interpolation distorts the magnitude if not the direction of changes that actually occurred between decades.

Although difficult to interpret, the findings indicate clearly that changes in the youthful population were more directly relevant to the punishment of whites than of blacks. Nevertheless, they often exercised the same influence on both black and white offenders. Growth moderated punishment, while declines induced harsher punishment. For whites, this influence grew apparent only after violent and property offenders underwent separate examination. Nevertheless, the general tendency for growth to prompt lenient treatment masked an exceptional period during which noticeable growth dovetailed with several other circumstances to prompt more punitive sanctions, directed exclusively at white property offenders.

Composition of Admitted Offenders

The analysis examined two attributes of offenders admitted to the penitentiary: their average seriousness and their average age. The expected link between seriousness and punishment is straightforward:

1. Punishment will grow more severe as more serious offenders are imprisoned.

The findings strongly supported this hypothesis. On average, sentences became proportionately longer simply because a larger proportion of offenders admitted to the penitentiary were convicted of serious offenses. Yet both race and offense affected the strength of the relationship and its trajectory over time. For example, the link between seriousness and the prison sentences imposed on black offenders was immediate, strong, and stable over time. The link for white offenders was equally immediate, but it dissipated slowly and became less powerful. By the 1920s, seriousness exercised an influence that was only half as strong as it had been in the nineteenth century. Offense conditioned the impact of seriousness as well. For violent offenders, seriousness was the major determinant of prison sentences. For property offenders, its influence was dramatically weaker. Nowhere was this clearer than for white offenders. Seriousness reduced the unexplained variance in the sentences imposed on violent offenders by 62 percent and in property offenders by less than 7 percent.

Not surprisingly, seriousness exercised its primary influence on prison sentences. Its role during the release process was more limited. Only for white property offenders was there support for the expectation that the admission of more serious offenders would discourage release. The admission of a more serious cohort of black property offenders quickly triggered the opposite response: the immediate release of more black property offenders. Taken together, these findings suggest that the logic underlying the link between cohort seriousness and the release decision is incomplete. The admission of more serious white property offenders may well have reduced the number of white property convicts eligible for release. It could also have increased the salience of a general deterrent message. But the admission of more serious black property offenders could have sent an altogether different signal. Compared with the current pool of convicts, the youth, robustness, and longer sentences imposed on more serious property offenders signaled a possible improvement in the quality of the convict labor force as a whole. The admission of more reliable labor could have provided the pretext for releasing older property convicts who had outlived their usefulness as laborers.

In sum, the admission of more serious offenders generally prompted more severe punishment. Sentences responded more often and more consistently to the admission of a serious cohort; release from prison responded less often and inconsistently. In both cases, the precise response depended on race and offense. The sentences imposed on black and violent offenders were more sensitive to offense seriousness than were the sentences imposed on their white and property counterparts. In contrast, the release of white property offenders depended more heavily and quite differently on seriousness than did the release of black property offenders.

Three hypotheses framed consideration of the second attribute of admitted offenders. Underlying the first was the presumption that entrepreneurs and counties would find a younger cohort of black offenders more useful as laborers than an older cohort. As a result,

2. A youthful cohort of black offenders will receive longer sentences.

The findings failed to support this logic. A younger cohort of black offenders never suffered for their youthfulness. Instead, property offenders who were admitted two years after a younger cohort were at a disadvantage. They received longer sentences. It is possible that counties and private entrepreneurs found young offenders less capable than older offenders of performing the difficult manual labor dictated by the lease or public works. To compensate for the loss of labor that a younger cohort implied, judges may have imposed longer sentences on later cohorts. An equally plausible interpretation is that judges imposed longer sentences on later cohorts as a delayed deterrent response to youthful crime.

Different reasoning informed the expected relationship between a youthful white cohort and their subsequent punishment. Presumably, younger white offenders were more reformable and less useful as laborers. As a result,

3. A youthful cohort of white offenders will receive shorter sentences.

The findings also failed to support this logic. Younger cohorts of white offenders received neither lenience nor severity. Rather, subsequent cohorts were placed at either an advantage or a disadvantage, depending on their offense and when they were imprisoned. The most immediate response to the admission of a younger cohort of violent offenders was to impose shorter sentences on violent offenders admitted two years later. This lenience was offset the following year by the imposition of longer sentences on the incoming cohort of white violent offenders. In contrast, the most immediate reaction to the admission of a younger cohort of white property offenders was to impose *longer* sentences on property offenders admitted two years later. This severity was offset the following year by the imposition of shorter sentences on the incoming cohort of white property offenders. For the most part, these opposing tendencies were hallmarks of the nineteenth century and became less pronounced in the twentieth century.

As noted above for black offenders, harshness directed at offenders admitted after an especially young cohort could reflect a delayed deterrent response to youthful crime. For white offenders, this interpretation is incomplete and leaves most questions unanswered. If harshness was designed to serve a deterrent function, why did less serious offenders, those convicted of property crimes, receive it more quickly than did more serious violent offenders? Were crimes of property considered more amenable to deterrence than those of violence? Or was there continued tolerance of violent crimes between whites? If, for whatever reason, a quicker deterrent response was warranted for property offenders, why was it offset by lenience toward the succeeding cohort? Did earlier punitiveness (viz., longer sentences and fewer releases, discussed below) strain social control capacities to a point where deterrence issues lost relevance? Finally, if there was continued tolerance of white violence, why was lenience, the most immediate reaction to the admission of a youthful cohort of violent offenders, quickly offset by harsher sentences? Answers to these questions clearly require a more complex explanation than general deterrence can give.

Underlying the final hypothesis is the presumption that the admission of noticeably younger offenders may also increase the salience of the deterrent function
of punishment. As a result,

4. The admission of a youthful cohort of offenders will discourage release from the
penitentiary.

There was some evidence to support this reasoning, but only for white offenders. Immediately upon the admission of a younger cohort of white property offenders, their counterparts already in prison found release more difficult to obtain.
Once parole was available, support for the hypothesis strengthened. The admission of a younger cohort limited the *conditional* release not only of white property
offenders but also of white men convicted of violence. If the results reflect the
operation of deterrence, they suggest that the use of release to serve a deterrent
function was limited to white offenders, where it became more salient once authorities had the discretion to release offenders conditionally.

In their entirety, the findings for age and seriousness cast doubt on a simplistic
or commonsense relationship between punishment and the character of offenders
admitted to the penitentiary. Seriousness had sharply different consequences for
the punishment of violent and property offenders. Not surprisingly, its tight coupling with the sentences imposed on violent offenders suggests the exercise of little
discretion during the sentencing of the state's most serious offenders. Its loose
coupling with the punishment of property offenders implies the exercise of considerably more discretion. The more surprising feature of these findings is the extent
to which the same relationship between seriousness and punishment varied over
time. That is, even when punishing the same group of offenders, the exercise of
discretion was not a constant phenomenon. This was especially the case for two
groups of offenders: black men convicted of violence and white men convicted of
theft and burglary. Until World War I, the seriousness of the offense became
increasingly less crucial to decisions about the appropriate sentences that black
violent offenders should receive. After World War I, seriousness grew increasingly
more central to these decisions. The reverse was the case for white property offenders. Many factors could account for these shifts in the relationship between
seriousness and punishment. External events could divert attention from seriousness. Qualitative differences among cohorts could redirect attention to seriousness.
For the moment, the precise reasons for the variation must remain hidden. Of
greater import at this point is empirical documentation of two phenomena: temporal shifts in the bond between seriousness and punishment and the central role
played by race and offense in conditioning the presence and magnitude of those

shifts. Both phenomena serve as forcible reminders that factors of explicit legal relevance are as problematic and worthy of theoretical attention as those social and economic factors whose theoretical place has already been established.

The same conclusion applies to the second attribute of admitted offenders: their age. Although grounded in an understanding of postbellum punishment, simple expectations fared poorly. There was no immediate link between the admission of a youthful cohort and its punishment. General deterrence was a logical but speculative interpretation of the delayed link between the admission of younger offenders and the more intense punishment of succeeding cohorts. Yet this reason was far too general. It failed to explain why the delay was different for white property and white violent offenders, why some succeeding cohorts received lenience, and why the relationship was more pronounced in the nineteenth century when white admission rates were low and stable. Like seriousness, then, the age of offenders admitted to the penitentiary deserves more sustained attention than it has received in the past.

Stability of Punishment

Underlying the stability of punishment thesis is the argument that levels of punishment are generally stable and that stability is achieved through the use of adaptive self-regulating mechanisms. The analysis examined the extent to which self-regulation was located within the system of punishment itself. The central hypothesis argues that an increase in the severity of one punishment will be compensated for by a decrease in the severity of the other punishments.

Regulation was indeed common, but for the most part, it was weak and variable over time. Once again, race and offense shaped the extent to which punishments affected, much less regulated, one another. The punishments imposed on white offenders were slightly more likely than those imposed on comparable blacks to act in a regulatory fashion. In fact, their regulatory force extended beyond the boundaries of other white punishments to include selected black punishments. The punishments imposed on property offenders were also slightly more likely than the punishments imposed on violent offenders to regulate one another. Indeed, they were linked more often and more tightly with each other than were the punishments imposed on violent offenders.

The regulatory force of punishments must be placed within its more general context, however. In some cases, regulation was undercut by earlier or later impacts that had the opposite effect. Destabilizing influences occurred just as often as regulatory influences, and typically they exerted greater force. More often than not, however, the punishments imposed on black and white offenders were not connected and were more likely to be affected by broader social and economic changes.

259

Prospects for Theory and Research

As chapter 3 made clear, the notion of threat has unified much theorizing and empirical work on punishment. From the Durkheimian tradition arises a focus on threatening "times," that is, various events that pose general and diffuse threats to the social order. From neo-Marxian roots springs a concern with threats posed by weaknesses in the cotton and industrial economies. From the interracial conflict perspective derives an interest in threats posed by the relative position of minorities in the economic and political arenas. The ultimate purpose of the analysis was not to declare any one of these perspectives the victor but rather to obtain the fullest understanding of the linkages between punishment and social change. To that end, the models tested in previous chapters drew on the chief insights of each theoretical perspective and research that has been undertaken on its behalf. The results of these tests draw into sharp relief the strengths and weaknesses of each perspective and the distance that separates perspectives from a general theory of punishment.

The stability of punishment literature yielded two insights that proved invaluable to this study of postbellum punishment. The first was that traumatic social events and dramatic changes in policy have the potential to alter punishment fundamentally. Punishment in Georgia reacted often and sharply to cataclysmic events and, to a lesser degree, to policy changes. In the final analysis, however, punishment responded selectively and only in the short term. Only temporarily did war and demobilization, for example, affect the frequency with which the state punished (viz., admissions to the penitentiary). Both events had few implications for the severity with which the state punished (viz., prison sentences) and for the level at which the state ceased punishment (viz., release rates). Depression-era federal policies affected the cessation of punishment in the short term, but were marginally implicated in its frequency or severity. Economic downturns were more consistently important because they affected all three dimensions of punishment examined here. In a sense, though, declines in the business cycle were no different than other traumatic events. Their impacts on punishment were temporary and selective, and they depended on whether the offender was white or black, whether his crime threatened others or their property, and whether the frequency, severity, or termination of punishment was at issue.

The second insight of the stability of punishment tradition was its recognition that punishment has its own internal dynamic and may regulate itself to achieve equilibrium. To compensate for more severe punishment, for example, officials punish less often. The analysis provided evidence that postbellum punishment did indeed regulate itself in this manner. Yet this type of regulation was neither at the core nor a consistent feature of punishment in Georgia. Regulatory impacts were simply one of many influences whose appearance and force depended on a familiar

260

constellation of factors: race, offense, and the quality of punishment being imposed. Moreover, self-regulation was not the only contributor to equilibrium. Social changes and events also played a role. Falling cotton prices, for example, increased the frequency, the severity, *and* the termination of black punishment. Growth in urbanization reduced the frequency with which black men were punished for violent crime, but increased its severity. It also increased the frequency with which black men were punished for property crime, but reduced its severity. Lenience after the admission of a younger cohort of white violent offenders was offset the following year by harshness. Harshness after the admission of a younger cohort of white property offenders was offset the following year by lenience.

Equilibrating tendencies characterized the impact of selected events as well. The depression of 1882–84, for example, reduced the frequency of black punishment but increased its severity. Other cyclical declines increased the severity of punishments imposed on some newly admitted offenders, even as they terminated the punishments imposed on comparable offenders already in the penitentiary. Passage of the Federal Aid Road Act lowered the frequency with which white men were punished but increased its severity. These counterbalancing tendencies occurred with sufficient regularity to suggest that social changes and events were alternative mechanisms for regulating punishment.

The stability of punishment literature, then, drew attention to two broad factors that proved to be necessary components of an understanding of punishment in Georgia: dramatic events and the interrelations among dimensions of punishment. The political economy perspective directed attention to other factors: the cotton economy, its labor market, and the health and progress of the industrial component within an agrarian economy. This attention was also well repaid. Elements of the cotton economy were integral features of punishment in Georgia, and they remained so even as the state became more industrialized. Elements of the industrial economy were also integral features of punishment, and they became even more so as agrarian pursuits became less central to the economy. Yet even in the nineteenth century, when cotton was king, the cotton economy was never the dominant determinant of punishment. Nor was its influence consistently felt across all facets of the punishment of all types of offenders. Even in the twentieth century, when the industrial economy developed rapidly, industrialization and urbanization never dominated punishment. No less than dramatic events and other facets of punishment, then, the political economy selectively affected punishment. Again, its precise influence required a consideration of race, offense, and the nature of the sanction under examination.

The final perspective, interracial competition, drew attention to the relative economic position of blacks and whites. A focus on racial economic inequality also bore fruit, though perhaps not as rich a harvest as an emphasis on the political economy. Declines in inequality were integral only for a narrow feature of punishment, namely, the frequency with which black men were punished. Its contribution to the severity and termination of punishment was indirect. As inequality declined, for example, white men incarcerated for violence tended to be younger and their crimes less serious (see appendix A). As we have just seen, these attributes had profound consequences for the severity and the termination of punishment.

In varying degrees, then, each perspective contributed to an understanding of punishment. As broad orientations, none was totally misguided. Yet their combination in this work brought into sharp relief the distance that lies between current theorizing and a general theory of punishment (Tittle 1995). No perspective was broad enough to support the development of propositions that accounted with equal success for the frequency of punishment, its severity, and its termination through release. We have repeatedly seen that an event or social change with the highest priority for shaping one aspect of punishment could be entirely tangential to a determination of its other aspects. The journey toward a general theory of punishment, then, must begin with a determination of the qualities that distinguish the frequency of punishment from its severity and cessation. It must also specify the precise ways in which these qualities dictate the relevance of social changes and events.

In addition to a lack of breadth, no perspective was comprehensive enough to generate hypotheses that incorporated all the elements necessary for a full explanation of postbellum punishment. Even cornerstones of the political economy, with its emphasis on labor markets and economic conditions, required assistance from demographic changes, global events, and other punishments to complete the portrait of punishment. Absent from each perspective was a place for the composition of the inmate population, which predicted the severity of punishment and its termination. In conjunction with a clearer conception of punishment, then, progress toward a general theory requires a clear and coherent integration of seemingly disparate social changes and events.

Not surprisingly, each perspective also lacked the precision needed to yield hypotheses that specified accurately the conditions under which relationships altered in strength if not in direction. We have repeatedly seen that an event or social change occupied center stage for the punishment of one group of offenders, only to be marginal or completely offstage during the punishment of another group. Just as punishment itself and social events and changes require clearer conceptualization, so also do the conditions that alter the bonds connecting punishment and its social context. For this exploration, race and offense groupings were paramount conditions. Doubtless, there are others (e.g., gender, age). Yet the extent to which race and offense could condition the bond between social change and punishment depended on two other conditions: the quality of punishment and the element of time. The admissions process, in a sense, gave race free rein to determine which social changes would affect the frequency with which the state punished. The process of setting terms of imprisonment gave the offense free rein to determine which social changes would alter the severity with which the state punished. Finally, the release process allowed race and offense to conspire together and determine the extent to which social change would bring punishment to an end. These findings bring us full circle to the initial steps toward a general theory of punishment: a specification of qualitative differences among the dimensions of punishment and a determination of how and why these differences give race, offense, and other factors the opportunity to interpose themselves between social change and punishment.

Throughout this exploration, time altered the bonds between social change and punishment. In reality, however, time was little more than a surrogate for a cluster of conditions—some known, some only surmised—that in concert with one another fundamentally altered the link between social change and punishment. The search for discrete factors capable of conditioning relationships must consider the possibility that they gain their conditioning ability only at the intersection of several social changes.

Finally, no perspective proved to be deep enough to explicate the logic underlying the links between social change and punishment. Unexpected relationships were a regular feature of the findings. The multiple threats posed by the economic distress of lower cotton prices, cyclical business downturns, and labor market difficulties did not always increase the coerciveness of social control. Often they had precisely the opposite effect. Punishment was not invariably imposed more frequently or more severely on the more vulnerable of two racial groupings. Under certain circumstances, white men were at a comparative disadvantage. Unsettled economic conditions did not prompt greater intolerance toward offenders whose crimes further disturbed the economic order. Under certain circumstances and for certain punishments, violent offenders were at a comparative disadvantage. The emergence of these unexpected tendencies underscores the limitations of the logic that underpins current perspectives. Revisions of that logic are essential and may require an exploration of social changes and conditions that now lie far beyond the traditional borders of current perspectives.

Conclusion

The journey toward a general theory of punishment cannot be undertaken by merely crossing the boundaries of existing perspectives and incorporating their most salient concepts. Rather, it requires creative theorizing about punishment itself and the ways in which its components differ from and affect one another. A

263

general theory requires the incorporation not only of a comprehensive and integrated range of events and social changes. It must also include rationales that explain their relevance for punishment. Of equal importance is the identification of the range of conditions that, alone or in concert, alter the direction and strength of the bonds between each facet of punishment and each relevant event and social change.

Theorizing of this magnitude cannot proceed without the development of a broad empirical base of knowledge about past and present punishment, undertaken in a variety of contexts. To inform a general theory of punishment, research must incorporate multiple facets of punishment, explore various conditioning influences, and include the element of time. As we have seen here, insensitivity to the conditioning influence of race and offense can convey misleading impressions about the link between punishment and its context. Insensitivity to the element of time produces precisely the same result. Although essential, longitudinal research must be counterbalanced by cross-sectional research, which, like a photograph, provides invaluable details that become visible only when research requires time to stand still. Cross-sectional and longitudinal research thus form a partnership whose joint contributions lay the empirical foundation for a general theory of punishment.

Appendix A

The Relationship among
Social Change Series

THE ANALYSIS DESCRIBED BELOW ENSURES THAT THE RELATIONSHIPS between social change and punishment are accurate and nonspurious. Intervention analysis removes the impact of events from social change series. The multivariate analysis frees each social change series from the influence exerted by other social change series.

Results of the Intervention Analysis

Intervention analysis could reasonably be undertaken only for series that were measured at the annual or biennial level. These were cotton price, cotton harvest, value added by manufacturing, racial inequality, and the seriousness and age of admissions to the penitentiary. The remaining series were measured every ten years, with linear interpolation providing interim estimates. The derivation of these series made estimation of short-term impacts less meaningful.

To determine which events had impacts, I inspected the differenced series for changes in level during and after the event. The cross-correlation function between the series and the event was also a useful diagnostic tool. A spike at the second lag, for example, suggested that the event had an impact on the social change series after a delay of two years. The initial assumption was that economic crises, World War I, and demobilization generated abrupt temporary changes in the price of cotton, the size of its harvest, the value added by manufacturing, racial inequality, and the attributes of offenders admitted to the penitentiary. Each impact was therefore coded as a binary pulse variable: one for the year of onset, zero otherwise. To determine whether this impact was felt over a period of years, a first-order transfer function was estimated $[\omega/(1-\delta B)]\ X_t$. The first parameter of this function, ω, measures the magnitude of the impact. The second parameter, δ, measures how long the impact was felt before the series returned to its preexisting level. A nonsignificant δ implies that the impact evaporated quickly. In this instance, a zero-order transfer function $\omega_n X_t$, which measures only the magnitude of the impact at lag n, should be estimated. A large significant δ suggests that the event had an impact that persisted over time. If δ approaches unity ($>.95$), the effect of the event is for all practical purposes permanent, and a zero-order step function should be estimated. Unlike a pulse function, a step function is zero for all years prior to the event and one for the year of the event and all years thereafter. It tests for the presence of an abrupt permanent impact.

The first expectation was that economic crises and demobilization precipitated lower cotton prices, whereas World War I, after a period of adjustment, stimulated demand and contributed to higher prices. For the most part, the direction of impacts met expectations (table A-1). The price of cotton fell in response to the 1890–91 recession, the 1920–21 depression, and the 1926–27 recession. In contrast, prices rose a year after the onset of the 1899 recession, with the beginning of economic recovery. They also rebounded in 1916 and with America's entry into World War I in 1917. Taken together, all estimated interventions reduced the error sum of squares by over 50 percent.

Undergoing intervention analysis next was the size of the cotton harvest. Like the price of cotton, smaller harvests tended to be a consequence of economic downturns, particularly during the twentieth century. The exceptions were the recessions of 1902–4 and 1923–24. Toward the end of each crisis, the cotton harvest increased. World War I also affected the size of the harvest, precipitating a short-term reduction due to closed European markets. Taken together, these impacts reduced the error sum of squares by 54 percent.

The third input series of interest was industrialization, which was most affected by World War I and postwar depressions. Significant increases in the value added by manufacturing occurred each year between 1915 and 1917. Manufacturing became less profitable during the worst year of the depression of 1920–21 and during the initial years of the Great Depression. The final important influence was the recession of 1890–91, which triggered a decline in the value added by manufacturing. Together, economic crises and the war accounted for a 62 percent reduction in unexplained variance.

Racial inequality was the fourth input series to undergo intervention analysis. The expectation was that economic upheavals would narrow the economic gap

Table A.1 Impact of events on social change and control series

Social Change		Event	Transfer Function	Estimate	T-ratio
Cotton Price					
		1890–91 recession	ω_1	−.03	−1.91
		1899–1900 recession	ω_1	.03	2.13
		1920–21 depression	ω_1	−.07	−5.04
		1926–27 recession	ω_0	−.03	−2.09
		World War I	$\omega_2 - \omega_3$	.03	1.92
				−.04	−3.00
Original SSE	.025				
Model SSE	.012				
% SSE reduction	52.00				
Cotton Harvest					
		1902–4 recession	ω_2	.40	2.28
		1910–12 recession	ω_2	−.44	−2.54
		1920–21 depression	ω_1	−.59	−3.35
		1923–24 recession	ω_1	.54	3.06
		1929–33 depression	$\omega_3/(1 - \delta B)$	−.46	−2.84
				−.62	−3.25
		1937–38 recession	ω_1	−.54	−2.99
		World War I	ω_1	−.35	−2.02
Original SSE	4.04				
Model SSE	1.84				
% SSE reduction	54.45				
Value Added by Manufacturing					
		1890–91 recession	ω_1	−.36	−2.85
		1920–21 depression	ω_1	−.81	−6.32
		1929–33 depression	$\omega_1 - \omega_2$	−.31	−2.42
				.43	3.41
		World War I	$\omega_1 - \omega_2 - \omega_3$	.31	2.47
				−.43	−3.41
				−.50	−3.95
Original SSE	2.66				
Model SSE	1.02				
% SSE reduction	61.65				
Racial Inequality					
		1890–91 recession	ω_0	−.09	−2.14
		1895–97 recession	ω_0	.06	1.52
		1910–12 recession	ω_0	−.08	−1.93

continued

Table A.1 *continued*

Social Change		Event	Transfer Function	Estimate	*T*-ratio
		1918–19 recession	ω_0	−.09	−2.18
		Demobilization	ω_0	−.09	−2.36
Original SSE	.127				
Model SSE	.093				
% SSE reduction	26.77				
Seriousness of Black Admissions					
		1873–79 depression	ω_0	−.14	−2.39
		1882–84 depression	ω_0	.12	1.97
		1893–94 depression	ω_1	−.10	−1.71
		1895–97 recession	ω_2	.17	2.78
		Lease abolition	ω_0	.11	1.88
Original SSE	.32				
Model SSE	.23				
% SSE reduction	28.13				
Age of Black Admissions					
		1882–84 depression	ω_0	.08	3.07
		1887–88 recession	ω_1	−.08	−2.93
		1890–91 recession	ω_0	−.05	−1.95
		1895–97 recession	ω_1	−.07	−2.63
		1926–27 recession	ω_1	−.05	−2.07
		World War I	ω_1	−.05	−2.10
Original SSE	.07				
Model SSE	.04				
% SSE reduction	42.86				
Seriousness of White Admissions					
		1873–79 depression	ω_0	−.41	−2.31
		1895–97 recession	ω_0	.31	1.83
		World War I	ω_1	−.29	−1.64
Original SSE	2.46				
Model SSE	2.10				
% SSE reduction	14.63				
Age of White Admissions					
		1882–84 depression	ω_2	.26	4.49
		1890–91 recession	ω_0	.12	2.16
Original SSE	.30				
Model SSE	.22				
% SSE reduction	26.67				

continued

Table A.1 *continued*

Social Change		Event	Transfer Function	Estimate	T-ratio
Seriousness of Black Violent Admissions					
		1873–79 depression	ω_0	−.19	−2.09
		1923–24 recession	ω_1	.15	1.64
		1937–38 recession	ω_1	.15	1.65
Original SSE	.65				
Model SSE	.57				
% SSE reduction	12.31				
Age of Black Violent Admissions					
		1873–79 depression	ω_1	−.11	−3.87
		1882–84 depression	ω_0	.06	2.28
		1887–88 recession	ω_1	−.07	−2.49
		1890–91 recession	ω_0	−.06	−2.13
		1895–97 recession	ω_1	−.08	−2.94
		1929–33 depression	ω_2	−.06	−2.18
Original SSE	.10				
Model SSE	.05				
% SSE reduction	50.00				
Seriousness of White Violent Admissions					
		1873–79 depression	ω_0	−.65	−3.20
		1890–91 recession	ω_0	.52	2.58
		1895–97 recession	ω_0	.43	2.11
		World War I	ω_1	−.35	1.74
Original SSE	3.70				
Model SSE	2.70				
% SSE reduction	27.03				
Age of White Violent Admissions					
		1882–84 depression	ω_0	.39	4.46
Original SSE	.68				
Model SSE	.53				
% SSE reduction	22.06				
Seriousness of Black Property Admissions					
		1882–84 depression	ω_1	−.11	−2.32
		1899–1900 recession	ω_1	−.09	−1.89
		1923–24 recession	ω_1	−.17	−3.71
		1926–27 recession	ω_0	−.18	−3.83
		Probation	ω_0	−.11	−2.33

continued

Table A.1 *continued*

Social Change		Event	Transfer Function	Estimate	T-ratio
Original SSE	.23				
Model SSE	.14				
% SSE reduction	39.13				
Age of Black Property Admissions					
		1882–84 depression	ω_0	.08	2.56
		1887–88 recession	ω_1	−.08	−2.41
		1890–91 recession	ω_0	−.07	−2.04
		1893–94 depression	ω_0	.07	2.24
		1895–97 recession	ω_1	−.07	2.14
		1902–4 recession	ω_2	−.07	−2.14
		1920–21 depression	ω_0	−.08	−2.48
		World War I	$\omega_0 - \omega_1$	.12	3.71
				.10	3.01
Original SSE	.13				
Model SSE	.07				
% SSE reduction	46.15				
Seriousness of White Property Admissions					
		1882–84 depression	ω_2	−.21	−1.92
		1890–91 recession	$\omega_0 - \omega_1$	.39	3.53
				.44	3.95
		1902–4 recession	ω_2	−.32	−2.92
Original SSE	1.28				
Model SSE	.79				
% SSE reduction	38.28				
Age of White Property Admissions					
		1882–84 depression	ω_1	.17	2.32
		1890–91 recession	ω_0	.17	2.38
		1895–97 recession	ω_2	.34	4.60
Original SSE	.58				
Model SSE	.35				
% SSE reduction	39.67				

Note: SSE denotes error sum of squares. Series were stationary in level and variance before cross-correlations were estimated.

between blacks and whites. Several did. The recessions of 1890–91, 1910–12, and 1918–19 reduced inequality, as did demobilization (1919). Inequality became more pronounced during only one recession (1895–97). Taken as a whole, economic events and the war were relatively weak predictors, capable of reducing the error sum of squares by slightly more than 25 percent.

The final input series, attributes of offenders admitted to the penitentiary, are relevant to prison sentences and subsequent release. To the extent that economic crises heightened perceptions of threat, less serious offenders, particularly if black, should be admitted to the penitentiary. This was the case during the 1873–79 and 1893–94 depressions. In contrast, more serious black offenders were imprisoned with the onset of the 1882–84 depression and during the final year of the 1895–97 recession. The final impact on seriousness was abolition of the lease in 1909, which was accompanied by the imprisonment of more serious black offenders. Together, these impacts were not particularly strong, accounting for a modest reduction in unexplained variance (28 percent).

Economic downturns and the war were better predictors of the age of admitted felons than of their seriousness. With one exception (1882–84 depression), economic crises tended to result in the admission of younger black offenders. So did World War I. Together, these factors reduced the error sum of squares by 43 percent.

In two respects, the findings for the seriousness of white admissions resembled their black counterparts. The lengthy depression between 1873 and 1879 temporarily prompted the admission of less serious white offenders. The recession two decades later (1895–97) had the opposite effect: it generated a delayed tendency to admit more serious white offenders. World War I exerted the only remaining impact. A year after the war began, less serious white offenders were imprisoned. None of these impacts was particularly strong. Together, they generated only a slight reduction in unexplained variance (15 percent).

Recall that for black men, economic crises tended to result in the incarceration of younger offenders. For white men, they had the opposite effect, stimulating the imprisonment of older offenders. Taken together, the 1882–84 depression and 1890–91 recession reduced the error sum of squares by 27 percent.

The remaining results focus on the seriousness and age of offenders admitted to the penitentiary for violent and property crimes. Economic crises were critical, particularly for black admissions. More often than not, crises precipitated the admission of both less serious and younger offenders. World War I and its aftermath were rarely relevant, nor were the policies of probation, parole, and abolition of the lease. Finally, the events of interest were often better predictors of the age of admitted offenders than of their seriousness.

271

Results of Multivariate Analysis

The second stage of the preliminary analysis identified and estimated relationships among the social change series. For series that underwent intervention analysis, multivariate analysis used the residuals from the intervention model. Where necessary, the remaining series were logged and differenced to achieve stationary levels and variances. The chief diagnostic tool for this stage of the analysis was the cross-correlation function, which provided evidence of the strength and direction of the relationship between two series.

Estimated first was the impact of value added by manufacturing on the size of the cotton harvest (table A-2). As manufacturing became more profitable, cotton harvests became slightly larger. Although significant, this relationship resulted in only a trivial reduction in unexplained variance (3 percent). No other social change affected the size of the harvest. Both the harvest and value added by manufacturing affected the price of cotton, however. The more profitable manufacturing was, the higher the price of cotton. The larger the size of the cotton harvest, the lower its price. Although statistically significant, neither influence was powerful. Together, they reduced the error sum of squares by only 17 percent.

Considered next was urbanization, whose only significant determinant was the size of the young white male population. As it declined, Georgia became more urbanized. Once purged of the impact of percentage young white male, urbanization affected a variety of demographic series. Along with a decline in cotton prices, growth in urbanization reduced the size of the black urban population. Together, these two factors reduced the unexplained variance by 50 percent. Along with industrialization and the young white male population, urbanization affected the size of the young black male population. As manufacturing became more profitable, the population of young black men declined. As urbanization and the population of young white males grew, so did the size of the young black male population. Together, these three factors were powerful predictors, reducing the unexplained variance by 86 percent. Finally, both urbanization and the black urban population affected the magnitude of racial inequality. As Georgia became more urbanized, racial inequality increased. As its black urban population shrank, so too did the magnitude of racial inequality. Neither influence was very strong, and together they reduced the unexplained variance in inequality by only 20 percent.

Social change series also had implications for the cohort of offenders admitted to the penitentiary. After some delay, lower cotton prices and a decline in the population of young black men prompted the admission of more serious black offenders. Urbanization precipitated the admission of older black offenders. Falling cotton prices and growth in urbanization also encouraged the admission of more serious white offenders. Declines in racial inequality and in the population of

Table A.2 Relationships between social change series

Social Change		Input Series	Transfer Function	Estimate	T-ratio
Cotton Harvest					
		Value added by manufacturing	ω_1	.26	1.43
Original SSE	1.84				
Model SSE	1.78				
% SSE reduction	3.26				
Cotton Price					
		Value added by manufacturing	ω_4	.04	2.82
		Cotton harvest	ω_1	−.02	−2.33
Original SSE	.012				
Model SSE	.010				
% SSE reduction	16.67				
Percentage Urban					
		Percentage young white male	ω_0	−.88	−13.85
Original SSE	.003				
Model SSE	.001				
% SSE reduction	66.67				
Percentage Black Male					
		Cotton price	ω_1	−.02	−1.39
		Percentage urban	ω_0	−.15	−2.23
Original SSE	.0002				
Model SSE	.0001				
% SSE reduction	50.00				
Percentage Black Urban					
		Percentage urban	ω_0	−.38	−4.67
Original SSE	.0004				
Model SSE	.0003				
% SSE reduction	25.00				
Percentage Young Black Male					
		Value added by manufacturing	ω_1	−.002	−1.59
		Percentage urban	ω_0	.26	4.30
		Percentage young white male	ω_0	.31	10.03
Original SSE	.0007				
Model SSE	.0001				
% SSE reduction	85.71				
Racial Inequality					
		Percentage urban	ω_1	3.94	2.53

continued

Table A.2 *continued*

Social Change		Input Series	Transfer Function	Estimate	T-ratio
		Percentage black urban	$\omega_0/(1 - \delta B)$	5.60	2.17
				.56	3.48
Original SSE	.093				
Model SSE	.074				
% SSE reduction	20.43				
Seriousness of Black Admissions					
		Cotton price	ω_5	−1.11	−2.12
		Percentage young black male	ω_5	−12.50	−2.67
Original SSE	.22				
Model SSE	.15				
% SSE reduction	31.82				
Age of Black Admissions					
		Percentage urban	ω_4	2.05	2.37
Original SSE	.04				
Model SSE	.03				
% SSE reduction	25.00				
Seriousness of White Admissions					
		Cotton price	$\omega_1/(1 - \delta B)$	−3.05	−2.01
				−.81	−6.01
		Percentage urban	ω_5	17.84	2.94
		Racial inequality	ω_4	1.71	3.25
		Percentage young white male	ω_0	−8.29	−2.6
Original SSE	1.68				
Model SSE	1.06				
% SSE reduction	36.90				
Age of White Admissions					
		Percentage urban	ω_4	−7.06	−3.2
		Racial inequality	ω_5	.49	2.5
Original SSE	.22				
Model SSE	.14				
% SSE reduction	36.36				
Seriousness of Black Violent Admissions					
		Cotton price	$\omega_1/(1 - \delta B)$	−2.00	−2.2
				−.69	−2.9
		Percentage urban	$\omega_0/(1 - \delta B)$	−4.01	−1.4
				−.81	−4.5

continued

ble A.2 *continued*

cial Change		Input Series	Transfer Function	Estimate	T-ratio
		Racial inequality	ω_5	.86	2.72
Original SSE	.52				
Model SSE	.37				
% SSE reduction	28.85				
e of Black Violent Admissions					
		Percentage urban	ω_4	1.69	1.57
		Racial inequality	ω_4	−.26	−2.70
Original SSE	.05				
Model SSE	.04				
% SSE reduction	20.00				
riousness of White Violent Admissions					
		Cotton price	$\omega_2/(1 - \delta B)$	3.22	1.96
				−.89	−10.21
		Racial inequality	ω_4	1.85	2.81
		Percentage young white male	ω_5	−9.85	−2.52
Original SSE	2.40				
Model SSE	1.71				
% SSE reduction	28.75				
ge of White Violent Admissions					
		Cotton price	ω_0	1.40	2.00
		Cotton harvest	ω_2	.14	2.52
		Racial inequality	$\omega_3/(1 - \delta B)$	.98	4.20
				−.74	−6.63
		Percentage young white male	ω_0	3.95	2.54
Original SSE	.50				
Model SSE	.25				
% SSE reduction	50.00				
riousness of Black Property Admissions					
		Cotton price	ω_4	1.06	2.35
		Black property admission rate	ω_0	.06	2.00
Original SSE	.13				
Model SSE	.11				
% SSE reduction	15.38				
ge of Black Property Admissions					
		Percentage black male	ω_2	4.97	2.06

continued

Table A.2 *continued*

Social Change		Input Series	Transfer Function	Estimate	T-rati
		Seriousness of admissions	ω_2	−.14	−1.6
Original SSE	.06				
Model SSE	.05				
% SSE reduction	16.67				
Seriousness of White Property Admissions					
		Value added by manufacturing	ω_3	.19	1.7
		Percentage urban	ω_4	9.87	2.5
		Percentage young white male	ω_2	−4.86	−2.2
Original SSE	.79				
Model SSE	.60				
% SSE reduction	24.05				
Age of White Property Admissions					
		Percentage black male	ω_1	−10.30	−2.4
		Racial inequality	$\omega_1 - \omega_2 - \omega_5$	−.69	−3.3
				−.92	−4.2
				−.61	−3.0
		Percentage young white male	ω_5	−3.71	−3.2
Original SSE	.28				
Model SSE	.14				
% SSE reduction	50.00				

Note: SSE denotes error sum of squares. Input series were stationary at the mean and variance and noise componen modeled before estimating cross-correlation functions. Italicized series are the residuals of the original series after th influence of other series had been removed. For example, percentage urban was purged of the influence of percentag young white male, and its residuals used in all later cross-correlation functions.

young white men, in contrast, fostered the admission of less serious white offenders. Finally, as urbanization increased and racial inequality declined, more youthful cohorts of white men were admitted.

The remaining findings report the influence of social change on offenders incarcerated for violent and property crimes. In general, social changes had weak implications for the seriousness of admitted offenders, accounting for less than 30 percent of the unexplained variance. Their impacts varied as a function of both race and offense. A decline in the price of cotton, for example, triggered the admission of more serious black violent offenders but *less serious* black property and white violent offenders. Growth in urbanization tended to encourage the admission of less serious black violent offenders and of more serious white property offenders.

Table A.3 Operative years for residualized social change series

Series	Operative Years
Cotton Economy	
Cotton price	1876–1940
Cotton harvest	1873–1940
Percentage black male	1877–1940
Industrial Economy	
Value added by manufacturing	1872–1940
Percentage urban	1871–1940
Percentage black urban	1871–1940
Inequality	
Racial inequality	1875–1937
Control Series	
Percentage young black male	1873–1940
Percentage young white male	1870–1940
Seriousness of black admissions	1881–1940
Age of black admissions	1875–1940
Seriousness of white admissions	1882–1940
Age of white admissions	1880–1940
Seriousness of black violent admissions	1880–1940
Age of black violent admissions	1879–1940
Seriousness of white violent admissions	1879–1940
Age of white violent admissions	1881–1940
Seriousness of black property admissions	1880–1938
Age of black property admissions	1882–1940
Seriousness of white property admissions	1875–1940
Age of white property admissions	1880–1938

Only racial inequality exerted a consistent influence. As the economic gap between blacks and whites narrowed, less serious violent offenders—both black and white—were admitted to the penitentiary.

Social changes had stronger implications for the age of admitted felons. Again, impacts varied by race and offense. Declining inequality, for example, resulted in the admission of older black violent and white property offenders. It had the opposite effect on the admission of white violent offenders, tending to result in the incarceration of a more youthful cohort. Similarly, a decline in population of black men prompted the admission of more youthful black property offenders and older white property offenders.

Conclusion

The analysis reported in chapters 5 through 8 uses the residuals from the multivariate stage of the analysis. These residuals represent social change series from which the influence of events and other social changes has been removed. Any remaining autocorrelations among the residuals of these series were also removed before estimating their relationship with punishment.

It merits emphasis that the preliminary analysis reported above altered the length of series for which analyses involving punishment could be conducted (table A-3). For example, the original cotton harvest series was available between 1870 and 1940. After estimating the delayed impact of value added by manufacturing, the residuals spanned a slightly shorter period (1873–1940). The original cotton price series was also available between 1870 and 1940. Yet after removing the delayed influence of cotton harvest (1873–1940) and value added by manufacturing (1870–1940), its residuals covered the period between 1876 and 1940. Seriousness and age series were available for even shorter periods. For example, after removing the delayed influence of cotton price (1876–1940), the seriousness of black admissions was available between 1881 and 1940.

The inclusion of shortened series in multivariate models had two consequences. First, it limited our ability to estimate the impact of the 1873–79 depression and, less frequently, the 1937–38 recession. For this reason, intervention analysis was conducted first and separately from the multivariate analysis. Second, shorter residualized series limited the years for which other, possibly longer, input series could be estimated. In some cases, the resulting loss of data points in the multivariate model diminished the impact of some series to insignificance. The series receives attention if its impact was statistically significant when estimated alone and if the series reduced unexplained variance by a nontrivial amount.

Appendix B

Conditional and Unconditional
Release from the Penitentiary

Table B.1 Impact of events on black conditional and unconditional release rate

Event	Transfer Function	Release Rate	
		Conditional	Unconditional
Economic Crises			
1882–84 depression	ω_1		−3.06
			(−3.12)
1895–97 recession	ω_0		−4.44
			(−4.53)
1899–1900 recession	ω_0		4.02
			(4.10)
1929–33 depression	ω_3	3.30	
		(3.51)	
1937–38 recession	ω_0	−3.16	
		(−3.36)	
Policies			
Agricultural Adjustment Act	ω_3	2.70	
		(2.87)	
χ^2 of residuals		7.53	2.56
(p)		(.27)	(.86)
Original SSE		51.23	110.59
Model SSE		23.04	65.36
% SSE reduction		55.03	40.90

Note: T-ratio of estimate in parentheses. SSE denotes error sum of squares.

Table B.2 Impact of social change on black conditional and unconditional release rate

Social Change	Transfer Function	Release Rate	
		Conditional	Unconditional
Cotton Economy			
Cotton price	a	−20.29	−22.96
		(−2.14)	(−2.55)
			−.73
			(−4.31)
Industrial Economy			
Value added by manufacturing	ω_0	2.02	
		(2.05)	
Percentage urban	ω_5	−99.39	−85.65
		(−1.86)	(−2.37)
Control Series			
Seriousness of admissions	ω_2	−6.51	
		(−2.06)	
χ^2 of residuals		4.51	6.77
(p)		(.61)	(.34)
Original SSE		23.04	53.68
Model SSE		11.99	38.91
% SSE reduction		47.96	27.51

Note: T-ratio of estimate in parentheses. SSE denotes error sum of squares.

[a]For conditional release rate, the transfer function is ω_2; for the unconditional release rate, $\omega_4/(1 - \delta B)$.

Table B.3 Impact of events on white conditional and unconditional release rate

Event	Transfer Function	Release Rate Conditional	Unconditional
Economic Crises			
1895–97 recession	ω_0		−.52
			(−2.47)
1899–1900 recession	ω_0		.42
			(2.00)
1910–12 recession	ω_0		−.50
			(−2.38)
1920–21 depression	ω_1	.70	
		(2.70)	
1929–33 depression	ω_3	.68	
		(2.62)	
1937–38 recession	$\omega_0 - \omega_1$	−.70	−.76
		(−2.70)	(−3.61)
			−1.10
			(−4.24)
Policies			
Agricultural Adjustment Act[a]	ω_t	−.90	.60
		(−3.47)	(2.85)
χ^2 of residuals		3.58	6.18
(p)		(.73)	(.40)
Original SSE		5.10	4.56
Model SSE		1.62	2.92
% SSE reduction		68.24	35.96

Note: T-ratio of estimate in parentheses. SSE denotes error sum of squares.

[a]For the conditional release rate, $t = 1$; for the unconditional rate, $t = 0$.

Table B.4   Impact of social change on white conditional and unconditional release rate

Social Change	Transfer Function	Release Rate	
		Conditional	Unconditional
Cotton Economy			
Percentage black male	ω_3		−33.00
			(−2.34)
Industrial Economy			
Percentage urban	ω_3	−38.27	
		(−2.39)	
Control Series			
Age of admissions	ω_3		−.94
			(−2.09)
χ^2 of residuals		4.17	5.81
(p)		(.62)	(.44)
Original SSE		1.62	2.02
Model SSE		1.34	1.58
% SSE reduction		17.28	21.78

Note: T-ratio of estimate in parentheses. SSE denotes error sum of squares.

282

Table B.5 Impact of events on black violent release rate

Event	Transfer Function	Release Rate Conditional	Release Rate Unconditional
Economic Crises			
1882–84 depression	ω_1		−.84
			(−2.49)
1895–97 recession	ω_0		−1.80
			(−5.34)
1899–1900 recession	ω_0		1.28
			(3.80)
1910–12 recession	ω_0		−.74
			(−2.20)
1920–21 depression	ω_0	1.00	
		(1.86)	
1929–33 depression	ω_3	1.08	
		(2.01)	
1937–38 recession	ω_0	−1.16	
		(−2.16)	
Policies			
Agricultural Adjustment Act	ω_1	−1.06	
		(−1.97)	
χ^2 of residuals		8.13	4.04
(p)		(.23)	(.67)
Original SSE		11.91	13.73
Model SSE		7.23	7.60
% SSE reduction		39.29	44.65

Note: T-ratio of estimate in parentheses. SSE denotes error sum of squares.

Table B.6   Impact of social change on black violent release rate

Social Change	Transfer Function	Release Rate Conditional	Release Rate Unconditional
Cotton Economy			
Percentage black male	ω_5	68.97	
		(1.69)	
Industrial Economy			
Value added by manufacturing	ω_0	1.16	
		(1.79)	
Percentage urban	ω_0		$-.22$
			(-1.77)
χ^2 of residuals		3.67	2.09
(p)		(.72)	(.91)
Original SSE		7.23	7.60
Model SSE		5.44	7.01
% SSE reduction		24.76	7.89

Note: *T*-ratio of estimate in parentheses. SSE denotes error sum of squares.

Table B.7 Impact of events on white violent release rate

Event	Transfer Function	Release Rate	
		Conditional	Unconditional
Economic Crises			
1882–84 depression	ω_1		−.22
			(−1.92)
1910–12 recession	$\omega_0 - \omega_1$		−.34
			(−2.97)
			−.28
			(−2.44)
1920–21 depression	ω_1	.30	
		(2.52)	
1929–33 depression	ω_3	.30	
		(2.52)	
1937–38 recession	a	−.32	−.42
		(−2.68)	(−3.66)
		−.38	
		(−3.19)	
War			
World War I	ω_0		.22
			(1.92)
Policies			
Agricultural Adjustment Act	$\omega_1 - \omega_2$	−.40	
		(−3.32)	
		−.38	
		(−3.19)	
χ^2 of residuals		2.57	5.77
(*p*)		(.86)	(.45)
Original SSE		1.06	1.33
Model SSE		.33	.87
% SSE reduction		68.87	34.59

Note: *T*-ratio of estimate in parentheses. SSE denotes error sum of squares.

[a]For the conditional release rate, the transfer function is $\omega_0 - \omega_1$; for the unconditional rate, ω_0.

Table B.8 Impact of social change on white violent release rate

Social Change	Transfer Function	Release Rate Conditional	Release Rate Unconditional
Industrial Economy			
Value added by manufacturing	ω_0	−.28	
		(−2.28)	
Inequality			
Racial inequality	ω_3		−.97
			(−2.72)
Control Series			
Percentage young	ω_0		−5.01
			(−2.31)
Age of admissions	ω_3	.85	
		(2.62)	
χ^2 of residuals		3.03	2.77
(p)		(.81)	(.84)
Original SSE		.33	.77
Model SSE		.23	.57
% SSE reduction		30.30	25.97

Note: T-ratio of estimate in parentheses. SSE denotes error sum of squares.

Table B.9 Impact of events on black property release rate

Event	Transfer Function	Release Rate	
		Conditional	Unconditional
Economic Crises			
1882–84 depression	ω_1		−2.22
			(−2.90)
1895–97 recession	ω_0		−2.64
			(−3.45)
1899–1900 recession	ω_0		2.74
			(3.58)
1929–33 depression	ω_3	2.22	
		(3.55)	
1937–38 recession	ω_0	−1.98	
		(−3.17)	
Policies			
Agricultural Adjustment Act	ω_3	1.74	
		(2.79)	
χ^2 of residuals		8.57	6.78
(p)		(.20)	(.34)
Original SSE		22.03	59.15
Model SSE		10.15	39.75
% SSE reduction		53.93	32.80

Note: T-ratio of estimate in parentheses. SSE denotes error sum of squares.

Table B.10 Impact of social change on black property release rate

| | Transfer | Release Rate | |
Social Change	Function	Conditional	Unconditional
Cotton Economy			
Cotton price	ω_2	−15.09	
		(−2.82)	
Industrial Economy			
Value added by manufacturing	$\omega_0 - \omega_1$	2.02	
		(3.65)	
		1.18	
		(1.75)	
Percentage urban	ω_5	−44.48	−91.46
		(−1.77)	(−3.48)
Control Series			
Percentage young	ω_2		120.94
			(2.20)
Seriousness of admissions	ω_0	3.95	
		(2.55)	
Age of admissions	ω_1	7.90	7.32
		(2.84)	(2.64)
χ^2 of residuals		1.97	6.86
(p)		(.92)	(.33)
Original SSE		10.15	26.87
Model SSE		2.13	19.22
% SSE reduction		79.01	28.47

Note: T-ratio of estimate in parentheses. SSE denotes error sum of squares.

Table B.11   Impact of events on white property release rate

Event	Transfer Function	Release Rate Conditional	Release Rate Unconditional
Economic Crises			
1882–84 depression	ω_1		−.24
			(−1.80)
1895–97 recession	ω_0		−.36
			(−2.70)
1929–33 depression	ω_1		.40
			(3.01)
1937–38 recession	$\omega_0 - \omega_1$	−.38	−.34
		(−1.74)	(−2.55)
		−.74	
		(−3.38)	
Policies			
Agricultural Adjustment Act	a	−.50	.42
		(−2.29)	(3.16)
			.36
			(2.70)
χ^2 of residuals		2.85	13.90
(*p*)		(.83)	(.03)
Original SSE		2.28	1.92
Model SSE		1.34	1.15
% SSE reduction		41.23	40.10

Note: *T*-ratio of estimate in parentheses. SSE denotes error sum of squares.

[a]For the conditional release rate, the transfer function is ω_1; for the unconditional release rate, $\omega_0 - \omega_1$.

Table B.12 Impact of social change on white property release rate

Social Change	Transfer Function	Release Rate Conditional	Release Rate Unconditional
Control Series			
Percentage young	ω_1	43.38	
		(2.90)	
Seriousness of admissions	ω_2		−.32
			(−2.23)
Age of admissions	ω_0	1.79	
		(2.16)	
Noise Component	θ_1		.35
			(2.92)
χ^2 of residuals		3.79	6.06
(p)		(.71)	(.30)
Original SSE		1.19	.91
Model SSE		.75	.74
% SSE reduction		36.97	18.68

Note: T-ratio of estimate in parentheses. SSE denotes error sum of squares.

Appendix C

Black Property Values and
Prison Sentences

Table C.1   Impact of black property value on black property prison sentence

Social Change	Transfer Function	Model 1	Model 2	Model 3
Industrial Economy				
Percentage urban	ω_0		14.03	10.54
			(3.50)	(3.46)
Percentage black urban	ω_0		−2.54	[a]
			(−.41)	
Inequality				
Black property value	ω_3	−.82	−.70	−.94
		(−3.25)	(−2.81)	(−4.64)
Control Series				
Seriousness of admissions	ω_0		.37	[a]
			(1.63)	
Age of admissions	ω_2		−.67	−1.17
			(−1.97)	(−4.64)
Noise Component	θ_1			.51
				(3.76)
χ^2 of residuals			11.29	5.20
(p)			(.08)	(.39)
Original SSE		.44	.42	.40
Model SSE		.38	.25	.22
% SSE reduction		13.64	40.48	45.00

Note: *T*-ratio of estimate in parentheses. SSE denotes error sum of squares. Variation in original SSE is due to variation in the time span of residualized input series. See Appendix A for details.

[a]Estimate was nonsignificant in earlier estimation, and excluded from the model.

Notes

1. Social Change and the Rise of the Penitentiary

1. The rise of the penitentiary in America was a corollary of similar processes occurring in England and on the continent (Foucault 1977; Hogg 1979; Dobash 1983; Spierenburg 1987). Similarly, the penitentiary was part of a larger process of institutionalizing economically unproductive populations such as the poor and insane (see, e.g., Foucault 1965; Spitzer 1975, 1979; Scull 1977; Sutton 1991).
2. Capitalism is defined by the production of commodities for sale rather than use, via a universal medium of exchange; labor as a commodity that is bought and sold; and control of production by the capitalist class (Dowd 1974). The basis of the process is the expropriation of agricultural producers from the soil and the consequent subordination of labor to the dictates of capital (Hindess and Hirst 1975).
3. Analysts have emphasized a second role of punishment within the capitalist mode of production. By design, labor in penitentiaries was a disciplinary mechanism whose purpose was to render certain elements of the workforce more amenable to exploitation under the capitalist regimen (Hogg 1979; Miller 1980; Melossi and Pavarini 1981; Gildemeister 1987). Work in the penitentiary was a mirror image of industrial production, with its emphasis on minute regulations governing arrival, departure, and comportment while working. Prohibitions against smoking, profanity, "useless talking," and "dawdling" were common in both venues (Levasseur 1900). It is debatable whether prison work regimens achieved their aim of producing an obedient and industrious workforce. Overemphasis on this role implies that the state was little more than a passive recipient of the capitalist agenda. An alternative view considers work regimens in prison one facet of the alliance between the "accumulative state" and capitalist entrepreneurs (Staples 1990). Prison labor survived the demise of this alliance because it helped keep facilities orderly and rein in the costs of expanding prison facilities. With varying degrees of success, then, prison

293

labor served two masters: capitalists seeking a docile labor force and state managers interested in reproducing the apparatus of the state.

4. Nearly 40 percent of all convicts employed in productive labor were under the contract system in 1885. Only 12 percent remained so in 1923. Conversely, a minority of all convicts at productive labor in 1885 worked to benefit the state or the public via road and public work construction. In 1923, 85 percent of all productively employed inmates were so engaged (Jackson 1927–28).

5. Unless noted otherwise, the following states are defined as southern; their reliance on the lease in 1885 is presented in parentheses (U.S. Department of the Interior 1887): Alabama (100%), Arkansas (100%), Florida (100%), Georgia (100%), Kentucky (85%), Louisiana (100%), Mississippi (100%), Oklahoma (not yet a state), North Carolina (66%), South Carolina (10%), Tennessee (100%), Texas (0%), and Virginia (0%). For overviews of the convict lease system in the South, see Zimmerman (1947), Lichtenstein (1996), and Mancini (1996). For studies of individual states, see Moos (1942) and Ward and Rogers (1987) for Alabama; Zimmerman (1949) for Arkansas; Pratt (1949) for Florida; Taylor (1942a, 1942b), Lichtenstein (1996), and Mancini (1996) for Georgia; Sneed (1860) for Kentucky; Carleton (1971) for Louisiana; Shivers (1930) for Mississippi; McKay (1942) for North Carolina; Shelden (1979, 1981) and Hutson (1936) for Tennessee; and Walker (1988) for Texas.

6. More nefarious links between private entrepreneurs and local and state government officials were also alleged. According to Green (1949: 119), "Pressure was brought to bear on officials to arrest, and the courts to convict, all offenders so that the lessees might secure more convict laborers for their fixed payments." Rebecca Felton, an outspoken critic of the lease, further accused the "Convict Kings" (McKelway 1908a: 222) of bribing members of Georgia's penitentiary committees to present "mildly" the atrocious conditions that characterized convict camps (Felton 1911).

2. Forms of Punishment in Georgia

1. Virginia and Kentucky began operating penitentiaries in 1800 (Sneed 1860; Lewis [1922] 1967). Maryland opened its first state prison in 1812. The remaining southern states did not open penitentiaries until later: Tennessee in 1831 (Lewis [1922] 1967), Louisiana in 1835 (Carleton 1971), Mississippi in 1840 (Shivers 1930), Alabama in 1841 (Ward and Rogers 1987), and Arkansas and Texas in 1849 (Zimmerman 1949; Walker 1988). At the beginning of the Civil War, three southern states (North Carolina, South Carolina, Florida) lacked state penitentiaries (Walden 1974). South Carolina, for example, hanged 10 percent of felons, fined about half, whipped, pilloried, or branded another 30 percent, and sentenced the rest to one of twenty-eight local jails (Williams 1959).

2. The lessees benefited more from long-term leases than did the state. They paid the state a fixed amount, regardless of the number of convicts. Between 1879 and 1890, the number of convicts increased from 1,200 to 1,700, the result being a decline in the per capita rate of hire from $20.00 to $14.50 (Ward 1947).

3. Principal physicians also offered their thoughts on the lease system. Dr. W. F. Westmoreland argued that full compliance with the law required that the state appoint and pay a physician in charge of each camp, who would maintain hygienic conditions (Principal Physician of the Penitentiary 1886). Principal Physician Bush considered the lease system a blot on Georgia's history, and he recommended a graded penitentiary, where convicts would be punished according to their crime. Should the lease continue, Bush

echoed Westmoreland's plea that camp physicians be appointed by the principal physician, with the consent of the governor, thereby ensuring their status as officers of the state (Principal Physician of the Penitentiary 1896).

4. By 1911, sixteen states permitted felons to be used for road work, with fifteen more joining them by 1917. Of the sixteen states permitting state convict labor on county roads in 1911, six were in the South (Georgia, Louisiana, North Carolina, Oklahoma, South Carolina, and Virginia). The rest were either western or midwestern (American Highway Association 1912). Between 1911 and 1917, three more southern states (Florida, Kentucky, Tennessee) joined the ranks of those permitting state convicts to be worked on county roads. The thirteen other states were dispersed throughout the nation (American Highway Association 1917).

5. Good-roads associations were not the only supporters of expanded public roads at the turn of the century (Mason 1957; Hilles 1958). Credited with initiating the movement was the League of American Wheelmen, an association for bicycling enthusiasts, founded in 1880. Other organizations included the Automobile Club of America, founded in 1899, and the American Road Makers Association, an organization of road engineers founded in 1902. In 1907, the National Grange met jointly with the Automobile Association of America (formerly the Automobile Club of America) to pledge their assistance to the good-roads movement. They were joined in 1910 by the Farmers' Educational and Cooperative Union, which represented southern farmers. Federal interest in good roads began in 1893 with the establishment of the Office of Road Inquiry within the Department of Agriculture. This office disseminated information through its bulletins and through the building, at local expense, of short object-lesson roads (roads that taught lessons about road building) (Mason 1957; Preston 1991). Its directors supported the use of convict labor for road building (Stone 1907; Hilles 1958).

6. Georgia law provided two choices for road construction and repair. The first, a labor tax system, required each male citizen between sixteen and fifty years of age to work on the roads no more than fifteen days a year. Defaulters paid a fine of three dollars a day (Jenks 1889). The alternative "cash tax" system, devised in 1891, allowed county grand juries to levy a road tax of not more than twenty cents per one hundred dollars of taxable property. Male citizens in counties with Public Road Funds could be exempted from road duty by paying a commutation tax of fifty cents per day for up to ten days of labor. In 1904, 74 of Georgia's 137 counties used this alternative; only 27 counties relied on convict labor (Page 1907). By 1910, most counties relied on state convicts (Wallenstein 1987).

7. The initial composition of the State Highway Commission reveals the strong link between punishment and road improvement. Its members included the entire Prison Commission, the state geologist, and two academics with expertise in road building. With the press of other duties, prison commissioners were no longer members when the Highway Commission was reorganized in 1919 as the State Highway Board. For a history of Georgia's highway department, see Foster (1949).

8. Of the crimes considered here, the following could not be reduced to misdemeanors: murder, feticide, manslaughter, rape and assault with intent to rape, sodomy, and mayhem.

3. Social Change and the Use of the Penitentiary

1. The industrial stage of capitalism entailed large-scale industry based on machine-powered production; competition among capitalists, which increased the rate of techno-

logical innovation and therewith the rate of surplus value; and the concentration and centralization of capital (Eaton 1966). Monopoly capitalism flowered fully after World War II. Among its defining attributes are capital concentrated in monopolies and oligopolies, international markets for capital and labor, imperialism, an expanded role for the state as guarantor of the conditions under which capitalism flourishes, and a persistent surplus of labor.

2. For consideration of a third axis, gender, see Myers (1995a).

4. Modeling Use of the Penitentiary in Georgia

1. Before merging data from Principal Keeper Reports and the Central Register of Convicts, I removed duplicates and reconciled inconsistencies. The typical inconsistencies involved year of conviction and type of offense. In the late 1800s, for example, rape and assault with intent to rape were often used interchangeably. Reports referred to manslaughter, while the Central Register identified the crime with greater specificity (e.g., voluntary manslaughter). To resolve inconsistencies, I recorded the more specific or the most frequent entry.

2. Several offenses were rarely encountered and too distinctive for inclusion in the more general property or violent crime category. The most prominent of these were robbery, arson, white-collar crimes (e.g., embezzlement, forgery), and receiving stolen goods. Offenders convicted of felonies against the public order (e.g., liquor and narcotics law violations) were also rare and excluded from consideration. The sample does include, however, offenders who committed any of these crimes in conjunction with a burglary, larceny, or violent crime.

3. Life imprisonment received a score of forty-two, while offenders receiving the death penalty were assigned a score of sixty.

4. Tenants and sharecroppers differed in degree and not in kind. Tenants supplied their own equipment, such as tools and animals, and relinquished one-quarter to one-third of the cotton crop. Sharecroppers offered only their labor. They received food, supplies, and equipment, relinquishing up to half of the crop as rent (Johnson, Embree, and Alexander 1935). Share tenants were classified as sharecroppers in Georgia, and neither had title to the crops they grew (Hahn 1983).

5. Other social scientists (e.g., Corzine, Huff-Corzine, and Creech 1988; Tolnay, Beck, and Massey 1992) use tenancy data to measure racial inequality, but these data are available only after 1900 and only at ten-year intervals. Not surprisingly, they are less successful predictors of punishment (Myers 1990b). The measure used here documents the same trends as do tenantry data: marginal increases in black prosperity and more consistent declines in the economic position of whites. It uses annual property tax assessments, conducted by the state's comptroller general (Georgia Comptroller General 1874–1936). While subject to undervaluation, tax data provide a reliable index of the rate of accumulation over time (Higgs 1982).

6. For expositions of ARIMA modeling and its requirements, see McCleary and Hay (1980), Makridakis, Wheelwright, and McGee (1983), and Wei (1990). The requirements for estimating accurate cross-correlation functions are discussed by Haugh and Box (1977), Montgomery and Weatherby (1980), and Harvey (1981). See Wei (1990), Box and Tiao (1975), and Harvey (1981) for explanations of transfer functions.

7. Trend is any systematic change in the level of a time series. It refers to deterministic behavior, whether upward or downward, that can be represented as a systematic or fixed function of time. Drift, in contrast, is stochastic behavior that can be expressed only as the outcome of a process operating through time. Future values of a deterministic process are constrained by the definition of the function, while future values of a stochastic process vary in a probabilistic manner. While conceptually distinct, drift and trend are often difficult to distinguish in actual practice. After differencing, series that trend will exhibit a mean that differs significantly from zero. The mean of a drifting series, in contrast, will be zero (McDowall and Loftin 1992).

8. Of the social change series, only cotton price was *not* log transformed. The three control series (percentage young, seriousness of admissions, age of admissions) were log transformed, as were black admission rates and all sentence length series.

9. The final possibility, not encountered here, is a mixed process (ARMA) that contains both autoregressive and moving average components. This process describes a situation where the value of the time series in any given year is a combined function of both the previous values of the series and previous random shocks.

10. For a first-order moving average or autoregressive process, the parameter estimate must lie between -1 and $+1$. If estimates exceed these bounds, then the model reflects a nonstationary process, wherein the impact of the previous values of an autoregressive process or the random shocks of a moving average process increases with time. This "growth" model is inconsistent with autoregressive or moving average behavior, which requires that the impact of previous values or shocks diminish with time.

11. To obtain an accurate indication of the influence of social change on punishment, analysis must not only disentangle the social change series from one another. It must also free each social change series from the impact of any events. For example, depressions may affect both the price of cotton and the rate at which black men were admitted to the penitentiary. To obtain a clear picture of the effect of cotton price on admissions *and* of depressions on admissions, the impact of depressions on cotton price must be removed. Appendix A presents the results of this analysis.

12. The final possible impact is an abrupt permanent change. It is estimated with a zero-order transfer function, $[\omega X_{t-n}]$, where the subscript n refers to the time lag before the impact is realized (e.g., $t-1$ implying a one-year lag). In this case, the series X is a binary step variable.

13. Graphs and results not presented in the body of the text are available to interested readers on request.

5. Admissions to the Penitentiary

1. To conserve space, graphs depicting the results of the moving average strategy are not presented if the overall relationship was weak or trivial. Results not shown in the text are available from the author.

2. To explore the relationship between cotton price and black admissions for violence, several transfer functions were estimated. Model 4 best met the criteria for inclusion in the table. It reached statistical significance [*$p < .05$], generated a greater percentage reduction in error sum of squares (SSE) than alternatives, and yielded a nonsignificant cross-correlation function between residuals of the model and the input series.

Model	Transfer Function	SSE	Cross-Correlation Check	
			χ^2	p
1	$\omega_0{}^*$	1.53	3.63	(.60)
2	ω_1	1.56	2.38	(.79)
3	$\omega_0{}^* - \omega_1{}^*$	1.47	2.49	(.65)
4	$\omega_0{}^*/(1 - \delta B)$	1.43	1.29	(.86)

3. Further analysis examined the impact of an absolute measure of white wealth, contained in Georgia Comptroller General Reports (1874–1936). Individual cross-correlations between white property value (1900 dollars) and the three white admission rates were modest ($<.20$) and insignificant. The strongest cross-correlation involved a contemporaneous marginally significant relationship between the white admission rate and *black* property value (CCF + 0 = .21). This finding suggests that as black property values increased, white admission rates rose. Estimated alone, the zero-order transfer function was significant ($\omega_0 = 1.04$, t-ratio = 1.69). Nevertheless, black property value reduced the unexplained variance in white admissions by only 4.5 percent. It lost statistical significance when included in the multivariate model.

6. Prison Sentences

1. Results not presented in the text are available from the author.
2. Where more than one impact appeared possible, I estimated several transfer functions. A function was acceptable for presentation if the parameter estimate reached statistical significance, generated a greater percentage reduction in error sum of squares (SSE) than alternatives, and yielded nonsignificant cross-correlations between residuals of the model and the input series.
3. Presented below are several possible estimates of the impact of age on the sentences of white property offenders. Although the asterisked estimates reached statistical significance, they did not always generate an impressive reduction in error sum of squares (SSE). Nor did they remove all cross-correlation between the residuals and the input series. Model 3 met the criteria for presentation.

Model	Transfer Function	SSE	Cross-Correlation Check	
			χ^2	p
1	$\omega_1{}^*$	2.09	11.05	(.05)
2	$\omega_2{}^*$	2.12	4.64	(.46)
3	$\omega_1{}^* - \omega_2{}^*$	1.84	2.89	(.58)
4	$\omega_1{}^*/(1 - \delta B)$	1.99	7.83	(.10)

4. The indicator of white economic position was the per capita value of white property in 1900 dollars (Georgia Comptroller General 1874–1936). This factor had no effect on the sentences imposed on white offenders in general or on white property and violent of-

fenders in particular. Also irrelevant were alterations in the economic position of black men, measured as the per capita value of black property in 1900 dollars. Full results are available on request.

7. Release from the Penitentiary

1. Presented below are several possible estimates of the impact of cotton price on the release of black convicts from the penitentiary. Only the estimates of asterisked parameters reached statistical significance. The second transfer function met the criteria for inclusion in the table.

Model	Transfer Function	SSE	Cross-Correlation Check	
			χ^2	p
1	ω_2^*	82.83	12.31	(.03)
2	$\omega_2^* - \omega_3^*$	73.66	5.98	(.20)
3	$\omega_2^*/(1 - \delta B)^*$	77.52	8.57	(.07)

2. The multivariate model included seriousness of black property admissions, whose residuals spanned 1880 to 1938. Subsequent analysis reveals why the industrial economy lost significance in this model (see appendix B). Industrialization influenced only the *conditional* release of black property offenders. Urbanization, in contrast, was particularly relevant for unconditional discharges, for which twelve years of data (1870–80, 1939–40) were lost by including seriousness in the multivariate model.
3. Further analysis examined the impact of an absolute measure of wealth, per capita black and white property value. These data were the components of the racial inequality measure, described in chapter 4. There were no significant relationships between black release rates and either black or white property value. Similarly, there were no significant relationships between white release rates and either white or black property value.

8. The Self-Regulation of Punishment

1. To conserve space, cross-correlation functions between white and black punishment are not presented. Graphs depicting the results of the moving average strategy for trivial relationships are also not presented. Results not shown in the text are available from the author.
2. The recalculated cross-correlation function between white property release rate and prison sentence yielded a significant association at the second lag (CCF + 2 = .31). The function as a whole was significant at p = .10.

References

Adamson, Christopher. 1983. "Punishment after Slavery: Southern State Penal Systems, 1865–1890." *Social Problems* 30:556–69.

———. 1984a. "Hard Labor and Solitary Confinement: Effects of the Business Cycle and Labor Supply on Prison Discipline in the United States, 1790–1835." *Research in Law, Deviance, and Social Control* 6:19–56.

———. 1984b. "Toward a Marxian Penology: Captive Criminal Populations as Economic Threats and Resources." *Social Problems* 31:435–58.

American Highway Association. 1912. *The Official Good Roads Yearbook of the United States, 1912.* Baltimore: Waverly Press.

———. 1913. *The Official Good Roads Yearbook of the United States, 1913.* Baltimore: Waverly Press.

———. 1917. *The Official Good Roads Yearbook of the United States, 1917.* Baltimore: Waverly Press.

Archer, Dane, and Rosemary Gartner. 1984. *Violence and Crime in Cross-National Perspective.* New Haven: Yale University Press.

Arnett, Alex Mathews. [1922] 1967. *The Populist Movement in Georgia: A View of the "Agrarian Crusade" in the Light of Solid-South Politics.* New York: AMS Press.

Ayers, Edward L. 1984. *Vengeance and Justice: Crime and Punishment in the Nineteenth-Century American South.* New York: Oxford University Press.

Baker, Ray Stannard. 1908. *Following the Color Line: An Account of Negro Citizenship in the American Democracy.* New York: Doubleday.

Banks, Enoch Marvin. 1905. *The Economics of Land Tenure in Georgia.* New York: Columbia University Press.

Barnes, Harry Elmer, and Negley K. Teeters. 1945. *New Horizons in Criminology: The American Crime Problem.* New York: Prentice Hall.

Baron, Harold M. 1971. "The Demand for Black Labor: Historical Notes on the Political Economy of Racism." *Radical America* 5(2):1–46.

Beck, E. M., and Stewart E. Tolnay. 1990. "The Killing Fields of the Deep South: The Market for Cotton and the Lynching of Blacks, 1882–1930." *American Sociological Review* 55:526–39.

Berk, Richard A., Sheldon L. Messinger, David Rauma, and John E. Berecochea. 1983. "Prisons as Self-Regulating Systems: A Comparison of Historical Patterns in California for Male and Female Offenders." *Law & Society Review* 17:547–86.

Berk, Richard A., David Rauma, Sheldon L. Messinger, and Thomas F. Cooley. 1981. "A Test of the Stability of Punishment Hypothesis: The Case of California, 1851–1970." *American Sociological Review* 46:805–29.

Biles, Roger. 1988. "Cotton Fields or Skyscrapers: The Case of Memphis, Tennessee." *The Historian* 50:210–33.

———. 1990. "The Urban South in the Great Depression." *Journal of Southern History* 56:71–100.

Blalock, Hubert M. 1967. *Toward a Theory of Minority-Group Relations.* New York: Wiley.

Blatner, William E. 1952. "Some Aspects of the Convict Lease System in the Southern States." Master's thesis, University of Oklahoma.

Bloom, Jack M. 1987. *Class, Race, and the Civil Rights Movement.* Bloomington: Indiana University Press.

Blumstein, Alfred, and Jacqueline Cohen. 1973. "A Theory of the Stability of Punishment." *Journal of Criminal Law and Criminology* 64:198–207.

Blumstein, Alfred, and Soumyo Moitra. 1979. "An Analysis of the Time Series of the Imprisonment Rate in the States of the United States: A Further Test of the Stability of Punishment Hypothesis." *Journal of Criminal Law and Criminology* 70:376–90.

———. 1980. "Growing or Stable Incarceration Rates: A Comment on Cahalan's 'Trends in Incarceration in the United States since 1880.'" *Crime and Delinquency* 26:91–94.

Blumstein, Alfred, Jacqueline Cohen, and Daniel Nagin. 1977. "The Dynamics of a Homeostatic Punishment Process." *Journal of Criminal Law and Criminology* 67:317–34.

Bonner, James C. 1971. "The Georgia Penitentiary at Milledgeville, 1817–1874." *Georgia Historical Quarterly* 55:303–28.

Box, G. E. P., and G. M. Jenkins. 1976. *Time Series Analysis: Forecasting and Control.* Rev. ed. San Francisco: Holden-Day.

Box, G. E. P., and G. C. Tiao. 1975. "Intervention Analysis with Applications to Economic and Environmental Problems." *Journal of the American Statistical Association* 70:70–79.

Brownell, Blaine A. 1975. *The Urban Ethos in the South, 1920–1930.* Baton Rouge: Louisiana State University Press.

Bursik, Robert J., Jr. 1988. "Social Disorganization and Theories of Crime and Delinquency: Problems and Prospects." *Criminology* 26:519–52.

Carleton, Mark. 1971. *Politics and Punishment: The History of the Louisiana State Penal System.* Baton Rouge: Louisiana State University Press.

Carter, Dan T. 1964. "Prisons, Politics, and Business: The Lease System in the Post–Civil War South." Master's thesis, University of Wisconsin.

Chamlin, Mitchell B. 1989. "A Macro Social Analysis of Change in Police Force Size, 1972–1982: Controlling for Static and Dynamic Influences." *Sociological Quarterly* 30:615–24.

Chamlin, Mitchell B., and Allen E. Liska. 1992. "Social Structure and Crime Control

Revisited: The Declining Significance of Intergroup Threat." Pp. 103–12 in *Social Threat and Social Control*, edited by Allen E. Liska. Albany: State University of New York Press.

Chiricos, Theodore G., and Miriam A. DeLone. 1992. "Labor Surplus and Punishment: A Review and Assessment of Theory and Evidence." *Social Problems* 39:421–46.

Clark, Thomas D., and Albert D. Kirwan. 1967. *The South since Appomattox: A Century of Regional Change*. New York: Oxford University Press.

Cobb, Howell. 1850. *A Compilation of the Penal Code of the State of Georgia*. Macon, Ga.: Joseph M. Boardman.

Cobb, James C. 1984. *Industrialization and Southern Society, 1877–1984*. Lexington: University Press of Kentucky.

———. 1988. "Beyond Planters and Industrialists: A New Perspective on the New South." *Journal of Southern History* 54:45–68.

Cohen, Stanley. 1985. *Visions of Social Control: Crime, Punishment and Classification*. Cambridge: Polity Press.

Coleman, Kenneth, ed. 1991. *A History of Georgia*. 2d ed. Athens: University of Georgia Press.

Collier, Tarleton. 1938. *Georgia Penal System*. Atlanta: Citizens Fact Finding Movement of Georgia.

———. 1940. *Penal System: A Reflection of Our Lives and Our Customs*. Atlanta: Citizens Fact Finding Movement of Georgia.

Commons, John R., David J. Saposs, Helen L. Sumner, E. B. Mittelman, H. E. Hoagland, John B. Andrews, and Selig Perlman. 1918. *History of Labour in the United States*. Vol. 1. New York: Macmillan.

Conley, John. 1980. "Prisons, Production, and Profit: Reconsidering the Importance of Prison Industries." *Journal of Social History* 14:257–75.

Conrad, David Eugene. 1965. *The Forgotten Farmers: The Story of Sharecroppers in the New Deal*. Urbana: University of Illinois Press.

Conway, Alan. 1966. *The Reconstruction of Georgia*. Minneapolis: University of Minnesota Press.

Corzine, Jay, Lin Huff-Corzine, and James C. Creech. 1988. "The Tenant Labor Market and Lynching in the South: A Test of Split Labor Market Theory." *Sociological Inquiry* 58:261–78.

Coulter, E. Merton. 1947. *The South during Reconstruction, 1865–1877*. Baton Rouge: Louisiana State University Press.

Cox, William B. 1928. "Convict Labor in the South." *American Prison Association Proceedings* 1928:207–16.

———. 1935. "Revenge or Reform?" *American Prison Association Proceedings* 1935:47–57.

Crowe, Charles. 1968. "Racial Violence and Social Reform: Origins of the Atlanta Riot of 1906." *Journal of Negro History* 53:234–56.

D'Alessio, Stewart J., and Lisa Stolzenberg. 1995. "Unemployment and the Incarceration of Pretrial Defendants." *American Sociological Review* 60:350–59.

Daniel, Pete. 1985. *Breaking the Land: The Transformation of Cotton, Tobacco, and Rice Cultures since 1880*. Urbana: University of Illinois Press.

———. 1994. "The Legal Basis of Agrarian Capitalism: The South since 1933." Pp. 79–110 in *Race and Class in the American South since 1890*, edited by Melvin Stokes and Rick Halpern. Oxford and Providence, R.I.: Berg.

Davis, Allison, Burleigh B. Gardner, and Mary R. Gardner. 1941. *Deep South: A Social Anthropological Study of Caste and Class.* Chicago: University of Chicago Press.

Dawson, William C. 1831. *A Compilation of the Laws of the State of Georgia Passed by the Georgia Assembly, since the Year 1819 to the Year 1829, Inclusive.* Milledgeville: Grantland and Orme.

Dearing, Charles L. 1941. *American Highway Policy.* Washington, D.C.: Brookings Institution.

DeCanio, Steven J. 1974. *Agriculture in the Postbellum South: The Economics of Production and Supply.* Cambridge: MIT Press.

Director of Corrections. 1943–44. *Annual Report.* Atlanta: Department of Corrections.

Dittmer, John. 1977. *Black Georgia in the Progressive Era, 1900–1920.* Urbana: University of Illinois Press.

Dobash, Russell P. 1983. "Labour and Discipline in Scottish and English Prisons: Moral Correction, Punishment and Useful Toil." *Sociology* 17:1–27.

Dollard, John. 1937. *Caste and Class in a Southern Town.* New York: Doubleday.

Dowd, Douglas F. 1974. *The Twisted Dream: Capitalist Development in the United States.* Cambridge, Mass.: Winthrop.

Doyle, Don H. 1980. *New Men, New Cities, New South: Atlanta, Nashville, Charleston, Mobile, 1860–1910.* Chapel Hill: University of North Carolina Press.

Durkheim, Emile. 1933. *The Division of Labor in Society.* Translated by George Simpson. New York: Macmillan.

———. 1961. *Moral Education: A Study in the Theory and Application of the Sociology of Education.* Translated by Everett K. Wilson and Herman Schnurer. New York: Free Press.

Eaton, John. 1966. *Political Economy: A Marxist Textbook.* New York: International Publishers.

Eldridge, Hope T., and Dorothy Swaine Thomas. 1964. *Demographic Analyses and Interrelations.* Vol. 3, *Population Redistribution and Economic Growth: United States, 1870–1950,* edited by Simon Kuznets and Dorothy Saine Thomas. Philadelphia: American Philosophical Society.

Evans, Arthur S. 1989. "The Relationship between Industrialization and White Hostility toward Blacks in Southern Cities, 1865–1910." *Urban Affairs Quarterly* 25:322–41.

Eve, W. F. 1895. "Report from Georgia." Pp. 15–16 in *Progress of Road Construction in the United States.* U.S. Department of Agriculture, Office of Road Inquiry Bulletin, no. 19. Washington, D.C.: Government Printing Office.

Feeley, Malcolm M., and Deborah L. Little. 1991. "The Vanishing Female: The Decline of Women in the Criminal Process, 1687–1912." *Law & Society Review* 25:719–57.

Felton, Rebecca Latimer. 1911. *My Memoirs of Georgia Politics.* Atlanta: Index Printing Co.

Fields, Barbara Jeanne. 1983. "The Nineteenth-Century American South: History and Theory." *Plantation Society in the Americas* 2:7–28.

Fierce, Milfred C. 1994. *Slavery Revisited: Blacks and the Southern Convict Lease System, 1865–1933.* New York: Africana Studies Research Center, Brooklyn College, City University of New York.

Fiselier, Jan P. S. 1992. "A Test of the Stability of Punishment Hypothesis: The Dutch Case." *Journal of Quantitative Criminology* 8:133–51.

Flamant, Maurice, and Jeanne Singer-Kerel. 1968. *Modern Economic Crises.* Translated by Pat Wardroper. London: Barrie and Jenkins.

Flamming, Douglas. 1992. *Creating the Modern South: Millhands and Managers in Dalton, Georgia, 1884–1984.* Chapel Hill: University of North Carolina Press.

Fligstein, Neil. 1981. *Going North: Migration of Blacks and Whites from the South, 1900–1950.* New York: Academic Press.

Flynn, Charles L. 1983. *White Land, Black Labor: Caste and Class in Late Nineteenth-Century Georgia.* Baton Rouge: Louisiana State University Press.

Foster, Albert Pafford. 1949. "The Georgia State Highway Department: Its Origin, Development, and Current Administration." Master's thesis, Emory University.

Foucault, Michel. 1965. *Madness and Civilization: A History of Insanity in the Age of Reason.* Translated by Richard Howard. New York: Pantheon Books.

———. 1977. *Discipline and Punish: The Birth of the Prison.* Translated by Alan Sheridan. New York: Vintage Books.

Frederickson, George M. 1971. *The Black Image in the White Mind: The Debate on Afro-American Character and Destiny, 1817–1914.* New York: Harper and Row.

Freeze, Gary R. 1991. "Poor Girls Who Might Otherwise Be Wretched: The Origins of Paternalism in North Carolina's Mills, 1836–1880." Pp. 21–32 in *Hanging by the Thread: Social Change in Southern Textiles,* edited by Jeffrey Leiter, Michael D. Schulman, and Rhonda Zingraff. Ithaca, N.Y.: ILR Press.

Fuller, Hugh N. 1929. *Criminal Court Statistics, Studies #2–#7.* Atlanta: Department of Public Welfare, State of Georgia.

Gardner, Gil. 1987. "The Emergence of the New York State Prison System: A Critique of the Rusche-Kirchheimer Model." *Crime and Social Justice* 29:88–109.

Garland, David. 1990. *Punishment and Modern Society: A Study in Social Theory.* Chicago: University of Chicago Press.

Gatrell, V. A. C. 1980. "The Decline of Theft in Victorian and Edwardian England." Pp. 238–70 in *Crime and the Law: The Social History of Crime in Western Europe since 1500,* edited by V. A. C. Gatrell, Bruce Lenman, and Geoffrey Parker. London: Europa.

Georgia Assembly. 1856–67. *Acts of the General Assembly of the State of Georgia.* Milledgeville: State Printer.

———. 1871–1941. *Acts and Resolutions of the General Assembly of the State of Georgia.* Atlanta: State Printer.

———. 1943a. *Acts and Resolutions of the General Assembly of the State of Georgia.* Atlanta: State Printer.

———. 1943b. *Acts and Resolutions of the Special Session of the General Assembly of the State of Georgia.* Atlanta: State Printer.

Georgia Code. 1867. *The Code of the State of Georgia.* Atlanta: Franklin Steam Printing House.

———. 1873. *The Code of the State of Georgia.* Macon: J. W. Burke.

———. 1882. *The Code of the State of Georgia.* Atlanta: Jas. P. Harrison.

———. 1896. *The Code of the State of Georgia, Adopted December 15, 1895.* Atlanta: Foote and Davies.

———. 1911. *The Code of the State of Georgia, Adopted August 15, 1910.* Atlanta: Foote and Davies.

———. 1926. *The Georgia Code of 1926.* Charlottesville, Va.: Michie.

———. 1935. *The Code of Georgia of 1933.* Atlanta: Harrison.

Georgia Comptroller General. 1874–1936. *Report of the Comptroller General of the State of Georgia.* Atlanta: State Printer.

Georgia Department of Public Welfare. 1925. "Crime and the Georgia Courts: A Statistical Analysis." *Journal of the American Institute of Criminal Law and Criminology* 16:1–52.

———. 1937. *Survey of Criminal Court Procedure in Georgia: A Works Progress Administration Project.* Atlanta: Department of Archives and History, State of Georgia.

Georgia Highway Board. 1932. *Fourteenth Report.* Atlanta: Stein Printing Co.

———. 1934. *Fifteenth Report.* Atlanta: Stein Printing Co.

———. 1937–38. *Seventeenth Report.* Atlanta: State Printer.

———. 1941–42. *Nineteenth Report.* Atlanta: State Printer.

Georgia Highway Department. 1919. *First Annual Report.* Atlanta: State Printer.

———. 1922. *Fourth Annual Report.* Atlanta: State Printer.

Georgia House of Representatives. 1843–1854. *Journal of the House of Representatives of the State of Georgia at the Regular Session of the Georgia Assembly.* Milledgeville: State Printer.

———. 1870–1944. *Journal of the House of Representatives of the State of Georgia at the Regular Session of the Georgia Assembly.* Atlanta: State Printer.

———. 1908. *Journal of the House of Representatives of the State of Georgia at the Extraordinary Session of the Georgia Assembly.* Atlanta: Chas. P. Byrd, State Printer.

Georgia Senate. 1818–1856. *Journal of the Senate of the State of Georgia at the Regular Session of the Georgia Assembly.* Milledgeville: State Printer.

———. 1878–1899. *Journal of the Senate of the State of Georgia at the Regular Session of the Georgia Assembly.* Atlanta: State Printer.

———. 1943. *Journal of the Senate of the State of Georgia at the Extraordinary Session of the Georgia Assembly.* Decatur, Ga.: Bowen Press.

Gildemeister, Glen A. 1987. *Prison Labor and Convict Competition with Free Workers in Industrializing America, 1840–1890.* New York: Garland.

Gillis, A. R. 1996. "Urbanization, Sociohistorical Context, and Crime." Pp. 47–74 in *Criminological Controversies: A Methodological Primer,* edited by John Hagan, A. R. Gillis, and David Brownfield. Boulder, Colo.: Westview Press.

Goldfield, David R. 1982. *Cotton Fields and Skyscrapers: Southern City and Region, 1607–1980.* Baton Rouge: Louisiana State University Press.

Gordon, Robert J. 1986. *The American Business Cycle: Continuity and Change.* Chicago: University of Chicago Press.

Gorn, Elliott J. 1985. "'Gouge and Bite, Pull Hair and Scratch': The Social Significance of Fighting in the Southern Backcountry." *American Historical Review* 90:18–43.

Grantham, Dewey W. 1983. *Southern Progressivism: The Reconciliation of Progress and Tradition.* Knoxville: University of Tennessee Press.

Green, Fletcher Melvin. 1949. "Some Aspects of the Convict-Lease System in the Southern States." *James Sprunt Studies in History and Political Science* 31:112–23.

Grossman, James R. 1989. *Land of Hope: Chicago, Black Southerners, and the Great Migration.* Chicago: University of Chicago Press.

Gurr, Ted Robert, Peter N. Brabosky, and Richard C. Hula. 1977. *The Politics of Crime and Conflict: A Comparative History of Four Cities.* Beverly Hills, Calif.: Sage.

Hahn, Steven. 1983. *The Roots of Southern Populism: Yeoman Farmers and the Transformation of the Georgia Upcountry, 1850–1890.* New York: Oxford University Press.

———. 1985. "The 'Unmaking' of the Southern Yeomanry: The Transformation of the Georgia Upcountry, 1860–1890." Pp. 179–203 in *The Countryside in the Age of Capitalist Transformation: Essays in the Social History of Rural America,* edited by Steven Hahn and Jonathan Prude. Chapel Hill: University of North Carolina Press.

Hall, Jacquelyn Dowd, James Leloudis, Robert Korstad, Mary Murphy, Lu Ann Jones, and Christopher Daly. 1987. *Like a Family: The Making of a Southern Cotton Mill World.* Chapel Hill: University of North Carolina Press.

Hammond, Matthew B. 1897. *The Cotton Industry: An Essay in American Economic History.* Pt. 1, *The Cotton Culture and the Cotton Trade.* Publications of the American Economic Association, n.s., no. 1. New York: Macmillan.

Harvey, A. C. 1981. *The Econometric Analysis of Time Series.* Oxford: Philip Allan.

Haugh, Larry D., and G. E. P. Box. 1977. "Identification of Dynamic Regression (Distributed Lag) Models Connecting Two Time Series." *Journal of the American Statistical Association* 72:121–30.

Hawk, Emory Q. 1934. *Economic History of the South.* New York: Prentice Hall.

Hawkins, Darnell F. 1984. "State versus County: Prison Policy and Conflicts of Interest in North Carolina." *Criminal Justice History* 5:91–128.

———. 1987. "Beyond Anomalies: Rethinking the Conflict Perspective on Race and Criminal Punishment." *Social Forces* 65:719–45.

Hay, Douglas. 1980. "Crime and Justice in Eighteenth- and Nineteenth-Century England." Pp. 45–84 in *Crime and Justice: An Annual Review of Research,* vol. 2., edited by Norval Morris and Michael Tonry. Chicago: University of Chicago Press.

Haynes, Frederick E. 1939. *The American Prison System.* New York: McGraw-Hill.

Henderson, Harold Paulk. 1991. *The Politics of Change in Georgia: A Political Biography of Ellis Arnall.* Athens: University of Georgia Press.

Herndon, Jane Walker. 1974. "Eurith Dickinson Rivers: A Political Biography." Ph.D. diss., University of Georgia.

Hepworth, Joseph T., and Stephen G. West. 1988. "Lynchings and the Economy: A Time-Series Reanalysis of Hovland and Sears (1940)." *Journal of Personality and Social Psychology* 55:239–47.

Higgs, Robert. 1973. "Race, Tenure, and Resource Allocation in Southern Agriculture, 1910." *Journal of Economic History* 33:149–69.

———. 1974. "Patterns of Farm Rental in the Georgia Cotton Belt, 1880–1900." *Journal of Economic History* 34:468–82.

———. 1977a. *Competition and Coercion: Blacks in the American Economy, 1865–1914.* Cambridge: Cambridge University Press.

———. 1977b. "Firm-Specific Evidence on Racial Wage Differentials and Workforce Segregation." *American Economic Review* 67:236–45.

———. 1982. "Accumulation of Property by Southern Blacks before World War I." *American Economic Review* 72:725–37.

Hilles, William C. 1958. "The Good Roads Movement in the United States, 1880–1916." Ph.D. diss., Duke University.

Hindess, Barry, and Paul Q. Hirst. 1975. *Precapitalist Modes of Production.* London: Routledge and Kegan Paul.

Hoffsommer, Harold. 1935. "The AAA and the Cropper." *Social Forces* 13:494–502.

Hogg, Russell. 1979. "Imprisonment and Society under Early British Capitalism." *Crime and Social Justice* 12:4–17.

Holmes, J. A. 1901a. "Functions of the Government, the State, and the County in American Highway Improvement." Pp. 39–45 in *Proceedings of the International Good Roads Congress.* U.S. Department of Agriculture, Public Road Inquiries Bulletin, no. 21. Washington, D.C.: Government Printing Office.

——. 1901b. "Road Building with Convict Labor in the Southern States." Pp. 320–25 in *Yearbook of Agriculture.* U.S. Department of Agriculture. Washington, D.C.: Government Printing Office.

Holt, W. Stull. 1923. *The Bureau of Public Roads: Its History, Activities, and Organization.* Institute for Government Research, Service Monographs of the U.S. Government, no. 26. Baltimore: Johns Hopkins University Press.

Hutson, A. C., Jr. 1936. "The Overthrow of the Convict Lease System in Tennessee." *Publications of the East Tennessee Historical Society* 8:82–103.

Isaac, Larry W., and Larry J. Griffin. 1989. "Ahistoricism in Time-Series Analyses of Historical Processes: Critique, Redirection, and Illustrations from U.S. History." *American Sociological Review* 54:873–90.

Jackson, Henry Theodore. 1927–28. "Prison Labor." *Journal of Criminal Law, Criminology, and Police Science* 18:218–318.

Jackson, Pamela Irving. 1992. "Minority Group Threat, Social Context, and Policing." Pp. 89–112 in *Social Threat and Social Control,* edited by Allen E. Liska. Albany: State University of New York Press.

Jacobs, David. 1978. "Inequality and the Legal Order: An Ecological Test of the Conflict Model." *Social Problems* 25:515–30.

Janiewski, Delores E. 1985. *Sisterhood Denied: Race, Gender, and Class in a New South Community.* Philadelphia: Temple University Press.

Jenks, Jeremiah W. 1889. "Road Legislation for the American State." *American Economic Association Publications* 4:145–227.

Johnson, Charles S., Edwin R. Embree, and W. W. Alexander. 1935. *The Collapse of Cotton Tenancy: Summary of Field Studies and Statistical Surveys 1933–35.* Chapel Hill: University of North Carolina Press.

Johnson, Daniel M., and Rex R. Campbell. 1981. *Black Migration in America: A Social Demographic History.* Durham, N.C.: Duke University Press.

Joint Committee on the Penitentiary. [1870] 1974. *Proceedings of the Joint Committee Appointed to Investigate the Condition of the Georgia Penitentiary.* New York: Arno Press.

Kessler-Harris, Alice. 1982. *Out to Work: A History of Wage-Earning Women in the United States.* New York: Oxford University Press.

Kirby, Jack Temple. 1984. "Black and White in the Rural South, 1915–1954." *Agricultural History* 58:411–22.

——. 1987. *Rural Worlds Lost: The American South, 1920–1960.* Baton Rouge: Louisiana State University Press.

LaFree, Gary, and Kriss A. Drass. 1996. "The Effect of Changes in Intraracial Income Inequality and Educational Attainment on Changes in Arrest Rates for African Americans and Whites, 1957 to 1990." *American Sociological Review* 61:614–34.

LaFree, Gary, Kriss A. Drass, and Patrick O'Day. 1992. "Race and Crime in Postwar America: Determinants of African-American and White Rates, 1957–1988." *Criminology* 30:157–88.

Lamar, Lucius Q. C. 1821. *A Compilation of the Laws of the State of Georgia Passed by the Legislature since the Year 1810 to the Year 1819, Inclusive.* Augusta, Ga.: T. S. Hannon.

Lane, Roger. 1970. "Urbanization and Criminal Violence in the Nineteenth Century: Massachusetts as a Test Case." Pp. 468–84 in *Violence in America: Historical and Comparative Perspectives: A Report to the National Commission on the Causes and Prevention of Violence,* rev. ed., edited by Hugh Davis Graham and Ted Robert Gurr. New York: Praeger.

———. 1974. "Crime and the Industrial Revolution: British and American Views." *Journal of Social History* 7:287–303.

———. 1979. *Violent Death in the City: Suicide, Accident, and Murder in Nineteenth-Century Philadelphia.* Cambridge: Harvard University Press.

———. 1980. "Urban Homicide in the Nineteenth Century: Some Lessons for the Twentieth." Pp. 91–109 in *History and Crime: Implications for Criminal Justice Policy,* edited by James A. Inciardi and Charles E. Faupel. Beverly Hills, Calif.: Sage.

Larsen, Lawrence H. 1990. *The Urban South: A History.* Lexington: University Press of Kentucky.

Lebergott, Stanley. 1964. *Manpower in Economic Growth: The American Record since 1800.* New York: McGraw-Hill.

———. 1984. *The Americans: An Economic Record.* New York: W. W. Norton.

Lessan, Gloria T., and Joseph F. Sheley. 1992. "Does Law Behave? A Macrolevel Test of Black's Propositions on Change in Law." *Social Forces* 70:655–78.

Levasseur, Emile. 1900. *The American Workman.* Translated by Thomas S. Adams. Baltimore: Johns Hopkins University Press.

Lewis, Orlando F. [1922] 1967. *The Development of American Prisons and Prison Customs, 1776–1845, with Special Reference to Early Institutions in the State of New York.* Montclair, N.J.: Patterson Smith.

Lewis, Ronald L. 1987. *Black Coal Miners in America: Race, Class, and Community Conflict, 1780–1980.* Lexington: University Press of Kentucky.

Lichtenstein, Alex. 1996. *Twice the Work of Free Labor: The Political Economy of Convict Labor in the New South.* London: Verso.

Lindsey, Edward. 1925. "Historical Sketch of the Indeterminate Sentence and Parole System." *Journal of the American Institute of Criminal Law and Criminology* 16:9–126.

Liska, Allen E. 1992. "Introduction to the Study of Social Control." Pp. 1–29 in *Social Threat and Social Control,* edited by Allen E. Liska. Albany: State University of New York Press.

———. 1994. "Modeling the Conflict Perspective of Social Control." Pp. 53–71 in *Inequality, Crime, and Social Control,* edited by George S. Bridges and Martha A. Myers. Boulder, Colo.: Westview Press.

Liska, Allen E., and Mitchell B. Chamlin. 1984. "Social Structure and Crime Control among Macrosocial Units." *American Journal of Sociology* 90:383–95.

McCallie, S. W. 1901. *A Preliminary Report on the Roads and Road-Building Materials of Georgia.* Geological Survey of Georgia Bulletin, no. 8. Atlanta: Franklin.

———. 1912. *A Third Report on the Public Roads of Georgia.* Geological Survey of Georgia Bulletin, no. 28. Atlanta: Chas. P. Byrd, State Printer.

McCleary, Richard, and Richard A. Hay, Jr. 1980. *Applied Time Series Analysis for the Social Sciences.* Beverly Hills, Calif.: Sage.

McDowall, David, and Colin Loftin. 1992. "Comparing the UCR and NCS over Time." *Criminology* 30:125–32.

McHugh, Cathy L. 1988. *Mill Family: The Labor System in the Southern Cotton Textile Industry, 1880–1915.* New York: Oxford University Press.

McKay, Herbert Stacey. 1942. "Convict Leasing in North Carolina, 1870–1934." Master's thesis, University of North Carolina.

McKelvey, Blake. 1935. "Penal Slavery and Southern Reconstruction." *Journal of Negro History* 20:153–55.

McKelway, A. J. 1908a. "Abolition of the Convict Lease System in Georgia." *Proceedings of the American Prison Association* 1908:219–26.

——— 1908b. "The Convict Lease System of Georgia." *Outlook* 90 (September):67–72.

Makridakis, Spyros, Steven C. Wheelwright, and Victor E. McGee. 1983. *Forecasting: Methods and Applications.* 2d ed. New York: Wiley.

Mancini, Matthew J. 1996. *One Dies, Get Another: Convict Leasing in the American South, 1866–1928.* Columbia: University of South Carolina Press.

Mann, Susan Archer. 1990. *Agrarian Capitalism in Theory and Practice.* Chapel Hill: University of North Carolina Press.

Marks, Carole. 1985. "Black Labor Migration, 1910–1920." *Insurgent Sociologist* 12:5–24.

Mason, Philip P. 1957. "The League of American Wheelmen and the Good Roads Movement, 1880–1905." Ph.D. diss., University of Michigan.

Melossi, Dario, and Massimo Pavarini. 1981. *The Prison and the Factory: Origins of the Penitentiary System.* Translated by Glynis Cousin. Totowa, N.J.: Barnes and Noble.

Miller, Martin B. 1980. "Sinking Gradually into the Proletariat: The Emergence of the Penitentiary in the United States." *Crime and Social Justice* 14:37–43.

Miller, Zane L. 1975. "Urban Blacks in the South, 1865–1920: The Richmond, Savannah, New Orleans, Louisville, and Birmingham Experience." Pp. 184–204 in *The New Urban History: Quantitative Explorations by American Historians,* edited by Leo F. Schnore. Princeton: Princeton University Press.

Mohler, Henry Calvin. 1924–25. "Convict Labor Policies." *Journal of Criminal Law, Criminology, and Police Science* 15:530–97.

Moitra, Soumyo D. 1987. *Crimes and Punishments: A Comparative Study of Temporal Variations.* Freiburg: Bundschuh.

Monkkonen, Eric H. 1975. *The Dangerous Class: Crime and Poverty in Columbus, Ohio, 1860–1885.* Cambridge: Cambridge University Press.

———. 1981. *Police in Urban America, 1860–1920.* Cambridge: Cambridge University Press.

Montgomery, Douglas G., and Ginner Weatherby. 1980. "Modeling and Forecasting Time Series Using Transfer Function and Intervention Methods." *AIIE Transactions* 12:289–306.

Moos, Malcolm C. 1942. *State Penal Administration in Alabama.* Tuscaloosa: University of Alabama, Bureau of Public Administration.

Morse, Wayne L., ed. 1939. *Attorney General's Survey of Release Procedures.* Vol. 1, *Digest of Federal and State Laws on Release Procedures.* Washington, D.C.: Government Printing Office.

Murray, Paul Thom. 1972. "Blacks and the Draft: An Analysis of Institutional Racism, 1917–1971." Ph.D. diss., Florida State University.

Myers, Martha A. 1990a. "Black Threat and Incarceration in Postbellum Georgia." *Social Forces* 69:373–93.

———. 1990b. "Economic Threat and Racial Disparities in Incarceration: The Case of Postbellum Georgia." *Criminology* 28:627–56.

———. 1991. "Economic Conditions and Punishment in Postbellum Georgia." *Journal of Quantitative Criminology* 7:99–121.

———. 1993. "Inequality and the Punishment of Minor Offenders in the Early 20th Century." *Law & Society Review* 27:401–31.

———. 1995a. "Gender and Southern Punishment after the Civil War." *Criminology* 33:17–46.

———. 1995b. "The New South's 'New' Black Criminal: Rape and Punishment in Georgia,

1870–1940." Pp. 145–66 in *Ethnicity, Race, and Crime: Perspectives across Time and Place*, edited by Darnell F. Hawkins. Albany: State University of New York Press.

Myers, Martha A., and James L. Massey. 1991. "Race, Labor, and Punishment in Postbellum Georgia." *Social Problems* 38:267–86.

Myers, Martha A., and Susette M. Talarico. 1987. *The Social Contexts of Criminal Sentencing*. New York: Springer-Verlag.

Myers, Samuel L., Jr., and William J. Sabol. 1986. "The Stability of Punishment Hypothesis: Regional Differences in Racially Disproportionate Prison Populations and Incarcerations, 1850–1980." Paper presented at annual meeting of the Law and Society Association, Chicago.

———. 1987. "Unemployment and Racial Differences in Imprisonment." *Review of Black Political Economy* 16:189–209.

Newby, Idus A. 1965. *Jim Crow's Defense: Anti-Negro Thought in America, 1900–1930*. Baton Rouge: Louisiana State University Press.

Norrell, Robert J. 1991. *James Bowron: The Autobiography of a New South Industrialist*. Chapel Hill: University of North Carolina Press.

Olzak, Susan. 1990. "The Political Context of Competition: Lynching and Urban Racial Violence, 1882–1914." *Social Forces* 69:395–421.

Oubre, Claude R. 1978. *Forty Acres and a Mule: The Freedmen's Bureau and Black Land Ownership*. Baton Rouge: Louisiana State University Press.

Page, Logan Waller. 1907. *Public Roads of Georgia: Mileage and Expenditures in 1904*. U.S. Department of Agriculture, Office of Public Roads Circular, no. 76. Washington, D.C.: Government Printing Office.

Page, Myra. 1935. "Men in Chains." *Nation*, November 13, 561–63.

Paternoster, Raymond. 1991. *Capital Punishment in America*. New York: Lexington Books.

Pennybacker, J. E., Jr., and Maurice O. Eldridge. 1912. *Mileage and Cost of Public Roads in the United States in 1909*. U.S. Department of Agriculture, Office of Road Inquiry Bulletin, no. 41. Washington, D.C.: Government Printing Office.

Petchesky, Rosalind P. 1981. "At Hard Labor: Penal Confinement and Production in Nineteenth-Century America." Pp. 341–57 in *Crime and Capitalism: Readings in Marxist Criminology*, edited by David F. Greenberg. Palo Alto, Calif.: Mayfield.

Pollard, Sidney. 1963. "Factory Discipline in the Industrial Revolution." *Economic History Review* 16:254–71.

Porter, Robert P. 1880. "State Debts and Repudiation." *International Review* 9:556–92.

Pratt, Kathleen Falconer. 1949. "The Development of the Florida Prison System." Master's thesis, Florida State University.

Preston, Howard Lawrence. 1991. *Dirt Roads to Dixie: Accessibility and Modernization in the South, 1885–1935*. Knoxville: University of Tennessee Press.

Prince, Oliver H. 1822. *Digest of the Laws of the State of Georgia*. Milledgeville: Grantland and Orme.

———. 1837. *Digest of the Laws of the State of Georgia*. 2d ed. Athens, Ga.: Privately printed.

Principal Keeper of the Penitentiary. 1870–75. *Report*. Atlanta: State Printer.

———. 1880–86. *Biennial Report*. Atlanta: Jas. P. Harrison.

———. 1896–97. *Annual Report*. Atlanta: Franklin.

Principal Physician of the Penitentiary. 1886. "Report of the Principal Physician to the Penitentiary." Pp. 105–40 in *Biennial Report, 1884–1886*, by Principal Keeper of the Penitentiary. Atlanta: Jas. P. Harrison.

———— 1890. *Biennial Report, 1888–1890.* Atlanta: Franklin.

————. 1896. *Annual Report, 1895–1896.* Atlanta: Franklin.

Prison Commission. 1898–1923. *Annual Report.* Atlanta: State Printer.

————. 1925–36. *Biennial Report.* Atlanta: State Printer.

Rabinowitz, Howard W. 1976. "The Conflict between Blacks and the Police in the Urban South, 1865–1900." *The Historian* 39:62–76.

Ransom, Roger L., and Richard Sutch. 1972. "Debt Peonage in the Cotton South after the Civil War." *Journal of Economic History* 32:641–69.

————. 1977. *One Kind of Freedom: The Economic Consequences of Emancipation.* Cambridge: Cambridge University Press.

Raper, Arthur F. 1936. *Preface to Peasantry: A Tale of Two Black Belt Counties.* Chapel Hill: University of North Carolina Press.

Raper, Arthur F., and Ira DeA. Reid. 1941. *Sharecroppers All.* Chapel Hill: University of North Carolina Press.

Rauma, David. 1981. "Crime and Punishment Reconsidered: Some Comments on Blumstein's Stability of Punishment Hypothesis." *Journal of Criminal Law and Criminology* 72:1772–98.

Roberts, Derrell C. 1960. "Joseph E. Brown and the Convict Lease System." *Georgia Historical Quarterly* 26:399–410.

Ross, Arthur M. 1940. "The Negro Worker in the Depression." *Social Forces* 18:550–59.

Royce, Edward. 1993. *The Origins of Southern Sharecropping.* Philadelphia: Temple University Press.

Rudwick, Elliot, and August Meier. 1966. "Negro Retaliatory Violence in the Twentieth Century." *New Politics* 5:41–51.

Rusche, Georg, and Otto Kirchheimer. 1939. *Punishment and Social Structure.* New York: Russell and Russell.

Russell, James Michael. 1988. *Atlanta, 1847–1890: City Building in the Old South and New.* Baton Rouge: Louisiana State University Press.

Sabol, William J. 1989. "The Dynamics of Unemployment and Imprisonment in England and Wales, 1946–1985." *Journal of Quantitative Criminology* 5:147–68.

Saloutos, Theodore. 1960. *Farmer Movements in the South, 1865–1933.* Berkeley: University of California Press.

Sampson, Robert J. 1985. "Structural Sources of Variation in Race-Age-Specific Rates of Offending across Major U.S. Cities." *Criminology* 23:647–73.

Schulman, Michael D., and Jeffrey Leiter. 1991. "Southern Textiles: Contested Puzzles and Continuing Paradoxes." Pp. 3–17 in *Hanging by the Thread: Social Change in Southern Textiles,* edited by Jeffrey Leiter, Michael D. Schulman, and Rhonda Zingraff. Ithaca, N.Y.: ILR Press.

Scott, Emmett J. 1919. *Scott's Official History of the American Negro in the World War: A Complete and Authentic Narration.* Chicago: Homewood Press.

————. 1920. *Negro Migration during the War.* New York: Oxford University Press.

Scull, Andrew T. 1977. "Madness and Segregative Control: The Rise of the Insane Asylum." *Social Problems* 24:337–51.

Shaw, Barton C. 1984. *The Wool-Hat Boys: Georgia's Populist Party.* Baton Rouge: Louisiana State University Press.

Sheffield, O. H. 1894. *Improvement of the Road System of Georgia.* U.S. Department of

Agriculture, Office of Road Inquiry Bulletin, no. 3. Washington, D.C.: Government Printing Office.

Shelden, Randall G. 1979. "From Slave to Caste Society: Penal Changes in Tennessee, 1830–1915." *Tennessee Historical Quarterly* 38:462–78.

———. 1981. "Convict Leasing: An Application of the Rusche-Kirchheimer Thesis to Penal Changes in Tennessee, 1830–1915." Pp. 358–66 in *Crime and Capitalism: Readings in Marxist Criminology*, edited by David F. Greenberg. Palo Alto, Calif.: Mayfield.

Shivers, Lyda Gordon. 1930. "A History of the Mississippi Penitentiary." Master's thesis, University of Mississippi.

Simon, Jonathan. 1993. *Poor Discipline: Parole and the Social Control of the Underclass, 1890–1990*. Chicago: University of Chicago Press.

Smith, Albert Colbey. 1975. "Violence in Georgia's Black Belt: A Study of Crime in Baldwin and Terrell Counties, 1866–1899." Master's thesis, University of Georgia.

———. 1982. "Down Freedom's Road: The Contours of Race, Class, and Property Crime in Black-Belt Georgia, 1866–1910." Ph.D. diss., University of Georgia.

Sneed, William C. 1860. *A Report on the History and Model of Management of the Kentucky Penitentiary from Its Origin, in 1798, to March 1, 1860*. Frankfort, Ky.: John B. Major, State Printer.

Spierenburg, Pieter. 1987. "From Amsterdam to Auburn: An Explanation for the Rise of the Prison in Seventeenth-Century Holland and Nineteenth-Century America." *Journal of Social History* 20:439–61.

Spitzer, Steven. 1975. "Toward a Marxian Theory of Deviance." *Social Problems* 22:638–51.

———. 1979. "The Rationalization of Crime Control in Capitalist Society." *Contemporary Crises* 3:187–206.

Staples, William G. 1990. *Castles of Our Conscience: Social Control and the American State, 1800–1985*. New Brunswick, N.J.: Rutgers University Press.

Steiner, Jesse, and Roy M. Brown. [1927] 1970. *The North Carolina Chain Gang: A Study of County Convict Road Work*. Westport, Conn.: Negro Universities Press.

Stern, Leon Thomas. 1940–41. "The Effect of the Depression on Prison Commitments and Sentences." *Journal of Criminal Law and Criminology* 31:696–711.

Stone, Roy. 1895. *State Laws Relating to the Management of Roads Enacted in 1894–95*. U.S. Department of Agriculture, Office of Road Inquiry Bulletin, no. 18. Washington, D.C.: Government Printing Office.

———. 1898. *Notes on the Employment of Convicts in Connection with Road Building*. U.S. Department of Agriculture, Office of Road Inquiry Bulletin, no. 16, rev. Washington, D.C.: Government Printing Office.

———. 1907. *Addresses on Road Improvement in Maine, New York, North Carolina, and Illinois*. U.S. Department of Agriculture, Office of Road Inquiry Circular, no. 28. Washington, D.C.: Government Printing Office.

Sutton, John. 1987. "Doing Time: Dynamics of Imprisonment in the Reformist State." *American Sociological Review* 52:612–30.

———. 1991. "The Political Economy of Madness: The Expansion of the Asylum in Progressive America." *American Sociological Review* 56:665–78.

Taylor, A. Elizabeth. 1940. "The Convict Lease System in Georgia, 1866–1908." Master's thesis, University of North Carolina.

313

———. 1942a. "The Abolition of the Convict Lease System in Georgia." *Georgia Historical Quarterly* 26:273–87.

———. 1942b. "The Origin and Development of the Convict Lease System in Georgia." *Georgia Historical Quarterly* 26:113–28.

Thompson, C. Mildred. 1915. *Reconstruction in Georgia: Economic, Social, Political, 1865–1872.* New York: Columbia University Press.

Thorp, Willard Long. 1926. *Business Annals.* New York: National Bureau of Economic Research.

Timasheff, Nicholas A. 1941. *One Hundred Years of Probation, 1841–1941.* Fordham University Studies, Social Science Series, no. 1. New York: Fordham University Press.

Tindall, George Brown. 1967. *The Emergence of the New South, 1913–1945.* Baton Rouge: Louisiana State University Press.

Tittle, Charles R. 1995. *Control Balance: Toward a General Theory of Deviance.* Boulder, Colo.: Westview Press.

Tolnay, Stewart E. 1985. "Black American Fertility Transition, 1880–1940." *Social Science Research* 70:1–7.

———. 1987. "The Decline of Black Marital Fertility in the Rural South, 1910–1940." *American Sociological Review* 52:211–17.

Tolnay, Stewart E., and E. M. Beck. 1990. "Black Flight: Lethal Violence and the Great Migration, 1900 to 1930." *Social Science History* 14:347–70.

———. 1992. "Toward a Threat Model of Southern Black Lynchings." Pp. 33–52 in *Social Threat and Social Control,* edited by Allen E. Liska. Albany: State University of New York Press.

———. 1994. *A Festival of Violence: An Analysis of the Lynching of African-Americans in the American South, 1882 to 1930.* Urbana: University of Illinois Press.

Tolnay, Stewart E., E. M. Beck, and James L. Massey. 1989. "Black Lynchings: The Power Threat Hypothesis Revisited." *Social Forces* 67:605–23.

———. 1992. "Black Competition and White Vengeance: Legal Execution of Blacks as Social Control in the Cotton South, 1890 to 1929." *Social Science Quarterly* 73:627–44.

Tremblay, Pierre. 1986. "The Stability of Punishment: A Follow-Up of Blumstein's Hypothesis." *Journal of Quantitative Criminology* 2:157–80.

U.S. Bureau of the Census. 1975. *Historical Statistics of the U.S.: Colonial Times to 1970.* Washington, D.C.: Government Printing Office.

U.S. Department of Agriculture. 1951–52. *Statistics on Cotton and Related Data.* Agricultural Economics Bureau Statistical Bulletin, no. 99. Washington, D.C.: Government Printing Office.

U.S. Department of Interior, Bureau of Labor. 1887. *Second Annual Report of Commissioner of Labor: Convict Labor.* Washington, D.C.: Government Printing Office.

———. 1906. *Twentieth Annual Report of Commissioner of Labor: Convict Labor.* Washington, D.C.: Government Printing Office.

U.S. Prison Industries Reorganization Administration. 1937. *The Prison Labor Problem in Georgia.* Washington, D.C.: Government Printing Office.

U.S. Statutes at Large. 1917. Vol. 39, pp. 355–59. *An Act to provide that the United States shall aid the States in the construction of rural post roads, and for other purposes.*

———. 1936. Vol. 49, p. 272. *An Act making appropriations for the Department of Agriculture and for the Farm Credit Administration for the fiscal year ending June 30, 1936, and for other purposes.*

Vance, Rupert. 1929. *Human Factors in Cotton Culture: A Study of the Social Geography of the American South*. Chapel Hill: University of North Carolina Press.

Vance, Rupert, and Nicholas J. Demerath, eds. 1954. *The Urban South*. Chapel Hill: University of North Carolina Press.

Varner, H. B. 1910a. "Convict Labor in Road Building." *Southern Good Roads* 2(4):18.

———. 1910b. "Good Roads Notes Gathered Here and There." *Southern Good Roads* 1(6):21.

———. 1915. "Good Roads Notes Gathered Here and There." *Southern Good Roads* 12(6):19.

Wade, Richard C. 1964. *Slavery in the Cities: The South, 1820–1860*. New York: Oxford University Press.

Walden, Mary Patricia. 1974. "History of the Georgia Penitentiary at Milledgeville, 1817–1868." Master's thesis, Georgia State University.

Walker, Donald R. 1988. *Penology for Profit: A History of the Texas Prison System, 1867–1912*. College Station: Texas A&M University Press.

Wallenstein, Peter. 1987. *From Slave South to New South: Public Policy in Nineteenth-Century Georgia*. Chapel Hill: University of North Carolina Press.

Waller, Irvin, and Janet Chan. 1974. "Prison Use: A Canadian and International Comparison." *Criminal Law Quarterly* 17:47–71.

Ward, Judson Clements, Jr. 1947. "Georgia under the Bourbon Democrats, 1872–1890." Ph.D. diss., University of North Carolina.

Ward, Robert David, and William Warren Rogers. 1987. *Convicts, Coal, and the Banner Mine Tragedy*. Tuscaloosa: University of Alabama Press.

Waskow, Arthur I. 1966. *From Race Riot to Sit-In, 1919 and the 1960s*. Garden City, N.Y.: Doubleday.

Watkins, Robert, and George Watkins. 1800. *A Digest of the Laws of the State of Georgia*. Philadelphia: R. Aitken.

Watts, Eugene J. 1973. "The Police in Atlanta, 1890–1905." *Journal of Southern History* 39:165–82.

Wei, William W. S. 1990. *Time Series Analysis: Univariate and Multivariate Methods*. Redwood City, Calif.: Addison-Wesley.

Whatley, Warren C. 1983. "Labor for the Picking: The New Deal in the South." *Journal of Economic History* 43:905–29.

Whitin, E. Stagg. 1912. *Penal Servitude*. New York: National Committee on Prison Labor.

Williams, Jack Kenny. 1959. *Vogues in Villainy: Crime and Retribution in Ante-bellum South Carolina*. Columbia: University of South Carolina Press.

Williams, Lee E. II. 1991. *Post-War Riots in America, 1919 and 1946: How the Pressures of War Exacerbated American Urban Tensions to the Breaking Point*. Lewiston, N.Y.: Edwin Mellen Press.

Wolters, Raymond. 1970. *Negroes and the Great Depression: The Problem of Economic Recovery*. Westport, Conn.: Greenwood Press.

Wood, Phillip J. 1986. *Southern Capitalism: The Political Economy of North Carolina, 1880–1980*. Durham, N.C.: Duke University Press.

Woodman, H. 1968. *King Cotton and His Retainers: Financing and Marketing the Cotton Crop of the South, 1800–1925*. Lexington: University Press of Kentucky.

Woodson, Carter G. 1918. *A Century of Negro Migration*. Washington, D.C.: Association for the Study of Negro Life and History.

Woodward, C. Vann. 1971. *Origins of the New South, 1877–1913*. Baton Rouge: Louisiana State University Press.

Woofter, Thomas Jackson. 1920. *Negro Migration: Changes in Rural Organization and Population of the Cotton Belt.* New York: W. D. Gray.

Wright, Gavin. 1986. *Old South, New South: Revolutions in the Southern Economy since the Civil War.* New York: Basic Books.

Wyatt-Brown, Bertram. 1986. *Honor and Violence in the Old South.* New York: Oxford University Press.

Wynne, Lewis Nicholas. 1986. *The Continuity of Cotton: Planter Politics in Georgia, 1865–1892.* Macon, Ga.: Mercer University Press.

Zimmerman, Jane. 1947. "Penal Systems and Penal Reforms in the South since the Civil War." Ph.D. diss., University of North Carolina.

———. 1949. "The Convict Lease System in Arkansas and the Fight for Abolition." *Arkansas Historical Quarterly* 8:171–88.

Index

AAA. *See* Agricultural Adjustment Act
abolition of the lease. *See* convict leasing, abolition of
admissions to the penitentiary, 3, 46–49, 81
offense differences in, 94, 102, 109–11, 113, 117–19, 227–29, 241–42, 247–48, 253, 261
racial differences in, 81, 93, 102, 109–19, 225–28, 234, 237, 241–44, 246, 249, 250, 253, 263
See also under specific types of offender
age of admissions, 46 table 4.1, 75
and black prison sentences, 73, 123, 125 table 6.2, 134 table 6.8, 143–45, 150, 158, 159, 256–57
and black release, 162, 164 table 7.2, 172 table 7.8, 181 table 7.14, 196, 288 table B.10
determinants of, 271, 274–77
operative years of, series, 277 table A.3
and white conditional release, 189, 196, 251, 286 table B.8, 290 table B.12
and white prison sentences, 123, 128–29, 130 table 6.6, 138 table 6.11, 147–48, 149 table 6.18, 158, 257, 261, 291 table C.1, 298 n. 3
and white release, 162, 168 table 7.5, 175 table 7.11, 184, 186, 196, 231, 282 table B.4
agrarian economy. *See* cotton economy
Agricultural Adjustment Act (AAA), 70–71
and admissions, 82–83, 85, 89–91, 98–99, 253
and black conditional release, 279 table B.1, 283 table B.5, 287 table B.9

and black release, 161, 162–63, 170–71, 178, 180 table 7.13, 181, 185, 187, 196, 253
and prison sentences, 122, 157
and white release, 161, 167, 169, 174–75, 179, 184–85, 196, 253, 281 table B.3, 285 table B.7, 289 table B.11
Alabama, 10, 21, 22, 294 nn. 1, 5
ARIMA modeling. *See* time series analysis
Assembly, state of Georgia. *See* state (Georgia)
Assistant Principal Keeper of the Penitentiary, 19
Atkinson, William Y., 24
Atlanta Georgian, 20

Black Belt, 66
black male population, size of, 3, 58–59
and black admissions, 83, 85 table 5.2, 94, 96 table 5.8, 105 table 5.14
and black prison sentences, 43, 122, 125 table 6.2, 134 table 6.8, 143 table 6.14, 152
and black release, 161, 164 table 7.2, 171–74, 178, 181–84, 190–91, 233–34, 236, 284 table B.6
determinants of, 78, 272, 273 table A.2
and incarceration rate, 39, 58
and lynching, 39
operative years of, series, 277 table A.3
and white admissions, 83, 91–93, 100–102, 108, 110, 112

black male population (*continued*)
and white prison sentences, 43, 123, 129 table
6.5, 138 table 6.11, 148 table 6.17, 152
and white release, 161, 164–65, 168–69, 170,
175–77, 179, 186 table 7.17, 187, 233, 236, 282
table B.4
black offenders
admissions of, 46–48, 84–89, 113–16, 118–19,
199–201, 203–4, 221–22, 225–27, 242–45,
249
age of admitted, 73, 75
conditional release of, 188–89, 191, 196, 251,
279 table B.1, 280 table B.2
prison sentences of, 49–51, 124–27, 133, 150,
152–57, 159, 199–201, 203, 222, 243, 244, 254,
255
release of, 51–53, 162–67, 169–70, 185, 187,
192–94, 196, 199–204, 221, 226–27, 234–35,
243–45, 247, 299 n. 1
seriousness of admitted, 73–74
unconditional release of, 188–89, 279 table
B.1, 280 table B.2
See also black property offenders; black violent offenders
black property offenders
admissions of, 47, 103–6, 109–19, 211–13, 216–
20, 222, 223, 228, 230, 234, 238, 240, 242–43,
251, 261
age of admitted, 75
conditional release of, 188–89, 191, 196, 251,
287 table B.9, 288 table B.10, 299 n. 2
prison sentences of, 49–51, 141–45, 146 fig.
6.8, 150–51, 153–59, 211–13, 216–23, 229–30,
234, 240, 245–49, 252, 256–57, 261
release of, 53, 179–84, 185, 187, 190–96, 211–13,
216–20, 222, 223, 228, 231, 234, 240, 246, 253,
256
seriousness of admitted, 73–74
unconditional release of, 188–89, 287 table
B.9, 288 table B.10, 299 n. 2
blacks
economic position of, 65–67
fertility of, 58
migration of, 58
population size, and social control, 38
punishment of, 39, 46–53
rural experiences of, 65–66
urban experiences of, 60–61
See also cotton economy
black urban population, 62 fig. 4.12, 63
and admissions, 83, 85 table 5.2, 96 table 5.8,
105 table 5.14, 113

determinants of, 272, 273 table A.2
operative years of, series, 277 table A.3
and prison sentences, 122–23, 125 table 6.2, 134
table 6.8, 143 table 6.14, 144 table 6.15, 145,
146 fig. 6.8, 153, 240, 291 table C.1
and release, 161, 172 table 7.8, 192
black violent offenders
admissions of, 47–49, 94–97, 110–19, 205–10,
222, 228, 234, 238, 240, 242, 243, 261, 297–
98 n. 2
age of admitted, 75
conditional release of, 188, 191, 251, 283 table
B.5, 284 table B.6
prison sentences of, 49–51, 133–36, 140–41,
150–51, 152, 154–56, 158–59, 205 table 8.6,
229–30, 235, 240, 245, 246, 248, 258–59, 261
release of, 53, 170–74, 178, 187, 190–91, 193–96,
205–6, 209 table 8.10, 210, 222, 228, 235,
236, 246
seriousness of admitted, 73–74
unconditional release of, 283 table B.5, 284
table B.6
Board of Pardons and Parole, 28
Board of Penal Administration, 2, 27, 28
Board of Penal Corrections, 28
Board of Prisons, 28
boll weevil, 54, 58
Brown, Joseph E., 10–11
burglary, 1, 29, 30 table 2.1, 42, 73
See also property offenders
Bush, E. B., 294–95 n. 3
business cycles. *See* economic crises

capital, scarcity of, 8, 54–55
capitalism
attributes of, 293 n. 2
phases of, 6, 295–96 n. 1
and punishment, 6–7, 293–94 n. 3
role of state in, 9–11, 293 n. 3
capital punishment, 6, 13, 46 table 4.1
Census of Manufactures, 63
Central Register of Convicts, 45, 296 n. 1
chain gangs, 21, 24–29, 40
chaplain to the penitentiary, 19
Civil War, 2, 8, 15, 32, 52, 54
conditional release
determinants of, 188–89, 190–93, 279–90
racial differences in, 51–53, 188–89
See also under specific types of offender
conscription. *See* World War I
contract labor, 6–7, 14, 294 n. 4

convict labor
and capitalism, 6, 293–94 n. 3
in Georgia penitentiary, 8, 13–15, 25
in the North, 6–7, 23, 25
and road building (*see* road building)
in the South, 8–11, 15, 21
See also contract labor; convict leasing
convict leasing
abolition of, 20–21, 69–70
abolition of, and admissions, 70, 82, 85, 89,
103–4, 109, 110, 118, 251
abolition of, and prison sentences, 70, 122, 157
abolition of, and release, 161, 195
abolition of, and seriousness of admissions,
268 table A.1, 271
criticisms of, 16–20, 294–95 n. 3
development of, 7–11, 14–16, 294 n. 5
efforts to end, 18
grand jury oversight of, 19
profitability of, 294 n. 2
regulations governing, 16–18
subleasing under, 20
corporal punishment, 6, 13, 14
cotton economy, 2, 3, 39, 53–59, 65–67
and punishment, 111–12, 151, 190–91, 226, 228,
229, 231, 232–36, 261
See also black male population; cotton harvest; cotton price
cotton harvest, 57–58
and black admissions, 83, 85 table 5.2, 94, 96
table 5.8, 105 table 5.14
and black prison sentences, 122, 125–27, 134
table 6.8, 135–36, 143 table 6.14, 152, 226, 235
and black release, 161, 164 table 7.2, 171–73,
178, 181 table 7.14, 190, 235
determinants of, 54, 265–66, 267 table A.1,
272, 273 table A.2
and good-roads movement, 233
and incarceration rate, 40
operative years of, series, 277 table A.3, 278
and white admissions, 83, 91, 100 table 5.11,
101–2, 108, 109 table 5.18
and white prison sentences, 123, 129 fig. 6.5,
138 table 6.11, 148 table 6.17
and white release, 161, 168 table 7.5, 175 table
7.11, 186 table 7.17
cotton price, 54–56
and black admissions, 83, 85 table 5.2, 86–87,
94, 96, 103, 105, 106 table 5.15, 112, 228, 232–
33, 261, 297–98 n. 2
and black conditional release, 188, 190, 251,
280 table B.2, 288 table B.10

and black prison sentences, 122, 125–27, 133,
134 table 6.8, 135, 136, 141, 143 table 6.14, 150,
151–52, 226, 232–33, 261
and black release, 161, 164–65, 166 fig. 7.1, 171–
73, 181–83, 190, 232–33, 261, 299 n. 1
and black unconditional release, 188, 190, 280
table B.2
and coercive social control, 39, 56
determinants of, 54, 78, 265–66, 267 table A.1,
272, 273 table A.2
impact of war on, 68
operative years of, series, 277 table A.3, 278
and white admissions, 83, 91, 93, 100 table
5.11, 101–2, 108 table 5.17, 110, 112
and white prison sentences, 123, 128–30, 131
fig. 6.3, 138 table 6.11, 141, 148 table 6.17, 152,
232
and white release, 161, 168 table 7.5, 175 table
7.11, 186 table 7.17, 190
counties, role in punishment, 12–13, 21–26, 30–
31
county camps. *See* chain gangs
Cox, William B., 27
crime, 8, 43, 71–72
See also property crime; violent crime; young
male population
criminal penalties, 12, 13, 16, 29, 30 table 2.1,
295 n. 8

Dade Coal Company, 11
Darnell, John, 16, 18
data sources, 44–45, 296 n. 1
demobilization, 68–69
and black admissions, 82, 84 table 5.1, 85, 93,
94–95, 102–4, 110, 117, 226, 228, 249–50
and black prison sentences, 122, 157
and black release, 161, 195
and cotton economy, 265, 266
and industrialization, 265
and punishment, 36, 117, 156–57, 195, 249–50,
260
and racial inequality, 265, 268 table A.1, 271
and white admissions, 82, 89–90, 98–99,
107–10, 117, 229, 249–50
and white prison sentences, 122, 146–47, 150,
157, 249
and white release, 161, 195
Department of Corrections, 28–29, 45
depression of 1873–79, 63, 64 table 4.2
and admissions, 84, 87, 89–90, 94–95, 98–99,
103–5, 107, 110, 114, 115, 225, 228, 243
and age of admissions, 269

depression of 1873–79 (*continued*)
and prison sentences, 133, 134 table 6.7, 137, 154, 245
and seriousness of admissions, 268–69 table A.1, 271
depression of 1882–84, 64 table 4.2
and admissions, 84, 93, 94–95, 103–4, 110, 114–16, 228, 243, 245, 261
and age of admissions, 268–70 table A.1, 271
and prison sentences, 124, 130, 133, 134 table 6.7, 140, 146–47, 154, 243, 261
and release, 162–63, 178
and seriousness of admissions, 268–70 table A.1, 271
and unconditional release, 279 table B.1, 283 table B.5, 285 table B.7, 287 table B.9, 289 table B.11
depression of 1893–94, 33, 63, 64 table 4.2
and admissions, 87, 94–95, 116, 201
and age of admissions, 270 table A.1
and prison sentences, 146–47, 155
and seriousness of admissions, 268 table A.1, 271
depression of 1907–8, 33, 64 table 4.2
and admissions, 87, 115
and prison sentences, 142
depression of 1920–21, 64 table 4.2
and admissions, 103–4, 107, 110
and age of admissions, 270 table A.1
and conditional release, 281 table B.3, 283 table B.5, 285 table B.7
and cotton economy, 266, 267 table A.1
and industrialization, 266, 267 table A.1
and prison sentences, 137, 155, 246
depression of 1929–33. *See* Great Depression
depressions. *See* economic crises; *and under specific depressions and recessions*
Director of Corrections, 29
drug law violations, 296 n. 2
Durkheim, Emile, 5, 35

economic crises, 63–65
and age of admissions, 268–70 table A.1
and black admissions, 81–82, 84–85, 87, 93, 94–95, 102, 103–4, 114–17, 119, 225–28, 230, 233, 242–48
and black conditional release, 188, 279 table B.1, 283 table B.5, 287 table B.9
and black prison sentences, 122, 124, 126, 133, 134 table 6.7, 141–42, 150, 154–56, 159, 226, 229–30, 242–48
and black release, 160–61, 162–64, 169–71,
178, 180–81, 187, 190, 193–95, 197, 226–27, 231, 242–48
and black unconditional release, 188, 189, 279 table B.1, 283 table B.5, 287 table B.9
comparative impact of, 115–16, 154, 155 table 6.19, 193, 194 table 7.19, 245–46
and convict leasing, 20, 33
and cotton economy, 265–66, 267 table A.1
and industrialization, 265–66, 267 table A.1
and punishment, 114–17, 164–56, 193–95, 225–32, 242–48, 260–61
and racial inequality, 265, 266, 267–68 table A.1, 271
and self-regulation of punishment, 223, 261
and seriousness of admissions, 268–70 table A.1
and white admissions, 81–82, 89–90, 93, 98–99, 102, 105, 107, 108, 114–17, 119, 225–26, 228–31, 242–48
and white conditional release, 188, 240, 281 table B.3, 285 table B.7, 289 table B.11
and white prison sentences, 122, 127–28, 137, 141, 146, 147 table 6.16, 150–51, 154–56, 159, 226, 230–31, 242–48, 254
and white release, 160–61, 167, 169–70, 174–75, 184–85, 187, 190, 193–95, 197, 226–27, 230, 231, 233–37, 239, 240, 242–48
and white unconditional release, 188, 189, 281 table B.3, 285 table B.7, 289 table B.11
See also under specific depressions and recessions
Emancipation, 2, 8, 58
error sum of squares (SSE), 80
See also time series analysis
executions, 40

Federal Aid Road Act, 25–26, 70
and admissions, 82, 85, 89–90, 98–99, 118, 252, 261
and convict labor, 70
and prison sentences, 122, 128, 137–38, 141, 151, 157, 252, 261
and release, 161, 195
See also road building
Federal Bureau of Prisons, 29

gender and punishment, 296 n. 2
Georgia, state of. *See* state (Georgia)
good-roads movement, 21–22, 295 n. 5
and admissions, 118
and prison sentences, 127, 148, 152, 158, 233, 248, 254
and release, 169, 184, 191

role of convict labor in, 22–23
and self-regulation of punishment, 201, 210, 213, 216, 219, 221–23
See also Federal Aid Road Act; road building
"good time," 31
Gordon, John B., 11, 23
governor, state of Georgia
    position on chain gangs, 23–24, 27
    position on convict leasing, 18, 20
    power to pardon, 2, 31
    role in punishment, 13, 27, 28
Grant, Alexander and Company, 16
Grant, William D., 1
Great Depression, 3, 27, 33, 63–64, 70–71
    and admissions, 3, 89–90, 93, 98–99, 107, 108, 110, 114, 116, 243
    and age of admissions, 269 table A.1
    and black release, 53, 160, 170–71, 180 table 7.13, 181, 183–84, 193–95, 197, 244–45, 248, 279 table B.1, 283 table B.5, 287 table B.9
    and cotton harvest, 267 table A.1
    and industrialization, 266, 267 table A.1
    and prison sentences, 136, 208
    and self-regulation of punishment, 222
    and white release, 53, 160, 167, 169, 174–75, 179, 184–85, 193–95, 197, 215, 217, 219, 243–45, 248, 281 table B.3, 285 table B.7, 289 table B.11
    See also Agricultural Adjustment Act
Great Migration, 58, 66, 68

Harris, George D., 17
highway camps, 26–27
    See also chain gangs
Highway Commission, state of Georgia, 26, 295 n. 7
Highway Department, state of Georgia, 26, 28
Howard, John, 17

incarceration rate
    components of, 36
    determinants of, 34, 36, 37, 39–40, 41
indeterminate sentencing, 31–32, 40–41, 69
indictments, 72
industrial economy, 7, 8, 9, 37–38, 59–63, 83
    and punishment, 112–13, 152–53, 191–92, 236–41, 261, 293 n. 3
    See also black urban population; industrialization; urbanization
industrialization, 8–9, 59–63
    and black admissions, 82, 85 table 5.2, 86, 96 table 5.8, 105 table 5.14

and black conditional release, 188–89, 191, 251, 280 table B.2, 284 table B.6, 288 table B.10, 299 n. 2
and black prison sentences, 125 table 6.2, 134 table 6.8, 143 table 6.14, 152–53
and black release, 161, 164, 171–73, 181–83
and coercive social control, 37, 59
determinants of, 265–66, 267 table A.1
operative years of, series, 277 table A.3, 278
and white admissions, 82, 91–93, 100 table 5.11, 101–2, 108, 109 table 5.18, 110, 112
and white conditional release, 189, 237, 286 table B.8
and white prison sentences, 123, 129 table 6.5, 138 table 6.11, 148 table 6.17, 152–53
and white release, 161, 168 table 7.5, 175–77, 179, 186 table 7.17, 189, 191, 231, 237, 251, 286 table B.8
interracial competition, 38–41, 43, 66–67
    and punishment, 113–14, 154, 192–93, 241–43, 261–62
    See also racial inequality

Joint Standing Committee on the Penitentiary, 13, 14, 18

Kentucky, 13, 294 nn. 1, 5, 295 n. 4
Kirchheimer, Otto, 5, 6, 36

labor market. *See* cotton economy; industrial economy
larceny, 29, 30 table 2.1
    See also property offenders
lien system, 54–56
lynching, 39, 40

Maryland, 13, 294 n. 1
migration, 78
    See also Great Migration
Milledgeville, state penitentiary at, 1, 13–14
Murphy, John W., 11

National Committee on Prison Labor, 23
National Good Roads Association, 22
National League for Good Roads, 22
North, the
    industrialization in, 8, 58
    urbanization in, 60
    punishment in, 6–7, 10–11, 39
    and the Southern economy, 8–9
North Carolina, 21, 294 nn. 1, 5, 295 n. 4

offense differences
in admissions, 47–49, 94, 102, 109–11, 113, 117–19, 227–29, 235, 241–42, 247–48, 253, 261
in prison sentences, 49–51, 122–23, 133, 140–41, 143, 145 fig. 6.7, 146, 150–53, 156, 158–59, 229–31, 235, 241–42, 247–48, 255–56, 261, 263
in release, 53, 161, 177–79, 185, 187, 190, 194, 197, 231, 235, 247–48, 253, 263
in self-regulation of punishment, 219–20, 223, 259
in seriousness over time, 73–75
in social control, 42
offense seriousness, 73
See also seriousness of admissions

parole, 27–28, 31, 40–41, 69
and admissions, 82, 85, 89, 103, 118, 250–51
and prison sentences, 122, 157, 250–51
and release, 161, 188–89, 191–92, 195, 237, 239, 251
See also conditional release
penitentiary
admissions to (see admissions to the penitentiary)
development of, 6, 13–15, 293–94 nn. 1, 3, 295 n. 1
labor in, 8, 13–15, 25
at Milledgeville, 1, 13–14
at Reidsville, 2, 28
release from (see release from the penitentiary)
sentences in (see prison sentences)
See also chain gangs; convict leasing
penitentiary committee
report on chain gangs, 24, 28
report on convict leasing, 16–20, 294 n. 5
report on the penitentiary, 14, 15
See also Joint Standing Committee on the Penitentiary
penitentiary companies, 10–11, 16–17, 294 n. 5
Piedmont, 22, 66
policies
federal, 63–64, 71–72
penal, 12, 29–32, 69–70
and punishment, 117–19, 157, 195–96, 226, 229, 231, 250–53, 260
See also Agricultural Adjustment Act; convict leasing; Federal Aid Road Act; indeterminate sentencing; parole; probation
political economy
perspective, 6, 36–38, 261
and punishment, 6–7, 32–33, 41, 43

regional differences in, 8–9, 37–38, 58
See also cotton economy; industrial economy
Populist Party, 17, 19
Principal Keeper of the Penitentiary
position of, 1, 2, 18
report of, 18, 23, 44
Principal Physician of the Penitentiary, 18, 19, 294–95 n. 3
prison. See penitentiary
Prison and Parole Commission, 27, 28
Prison Commission, 2, 19–20, 27, 295 n. 7
report of, 18, 25, 31–32, 44–45
prison labor. See contract labor; convict leasing; chain gangs; public account system
prison sentences, 46 table 4.1, 49–51, 296 n. 3
offense differences in, 122–23, 133, 140–41, 143, 145 fig. 6.7, 146, 150–53, 156, 158, 159, 229–31, 241–42, 247–48, 255–56, 261, 263
racial differences in, 121, 122–23, 133, 152, 153, 155–56, 157–59, 226, 241–42, 244, 246–47, 255–56
role of judge in, 29, 32
role of jury in, 29–30
See also under specific types of offender
probation, adult, 29–30, 70
and admissions, 40–41, 82, 85, 89, 98–99, 102–3, 110, 118, 252
and prison sentences, 122, 142, 151, 157, 252
and release, 161, 195, 252
and seriousness of admissions, 269 table A.1
property, 8
black, and punishment, 154, 193, 291 table C.1, 298 n. 3, 298 n. 4, 299 n. 3
white, and punishment, 114, 193, 298 nn. 3, 4, 299 n. 3
See also racial inequality
property crime, 1, 3, 29, 30, 42
See also property offenders
property offenders, 43, 45, 46 table 4.1
See also black property offenders; white property offenders
public account system, 7
public work camps, 28–29
See also chain gangs
punishment, 2, 46–53
forms of, 12
dimensions of, 36, 41
race and (see under racial differences)
region and, 39, 42–43
self-regulation of (see self-regulation of punishment)

See also admissions to the penitentiary; prison sentences; release from the penitentiary

racial differences
in admissions, 46–48, 81, 93, 102, 109–19, 225–28, 234, 237, 241–44, 246, 249, 250, 253, 263
in cotton economy, 58, 65–67
in crime, 43
in industrial economy, 60
in military experience, 68–69
in offense seriousness, 45–46, 73, 74, 75 fig. 4.16
in prison sentences, 49–51, 121, 122–23, 133, 139, 140 fig. 6.6, 152, 153, 155–56, 157–59, 226, 241–42, 244, 246–47, 255–56
in property ownership (*see* racial inequality)
in punishment, 1–3, 42–43
in release, 51–53, 161, 169, 170, 176, 177 fig. 7.5, 188–91, 194–97, 225–27, 231, 234–35, 237, 245–47, 250, 256, 263
in sample, 45–46
in self-regulation of punishment, 205, 210–11, 221–23, 224, 259
in social control, 42–43
in tenantry, 58, 65–66, 70–71
in urban experiences, 60–61
racial inequality, 65–67, 296 n. 5
and black admissions, 83, 85 table 5.2, 86–87, 88 fig. 5.3, 93, 94, 96–97, 103, 105, 106 table 5.15, 110, 113–14, 226, 228, 241
and black prison sentences, 123, 125 table 6.2, 134 table 6.8, 143–45, 154
and black release, 161, 164 table 7.2, 172 table 7.8, 181 table 7.14, 193
determinants of, 78, 265, 266, 267–68 table A.1, 271–74
operative years of, series, 277 table A.3
and punishment, 43, 113–14, 154, 192–93, 236–41
and white admissions, 83, 91, 94, 100 table 5.11, 101–2, 108 table 5.17, 110, 114, 226
and white prison sentences, 123, 129 table 6.5, 138 table 6.11, 148 table 6.17, 154
and white release, 161, 168 table 7.5, 175–79, 186 table 7.17, 187, 231, 242, 286 table B.8
railroads, 8, 9, 16
recession of 1887–88, 64 table 4.2
and admissions, 94–95
and age of admissions, 268–70 table A.1
and prison sentences, 127–28, 137, 155, 246

recession of 1890–91, 64 table 4.2
and admissions, 115
and age of admissions, 268–70 table A.1
and cotton price, 266, 267 table A.1
and industrialization, 266, 267 table A.1
and prison sentences, 137, 146–47, 155, 246
and racial inequality, 267 table A.1, 271
and seriousness of admissions, 269–70 table A.1
recession of 1895–97, 64 table 4.2
and admissions, 84, 103–4, 110, 116, 243
and age of admissions, 268–70 table A.1
and black release, 162–63, 170–71, 180 table 7.13, 181, 193, 243–44
and black unconditional release, 279 table B.1, 283 table B.5, 287 table B.9
and prison sentences, 124, 137, 141, 146–47, 154, 243, 247
and racial inequality, 267 table A.1
and seriousness of admissions, 268–69 table A.1, 271
and white unconditional release, 281 table B.3, 289 table B.11
recession of 1899–1900, 64 table 4.2
and admissions, 115, 244
and black release, 162–63, 170–71, 180 table 7.13, 181, 193, 244, 246, 279 table B.1, 283 table B.5, 287 table B.9
and cotton price, 266, 267 table A.1
and prison sentences, 142
and seriousness of admissions, 269 table A.1
and white unconditional release, 281 table B.3
recession of 1902–4, 64 table 4.2, 266, 267 table A.1, 270 table A.1
recession of 1910–12, 64 table 4.2
and admissions, 89–90, 98–99, 243–44
and black release, 283 table B.5
and cotton harvest, 267 table A.1
and prison sentences, 146–47, 154, 157, 246
and racial inequality, 267 table A.1, 271
and white release, 167, 169, 174–75, 179, 243–44, 281 table B.3, 285 table B.7
recession of 1913–14, 64 table 4.2, 252
recession of 1918–19, 64 table 4.2, 244, 249, 268 table A.1, 271
recession of 1923–24, 64 table 4.2
and admissions, 84, 89–90, 94–95, 98–99, 107, 114, 116, 225–26, 243
and black release, 162–63, 178, 180 table 7.13, 181, 243
and cotton harvest, 266, 267 table A.1

recession of 1923–24 (*continued*)
  and prison sentences, 124, 133, 134 table 6.7, 140, 243
  and seriousness of admissions, 269 table A.1
recession of 1926–27, 64 table 4.2
  and admissions, 89–90, 107, 108
  and age of admissions, 268 table A.1
  and black release, 180 table 7.13, 181, 244
  and cotton price, 266, 267 table A.1
  and prison sentences, 142, 244
  and seriousness of admissions, 269 table A.1
recession of 1937–38, 64 table 4.2
  and admissions, 107 table 5.16, 108
  and black release, 162–63, 170–71, 180 table 7.13, 181, 193, 279 table B.1, 283 table B.5, 287 table B.9
  and cotton harvest, 267 table A.1
  and seriousness of admissions, 269 table A.1
  and white release, 167, 169, 174–75, 184–85, 193–94, 244, 281 table B.3, 285 table B.7, 289 table B.11
recessions. *See* economic crises; *and under specific recessions*
Reconstruction, 8
Reidsville, state penitentiary at, 2, 28
release from the penitentiary, 51–53, 160, 188
  offense differences in, 161, 177–79, 185, 187, 190, 194, 197, 231, 235, 247–48, 253, 263
  racial differences in, 161, 169, 170, 190, 191, 194–97, 225–27, 231, 234–35, 237, 245–47, 250, 256, 263
  See also conditional release; parole; unconditional release; *and under specific types of offender*
Rivers, Eurith, 27
road building
  and convict labor, 10, 11, 21–27, 69–70, 295 nn. 4, 5, 6
  See also Federal Aid Road Act; good-roads movement
robbery, 29, 30 table 2.1, 296 n. 2
Rusche, Georg, 5, 6, 36

sampling procedure, 44–45, 46 table 4.1, 296 n. 2
self-regulation of punishment, 36, 42, 75, 198–224, 259, 260–61
  See also under offense differences; racial differences
sentences. *See* prison sentences
seriousness of admissions, 46 table 4.1, 72–75
  and black conditional release, 189, 280 table B.2, 288 table B.10
  and black prison sentences, 123, 125–27, 132–

33, 134 table 6.8, 135–36, 140, 143–44, 150, 151, 158, 226, 229, 255–56
  and black release, 162, 164 table 7.2, 172 table 7.8, 181–82, 184, 187, 196
  determinants of, 268–72, 274–77
  operative years of, series, 277 table A.3, 278
  and white prison sentences, 123, 128–30, 131 fig. 6.2, 132–33, 138–39, 140, 147–48, 149 table 6.18, 150–51, 158–59, 226, 230–31, 255–56, 291 table C.1
  and white release, 162, 168 table 7.5, 175 table 7.11, 184, 186, 231, 290 table B.12
sharecropping, 65–67, 70–71, 296 n. 4
Sherman, William T., 15
Smith, James M., 11
Smith, James Monroe, ix
South, the
  industrialization in, 59–63
  political economy of, 8–9
  punishment in, 39, 294 nn. 1, 5
  urbanization in, 60–62
South Carolina, 21, 294 nn. 1, 5, 295 n. 4
Southern Good Roads, 22
Southern Road Congress, 22
stability of punishment, 35–36, 39, 69
  See also self-regulation of punishment
state (Georgia)
  oversight of the penitentiary, 13
  oversight of chain gangs, 21, 23–24, 27–29, 31–32
  oversight of convict leasing, 14–20
  role in punishment, 33
  See also Joint Standing Committee on the Penitentiary; penitentiary committee
state, the
  role in punishment, 9–11, 40–41, 293 n. 3
state farm, 25
state highway camps. *See* highway camps

Talmadge, Eugene, 27
tenantry, 296 nn. 4, 5
  See also sharecropping
Tennessee, 16, 294 nn. 1, 5, 295 n. 4
theft, 29, 30 table 2.1
  See also property crime; property offenders
theoretical implications, 262–64
  cotton economy, 111–12, 151, 190–91, 232–36
  industrial economy, 112–13, 152–53, 191–92, 236–41
  interracial competition, 113–14, 154, 192–93, 241–42
  stability of punishment, 221–24, 260–61

threat, notion of
and punishment, 34, 38, 260
time series analysis
ARIMA, 76–80, 278, 296 n. 6, 297 nn. 7–10, 12
cross-correlation function in, 76–80, 296 n. 6
intervention, 79, 265–71, 296 n. 6, 297 nn. 11, 12
moving average, 80
multivariate, 79–80, 272–77
operative years of, 277 table A.3
transfer functions in, 78–79, 265–66, 296 n. 6, 297 n. 12, 298 n. 2
time served, 46 table 4.1

unconditional release, 51–53, 188
determinants of, 189, 190, 279–90
racial differences in, 51–53
See also conditional release
unemployment rate, 37
urbanization, 2–3, 60–63, 167
and black admissions, 83, 85 table 5.2, 86–87, 88 fig. 52, 93, 94, 96–98, 102, 103, 105, 106, 109, 110, 112–13, 119, 226, 228, 238, 240, 261
and black conditional release, 280 table B.2, 288 table B.10
and black prison sentences, 122, 125 table 6.2, 134 table 6.8, 135, 136, 141, 143–45, 150, 151, 153, 159, 238, 240, 261
and black release, 161, 164–65, 166 fig. 7.2, 167, 170, 172 table 7.8, 178, 181–83, 187, 192, 238
and black unconditional release, 189, 280 table B.2, 284 table B.6, 288 table B.10, 299 n. 2
determinants of, 272, 273 table A.2
operative years of, series, 277 table A.3
and white admissions, 83, 91, 93, 94, 100, 101, 108 table 5.17, 110, 112–13, 226, 240
and white conditional release, 189, 192, 251, 282 table B.4
and white prison sentences, 123, 128–30, 132 fig. 6.4, 138–39, 138 table 6.11, 140 fig. 6.6, 141, 148 table 6.17, 150, 151, 153, 230, 239, 240, 291 table C.1
and white release, 161, 168 table 7.5, 175–77, 179, 186 table 7.17, 187, 192, 231, 239, 235
See also black urban population

value added by manufacturing. See industrialization
Varner, H. B., 22

violent crime, 29, 30, 42, 62
See also violent offenders
violent offenders, 43, 45
See also black violent offenders; white violent offenders
Virginia, 13, 21, 294 nn. 1, 5, 295 n. 4

Wallis, Haley and Company, 17
Walnut Street jail, Philadelphia, 13
war, punishment during, 36
See also World War I
Westmoreland, W. F., 294 n. 3
whipping boss, 17, 19
white offenders
admissions of, 46–48, 89–93, 112–19, 201 table 8.3, 203–4, 221, 225–26, 229, 243–46, 249, 252, 298 n.3
age of admitted, 73, 75
prison sentences of, 49–51, 127–32, 133, 150, 152–53, 154–57, 201–4, 221, 222, 230–31, 234, 245–46, 252, 254
release of, 51–53, 167–70, 187, 189, 190, 192–94, 201–4, 222, 226–27, 231, 243–47, 251, 281 table B.3, 282 table B.4
seriousness of admitted, 73–74
See also white property offenders; white violent offenders
white property offenders
admissions of, 47–48, 105–9, 112–19, 214–16, 219–21, 223, 228–29, 234, 243, 246, 247, 253
age of admitted, 75
prison sentences of, 49–51, 146–49, 150, 151, 153–59, 214–16, 217 table 8.15, 220–23, 230–31, 246–47, 294, 254–59, 261, 298 n. 3, 299 n. 2
release of, 53, 184–89, 194, 196, 214–23, 230, 231, 243, 247, 251, 256, 258, 289 table B.11, 290 table B.12, 299 n. 2
seriousness of admitted, 73–74
whites
fertility of, 66
rural experiences of, 62, 66
and sharecropping, 65–67
urban experiences of, 60–62, 238–39
white violent offenders
admissions of, 47–48, 97–102, 112–19, 206–10, 222, 228–31, 234–36, 243, 252, 253
age of admitted, 75
prison sentences of, 49–51, 137–41, 151, 153–59, 207–8, 221, 239, 240, 246–47, 249–50, 254–57, 261

white violent offenders (*continued*)
release of, 53, 174–79, 187, 189–96, 209 table
8.10, 210, 221, 231, 233–37, 239, 240, 242–43,
247, 249, 250, 251, 258, 253, 285 table B.7, 286
table B.8
seriousness of admitted, 73–74
Whitin, E. Stagg, 23
Works Public Administration, 28
World War I, 67–68, 73
and age of admissions, 268 table A.1, 270 table
A.1, 271
and black admissions, 3, 47, 82, 84 table 5.1, 85,
93, 94–95, 102, 103–4, 110, 117, 226, 228,
249–50
and black prison sentences, 122, 142, 151, 156
and black release, 51, 161, 170, 195
and cotton economy, 265, 266, 267 table A.1
demobilization from (*see* demobilization)
and industrialization, 265, 266, 267 table A.1
and migration, 58, 68
and punishment, 117, 156–57, 195, 249–50,
260
and racial inequality, 265, 272
and self-regulation of punishment, 201, 213,
216, 222

and seriousness of admissions, 268–69 table
A.1, 271
and white admissions, 89, 98, 117, 226
and white prison sentences, 122, 128, 137–38,
146, 150, 151, 156, 230, 250
and white release, 51, 161, 170, 174 table 7.10,
175, 187, 195, 285 table B.7

young male population, 71–72, 75, 127, 148
and black admissions, 83, 85 table 5.2, 96 table
5.8, 105 table 5.14, 119
and black prison sentences, 123, 125–27, 134
table 6.8, 141, 143 table 6.14, 150, 157, 254
and black release, 161–62, 164 table 7.2, 172
table 7.8, 181 table 7.14, 196, 288 table B.10
determinants of, 255, 272, 273 table A.2
and incarceration rate, 72
operative years of, series, 277 table A.3
and white admissions, 83, 91 table 5.5, 100
table 5.11, 108 table 5.17, 119
and white prison sentences, 123, 128–30, 147–
49, 158
and white release, 161–62, 168 table 7.5, 175–
76, 178, 179, 186 table 7.17, 196, 286 table
B.8, 290 table B.12